IFAC

International Federation of Automatic Control

URBAN, REGIONAL AND NATIONAL PLANNING (UNRENAP)

Environmental Aspects

IFAC 1977 Conference Proceedings .

ATHERTON: Multivariable Technological Systems
BANKS & PRITCHARD: Control of Distributed Parameter Systems
CICHOCKI & STRASZAK: Systems Analysis Applications to Complex Programs
DUBUISSON: Information and Systems
GHONAIMY: Systems Approach for Development
HASEGAWA & INOUE: Urban, Regional and National Planning - Environmental Aspects
LEONHARD: Control in Power Electronics and Electrical Drives
OSHIMA: Information Control Problems in Manufacturing Technology
RIJNSDORP: Case Studies in Automation Related to Humanization of Work
SAWARAGI & AKASHI: Environmental Systems Planning, Design and Control
SINGH & TITLI: Control and Management of Integrated Industrial Complexes
SMEDEMA: Real Time Programming 1977

URBAN, REGIONAL AND NATIONAL PLANNING (UNRENAP)

Proceedings of the IFAC Workshop
Kyoto, Japan, 5 - 6 August 1977

Edited by

T. HASEGAWA

and

K. INOUE

Kyoto University, Japan

Published for the

INTERNATIONAL FEDERATION OF AUTOMATIC CONTROL

by

PERGAMON PRESS

OXFORD · NEW YORK · TORONTO · SYDNEY · PARIS · FRANKFURT

U.K.	Pergamon Press Ltd., Headington Hill Hall, Oxford OX3 0BW, England
U.S.A.	Pergamon Press Inc., Maxwell House, Fairview Park, Elmsford, New York 10523, U.S.A.
CANADA	Pergamon of Canada Ltd., 75 The East Mall, Toronto, Ontario, Canada
AUSTRALIA	Pergamon Press (Aust.) Pty. Ltd., 19a Boundary Street, Rushcutters Bay, N.S.W. 2011, Australia
FRANCE	Pergamon Press SARL, 24 rue des Ecoles, 75240 Paris, Cedex 05, France
FEDERAL REPUBLIC OF GERMANY	Pergamon Press GmbH, 6242 Kronberg-Taunus, Pferdstrasse 1, Federal Republic of Germany

First edition 1978

British Library Cataloguing in Publication Data

IFAC Workshop on Urban, Regional and National Planning,
Kyoto, 1977
Urban, regional and national planning.
1. City planning - Congresses 2. Regional planning
- Congresses 3. System analysis - Congresses
I. Title II. Hasegawa, Toshiharu
III. Inoue, K
711'.028'51 HT166 78-40573

ISBN 0-08-022013-4

In order to make this volume available as economically and as rapidly as possible the authors' typescripts have been reproduced in their original forms. This method unfortunately has its typographical limitations but it is hoped that they in no way distract the reader.

Printed in Great Britain by A. Wheaton & Co. Ltd., Exeter

IFAC WORKSHOP ON URBAN, REGIONAL AND NATIONAL PLANNING (UNRENAP); ENVIRONMENTAL ASPECTS

Sponsored by
The International Federation of Automatic Control Systems Engineering Committee
The International Federation of Automatic Control Environmental Systems Symposium Committee
International Institute for Applied Systems Analysis

Organized by
IFAC Workshop on UNRENAP Organizing Committee

Prepared by
IFAC SECOM Working Group on UNRENAP

CONTENTS

Session 4. Simulation

Session 5. Optimization

Papers added in press

*This paper was not presented at the Workshop

FOREWORD

Owing to the ever growing complexity of our society, problems concerning urban, regional and national planning have come to be of grave importance. There exist many problems to which systems science has been contributing. IFAC (International Federation of Automatic Control) has been working as one of the key institutions to cope with this type of problem, from the viewpoint of systems science. The IFAC Systems Engineering Committee (SECOM) Working Group on Urban, Regional and National Planning (UNRENAP) is one of the activities of IFAC in this field.

IFAC SECOM Working Group on UNRENAP decided to hold the first Workshop on Urban, Regional and National Planning in order to stimulate its activities under the cosponsorship of IFAC SECOM, the International Institute for Applied Systems Analysis (IIASA), Laxenburg, Austria and the IFAC Environmental Systems Symposium Committee, in Kyoto, Japan on 5 and 6 of August, 1977, after the IFAC Symposium on Environmental Systems Planning, Design and Control held at the same place.

As the fields which are covered by the IFAC Working Group on UNRENAP are too wide to be covered by a single workshop, the subjects in this workshop have been mostly confined to the environmental aspects and problems such as;

(1) What kind of model can be constructed to describe environmental aspects of UNRENAP problems?
(2) What kind of methodology can be used to solve the problems?

The purpose of this workshop is to provide the participants with an opportunity to have rather informal discussions on their knowledge, experience, new ideas and other valuable information.

Many colleagues and co-workers have contributed their time and abilities to the success of the workshop. It should be stated here that their efforts have made the workshop possible.

IFAC Workshop on UNRENAP
Organizing Committee
Takeo Shiina
Toshiharu Hasegawa

MODELING OF THE ENVIRONMENT THROUGH A SYSTEM OF MODELS

Felipe Lara and Wladimir M. Sachs

Fundación Javier Barros Sierra, A.C. Centro de Investigación Prospectiva, Tacuba 5, México 1, D.F.

ABSTRACT

Formal planning models usually include environment, i.e., factors influencing the planned system's behavior which are not part of it. However, the predictive value of these models is poor. This may be largely attributed (a) to the complexity of the environment which makes its modeling virtually impossible, and (b) to the existence of autonomous environmental agents whose behavior is unpredictable. The paper outlines an alternative approach to environmental modeling.

It is suggested that comprehensive models be replaced by a network of simpler models, focused on specific aspects of the reality and sponsored by corresponding decision-making organizations. Such models, rather than "objective" would be autonomous "subjective" expressions of the perception of the reality by the sponsoring organizations. Any model could use as inputs the outputs of another model. The environment of a model would consist of the models of environmental components. The modelbuilders would thus avoid the task of modelling the environment. The autonomy of the environmental components would be accounted for. If a particular organization would detect the undesirability of another organization's behavior it could initiate a process aimed at resolving the conflict.

INTRODUCTION

The accelerating rate of change is perhaps one of the central worries of those scientific disciplines that deal with management and control. A glance at the headlines of the daily press makes it clear that we are not good managers of the world in which we live. Crises are overcome only to be replaced by new ones of ever increasing magnitudes. Planners and prophets tell us that the worst is yet to come.

The scientific community and the public at large have been allerted to the problematique of change through dramatic "manifestos" such as Toffler's (1) *Future Shock* and through "models of doom" like the Club of Rome's (2) *Limits to Growth*. However, we do not as yet truly understand the nature of change, let alone are capable to cope with it constructively.

Donald Schon (3) offers an interesting hypothesis as to the roots of the management and control crisis. He argues that the responsibility cannot be allocated to the rate of change alone. Rather, it is the obsolescence of our conceptual schemes that generates the chaos. Our methods for management and control have evolved in a stable world in which change was slow and regular enough to be easily coped with. The stable world belongs to the past, and yet we continue to approach it in the "old ways."

In summary, there is nothing inherent in the phenomenon of change which makes it unmanageable. The challenge is to design new methods to cope with it. This essay is meant to be a modest contribution to the meeting of that challenge.

More specifically, the essay is devoted to an assessment of the adequacy of the traditional modeling methods as means for control of social systems and their environments, and to outlining an alternative approach to modeling. The first step is to describe briefly some essential characteristics of the social reality to be contrasted later with the nature of mathematical models.

SOCIAL SYSTEMS AND THEIR ENVIRONMENTS

Three points are argued in this section. First, that the behavior of social systems should be viewed as purposeful, that is, resulting from autonomous decision-making. The existence of purposeful entities in the environments of social systems makes them extremely uncertain and complex. Finally, it is argued that it is not possible to truly understand the behavior of social systems considered in isolation, that is, that they should be studied within the context to which they belong.

A system is purposeful when it can choose freely among several possible ways of behaving. More specifically, Ackoff and Emery (4) define a system as purposeful when it can display not only choice of means employed for achievement of specified goal, but also choice of ends (i.e., it can establish its own goals). The above concept of purposefulness is based on the comparison of behavior in different contexts. If a system's behavior is seen as nonpurposeful, that is, entailed by its built-in and environmental characteristics, then it cannot display significantly different types of behavior in the same situation.

In other words, it is in principle possible to build a mathematical model of nonpurposeful behavior which allows one to determine in any given situation what would the specific behavior of the system be (5). Such a model is not possible in the case of purposeful behavior. If it were, the system would not be purposeful, since its behavior would be governed by specific rules or laws, leaving no place for free choice.

The discussion above is not meant to convey that no aspects of purposeful behavior can be explained or predicted. However, the totality of such behavior cannot be expressed in form of an explicit mathematical model (5).

That social systems should be viewed in most situations as purposeful entities is not a factual or an ontological statement. Rather, it is a methodological postulate. Indeed, the two views being compatible, any behavior can be conceptualized either as mechanistic or as purposeful (4,6,7). However, it is more fruitful to conceptualize social behavior as purposeful, since such a view leads to more significant and useful research results. It is so, if for no other reason, because the current state of knowledge lends itself badly to construction of valid predictive models of social behavior.

Consider now the relationship of a system with its environment. Objective reality is a complex "mess" where everything is related to everything else.

Therefore, if an individual is faced with a problem, theoretically he should approach its solution considering the whole physical universe with all its interrelationships. Obviously, such an approach is impossible. The individual, in order to handle the reality, must abstract from it a relevant portion over which he has some degree of control and/or which can influence his purposeful behavior. Within this relevant reality the individual must identify a set of related entities such that collectively they display a property that is most relevant to his purpose, and which none of them or no subcollection does. This collection constitutes a system which will be called the focal system relative to the problem. All other identifiable systems within the relevant reality are called environmental. For instance, if we are interested in the Mexican foreign trade, we could identify Mexico as the focal system and North America, the European Common Market, and so on, as the environmental systems.

The environment of a social system generally contains other social systems. That is to say, the environment is populated with a multitude of purposeful entities, remaining in mutual interactions, be it of conflictual or cooperative nature. All those purposeful entities, including the focal system, entertain among themselves direct or indirect transactions, in which goods are coproduced, exchanged, and fought for, and the values influencing the choices made undergo continual change.

Thus the environment of a purposeful system is characterized by the fact that a great number of decisions --choices among possible behaviors -- are made constantly, every one of them changing the state of reality. Since those decisions are free, hence unpredictable, the environment is not only uncertain, but its uncertainty is to a great extent uncalculable (5). To use Emery and Trist's (8,9) terminology, the environment is turbulent, and the decision of the focal system cannot be based on reliable predic tions of the contextual conditions.

In conditions of turbulence the interactions of the system with the environment are not assuming any definite or regular pattern, hence they become vitally determinant of the system's behavior. That is to say, to assure its continuing functioning, the system has to regulate its relationship with the environment, constantly adapting its own behavior to environmental changes. The system's survival or performance are dependent more on the contextual conditions and the interactions with the environment than on its intrinsic or proper characteristics (9).

In summary, it is argued above that social systems and their environments should be viewed as composed of numerous autonomous decision-making entities, which makes prediction of their behavior possible only in very limited cases. The implications of the above for modeling are examined in the next section.

MODELS OF SOCIAL SYSTEMS

The above discussion brings to light two severe limitations of the usual modeling approach to the problem of management and control of social systems. The first one is that most models are mechanistic or probabilistic is nature, not reflecting the purposeful behavior of the real entity. To use such a model for management and control is in a way a contradiction. It consists in first predicting what the system's behavior will be in order to take decisions which would make those predictions untrue.

At present time there do not exist satisfactory modeling techniques which would allow to incorporate purposeful decision-making into a formal representation of the reality. Indeed, both control and game-theoretic approaches are highly simplified, serving heuristic rather than modeling functions (10). That is, they provide one with useful insights and systematization of knowledge concerning purposeful behavior, but the models with which they operate are unrealistic.

There seem to be two procedures through which models can approximate in a practical way the taking into account of purposeful behavior. Consider them below.

The simplest of the two is the scenario variable procedure (11). It substitutes a so called scenario variable (a course-of-action variable) for the decision-maker in every relevant choice situation. The model must then be run for every relevant combination of values of the scenario variables. This procedure has two principal drawbacks: it is very difficult, if not impossible, for an individual to be aware of all courses of action available to another purposeful individual in a given choice situation; and when there are many relevant choice situations, the number of different alternatives to explore makes the exercise unmanageable.

The second procedure is the interactive simulation one. It requires that several decision-makers, having responsibility for different aspects of the reality, cooperate for simulating a real world scenario. The model runs until a certain choice situation is arrived at in which the corresponding decision-maker chooses what he considers the most efficient course of action. The model simulates the outcomes and runs until the next choice situation, and so on (12). The crucial problem when this procedure is used is to get the cooperation of real decision-makers. Once they agree, however,the advantages of this technique are obvious. In the following sections we will discuss how to organize such cooperation.

The second limitation of usual modeling approaches resides in our inability to reflect the importance and the complexity of the environment in models. Most models "internalize" the environment through either incorporation of exogeneous variables or through the receival of a continual flow of environmental information. However, the internal variables of the system are usually given more weight, and the essentiality of interactions with the environment is not handled very well.

This state of affairs is not surprising, considering the environmental complexity discussed in the previous section. It seems difficult to imagine a single model able to treat adequately all relevant aspects of the environment and of its interactions with the system. Indeed, it would imply that nearly as much attention be given to a number of environmental entities as is given to the focal system itself. Which, in turn, implies an exponential increase in the amount of work involved in constructing the model.

In summary, it is argued that because of the current state of the art, and because of the complexity involved it is impossible in most non-trivial cases to construct models of social reality which would be veridic and of predictive value. In other words, the possibility of models being an "objective" reflection of the reality is limited. Does it mean that modeling should be abandoned? The answer is negative. Rather, the role of models should be re-thought and an alternative approach to modeling designed.

The value of modeling may be assessed from two different points of view: that of the model-builder, and that of other users of the model. For the first one, it is a heuristic device forcing rigor and precision in his thinking. For the second one, it is information about the builder's world-view.

Thus models should be viewed as a subjective expression of the model-builder's knowledge of, and beliefs about the reality. That is, they are a rigorous expression of what their builders think about the reality that is being modeled. As such they are a valuable means of communications allowing one to determine with precision what are the basic assumptions, value judgments and knowledge of those who build them.

The above point of view implies that model-building and decision-making should be closely related. More specifically, the team constructing a model and the one making decisions should be, if not identical, at least in close working relationship, which guarantees an identity of views. In this way the model serves the heuristic purposes in making of decisions and becomes a concise expression of assumptions which underly the decision-making.

Such an approach implies also that models will not be overly complex or concerned with overly "big" systems. Indeed, every model would be limited by the scope of the decision-making to which it is associated.

On the other hand, if every significant decision-making body constructs its own model of the system over which it exercises total or partial control, there would be a network of models created. Every and each of them would represent an aspect of the environment of all the others. Thus, any model could use the other ones as models of its environment. Hence, every modeling team would dispose of the labor of environmental modeling.

A discussion of a system of models along the lines suggested above is contained in the following two sections.

CONFLICTING AND COOPERATIVE DECISION-MAKERS

Consider two decision-makers A and B. Ackoff and Emery (4) define B as in conflict with A when A's expected payoff in a certain situation given the presence of B is smaller than it would be if B were absent. For instance, if A and B are coffee producers, and both want to sell their production then A can consider B to be in conflict with him because he would prefer to be alone on the market.

In the same way Ackoff and Emery (4) define B to be cooperative with A when A's expected payoff in a certain situation given the presence of B is greater than it would be if B were absent. For instance, if A wants to sell his oil production and B, also an oil producer, associates with him to constitute a monopoly or for distributing the market areas between them, then they can transform their former conflictual relationship into a cooperative one. In fact, through communication both decision-makers become aware of mutual interests that otherwise they would ignore.

The interactive simulation procedure is a technique to enhance cooperation between decision-makers using communication *via* a participative process of designing a common future. The instrument is a model of a portion of reality relevant to all of them. This model allows each of them to simulate decisions that affect others. Corresponding outcomes or effects are determined by the model. This process generates debates and negotiations that can be oriented toward resolution of conflicts. At the end, one eventually reaches a design of a common future more or less desirable to all participants, that is, one minimizes the importance of actual or potential conflicts.

ENVIRONMENTAL SIMULATION THROUGH A SYSTEM OF MODELS

The trouble with the described procedure lies in the requirements that it imposes on the model. The latter should be general enough to take into account the relevant common variables for all participants, but also detailed enough to be useful for each decision-maker. This conflict between general and particular utility cannot be solved with a single model because of the uniqueness of each participant.

The way in which we propose to solve the above problem is to form a system of interacting models. This could be done as follows.

1) Each participant (at an institutional level) would develop a model of his focal system.
2) The design of these models would be free enough to allow for the accomplishment of the purposes of each individual decision-maker. The only constraints are that the models would have to be built in a pre-established computer language to allow a common implementation, and that they would have to use environmental variables coming from a pre-established list so that the outputs of one model could be used as inputs to another.
3) There would be an organizational entity responsible for a systemic synthesis of the network of models. This entity would produce a special compiler for manipulating the different models so that the communication between computer models and decision-makers be as simple and operational as possible.
4) The particular models and the compiler should be designed to allow continuous adaptation and improvement. Each party should take the responsability of updating and improving its own model without interfering with the general compatibility of the models.
5) Each party should design and implement its own information system to make possible a continuous verification, updating and improvement of the parameters, assumptions and relations pertaining to its model.

APPLICATIONS

The Club of Rome has made a series of efforts to implement an interactive simulation procedure with participation of top decision-makers belonging to different nations. One of those efforts is coordinated by Mihajlo Mesarović from Case Western Reserve University in U.S.A. However, he uses a model developed by his team rather than the participants. The results regarding communication and cooperation between decision-makers from different countries have been very promising (12).

Another serious effort in this direction is the Project Link coordinated by Lawrence Klein from the University of Pennsylvania. He also uses models developed by his team and synthetizes them into a World Trade model. This model is not interactive however (13).

The Fundación Javier Barros Sierra in Mexico is engaged in a synthesis of an interactive system of models as proposed in this paper. A nuclear set of three compatible models dealing with various aspects of national life (population, economy and food), has been implemented (14). Each of this elementary models will be assigned to a specialized public agency. The responsibility of each agency will be the further development and improvement of the assigned model to satisfy its particular purposes. The Fundación Javier Barros Sierra will coordinate these developments to supervise the overall compatibility of the models and will develop the required software for the interactive runs. As end product of this effort a set of particular models will be available as tools for sectoral decision-making as well as a system of interacting models proper for cooperative decision-making at the national level.

NOTES AND REFERENCES

(1) Toffler, A. *Future Shock*. New York: Bantam Books, 1970.

(2) Meadows, D.H. *et al. The Limits to Growth*. New York: Signet, 1972.

(3) Schon, D.A. *Beyond the Stable State*. New York: W.W. Norton, 1971.

(4) Ackoff, R.L., F.E. Emery. *On Purposeful Systems*. Chicago: Aldine-Atherton, 1972.

(5) Sachs, W.M. *Man, Design, Machine*. PhD Thesis. Philadelphia: Busch Center, Wharton School, University of Pennsylvania, 1976.

(6) Churchman, C.W. *The Design of Inquiring Systems*. New York: Basic Books, 1971.

(7) Singer, E.A. Jr. *Mind as Behavior*. Columbus: R.G. Adams, 1924.

(8) Emery, F.E., E.L. Trist. "The Causal Texture of Organizational Environments." *Human Relations*, Vol. 18, 1965, pp. 21-32.

(9) Emery, F.E. , E.L. Trist. *Towards a Social Ecology*. London: Plenum Press, 1973.

(10) Rapoport, A. *Conflict in Man-Made*

Environment. London: Penguin, 1974.

(11) Systems Research Center, Case Institute of Technology, Case Western Reserve University. *APT-System: A Computer Based Tool for Assessment of Alternative Policies: An Aid in Planning.* Cleveland: Case Western Reserve University, 1975.

(12) This approach was used in the Seminar for Longe-Range Development Prospects for the Asian-Pacific Region at the East-West Center in Hawaii, January 16-20, 1977 where representatives of eleven nations participated in a cooperative way to formulate common futures, under the coordination of Mihajlo Mesarovič.

(13) McLeod, J. "Project Link. *Simulation,* Vol. 19, No. 6, Diciembre 1972, pp 192-194.

(14) Lara, F., *et al. Modelo para la elaboración de escenarios de referencia sobre el desarrollo de México.* México: Fundación Javier Barros Sierra, A.C., reporte interno, 1976.

SOME SOCIO-ECONOMIC ASPECTS OF HEALTH CARE PLANNING

A. Petrovsky, P. Kitzul, W. Olshansky and A. Yashin

Institute of Control Sciences, Moscow 117806, USSR

ABSTRACT

For planning the socio-economic development of regions interacting with the environment, the methods of global modeling are used at the increasing scale. In the existing global models, however, the health delivery aspect has not been given sufficient attention. The investments in this important field of economy and rational allocation of resources and planning thereof significantly influence the population health, and thus all the socio-economic indices of the regional development such as the gross regional product, the potential and actual labor resources, life expectation at birth, the level of social tension, etc. Rational planning in this field also requires taking into account the environmental factors.

All these factors call for more careful health care planning and investigating the influence of the health care system upon all the indices of regional socio-economic development.

The paper describes an approach to investigation of these problems with the method of systems modeling. The mathematical tools for describing the processes in a region are systems of partial differential, integro-differential and lagging equations. The algorithms are described and a numeric example is given.

INTRODUCTION

The need to foresee the results of simultaneous actions of many countries has generated a new direction of systems analysis which is called Global Modeling.

In the existing global models one can see two kinds of submodels - of productive subsystems (industries, food and agriculture, mining and energy, etc.) and of non-productive subsystems (education, health care, social welfare, law-enforcement, etc.).

The models are supposed to determine some sufficiently general trends in socio-economic development of different countries (Refs. 1-4). Nevertheless, the global nature of these models does not allow analyzing the details in functioning of regions and particular subsystems.

Meanwhile, there exists a significantly large number of autonomous models of subsystems which do not allow for effects of processes outside these subsystems.

There is an evident need to develop models that would retain the possibilities to analyse the decision-making within certain subsystems with the desired detail while recognizing the effect of processes in "external" subsystems. Such models may be named problem-oriented global models.

If the models of the productive subsystems have been thoroughly developed, the methodology for building models of non-productive subsystems is still wanting.

The importance of non-productive sectors for regional and global development is seen in the fact that these sectors affect not only the economic indices of productive sectors, but creates the necessary socio-cultural background (measured with appropriate indicators) for the evolution of the society.

One of the important subsystems is the health care system which not only affects the set of indicators characterizing the development of a certain region but is itself influenced by exogeneous socio-economic factors.

The health care - oriented global models while representing the regional specificity, should possess a certain amount of universality (Ref.5).

We have elaborated a simulation model "Population-Health Care" which recognizes the following kinds of interaction with external economico-ecological environment:
a) the gross regional product and its reproduction;
b) investment in health care and labor force reproduction;
c) food supply;
d) environment pollution;
e) inter-regional links.

This work was conducted as a joint program at the International Institute for Applied Systems Analysis (IIASA), Laxenburg, Austria and at the Institute of Control Science, Moscow.

THE STRUCTURE OF THE MODEL

To describe the population dynamics in the health care system model mathematical techniques are used which are very similar to those of certain demographic models. This description relies on partial differential equations of a special type. However, in health care system modeling this description becomes very involved because in addition to the sex-age structure of the population this structure has to incorporate health status indicators.

The population is classified into age-health groups. The number of age groups depends on the desired detailization of the age pyramid.

The minimal number of health categories is four -

1. healthy population;
2. the latent sick - those who are not aware of their disease or those who are aware but do not require medical help;
3. The detectee, sick who are aware of their disease but are not treated;
4. the patients who are treated.

The categories 2-4 may be subdivided into subcategories according to types of disease, stages of disease, types of the required service (in-patients, out-patients, custody, etc.) (Refs. 6,7).

At the initial step in studying models of health care, it is reasonable to develop models requiring the minimal amount of information. In a certain sense these requirements are met by a model with the four health categories.

Such a model has been studied by Atsumi and Kaihara (8). That model was developed to analyze the exchange rates among the categories using the statistical data available in Japan, and to forecast the future needs in medical care in Japan.

That model did not study the allocation of resources in health care or the feedbacks from the number of people in the categories to the exchange rates among the categories. However, considering these problems would make it possible to study some subtle non-linear effects due to, say, limited capacities of the health care system, health care availability and work-load, etc.

Age-health dynamics in our model is described by a system of partial differential equations (1)

$$\frac{\partial u(i,x,t)}{\partial t} = -\frac{\partial u(i,x,t)}{\partial x} + \sum_{j=1}^{K} q_{ji}(x,\vec{u},\vec{r},R) \times u(j,x,t),$$

$$u(i,x,0) = f_i(x),$$

$$u(i,0,t) = \sum_{j=1}^{K} \int_0^{\infty} \varphi_{ij}(u,x,t)\, u(j,x,t)\, dx,$$

$$i = 1,\ldots,K; \qquad (1)$$

where K is the number of health categories (including the dead), $u(i,x,t)$ are the people in the i-th health category, of the age x, at time t ; $q_{ji}(x,u,r,R)$ are the probabilities of transition from the category j into the category i depending on the vector of health care resources r, and on the time-vector

$$\vec{u} = (u(1,x,s),\ldots,u(K,x,s)),$$

$$0 \le x < \infty, \quad 0 \le s \le t;$$

$\varphi_{ij}(u,x,t)$ is the classified birth rate, R are the external factors,

Equation (1) is solved with the method of characteristics. The continuous age x is quantified so that the population is divided into N age groups.

The transition coefficients among the health categories are dictated in the model by the current medico-demographic structure of the population, the resourses for health care (prevention, medical education, professional medical education, detection measures, intensive treatment, progress of medical science, etc.) and by exogeneous factors (life standards, the nutrition level, the environment pollution level).

To work with the model, one has to specify the initial and boundary conditions, i.e. the medico-demographic characteristics of a region. The transition coefficients are partly specified in advance and partly are varied by the decision-maker in his work with the model. This work consists of a review of interesting for the decision-maker sets of numeric characteristics of population health as a function of various kinds of the transition coefficients variations.

To analyse the health care activities and to obtain reasonable controls, one must interact with this system bearing in mind the external systems.

This may be done in two ways -

(1) to develop a closed-loop model of health care system;
(2) to specify the external actions in compliance with a scenario.

The natural evolution of the model goes along the lines of progress in global modeling:

- At the first stage, it is a generalized model (somewhat analogous to models by Forrester and Meadows (Ref. 1);
- At the second stage, it is a regionalized model (an analog of one of the levels in the Mesarovic - Pestel model (Ref. 3).

The regionalized model will be a more adequate representation of mixed central - local allocation of investments in health delivery existing in some countries.

Links with External Systems

The model of health care system has the following input from external systems

- gross national/regional product per capita;
- environment pollution level;
- nutrition level;
- investments in health care.

The influence of these factors on parameters of population calls for further investigations. At the early stage of this model, we use the factors of environment pollution and nutrition level in the fashion of Ref. 3.

The outputs of the health care system affecting the external systems are the active labor resources and the index of health care social performance (see below).

To get a closed-loop model we are to build a model for the external systems and a set of controls (scenarios).

The External Systems

The easiest way to develop the model for the "external" systems is to use production functions that formally relate the resource productivities and amounts with the product.

The labor resources are divided into labor for industries, services, and agriculture. These resourses enter the associated production functions.

The production functions determine the gross regional product and provide the investments in industries, service, agriculture, and for the consumption.

In the model of health care the industries determine the environment pollution, and the agriculture - the nutrition level.

The minimal nutritional needs are specified so as to meet the conditions of life preservation as given in the recommendations of the World Health Organization. The actual needs in food increase with the gross industrial output per capita. Comparison of the nutritional needs with food production and availability leads to the nutrition deficit which affects the morbidity and death rates.

The gross regional product provides the investments in health care which should be intelligently allocated among the services and the functions of the health care system itself.

Health Care Management

Investments in health care are divided in the model into investments in the prevention/treatment activities:

- disease prevention and medical education;
- detection of the sick;
- treatment of the sick;

and the investments in management, equipment, professional medical education, and medical science.

In allocating the resourses in prevention, detection and treatment, priorities are specified for the resourses earmarked for each age group. For instance, the resources for children health care are larger compared with those for the other age groups, thus decreasing children morbidity and prevalence.

In the resourses allocation, some indicutors of public opinion reflecting marginal social tension due to inadequacy of health delivery are also allowed for.

Economic Efficiency of Health Care

The production function of industries (like in Ref. 1) is the following

$$y_{t+1} = CK_t m(K_t, y_t/P_t, L_t) \qquad (2)$$

$$m(K, y/p, L) = \begin{cases} 1, & L^*/L \leq 1; \\ \frac{1-h}{2}(\cos b(L^*/L - 1) + 1) + h, & 1 < L^*/L \leq \pi/b + 1; \\ h, & L^*/L > \pi/b + 1, \end{cases} \qquad (3)$$

$$L^*/K = \Lambda/(y/p - y_0), \qquad (4)$$

where t is time, y is the regional industrial output; C is the output-capital ratio; K is the capital; $m(\cdot, \cdot, \cdot)$ is the capital utilization factor; P is the total population, L is the active labor force supply; L^* is the labor force demand; h, b, y_0, Λ are empirical constants.

The investments in health care (resulting in the increase of active labor force due to the decrease in disablement and the increase of life expectation at birth increase the active labor force supply L —

$$L_t = \sum_{i=0}^{K} \int_0^{\infty} \lambda_i(x, S_t)\, u(i, x, t)\, dx,$$

where λ is the labor activity, S is the index of social performance of health care.

Investments I_{HC} increase L additionally by increasing the labor active fraction of the population by improving the socio-cultural indicators of the region.

It is natural to define the economic efficiency E_e of the investment in health care as the ratio of the regional industrial output increment due to the increment of the investments I_{HC} to these investments:

$$E_e = \frac{\partial Y}{\partial I_{HC}}. \qquad (6)$$

Within the framework of the economic model Eqs (2)-(4), the efficiency E_e may be different from zero only when the employment ratio $L^*/L > 1$. Under the conditions of the employment ratio $L^*/L \leq 1$, the investments in health care can only be justified by increasing the marginal social tension by deterioration of socio-cultural indicators if these investments were not appropriated.

Social Efficiency of Health Care

Marginal social tension due to inadequacy of health care will be specified by the index of social performance of health care S:

$$S_t = \frac{\sum_{i=1}^{K} \int_0^{\infty} \sigma_i(x)\, u(i,x,t)\, dx}{\sum_{i=1}^{K} \int_0^{\infty} u(i,x,t)\, dx} \cdot \frac{LE}{70}, \qquad (7)$$

where σ are empirical coefficients LE is life expectation at birth.

It is natural to determine the social efficiency E_s of the investment in health care as the ratio of the increment of the index of social performance of health care due to the increment of the investments I_{HC} to these investments:

$$E_s = \frac{\partial S}{\partial I_{HC}}. \qquad (8)$$

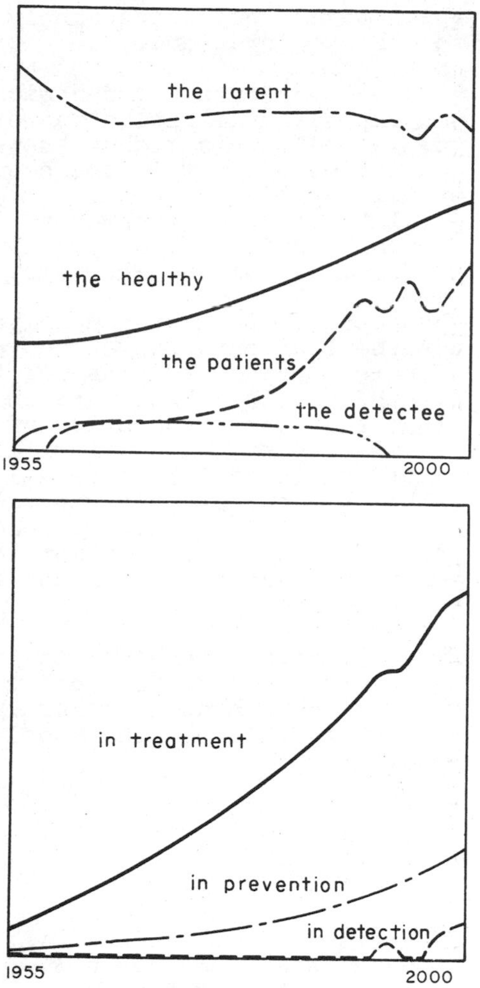

Fig. 1. Health care program 1:
(a) health categories prevalence dynamics;
(b) health care resources distribution.

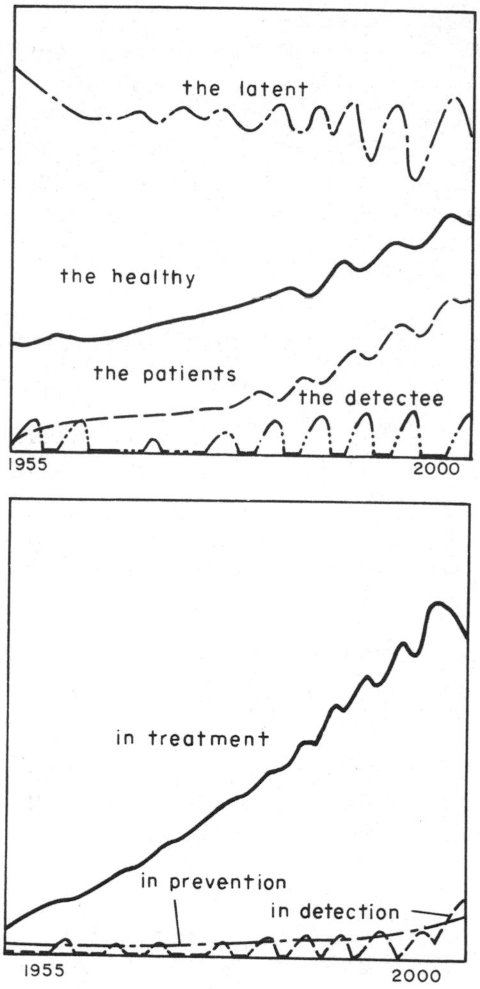

Fig. 2. Health care program 2:
(a) health categories prevalence dynamics;
(b) health care resources distribution.

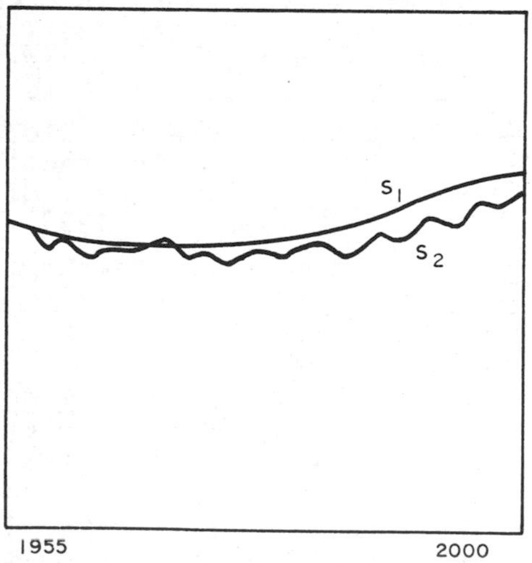

Fig. 3. The index of social performance of health care and the active labor force supply.

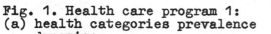

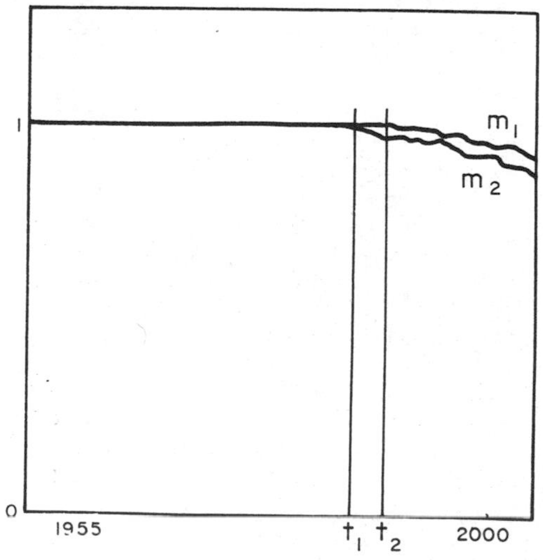

Fig. 4. The capital utilization factor dynamics in the two health programs.

CONCLUSIONS

The above methological approach to planning regional development allows us to determine the rôle of the health care system in the general socio-economic system of the region, and also to solve various problems of organization of the health delivery itself with due regard for exogeneous factors.

The first version of the health care-oriented model has been implemented on a computer. External subsystems are simulated by a modification of the WORLD 3 model (Ref. 1), the analysis of inter-regional relations follows the line of the GLOBE 6 model (Ref. 4).

The health delivery itself is described by Equations (1).

The model has been tried on the data on a certain hypothetical region (simulating a developing country).

The health care resources were allocated in the following way-specified fractions of the investments were appropriated to professional medical education, management, equipment, medical science, disease prevention and medical education, wages, salaries, and fees of the personnel engaged in treatment and detection;

> the personnel engaged in treatment and detection is reallocated between these two functions so that the number of detectees (i.e. the sick who know about their disease but do not receive proper treatment) is minimal under the absence of the underload of the treatment capacities (which are determined by the treatment resources productivity).

Figures 1 and 2 show the four categories prevalence dynamics and the dynamics of the resources of health care (the total investments increasing by 5% per year) allotted in (1) disease prevention and popular medical education, (2) detection of the latent sick, (3) patients treatment - using two different programs of allocation.

Investments in health care in the two programs are the same but in Program 1 prevention and medical education receive 2.5% of the total investments (Fig. 1), and in Program 2 - 9%. (Fig. 2).

Fig. 3 shows the index of social performance of health care S and the active labor force supply L for the two programs.

Figure 4 presents the dynamics of the capital utilization factor (Eqs. 3, 4). This Figure shows that until time t' or t'' the economic efficiency of health care E_e is equal to zero. After time t' the economic efficiency of Program 2 is better than that of Program 1.

The results of numeric modeling on hypothetical data prove the validity of this approach to planning the health care in a large region. It is clear that the preparation of actual data to run such a model will require considerable time because all the relevant data are not generally registered and, moreover, some data (e.g., about the latent morbidity and prevalence rate) can not be acquired directly.

Together with extensive and intensive development of the model we are working on methods to determine parameters relevant for model functioning.

REFERENCES

(1) Meadows D.H., Meadows D.L., Randers J., Behrens W.W. Dynamics of Growth in a Finite World, Wright-Allen Press, Cambridge, Mass. (1974).

(2) Fundacion Bariloche, Latin American World Model, Preliminary report presented at IIASA symposium, Baden, Austria (1974).

(3) Mesarovic M., Pestel E. (eds.), Multilevel Computer Model of World Development System, (vols 1-6), IIASA, Laxenburg, Austria (1974).

(4) Burnet R., Dionne P., Globe 6: A Multi-regional Interactive World Simulation Model, Simulation, 20, 6, 192-197 (1973).

(5) Venediktov D.D., Modeling of Health Care Systems, IIASA Conference '76, 2, 101-115 (1976), Laxenburg, Austria.

(6) Olshansky W., A Basic Model of Health Care Systems, Internal report, IIASA, Laxenburg, Austria (1976).

(7) Klementyev A. Mathematical Approach to Developing a Simulation Model of a Health Care System, Research memo, IIASA, Laxenburg, Austria (1976).

(8) Kaihara S., Atsumi K., A Simulation Model of Medical Demand in

Japan, 2nd USA-Japan Computer Conference Proceedings, 220-222, Information Processing Society of Japan (1975).

STRUCTURAL MODELING IN A CLASS OF SYSTEMS BY FUZZY SETS THEORY

E. Tazaki and M. Amagasa

Associate Professor and Research Associate, Faculty of Science and Technology, Tokyo University of Science, Noda city, Chiba 278, Japan

ABSTRACT

On the basis of fuzzy sets theory, we propose a method for structuring hierarchy for the several problems , that is Fuzzy Structural Modeling (FSM) method. An important requirement for structural modeling of complex systems is that the necessary data is acquired and organized into a form which a structural model can be developed.
The main purpose of this method is to describe and illustrate a formal procedure for constructing the graphic presentation of the hierarchical arrangement, given the necessary information concerning the relation of each element to each other element. The procedure permits the automatic development of the graphic structure that portrays the hierarchy.

INTRODUCTION

In studying complex problems, in developing plans, in managing organizations, in working with systems and in various other kinds of human endeavor, it is often desirable and sometimes essential to synthesize hierarchies. The process of arranging elements in a hierarchy is usually dealt with intuitively.
In order to deal with such a system systematically, ISM, DEMATEL and KJ method etc, have been proposed. In particular ISM and DEMATEL are developed on the basis of graph theory.
A matrix representing a subordination relation among elements of system is called a subordination matrix and the elements are filled with a binary relation. However it will not be always reasonable to use the binary relation among elements.
On the other hand, the concept of fuzzy sets gives an important mathematical clue for an approach to studies of such systems with no sharp boundaries.
On the basis of fuzzy sets theory, we propose a method for structuring hierarchy for the several problems mentioned above, that is Fuzzy Structural Modeling (FSM) method.
An important requirement for structural modeling of complex systems is that the necessary data is acquired and organized into a form which a structural model can be developed.
A fuzzy reachability matrix is one such form.

The main purpose of this method is to describe and illustrate a formal procedure for constructing the graphic presentation of the hierarchical arrangement, given the necessary information concerning the relation of each element to each other element. The procedure permits the automatic development of the graphic structure that portrays the hierarchy.
The entries in the matrix are taken to values on the interval [0,1] by virtue of a fuzzy binary relation. According to the matrix, a fuzzy digraph describes a contextual relation among the elements of the system and can be transformed into an interpretive structural model of the system with respect to the relation.
A significant step in the development of the proposed fuzzy structural modeling consists of the relaxation of transitivity, irreflexivity and asymmetry with respect to the construction of subordination matrix. The relaxation extends the flexibility and applicability for the structural modeling of systems.
In order to show how the proposed method works, a few examples have been illustrated and the structure for the system has been successfully identified.

PRELIMINARY FOR FUZZY STRUCTURAL MODELING

Several properties with respect to fuzzy subsets and fuzzy relations are shown as mathematical preliminaries for a fuzzy structural modeling.
[Definition 1] Let X be a arbitrary set which is treated in the ordinary sets theory. Denote an element of X by x. Let us consider $[0,1]^X$, i.e. the set of all mappings such that

$$\mu : X \rightarrow [0,1] \tag{1}$$

A label to an element of $[0,1]^X$ is written by μ_A. Then A is called a fuzzy subset of X and μ_A membership function of A.

[Definition 2] A fuzzy complement of a fuzzy subset A, denoted $\bar{A}$, is characterized by virtue of $\mu_{\bar{A}}$ as follows:

$$\mu_{\bar{A}} = \frac{1 - \mu_A}{1 + \lambda \cdot \mu_A} \tag{2}$$

,where a parameter λ in eq.(2) is a real number $-1<\lambda<\infty$.

[Definition 3] Let B and Y be a fuzzy matrix and a fuzzy vector, respectively such that

$$B = \begin{bmatrix} b_{11} & b_{12} & ---- & b_{1n} \\ --- & --- & ---- & --- \\ --- & --- & b_{ij} & --- \\ --- & --- & --- & ---- \\ b_{n1} & b_{n2} & ----- & b_{nn} \end{bmatrix}, \quad Y = [y_1, y_2, ---, y_n]^T \tag{3}$$

and both of b_{ij} and y_j are in a closed interval [0,1]. Then the fuzzy composition C of B and Y is defined as follows;

$$c_i = \bigvee_{j=1}^{n} (b_{ij} \wedge y_j), \ i=1,2,---,n \qquad (4)$$

,where $\bigvee_{i=1}^{n} a_i$ means $\max_{1 \leq i \leq n} \{ a_i \}$ and $a \wedge b$ min(a,b).

Eq.(4) is also written by

$$C = B \circ Y \qquad (5)$$

, where $C = (c_1, c_2, ---, c_n)$.

[Definition 4] A fuzzy logical sum D and a fuzzy logical product E of fuzzy matrices A and B are defined as follows:

$$D = A \oplus B \Leftrightarrow d_{ij} = \max[a_{ij}, b_{ij}] = a_{ij} \vee b_{ij}$$
$$E = A \otimes B \Leftrightarrow e_{ij} = \min[a_{ij}, b_{ij}] = a_{ij} \wedge b_{ij} \qquad (6)$$

[Definition 5] A fuzzy binary relation and its complement in S x S are characterized by f_R and $f_{\bar{R}}$, respectively as follows:

$$f_R : S \times S \rightarrow [0,1]$$
$$f_{\bar{R}} : S \times S \rightarrow [0,1] \qquad (7)$$

The complement of R, denoted $\bar{R}$, is the relation such that

$$f_{\bar{R}}(s_i, s_j) = \frac{1 - f_R(s_i, s_j)}{1 + \lambda \cdot f_R(s_i, s_j)}, \qquad (8)$$
$$\text{for } \forall (s_i, s_j) \in S \times S$$

Let p be a real number given on a semi-open interval (0,1]. Then some definitions of the fuzzy binary relations in S x S are given on the basis of such a p.

[Definition 6] (Fuzzy reflexive law)
When $f_R(s_i, s_i) \geq p$ for $\forall (s_i, s_i) \in S \times S$ is satisfied, it is called a fuzzy reflexive.

[Definition 7] (Fuzzy irreflexive law)
When $f_R(s_i, s_i) < p$ for $\forall (s_i, s_i) \in S \times S$ is satisfied, it is called a fuzzy irreflexive.

[Definition 8] (Fuzzy symmetric law)
When $f_R(s_j, s_i) \geq p$ is satisfied for $\forall (s_i, s_j) \in S \times S$, $i \neq j$, it is called a fuzzy symmetric.

[Definition 9] (Fuzzy asymmetric law)
For $\forall (s_i, s_j) \in S \times S$, $i \neq j$, when at least either $f_R(s_i, s_j) < p$ or $f_R(s_j, s_i) < p$ is satisfied, it is called a fuzzy asymmetric.

[Definition 10] (Fuzzy transitive law)
Let $s_i, s_j, s_k \in S$, $i \neq j \neq k$.
When $f_R(s_i, s_k) \geq \max_{s_j}[\min(f_R(s_i, s_j), f_R(s_j, s_k))]$

$$\text{for } \forall (s_i, s_j), (s_j, s_k), (s_i, s_k) \in S \times S$$

is satisfied , it is called a fuzzy transitive.

[Definition 11] (Fuzzy semi-transitive law)
Let $m_{ik} = \bigvee_{j=1}^{n} (f_R(s_i, s_j) \wedge f_R(s_j, s_k))$ for $\forall (s_i, s_j)$, (s_j, s_k), $(s_i, s_k) \in S \times S$. When $f_R(s_i, s_k) \geq m_{ik}$ for all of (s_i, s_k), $i \neq k$, satisfying $m_{ik} \geq p$, it is called a fuzzy semi-transitive.

RULE OF STRUCTURAL MODELING AND ALGORITHM

Let a system object be $S = \{s_1, s_2, ---, s_n\}$. We construct a fuzzy subordination matrix A which represents a fuzzy subordination relation among elements of the S on the basis of a certain contextual relation.

$$A = [a_{ij}] , \ (i,j = 1,2,---,n) \qquad (9)$$

,where the A is a square n x n matrix and the element a_{ij} of A is given by the membership function f_R of the fuzzy binary relation shown in definition 5 as follows;

$$a_{ij} = f_R(s_i, s_j), \ 0 \leq a_{ij} \leq 1, \ (i,j=1,2,---,n) \qquad (10)$$

This shows the grade which s_i is subordinate to s_j.

In order to show that the subordination relation is greater than a certain grade, we set up the parameter p as a threshold. Such a threshold must be given on the semi-open interval (0,1].

A fuzzy semi-reachability matrix is defined corresponding to the fuzzy subordination matrix.

[Definition 12] When a fuzzy subordination matrix A satisfies the fuzzy semi-transitive law, A is called a fuzzy semi-reachability matrix.

A method for finding such a matrix is proposed as follows;

Determination of fuzzy semi-reachability matrix

(STEP1') The powers matrices for the subordination matrix A are taken as follows;

$$A^1 = A, \ A^2 = A^1 \circ A, \ A^3 = A^2 \circ A, --- ,$$
$$A^i = A^{i-1} \circ A, ---, \ A^n = A^{n-1} \circ A \qquad (11)$$

A logical sum of the powers matrices A^1, A^2, ---, A^n is given by

$$\oplus A^i = A^1 \oplus A^2 \oplus --- \oplus A^n \qquad (12)$$

Further replace $\oplus A^i$ in (12) with A^*.
(STEP2') If the element a^*_{ij} of A* is less than p, the a^*_{ij} is set to zero.
(STEP3') The matrix obtained by the logical sum of the original matrix A and the A* becomes a fuzzy semi-reachability matrix $A' = [a'_{ij}]$.

$$A' = A \oplus A^*, \ a'_{ij} = a_{ij} \vee a^*_{ij}, \ (i,j=1,2,---,n) \qquad (13)$$

Next it is shown that the fuzzy semi-transitive law is satisfied such a matrix A'.
Suppose that the fuzzy subordination matrix $A = [a_{ij}]$ for $S = \{s_1, ---, s_{k_1}, s_{k_2}, ---, s_{k_6}, --- , s_n\}$. Each element of $a_{k_1k_2}$, $a_{k_2k_3}$, $a_{k_3k_4}$, $a_{k_1k_5}$, $a_{k_5k_6}$ is greater than or equal to the p and the other elements a_{ij} are less than the p.
In such a fuzzy subordination matrix,
$a_{k_1k_6} \geq p$ and $a_{k_1k_5} \wedge a_{k_5k_6} \geq p$.
It is necessary to satisfy the following relations for the fuzzy subordination matrix.

$$a_{k_1k_6} \geq a_{k_1k_5} \wedge a_{k_5k_6}$$

Further, for this matrix, though $a_{k_1k_2} \wedge a_{k_2k_3} \geq p$ and $a_{k_2k_3} \wedge a_{k_3k_4} \geq p$,
the following relations are also satisfied.

$a_{k_1k_3} < p,\ a_{k_2k_4} < p$

These mean that the fuzzy semi-transitive law is not satisfied in this matrix.
The fuzzy semi-reachability matrix is determind by using the algorithm mentioned above. Let consider the following powers matrices.

$$a^2_{k_1k_3} = \bigvee_{i=1}^{n} (a_{k_1i} \wedge a_{ik_3}) = a_{k_1k_2} \wedge a_{k_2k_3} \geq p \quad (14)$$

$$a^2_{k_2k_4} = a_{k_2k_3} \wedge a_{k_3k_4} \geq p \quad (15)$$

$$a_{k_1k_6} = a_{k_1k_5} \wedge a_{k_5k_6} \geq p \quad (16)$$

All of the other elements are less than p. Further, all of the elements of power matrix A^3 are also less than p except the following one element.

$$a^3_{k_1k_4} = \bigvee_{i=1}^{n} (a^2_{k_1i} \wedge a_{ik_4}) = a^2_{k_1k_3} \wedge a_{k_3k_4}$$
$$= a_{k_1k_2} \wedge a_{k_2k_3} \wedge a_{k_3k_4} \geq p \quad (17)$$

Similarly all of the elements of powers matrices A^4,---,A^n are also less than p.
$A^* = \bigoplus_{i=1}^{n} A^i$ is computed and each element satisfying a^*_{ij} p is put to zero. After such a computing process , six elements in the original matrix A and three elements $a^*_{k_1k_3}$, $a^*_{k_1k_4}$, $a^*_{k_2k_4}$ in the A* become greater than p, and the other elements are put to zero. From the definition $A' = A \oplus A^*$, the following subordination relations are satisfied in the A'.

$$a'_{k_1k_2} = a_{k_1k_2} \geq p \quad (18)$$

$$a'_{k_1k_3} = a_{k_1k_2} \wedge a_{k_2k_3} \geq p \quad (19)$$

$$a'_{k_1k_4} = a_{k_1k_2} \wedge a_{k_2k_3} \wedge a_{k_3k_4} \geq p \quad (20)$$

$$a'_{k_1k_5} = a_{k_1k_5} \geq p \quad (21)$$

$$a'_{k_1k_6} = a_{k_1k_6} \vee (a_{k_1k_5} \wedge a_{k_5k_6}) \geq p \quad (22)$$

$$a'_{k_2k_3} = a'_{k_2k_3} \geq p \quad (23)$$

$$a'_{k_2k_4} = a_{k_2k_3} \wedge a_{k_3k_4} \geq p \quad (24)$$

$$a'_{k_3k_4} = a_{k_3k_4} \geq p \quad (25)$$

$$a'_{k_5k_6} = a_{k_5k_6} \geq p \quad (26)$$

Further each of the other elements satisfies the following relation.

$$a'_{ij} = a_{ij} < p \quad (27)$$

Therefore,the fuzzy semi-transitive law is satisfied with the fuzzy semi-reachability matrix A'. In particular it is noted that the element $a'_{k_1k_6}$ satisfies the following relation by virtue of (21),(22) and (26).

$$a'_{k_1k_6} \geq (a'_{k_1k_5} \wedge a'_{k_5k_6})$$
$$= (a_{k_1k_5} \wedge a_{k_5k_6}) \geq p \quad (28)$$

We can see that the fuzzy semi-reachability matrix is a matrix modified so as to satisfy the fuzzy semi-transitive law without changing the property of the original fuzzy subordination relation. On the other hand, such a matrix may represent several hierarchies.

[Definition 13] A top level set $L_t(s)$, an intermediate level set $L_i(s)$, a bottom level set $L_b(s)$ and an isolation level set $L_{is}(s)$ are defined as follows;

$$L_t(s) = \{ s_i \mid \bigvee_{j=1}^{n} a_{ij} < p \leq \bigvee_{j=1}^{n} a_{ji} \} \quad (29)$$

$$L_i(s) = \{ s_j \mid \bigvee_{k=1}^{n} a_{kj} \geq p\ ,\ \bigvee_{k=1}^{n} a_{jk} \geq p \} \quad (30)$$

$$L_b(s) = \{ s_i \mid \bigvee_{j=1}^{n} a_{ji} < p \leq \bigvee_{j=1}^{n} a_{ij} \} \quad (31)$$

$$L_{is}(s) = \{ s_j \mid \bigvee_{k=1}^{n} a_{kj} < p\ ,\ \bigvee_{k=1}^{n} a_{jk} < p \} \quad (32)$$

Each element of the top level set is not subordinate to anyone. The elements of the intermediate level set is subordinate to anyone and has anyone subordinate to itself. Each of the bottom level set has nothing subordinate to itself. Each of the isolation level set is not subordinate to anyone, and has nothing subordinate to itself. These sets are shown in Fig.1.

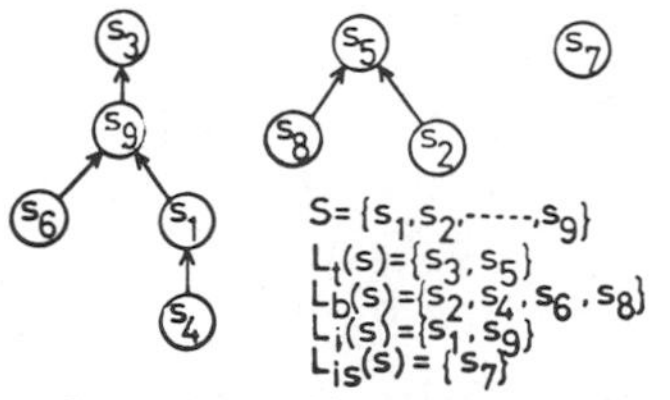

Fig.1 Single hierarchies and level sets

On the other hand,several hierarchies can be constructed by performing the structural modeling for a system object. The top level set must be separated corresponding to each hierarchy beforehand. For example, in Fig.1, there are two single hierarchies such that each element s_3 and s_5 is in the top level set of each hierarchy.
The matrix representing such a single hierarchy is called a single hierarchy matrix.

[Definition 14] Let $R(s_i)$ be a set to which any element s_j is directly or indirectly subordinate. Then the $R(s_i)$ is called a reachability set,and represented as follows;

$$R(s_i) = \{ s_j \mid a'_{ij} \geq p \} \quad (33)$$

For example, $R(s_1) = \{ s_3, s_9 \}$ in Fig.1.

Let $B(s_i)$ be elements set of the top level set to which s_i of the bottom level set is subordinate. Then it is defined as follows;

$$B(s_i) = \{ s_j \mid a'_{ij} \geq p,\ s_i \in L_b(s),\ s_j \in L_t(s) \} \quad (34)$$

It is clear that the following relation is held between $B(s_i)$ and $R(s_i)$.

$$B(s_i) \subseteq R(s_i),\ s_i \in L_b(s) \quad (35)$$

The equality sign in (35) is held when $a'_{ij} \geq p$, $s_j \in L_t(s)$ and $a'_{ik} < p$, $s_k \notin L_t(s)$.
This means that s_i is directly subordinate to at least one element of the top level set.

[Definition 15] The top level set of a single hierarchy is called a brock set and represented by Q_j, where an index j shows j-th hierarchy. It is clear that the following relation is held.

$$Q_j \subseteq L_t(s) \tag{36}$$

The equality sign is satisfied if and only if a single hierarchy exists. The block set contains the necessary information to determine how many hierarchies are represented by A and their separate top level set.
The block set is identified as follows;

Identification of block sets

Let D be a set family which is composed of the set $B(s_i)$ shown in (34).

$$D = \{B(s_i) \mid s_i \in L_b(s)\} \tag{37}$$

(STEP1") Let j=1 .
(STEP2") Take out any element $B(s_i)$ from D and delete it from D.

$$D \leftarrow D - B(s_i)$$

,where $\leftarrow$ means " replacing ".
Further let Q_j be the set of all the elements of $B(s_i)$. When $D=\emptyset$, the block set Q_j can be obtained. The procedure terminates.
Otherwise go to STEP3.
(STEP3") Take out the $B(s_k)$ successively from D obtained in STEP2, and perform the following operation for the $B(s_k)$ and the Q_j.

1) If $Q_j \cap B(s_k) \neq \emptyset$, delete the $B(s_k)$ from D and replace the Q_j with $Q_j \cup B(s_k)$.

2) If $Q_j \cap B(s_k) = \emptyset$, the operation is not performed at all.

(STEP4") If D is a null set, the procedure terminates, otherwise replace j with j+1 and return to STEP2".

[Definition 16] The submatrix among elements which shows the subordination relation is constructed of the elements subordinate to the same Q_j. The submatrix represents a single hierarchy structure, and is called a single hierarchy matrix $A^{(j)}$.
The matrix $A^{(j)}$ is found in the following operations.

Rows with respect to the elements of the top level set, columns with respect to the elements of the bottom level set, and rows and columns with respect to the elements of the isolation level set are eliminated from the fuzzy semi-reachability matrix.
In the $Q^{(j)}$, we find all of the elements which is not subordinate to the elements of the $Q^{(j)}$, and eliminate their rows and columns from the $A^{(j)}$. The matrix consisting of rows and columns remained after such a process is a single hierarchy matrix $A^{(j)}$.

[Definition 17] A row (column) is said to be regular if it contains only a single $a_{ij}^{(k)}$ which satisfies $a_{ij}^{(k)} \geq p$ in the $A^{(k)}$.

This regular row (column) represents an unique subordination relation between s_i and s_j. There is no need the regular row (column) by placing the regular row (column)'s index on the graph. Therefore such a regular row (column) can be eliminated from the $A^{(j)}$.

On the other hand, in such a process, it is sometimes that there exists no the regular row or column in the $A^{(j)}$. In such a case, one must split the lowest order row into the regular rows.
The rules for developing a graph from the reachability matrix will now be described.

[Rule1] Both of a fuzzy irreflexive law and a fuzzy asymmetric law must be satisfied on the fuzzy subordination matrix and the fuzzy semi-reachability matrix.

[Rule2] If there exists no the regular row or the regular column in the single hierarchy matrix, the lowest order row must be split into the regular rows.

We suppose that the $A^{(r)}$ is obtained after the elimination of the regular row or column.

$$A^{(r)} = \begin{array}{c} \\ s_i \\ s_j \\ s_k \end{array} \begin{array}{c} \begin{array}{ccc} s_1 & s_m & s_n \end{array} \\ \left[\begin{array}{ccc} p_1 & p_2 & a_{in}^{(r)} \\ p_3 & p_4 & p_5 \\ p_6 & p_7 & p_8 \end{array}\right] \end{array} \tag{38}$$

,where it is assumed that $p_i \geq p$, (i=1,---,8) and $a_{in}^{(r)} < p$ in (38).
In this case, each row s_i, s_j and s_k is irregular, each column s_1, s_m, s_n is also irregular. Therefore the lowest order row of their irregular rows is split into the regular rows. In this instance, select the row s_i and split it into two regular rows s_{i_1}, s_{i_2}. This gives a new matrix as shown in (39).

$$A^{(r)} = \begin{array}{c} \\ s_{i_1} \\ s_{i_2} \\ s_j \\ s_k \end{array} \begin{array}{c} \begin{array}{ccc} s_1 & s_m & s_n \end{array} \\ \left[\begin{array}{ccc} p_1 & 0 & a_{in}^{(r)} \\ 0 & p_2 & a_{i_n}^{(r)} \\ p_3 & p_4 & p_5 \\ p_6 & p_7 & p_8 \end{array}\right] \end{array} \tag{39}$$

The following rule3 is applied to (39).

[Rule3] When every regular rows s_{i_1}, s_{i_2}, -----, s_{i_m} obtained by splitting the row s_i are eliminated, the rows s_{i_1}, s_{i_2}, ---, s_{i_m} must be recombined to the s_i on the graph.

[Proposition 1] When the fuzzy subordination matrix A is modified so as to satisfy the fuzzy semi-transitive law for the threshold p, the elements of $L_i(s)$ and the elements of $L_b(s)$ are subordinate to at least one element of $L_t(s)$.

[Proof] Let a system object be $S=\{s_1, s_2, -----, s_{k_1}, s_{k_2}, ---, s_{k_6}, ---, s_n\}$,and consider the fuzzy subordination matrix $[a_{ij}]$ given on the basis of a certain contextual relation for such a system.
Then suppose that $L_t(s)=\{s_{k_1}, s_{k_2}\}$, $L_i(s)=\{s_{k_3}, s_{k_4}\}$, $L_b(s)=\{s_{k_5}, s_{k_6}\}$ and the other elements belong to the isolation level set $L_{is}(s)$.
The rows with respect to elements of $L_t(s)$, the columns with respect to elements of $L_b(s)$

and the rows and the columns with respect to elements of $L_{is}(s)$ can be eliminated from A. Without loss of generality, it is assumed that $p \leq p_1 \leq p_2 \leq \cdots \leq p_6 \leq 1$ and the other elements a_{ij} are less than p. Then the A is represented as follows;

$$A = \begin{array}{c} \\ s_{k_3} \\ s_{k_4} \\ s_{k_5} \\ s_{k_6} \end{array} \begin{array}{c} \begin{array}{cccc} s_{k_1} & s_{k_2} & s_{k_3} & s_{k_4} \end{array} \\ \left[\begin{array}{cccc} p_1 & p_2 & 0 & a_{k_3k_4} \\ a_{k_4k_1} & p_3 & a_{k_4k_3} & 0 \\ a_{k_5k_1} & a_{k_5k_2} & p_4 & a_{k_5k_4} \\ a_{k_6k_1} & a_{k_6k_2} & p_5 & p_6 \end{array}\right] \end{array} \qquad (40)$$

Regarding A in (40), the fuzzy transitive law is not satisfied because $a_{k_4k_2} \wedge a_{k_3k_1} = p_3 \wedge p_1 = p_1 \geq p$ and $a_{k_4k_1} < p$. Then A is modified so as to satisfy the fuzzy semi-transitive law and is replaced with a new matrix A' as follows;

$$A' = \begin{array}{c} \\ s_{k_3} \\ s_{k_4} \\ s_{k_5} \\ s_{k_6} \end{array} \begin{array}{c} \begin{array}{cccc} s_{k_1} & s_{k_2} & s_{k_3} & s_{k_4} \end{array} \\ \left[\begin{array}{cccc} p_1 & p_2 & 0 & a_{k_3k_4} \\ a_{k_4k_1} & p_3 & a_{k_4k_3} & 0 \\ p_1 & p_2 & p_4 & a_{k_5k_4} \\ p_1 & p_3 & p_5 & p_6 \end{array}\right] \end{array} \qquad (41)$$

With respect to the A', all of the elements $s_{k_3}, s_{k_5}, s_{k_6}$ are subordinate to s_{k_3}. This shows that if the fuzzy semi-transitive law is satisfied with the fuzzy subordination matrix, each element of $L_i(s), L_b(s)$ is subordinate to at least one element of $L_t(s)$.

[Proposition 2] Let the regular rows corresponding to s_i in a single hierarchy $A^{(r)}$ be s_{j_k}, k=1, 2,---, m ($m \leq n$). Further, the following operation is defined.

$$a^*_{\cdot i} = a^{(r)}_{\cdot i} \otimes \left(\bigotimes_{k=1}^{m} \overline{a^{(r)}_{\cdot j_k}} \right) \qquad (42)$$

$$\text{,where } \bigotimes_{k=1}^{m} a_{\cdot k} = a_{\cdot 1} \otimes a_{\cdot 2} \otimes \cdots \otimes a_{\cdot m} \qquad (43)$$

$$, \overline{a^{(r)}_{ij_k}} = (1 - a^{(r)}_{ij_k})/(1 + \lambda \cdot a^{(r)}_{ij_k}) \qquad (44)$$

When the column s_i of $A^{(r)}$ is replaced with $a^*_{\cdot i}$, the elements which are directly subordinate to s_i can be uniquely determined depending on a given λ except regular rows of s_i. With respect to the regular column corresponding to s_i, the elements to s_i can be uniquely determined in a similar way.

[Proof] Consider the submatrix A_{sub} which consist of s_i, s_j, s_k and s_1 belonging to a single hierarchy A as follows;

$$A_{sub} = \begin{array}{c} \\ s_j \\ s_k \\ s_1 \end{array} \begin{array}{c} \begin{array}{ccc} s_i & s_j & s_k \end{array} \\ \left[\begin{array}{ccc} p_{ji} & 0 & a_{jk} \\ p_{ki} & a_{kj} & 0 \\ p_{1i} & p_{1j} & p_{1k} \end{array}\right] \end{array} \qquad (45)$$

,where it is assumed that $a_{jk}, a_{kj} < p$ and $p_{ji}, p_{ki}, p_{kj}, p_{1i}, p_{1j}, p_{1k} \geq p$ in the matrix. Then regular rows corresponding to s_i are s_j and s_k. Therefore the following operation is carried out.

$$a^*_{\cdot i} = a_{\cdot i} \otimes \overline{a_{\cdot j}} \otimes \overline{a_{\cdot k}} = \begin{array}{c} \\ s_j \\ s_k \\ s_1 \end{array} \begin{array}{c} s_i \\ \left[\begin{array}{c} p_{ji} \wedge 1 \wedge \overline{a_{jk}} \\ p_{ki} \wedge \overline{a_{kj}} \wedge 1 \\ p_{1i} \wedge \overline{p_{1j}} \wedge \overline{p_{1k}} \end{array}\right] \end{array}$$

The following case is considered concerning irregular row s_1 corresponding to the s_i.

i) If $(1-p_{1j})/(1+\lambda \cdot p_{1j}) \geq p$ and $(1-p_{1k})/(1+\lambda \cdot p_{1k}) \geq p$, $a_{1i} = a^*_{1i} = p_{1i} \wedge \overline{p_{1j}} \wedge \overline{p_{1k}} \geq p$. Then this follows that the element s_1 is subordinate directly to s_i.

ii) If $(1-p_{1j})/(1+\lambda \cdot p_{1j}) < p$ or $(1-p_{1k})/(1+\lambda \cdot p_{1k}) < p$, $a^*_{1i} = \overline{p_{1j}} \wedge \overline{p_{1k}} < p$.

This follows that the element s_1 is not subordinate directly to s_i. Therefore we can see that the elements subordinate directly to s_j in each of the elements of irregular rows can be determined depending on the . It will be possible to prove the proposition 2 analogous to the above proof.
These facts enable us to obtain the following theorem for a structural modeling of system.

[Theorem 1] the structure of system object can be uniquely determined if the rules 1,2, 3 and the propositions 1, 2 are satisfied in the sub ordination matrix.
From the theorem 1, an algorithm for the structural modeling of system is proposed as follows;

<u>Algorithm for structural modeling</u>

<u>STEP1</u> Give the fuzzy subordination matrix $A = [a_{ij}]$ and construct the fuzzy semi-reachability matrix A' satisfying the fuzzy semi-transitive law from A.

<u>STEP2</u> Identify the level sets $L_t(s)$, $L_b(s)$ and $L_{is}(s)$ according to A'. Further, determine the subordination relation sets $B(s_i)$,($s_i \in L_b(s)$) between $L_t(s)$ and $L_b(s)$, and the block sets Q_j.

<u>STEP3</u> Eliminate all of the columns including elements belonging to $L_b(s)$ and the rows and columns including elements belonging to $L_{is}(s)$. The fuzzy subordination matrix consisting of remaining rows and columns is reconstructed as A'.

<u>STEP4</u> From A' obtained in STEP3, costruct the single hierarchy matrix $A^{(j)}$ corresponding to each block set Q_j.

<u>STEP5</u> Set up the fuzzy structure parameter and identify the graphic structure concerning with each single hierarchy $A^{(j)}$ by means of the flowchart shown in Fig.2.
Here assume that the regular rows corresponding to the s_i are s_{1k}, k=1,2,--,m ($m \leq n$) in A'. Let's define the following operation $a^*_{\cdot i} = a^{(j)}_{\cdot i} \otimes (\bigotimes_{k=1}^{m} \overline{a^{(j)}_{\cdot 1_k}})$. Then all of the rows

s_{l_k}, $k=1,2,\cdots,m$ can be eliminated by replacing $a_{\cdot i}^{(j)}$ with $a^{*}_{\cdot i}$. The same operation can be also applied in order to eliminate the columns.

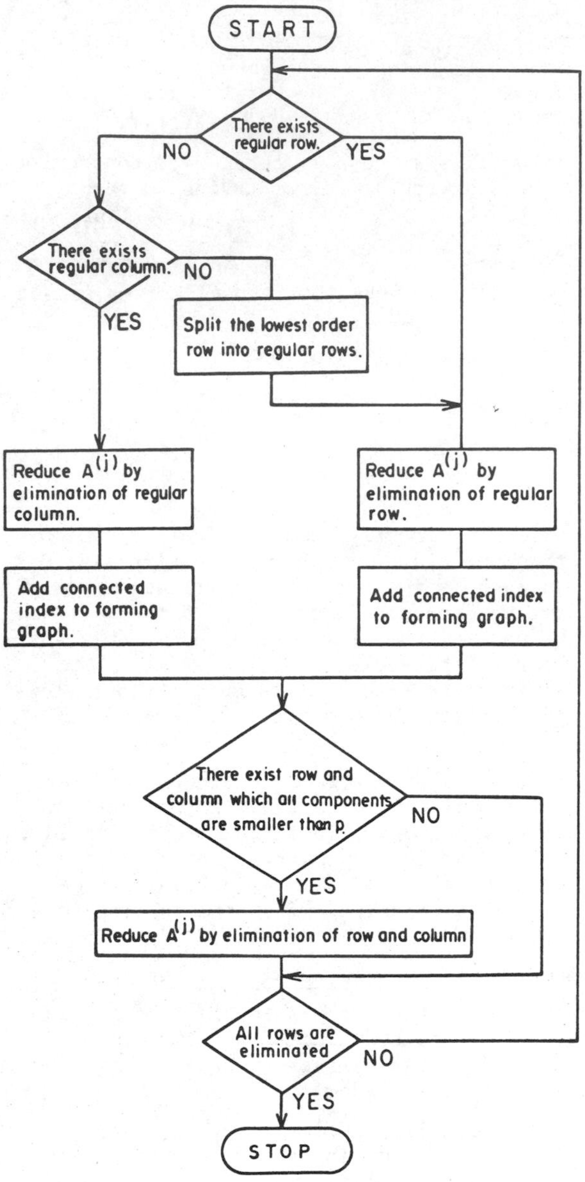

Fig.2 Flowchart for graphic construction of system in step5

ILLUSTRATIVE EXAMPLES

The following examples are illustrated in order to show how the proposed method works. Let $A = [a_{ij}]_{15\times 15}$ be the fuzzy subordination matrix for a given system object as shown in (46).
Using the algorithm described in the previous section, we construct the structural model with respect to the A and compare it with the result of ISM.

$A =$

	s_1	s_2	s_3	s_4	s_5	s_6	s_7	s_8	s_9	s_{10}	s_{11}	s_{12}	s_{13}	s_{14}	s_{15}
s_1	0.0	0.0	0.0	0.1	0.1	0.1	0.0	0.1	0.1	0.0	0.2	0.2	0.1	0.2	0.1
s_2	0.1	0.0	0.0	0.0	0.0	0.4	0.3	0.0	0.2	0.1	0.1	0.2	0.0	0.6	0.2
s_3	0.6	0.2	0.0	0.1	0.0	0.4	0.0	0.0	0.0	0.2	0.1	0.1	0.1	0.2	0.3
s_4	0.0	0.6	0.1	0.0	0.2	0.3	0.7	0.1	0.0	0.2	0.2	0.1	0.6	0.3	0.1
s_5	0.0	0.0	0.2	0.0	0.0	0.4	0.6	0.0	0.1	0.0	0.7	0.2	0.0	0.6	0.2
s_6	0.1	0.1	0.1	0.1	0.2	0.0	0.0	0.1	0.1	0.1	0.2	0.1	0.2	0.5	0.1
s_7	0.0	0.2	0.1	0.0	0.1	0.4	0.0	0.1	0.1	0.1	0.2	0.1	0.2	0.5	0.1
s_8	0.5	0.0	0.0	0.1	0.1	0.1	0.1	0.0	0.0	0.2	0.2	0.1	0.1	0.1	0.6
s_9	0.2	0.0	0.0	0.4	0.0	0.5	0.3	0.2	0.0	0.1	0.7	0.2	0.1	0.7	0.1
s_{10}	0.1	0.3	0.0	0.1	0.0	0.4	0.6	0.1	0.2	0.0	0.1	0.4	0.5	0.5	0.1
s_{11}	0.1	0.0	0.1	0.0	0.1	0.6	0.5	0.0	0.1	0.1	0.0	0.1	0.1	0.4	0.0
s_{12}	0.0	0.4	0.2	0.0	0.1	0.1	0.3	0.1	0.1	0.1	0.1	0.0	0.1	0.4	0.1
s_{13}	0.0	0.7	0.0	0.1	0.0	0.4	0.6	0.0	0.2	0.0	0.4	0.1	0.0	0.6	0.1
s_{14}	0.1	0.0	0.0	0.1	0.2	0.1	0.1	0.1	0.1	0.2	0.1	0.1	0.2	0.0	0.1
s_{15}	0.7	0.1	0.1	0.0	0.1	0.0	0.1	0.2	0.0	0.1	0.0	0.1	0.2	0.2	0.0

(46)

1) Case of p = 0.4, = 2.0 (FSM)

The graphic structure of this case is given in Fig.3.

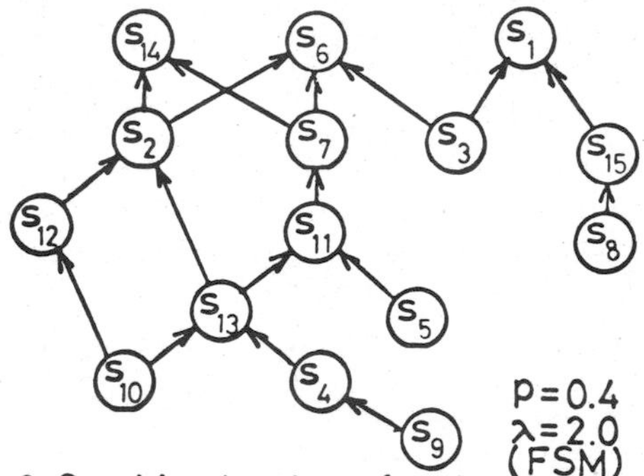

Fig.3 Graphic structure for the example

2) Case of p = 0.5, = -0.3 (FSM)

The graphic structure of this case is given in Fig.4, where the subordination matrix A is same in (1).

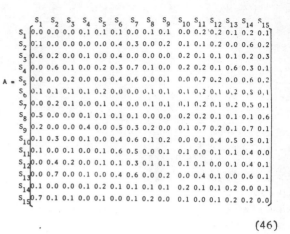

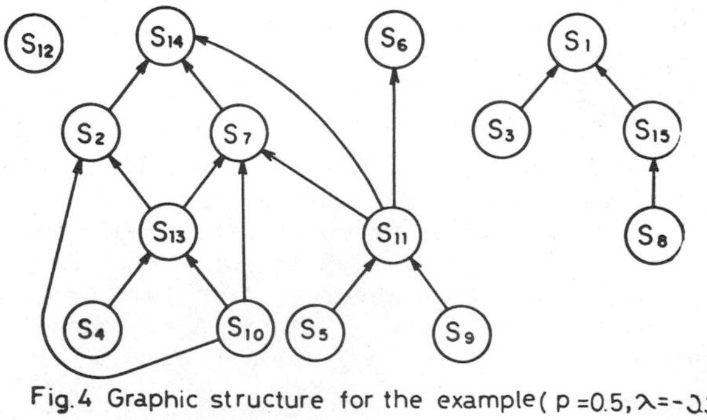

Fig.4 Graphic structure for the example(p =0.5, λ=-0.3)

In order to inspect the effect of changing for the structure of system, another example is illustrated, where the subordination matrix A is same in (2).

3) Case of p = 0.5, = 0.5 (FSM)

The graphic structure of this case is given in Fig.5.

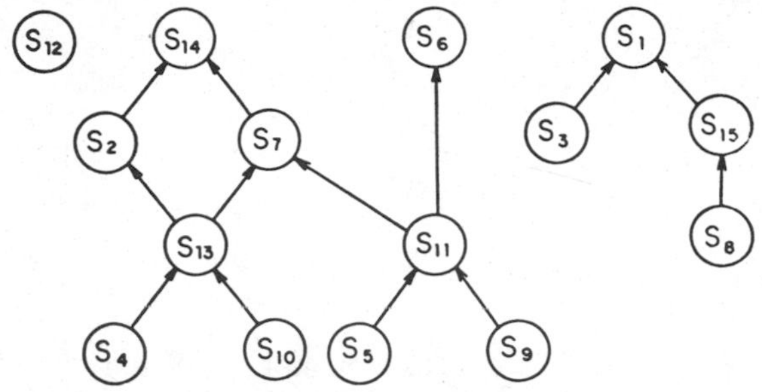

Fig.5 Graphic structure for the example(P=0.5, λ=0.5), and ISM(P=0.5)

Further, in order to compare the result of FSM with that of ISM, we put p=0.5 (λ=0) and apply ISM to this case.
The graphic structure of this case is given in Fig.5. The result coincides with that of the case p=0.5,λ=0.5 by FSM.

CONCLUSION

Hierarchy is fundamental to many fields of science engineering and human situations. It is one of several basic concepts needed in working with complex systems. We have proposed a method for structuring systematically such a hierarchy to the several systems, that is Fuzzy Structural Modeling (FSM) on the basis of fuzzy sets theory. It is a method for developing a hierarchy from a semi-reachability matrix. A significant step in the development of the proposed method consists of the relaxation of transitivity, irreflexivity, and asymmetry with respect to the construction of the subordination matrix. The relaxation has extended the flexibility and applicability for the structural modeling of the system. Further it has been shown that the structure of system can be uniquely determined depending on a threshold p and a structure parameter λ, especially, the same structure given in the case of ISM can be also obtained in a special case of p and λ. In order to show how the proposed method works, a few examples have been illustrated and the structure of system has been successfully identified.

REFERENCES

(1) J. N. Warfield et al., A unified systems engineering concept, Battele M. Inst. (1972).
(2) A. Gabus and E. Fontela, DEMATEL Report No.1, No.2 (1973), No.3 (1975), Batteie M. Inst.
(3) J. Kawakita, KJ Method, in Japanese, Cyuuou kouron shinsyo (1972).
(4) N. Christofides, Graph Theory. An Algorithmic Approach, Academic Press (1975).
(5) L. A. Zadeh, Fuzzy sets, Information and Control, 8, pp338-353 (1965).
(6) A. Kaufman et al., Introduction to the Theory of Fuzzy Subsets, Academic Press (1975).
(7) E. Tazaki, M. Amagasa and M. Takizawa, Fuzzy Structural Modeling, Transaction of the Operations Research Society of Japan, (1977) to appear.

REGIONAL PLANNING SUBJECTED TO ENVIRONMENTAL CONSTRAINTS

J. E. Rabinovich

Centro de Ecología, IVIC, Apartado 1827, Caracas 101, Venezuela

INTRODUCTION

The Rio Orinoco basin, the second largest in South America after the Amazon, has an extension of almost 1,100,000 Km^2, with an average annual flow of 1,400,000,000 m^3. Within this basin, south of the Orinoco River and in Venezuelan territory, we find the Río Caroní watershed, with an area of approximately 100,000 Km^2. This region has a population of 400,000 people, of which about 70% inhabit two of the most important cities: Ciudad Bolívar, capital of the State of Bolívar, and Ciudad Guayana, a development pole and industrial center. Up to now there seems to be no important areas of agricultural land of good quality in the region, although it is expected that some soils, although acid and of low fertility, but with good physical composition, could be put under production if used under adequate management.

North of the confluence of the Caroní and Paragua Rivers is the Raúl Leoni Dam, also called Guri Hydroelectric Project, to be completed in two steps. The first step was inaugurated in November 1968, with a total installed capacity of 2,650,000 KW, and it is expected to be concluded by 1977. The second step will take the level of the reservoir to the height of 270 m to complete a total of almost 9,000,000 KW installed in the site. In terms of hydroelectric development the investments anticipated in the construction of the enlargement of the dam to take it to its final step by 1982, are of the order of 1,400 million US$, and in the associated transmission systems of about 500 million US$.

In the 1975-1979 quinquennium the total amount of public and private investments in Guayana will reach over 7,000 million US$. The plan IV of the steel expansion, represents by itself an investment of the order of 3,000 million US$, while the investments in the plans for increasing the aluminum production will reach a figure of above 700 million US$.

More than half of the Río Caroní watershed from where the large hydroelectric potential needed by Guayana's industries is obtained, is covered by highly valuable commercial forests. This has resulted in a high pressure for exploiting the more valuable woods, which fortunately, in this area, is being carried out in a very selective way. The large demographic growth represented by the development pole, has also demanded a regional self-sufficiency in the production of food. This implies turning land into agricultural production to a certain magnitude. However, it is well known that the local soils are relatively poor, and that agricultural production in land that had been covered by stable tropical forests is of short duration. Thus a sustained food production would imply a progressive advance towards the higher parts of the watershed, producing an important and increasing change in the vegetation cover of the area.

These vegetation changes could eventually jeopardize the hydroelectric production complex in two ways: on one hand we can anticipate regime changes, with some increase of the river flows in the rainy season, and reductions in the dry season; on the other hand, with a reduction in the vegetation cover there is a potentially dangerous increase in erosion that, in a region like Guayana, with a relatively abrupt terrain, could reach one, two, and even three orders of magnitude. The first factor might affect the hydroelectric production in case the hydrologic regime would force to introduce important changes in the operation of the dam. The second factor could eventually silt up the reservoir up to the level of the intake of some of the turbines, reducing the life of the dam, or at least reducing its productive capacity if certain turbines have to be taken out of production.

This potential conflict between possible land uses, due to the size of the development programs already on their way, can not be analyzed on the terrain. Mathematical models, particularly computer simulation models, allow a quantitative comparative analysis between different possible strategies of action. With this goal in mind a simulation model was constructed to describe quantitatively the rain-vegetation-soil-river relationship, with the information and type of circumstances that characterize the Río Caroní watershed.

Given precipitation statistics in the region of the Río Caroní watershed, the model simulates in a digital computer the river flows that feed the Guri reservoir. Due to the character of potential conflict between land uses and hydroelectric production, the model was designed to facilitate the simulation of possible intervention strategies in the watershed in terms of changes produced in the vegetation cover. The model contemplates possible intervention strategies through actions at different intensity levels. For simplicity two types of actions were evaluated as possible environmental intervention: the rate of timber exploitation and the percentage of the area exploited for timber that is turned into agricultural production.

DEFINITION OF THE SYSTEM

The Río Caroní watershed is located on the right margin of the Orinoco River, in the State of Bolívar (southeast of Venezuela) in a geological formation known as Guayana Shield, one of the oldest geologic formations of the continent. From a panoramic point of view the topography of Guayana impresses as totally chaotic. Its mesas are cut in staircase shape, the tabular peaks are slightly inclined, and contrast with other mountains with rounded peaks; it is, in general, a vast mountainous block cut by rivers and canyons, without true orographic systems really defined.

The Caroní watershed is within the influence of an equatorial climate, characterized by high precipitations, fairly well spread during the year, and temperatures with small annual seasonality. This climate, that does not show months actually dry, can be considered as very humid. Precipitation shows a clear increment from north to south: the average values are very low (849 mm) west of Ciudad Bolívar, increasing progressively up to relatively high values, of the order of 4,000 mm/year, towards the border with Brazil.

The soils are one of the main unknown in our knowledge of the resources of the Venezuelan Guayana. However, it is accepted that the soils are highly mineralized, of low natural fertility, and highly susceptible to erosion; furthermore, the soils do not show good physico-chemical characteristics, such as texture, water retention, acidity, etc. The low fertility of these soils, that determines a low yield in agricultural land uses, does not contradict with the tall vegetation that, under natural conditions, we find in most parts of the watershed: the essential mineral elements for this outstanding development of vegetation are found in a permanent state of circulation, that takes place at a high turnover rate, so that their permanence in the soil is almost sporadic.

From the vegetation map of Venezuela (Hueck, (1960), thefollowing 10 vegetation types were recognized in the Caroní watershed: 1) hygrophillous evergreen forest; 2) hygrophillous evergreen forest periodically flooded; 3) deciduous forest; 4) hygrophillous forest interrupted by savannas; 5) chaparral; 6) gramineous praires; 7) praires and bogs; 8) gramineous praires with chaparral; 9) savanna; and 10) mangroves.

THE GURI MODEL

The point model that simulates the dynamics of water has been described elsewhere (Rabinovich, 1976); it is basically composed by 7 mathematical functions describing 5 key processes: 1) INTERCEPTION OF RAIN (as a function of vegetation biomass and amount of rain fallen in 24 hs), 2) INFILTRATION IN THE SOIL (as a function of amount of water in the soil, soil texture, and slope), 3) EVAPOTRANSPIRATION (as a function plant biomass unless the calculated value is smaller than potential evapotranspiration, in which case the latter is used), 4) PERCOLATION (as a function of soil texture), and 5) EROSION (as a function of soil texture, plant biomass, slope and runoff). Given the system's parameters (soil texture and slope) and the initial condition of the watershed (plant biomass, soil depth, and amount of water in the soil), for any rain input the point model calculates the fraction of rain that is intercepted by vegetation, and from the remaining what fraction infiltrates, percolates, runs-off and is evapotranspirated. Also the erosion cuased by the superficial runoff is calculated. The inputs and outputs of the point model were produced dividing the watershed by a grid of 40 contiguous cells of 55 by 55 Km. In every cell the point model was applied, using the day as a time unit. The daily superficial and subsuperficial runoffs produced by the point model were integrated in time and space applying time lags estimated from cross-correlations between rain and riverflow time series; the time lags were applied as a function of the reservoir.

In addition to the physical-biological point model, the GURI model also considers the economic aspects of the region. A TIMBER subroutine estimates the benefits from wood extraction activities; an AGRO subroutine estimates the benefits from agricultural and cattle activities (only corn, manioc and bovine cattle were considered); a HYDRO subroutine estimates the benefits from hydroelectric production. All these benefits are NET benefits accumulated through the simulation at a discount rate of 8%. Due to the potential conflict between land uses and hydroelectric production, the model was organized to facilitate the simulation of possible intervention strategies in the watershed in terms of changes produced in the vegetation cover as a result of action decisions. For simplicity two types of actions were evaluated as possible environmental interventions: the rate of timber exploitation (action A), and the percentage of the area exploited for timber that is turned into agricultural production (action B). Action A was implemented at 5 different levels of intensity (1 through 5) reflecting each of them the rate of increase of the area under exploitation in a 50 year period (thus, A= 2 means that in 50 years the area under exploitation is doubled). Action B was also implemented at 5 levels of intensity (0, 20, 40, 60, and 80) in units of percentages (thus, B= 20 means that 20% of the area exploited for timber will be turned into agricultural and cattle production).

The 5 levels of each of 2 types of decision actions produces a total of 25 intervention strategies; for each of them the GURI model was processed and the yearly results of physical, biological and economic consequences recorded. The results were analyzed for different time horizons using Peterman's (1975) desk-top optimization method, which involved the isoline representation of the output.

PHYSICAL AND ECONOMIC RESULTS OF SIMULATION

A higher level of actions A and B produces a larger vegetation cover modification; the latter, through 50 years of simulation, results in hydrological changes and in an increase in erosion. The river regime was slightly modified, with a reduction of flow in the dry months and an increase in the

TABLE 1 Mean Monthly River Flow (m^3/sec) in Year 50 of Simulation

B	Action A 1	2	3	4	5
0	4,094	4,984	4,989	4,989	4,989
20	5,110	5,223	5,250	5,250	5,250
40	5,356	5,529	5,675	5,675	5,675
60	5,677	6,096	6,224	6,224	6,224
80	6,073	6,701	6,905	6,905	6,905

rainy months. However, the increases were of greater magnitude than the decreases, producing a net annual increase, as shown in Table 1. The size of the reservoir and the design of the dam were such that the increase in total river flow actually represented a higher production of hydroelectric energy.

The increase in erosion is shown in Table 2; between the minimum and maximum intervention

TABLE 2 Total Erosion ($10^9 m^3$) Accumulated in 50 Years

B	Action A 1	2	3	4	5
0	1.0	1.2	1.3	1.4	1.5
20	2.6	3.7	3.7	4.5	5.5
40	4.6	6.9	8.7	9.8	10.5
60	6.8	10.2	12.9	14.6	15.7
80	9.0	13.6	17.2	19.5	21.0

strategies there is a 21-fold increase, which is consistent with many field measurements in the tropics under similar conditions. As most of the eroded material comes from soil horizons lost by the runoff effect, the 50 years accumulated amount of erosion was used as an index of environmental deterioration; using A= 5 and B= 80 as the 100% of environmental deterioration, the other 24 decision strategies were assigned a proportional percentage (Table 3). This index proved

TABLE 3 Environmental Deterioration Index (%) Based on Total Accumulated Erosion in 50 Years

B	Action A 1	2	3	4	5
0	4.7	5.7	6.5	24.4	26.2
20	12.4	17.6	21.8	24.4	26.2
40	22.2	32.8	41.3	46.5	50.1
60	32.4	48.5	61.3	69.3	74.7
80	43.0	64.6	81.9	92.6	100.0

to be very useful as a way of imposing the environmental constrain.

The height-volume curve of the reservoir, coupled with the information of the height of the intake of each turbine, allowed the

TABLE 4 Simulated Year in which the number of Active Turbines is Reduced to 10

B	Action A 1	2	3	4	5
0	-	-	-	-	-
20	-	44	40	37	35
40	40	35	32	30	29
60	35	31	28	27	25
80	31	28	26	24	23

estimation of the simulated year in which a given number of turbines would become eventually blocked by siltation of the reservoir (Table 4). The results of this effect upon the production capacity of the dam are shown in Fig. 1; in this figure, as in the

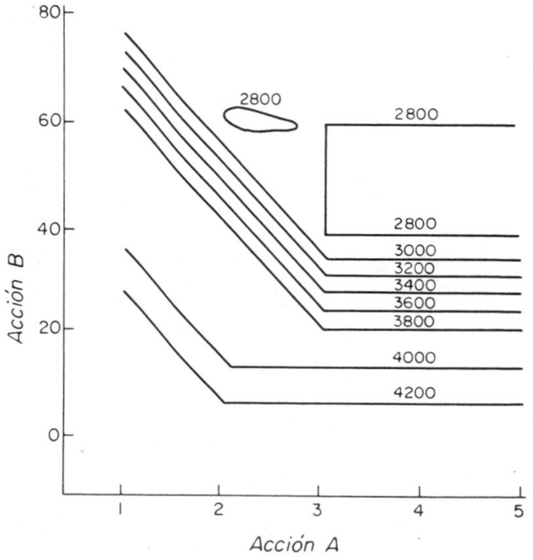

Fig. 1 Isolines for the average monthly hydroelectric production (GWH) for year 50 of simulation

following of the same kind, the axis labeled A represents action A (rate of timber extraction) with its 5 levels, and the axis labeled B represents action B (percentage of area exploited for timber that is turned into agriculture and cattle production). It is

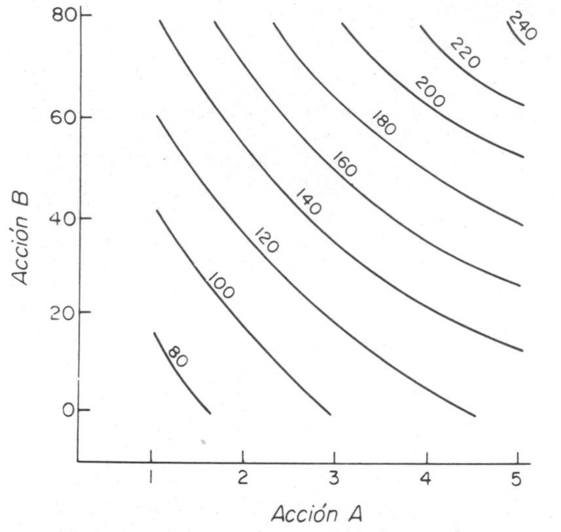

Fig. 2 Net benefits from agricultural, cattle raising, and timber activities (millions of Bolivars) accumulated for 50 years of simulation

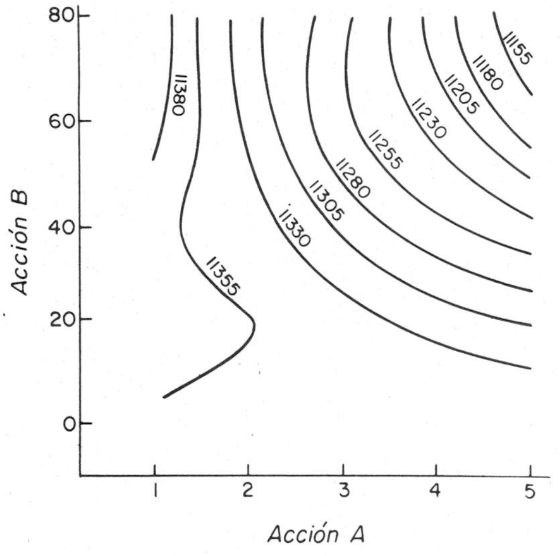

Fig. 3 Net benefits from hydroelectric production (millions of Bolivars) accumulated for 50 years of simulation

observed that there is a general trend of a reduction of the dam's capacity towards the upper right corner of the graph, that is to say, towards a more intensive land use. The reason that all the curves become horizontal for values 3, 4, and 5 of action A is that the results are plotted for the 50 years time horizon; for this time lapse all the watershed has been exploited independently of the level of action A (for A= 3, 4 and 5). Similar graphs can be drawn for other physical variables, for example, the erosion values expressed as the environmental degradation index (Table 3); such a graph was used later to impose the environmental constrain for the decision making.

The economic aspects of the results are shown in Figs. 2-4. The lumped net benefits from timber and agricultural and cattle activities (Fig. 2) show a consistent increase towards the upper right corner of the graph; although this outcome could be anticipated it proves: (a) the simplicity of this representation for decision makers (the same net benefits can be obtained by different decisions, thus allowing the consideration of other factors); (b) the nature of the conflict (as benefits resulting from intensive land use increase, the capacity of the dam decreases). However,

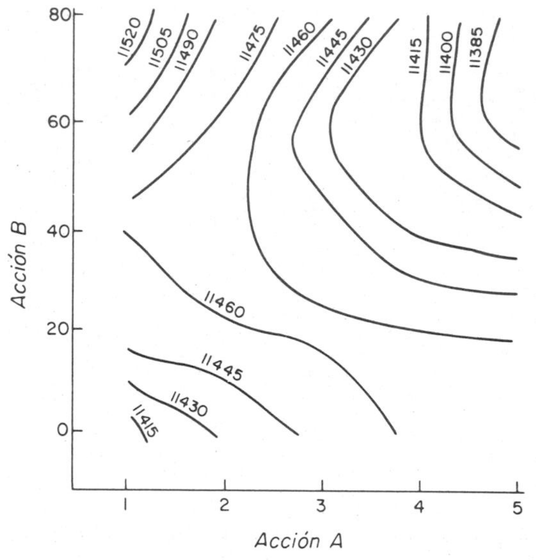

Fig. 4 Total net benefits (millions of Bolivars) accumulated for 50 years of simulation

as the economics of the hydroelectric production show the same trend as the physical production (Fig. 3) the conflict can be also represented in economic terms by calculating the TOTAL net benefits from all activities (Fig. 4); this combined representation shows an increasing trend along the diagonal that goes from the lower-left to the upper-right corner, but that after reaching A= 2 it turns towards the left again to become an absolute maximum for A= 1 and B= 80.

USE OF THE MODEL IN THE DECISION MAKING PROCESS

As both the input and the output of the model had been designed to answer specific questions involved in the decision making process, we can try to evaluate how well it serves this purpose. We will analyze separately the importance of the time horizon in regional planning involving environmental considerations, and the use of isoline graphs as a method for optimizing decisions.

Importance of the Time Horizon

As the results of the simulation model were produced for every simulated year (both absolute and accumulated), it was possible to express the results for different time horizons. As we are interested in long term regional planning, horizons of 35, 40, 45 and 50 years were compared. The comparison can be visually made in Fig. 5, where the total net benefits accumulated for each time horizon were graphed against the environmental degradation index. For each set of points

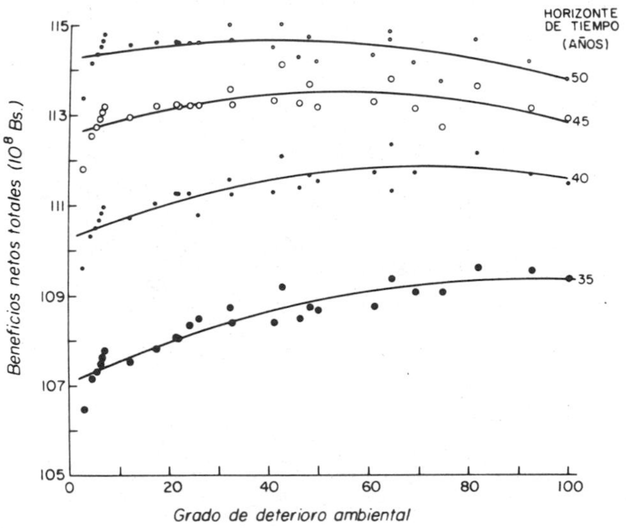

Fig. 5 Accumulated total net benefits (millions of Bolivars) as a function of the degree of ecological degradation (%) for 4 time horizons (35, 40, 45, and 50 years)

a second degree polinomial was fitted providing an analytical expression to solve for the inflection point, that is to say, the environmental degradation value that would produce, for each time horizon, the maximum net benefit.

Table 5 Relationship between the Planning Time Horizon and the Degree of Ecological Degradation

Time horizon (years)	Degree of ecological degradation (%) that produces the maximum total net benefit
35	92,5
40	70.5
45	54.1
50	40.8

The results of Table 5 show that as our time horizon used for planning increases, we will still be obtaining maximum benefits, but at the expense of a lower environmental degradation.

Optimization and Decision Making

The decision maker would often like to make optimum decisions based upon some criterium that is subjected to local constrains. Although many possible criteria can be applied to the example that has been developed here, and many different real world constrains will probably be imposing restrictions upon the decision maker, for the sake of simplicity we show now the way the results of this simulation model can be optimized for long range environmental impact analysis and natural resources planning.

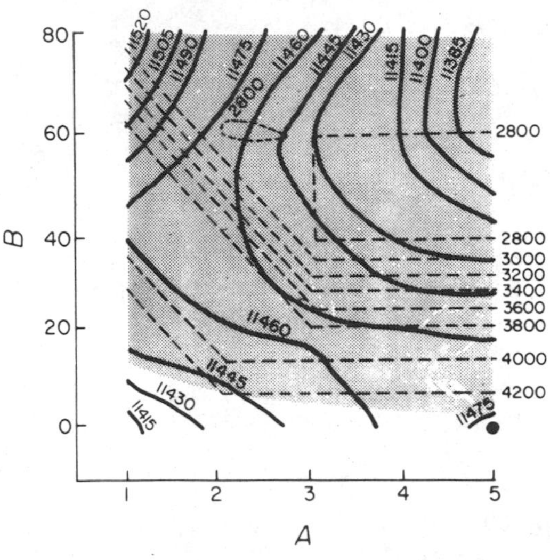

Fig. 6 Overlay of net benefits and hydroelectric production with a 10% ecological degradation constrain. See text for identification of lines and symbols

As most of the output of the simulation model has been expressed in terms of the 25 intervention strategies in a plane combinning actions A and B, the possibility of using the desk-top optimizer proposed by Peterman (1975) was opened. It was implemented in the following fashion: the variable to be maximized was the total net benefit accumulated in 50 years at a discount rate of 8%; two types of constrains were imposed upon the decision of maximizing such a variable: on one hand the goal of the electric company to maintain an average monthly energy production of 3,750 GWH; on the other hand, a given percentage of environmental degradation.

Figures 6-10 show the results of maximizing the net total benefit, subjected to the above-mentioned constrains. Solid lines represent the total accumulated net benefit (as in Fig. 4); broken lines represent the physical hydroelectric output (in monthly GWH, as in Fig. 1); the shaded area represents the set of all decisions in violation of the ecological constrains; the black dot represents the optimum solution, that is to say, the combination of decisions about actions A and B that maximizes total net benefits without violating hydroelectric production goals nor surpassing specified ecological degradation limits.

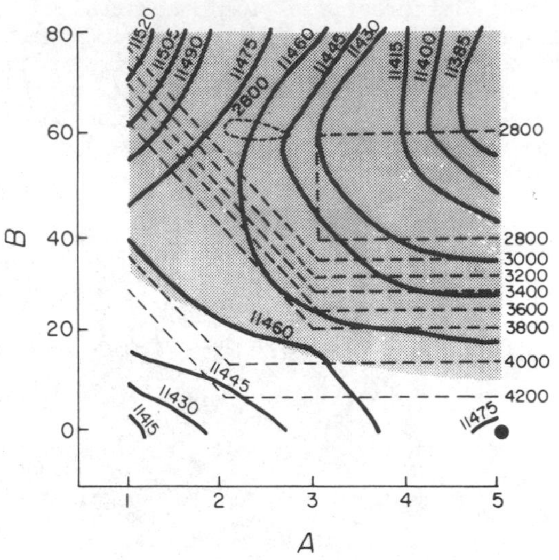

Fig. 7 Same as Fig. 6 for a 20% ecological degradation constrain

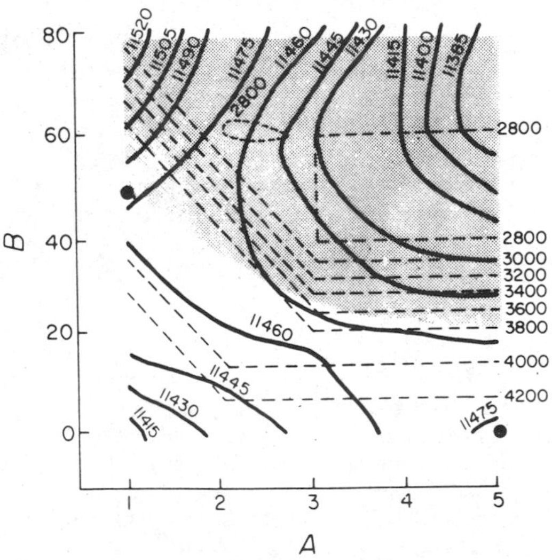

Fig. 8 Same as Fig. 6 for a 30% ecological degradation constrain

Figure 6 shows that, with environmental constrains of 10%, the optimum decision would be at action A level 5, and action B level 0. Figure 7 shows that when the environmental degradation constrain goes up to 20% the decision would be still the same : level 5 of action A, and level 0 of action B.

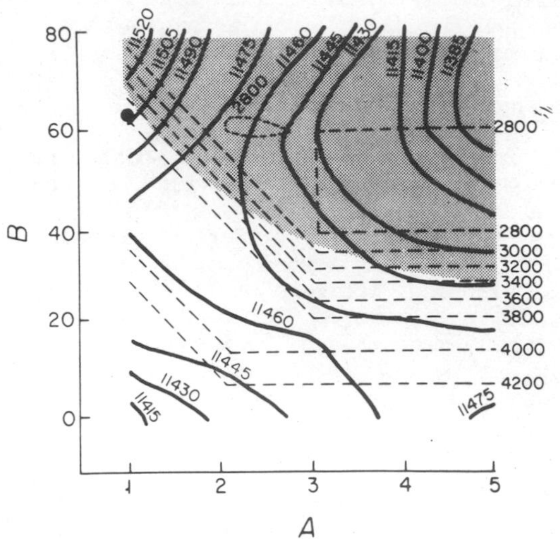

Fig. 9 Same as Fig. 6 for a 40% ecological degradation constrain

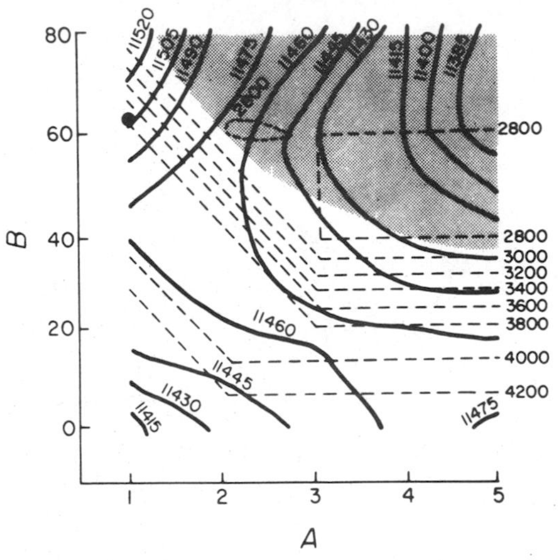

Fig. 10 Same as Fig. 6 for a 50% ecological degradation constrain

However when the environmental degradation constrain goes up to 30%, there are two equally satisfactory solutions for maximizing the total benefits and also keeping the constrain of 3,750 GWH in the hydroelectric energy production; the solutions are: level 5 of action A and level 0 of action B or, alternatively, level 1 of action A and level 52% of action B (Fig. 8). When the environmental degradation constrain is increased to 40% there is again only one optimum solution represented by level 1 of action A and 64% of action B (fig. 9). The same solution is obtained by any other constrain on ecological deterioration larger than 40%, as it is shown in Fig. 10 for 50%.

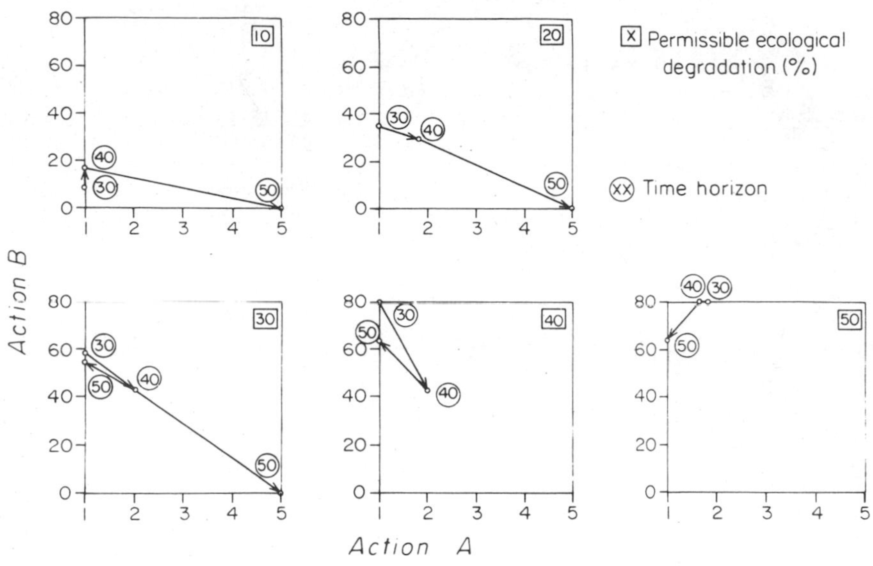

Fig. 11 Decision trajectories for 3 time horizons, subjected to 5 levels of ecological degradation constrains

A similar analysis can be performed for total net benefits accumulated for different time horizons, after applying Peterman's desk-top optimizer technique to years 30 and 40 of simulation. Table 6 was constructed from the graphical results; allowing the comparison between the optimum decision for the three selected time horizons. The comparison shows that there is a trend towards higher levels of intensity in both actions as the environmental constrain is relaxed. However, time horizons 40 and 50 show that there is an important interaction between actions A and B that produces QUALITATIVE changes in the type of final decisions; this occurs weakly at 50% ecological deterioration level for the time horizon of 40 years, and strongly at 30% ecological deterioration level for the time horizon of 50 years. In the latter case, there is a drastic change in the optimum decision, jumping from the extreme of maximum timber exploitation and zero agriculture, to the extreme of minimum timber exploitation and a relatively intense agricultural land use. When the optimum decision is compared across time horizons for a rigorous environmental constrain level (10 or 20%) also a drastic change can be detected: extending the time horizon from 40 to 50 years would make the decision maker switch from minimum timber extraction and intermediate agricultural land use to maximum timber extraction and zero agriculture activity.

TABLE 6 Levels of actions A and B for the optimum decision, resulting from the application of the desk-top optimizer for maximizing total net benefits with a variable ecological constrain and a fixed hydroelectric production constrain (3,750 GWH/month), for three time horizons

MAXIMUM ECOLOGICAL DETERIORATION (%)	TIME HORIZON (YEARS) 30 ACTION A	B	40 ACTION A	B	50 ACTION A	B
10	1	9	1	17	5	0
20	1	35	1.8	30	5	0
30	1	59	2	43	5(1)	0(52)
40	1	80	2	43	1	64
50	1.8	80	1.7	80	1	64

Figure 11 summarizes this interactive effect, showing the trajectories followed by the optimum decisions made for 3 different time horizons, subjected to 5 levels of ecological degradation constrain. It is quite clear how strongly the optimum decision shifts depending both upon the time horizon and the ecological degradation constrain. This result is, of course, the output of a fixed-decision model, that is to say, the 50 years of simulation depend of the originally selected decision, given as an initial condition. Once this condition is set, future courses of events are completely determined. It is left for future work the development of a flexible model, that allows the consideration of ecological constrains in a step by step planning process.

REFERENCES

Hueck, K., Mapa de la Vegetación de la República de Venezuela. Bol. Inst. For. Lat. Amer. Inv. Cap. 7:3-15 (1960)

Peterman, R. M., New Techniques for Policy Evaluation in Ecological Systems: Methodology for a Case Study of Pacific Salmon Fisheries. J. Fish. Res. Board Can. 32(11):2179-2188 (1975)

Rabinovich, J. E. (1976) El Modelo GURI: análisis de un potencial conflicto en el uso de recursos naturales en una cuenca tropical. Informe de trabajo. Comisión Económica para América Latina (CEPAL). Santiago, Chile. 73 pp.

INTEGRATED MANAGEMENT OF THE ENVIRONMENT IN THE NEW TOWN OF L'ISLE D'ABEAU (FRANCE)

Robert Spizzichino

Crepah-3, rue Lord Byron - 75008 Paris, France

INTRODUCTION

The new town of "l'Isle-d'Abeau" can be considered as the centre of expansion for Lyon, both population-wise (210,000 - 250,000 inhabitants by the end of the century including the already existing towns) and economically with 1,200 hectares of industrial zoning and an important service area now being constructed.

The directing scheme (in its December 1973 project) foresees the following urbanistic direction:

To take into account the delicate, fragile and scattered site by creating, separated urban quarters and leaving large unconstructed spaces. This will allow an inter-action of country and city, which explains why l'Isle-d'Abeau was advertised as "a city in the country". Such a decision on such an operational area (20,000 ha) has no meaning unless it really becomes an act of concerned zoning for which quality counts as much as quantity. The creation of housing has to be considered as well as the creation of jobs and services, and the technological ambitions of electronics, t.v. control and t.v. distribution,...

From this perspective, the qualitative cases have nothing to do with aesthetics. In this case, it contributes to a certain way of life that should be encouraged by the design of the city:

To respect the multiplicity of individual choices, concerning notably the pattern of consumption and laws, the multiplicity of possible contacts between the different socio-cultural groups, management of the conflicts which arise between opposite values like "city-country", "work leisure", "individual-collective".

These must be concretely regulated by creating a transportation system, urban districts, and collective services.

It is necessary to take into account the dimension "quality of the environment" in all planning interventions.

The quality of the environment is indefinable, because it is defined in a different way for everyone corresponding to his own system of values, and to our cultural models in a given situation. One cannot find unanamity and one can only find certain general tendencies in the relation of man environment.

This explains the temptation to skirt the issue by its opposite: the absence of nuisances, often reduced by excessive pollution control.

In fact, one knows now that this method is notably insufficient: there could very well exist a town without nuisances of which the quality of the environment would be seen as deplorable for all who live there. A double problem exists for the settlers:

- to avoid bad results coming from urban activities,
- to produce the living conditions apt to favour the taking over of the environment by the "environed".

One sees a difficulty in reducing the problem to a range of technical-economical choices.

In these conditions, the taking into account of the quality of the environment cannot be a part of the process of settlement. Neither can it be delegated to the specialists ("environmentalists" don't exist).

It cannot consist in the superposition of sectorial approaches (water, air, noise, urban equipment, waste). It has an impact on total procedure and touches directly on the act and the way of settling.

What is called the "integrated management of the environment" comes from a very pragmatic system. That means the same as to integrate in the choices and in the acts of settlements, a certain number of questions touching the environment and to establish connections between the very diverse factors, often conflicting:

To solve a problem of work, one is led to accept the companies which by the nuisances created can produce in the long run a problem of water distributed.

What do diverse categories feel in such conditions ("sensory perception of the environment") ?

At the time of making a general plan of the zone, have all physical, economical and social dimensions (site, climate, appropriation of spacem maintenance costs,...) been taken into account (system analysis) ?

Would not the elements of the problem be modified in the years to come (flexibility of solutions) ?

The insufficiency of existing methodological tools shows up when one applies those simple and even simplistic principles. Aware of these difficulties and stakes, the people responsible for the new town decided in March 1973 to start an operation destined to realise, in a practical manner, "an integrated management of the environment at l'Isle-d'Abeau."

The operational character of this experience became even more necessary since the first quarter of housing was in the process of construction, the first industrial zones were being filled, the restructuring of the land went quickly, the equipment began to be in service, etc.

It was then not a question, as for some other new towns, to take time to proceed to important preliminary studies, and to a systematic collection of all the necessary elements.

The experience was helped and followed by a directing committee composed not only of the EPIDA and the SGCVN, but also the DATAR and the Ministry of the Quality of Life. Shown are two diagrams, one describing the unfolding of the operation and other the principles concerning its organisation. These two diagrams are obviously very simplified.

The studies were made by a group of consultants (ARIANE) coming from 5 French firms complementary in the fields of environmental approaches: BERU, BERTIN, COYNE et BELLIER, MATRA, SEMA.

Doing this, one is conscious of the reduction that the present note shows in relation to the content of the works, and of the danger that exists in wanting to communicate to the largest possible audience, but one cannot escape the criticisms of the specialists. But, a pilot project like that at l'Isle d'Abeau has only a meaning if its unfolding is sufficiently known, even if it is criticized. It is necessary then to submit fully to the rules of the game.

EPIDA: Etablissement Public d'Aménagement de l'Isle d'Abeau.

SGCVN: Secrétariat du Groupe Central des Villes Nouvelles.

DATAR: Délégation à l'Aménagement du Territoire.

This note also briefly exposes only one element of intervention which seemed to us exemplary, by the general aspects of the case and by the adopted methodology the "city-country" dossier.

THE CITY-COUNTRY DOSSIER

The creation of the new town does not mean "sticking" housing on the land, equipments or factories. There are many involvements in such an operation, and those on environment are not the least. This change dictated to by nature must be taken into account, and for the sake of the town, you must not at any price let its natural environment die. It will be different, of course, but alive.

The balance city-country implies a number of actions allowing for a better meaning of country with city. The definition of those actions and their criticism by all the interested partners were the subject of a concerted action in the course of the years 1975 and 1976. One will find in the documents the answers to three types of finalities: social, economical and spatial: four priority aims have been determined at short term.

- to keep a land market (prices and surfaces).
- to increase profitability of exploitations capable to live at long term,
- to re-establish psychological conditions encouraging the rural life,
- to create a good system of management for the agricultural free spaces.

If these aims are not taken strictly into account, this will lead, not only to an accelerated damage of agriculture, but also to important lacks of balance in the realisation of the new town.

During 14 months, three committees have orientated and supervised the study led by the consulting firm "ARIANE" and by several local organisms:

- a National Control Committees regrouping the representatives of the different Ministries concerned and the Secretariat of the Central Group New Towns.

- a local Director Committee composed by representatives of the "Commission Agricole", the "EPIDA", the "SCANDINA", the "Syndicat des Marias de Bourgoin", the "D.D.E" and the "D.D.A.".*

- a Technical Committee, with most of the organisms which have worked in the area.

It would take too long to explain exactly the contents of the documents, but certain important points have to be remembered. Six priority programmes have been selected:

- Planning of agricultural areas;

- Sketch - plan of rural planning of the "Planteaux Sud";
- Land actions;
- Creation and management of open spaces;
- Planning of the village development;
- Social rural life.

The first programme has a very special purpose, since a study of preliminary design on the Agricultural Central Area (1,500 ha) has already been made.

This area was defined in the new town planning as a place which should be planned for the agriculture.

THE PLANNING OF THE CENTRAL AGRICULTURAL AREA

The intention of this operation is to place a first strong agricultural area for the cultivators who don't want to leave this place.

This area will form the subject of a re-structuring of the agricultural enterprises and also a land restructuring with allied works, first by an amicable procedure of exchange, then by a grouped operation of land planning. Hydraulic planning of drainage and irrigation, and studies and works destined to the mastery of the water surface will also be undertaken.

These realisations will be accompanied by an intensification programme of the existing production, with the progressive introduction of new speculations. Especially, the advisability of the creation of horticultural and market gardening zone will be tested.

The operation which can only be started in a progressive way and with important help from the state (now solicited) would concern successively a test area, then a 200 ha area for intensive irrigated cultures, market gardening and seed-bed. It might be enlarged later. It is of course a concerted operation taken over by the profession itself, with the participation for the main part of the clients: SAFER, Syndicates of the "MARAIS", Ministry of Agriculture, and Technicians from the DDA, etc.

THE RURAL PLANNING SCHEMES OF THE SOUTH PLATEAUS

The south plateaus of l'Isle d'Abeau are the first to be urbanised. A sector planning of all the urbanisations of the south plateaus has been realised. Comprehensive development area maps are now being elaborated.

Taking into accoubt an ecologic analysis, an inspection of the landscape and an odentification of the best agricultural areas: right now a better integration of those elements in the urban conception is proposed.

- to give precise details about the comprehensive development area maps;

- to elaborate the rural planning scheme of the non urbanised land, and of the land which could be urbanised in long term.

LAND ACTION

The point is to carry on the very active politics of the land in l'Isle d'Abeau by a better integration of the specific exigencies of agriculture and natural spaces. Three main actions have been proposed:

- the constitution of a tool for the establishment of a land band;
- the preparation of a land-planning programme;
- the constitution of a land-planning grouped operation (O.G.A.F.).

CREATION AND MANAGEMENT OF OPEN SPACES

The large number of spaces destined neither to urbanisation nor to agriculture, the will to have a development strategy connecting natural space and built space would lead, with classical solutions, to very important expenses for the creation and the management of open spaces.

So, it is necessary:

(1) to make an acquisition and a planning programme arranging the priorities;

(2) to propose the SCADINA inventive propositions for the maintenance of the open spaces, especially maintenance contracts with some cultivators.

RURAL HABITAT AND PLANNING OF THE VILLAGES

Country people must have a quality of habitat not too much unequal in comparison with the new constructions. Moreover, the revaluation of the already existing villages is an element which can help the development of the new town. A first evaluation permitted to give the dimension of a rehabilitation programme about 1,000 lodgements in ten years.

SOCIAL LIFE

It is essential to establish a general reanimation programme of social rural life accompanying the efforts made for the new arrivals. It implicates: a general information campaign destined to the rural world about the city country dossier.

It implies taking into consideration the existence of all those who have a double activity (which is the case of 70% of the cultivators). This presentation of the programmes is extremely thematic, however, it is necessary to notice that there exists many relations between those different programmes. The Local Direction Committee during the meeting on June 15th, 1976 confirmed the orientations and the priorities of the city-country dossier. It declared itself in favour of global action, concerted, destined for the most important number of people, and especially to yound people.

The National Direction Committee should declare itself before the end of the year. This would permit a start in the course of 1977, the first concrete action.

ABBREVIATIONS

* DDE: Direction Départementale de l'Equipement

DDA: Direction Départementale de l'Agriculture

SAFER: Société d'Action Foncière et d'Economie Rurale

OGAF: Opération groupée d'Aménagement Foncier.

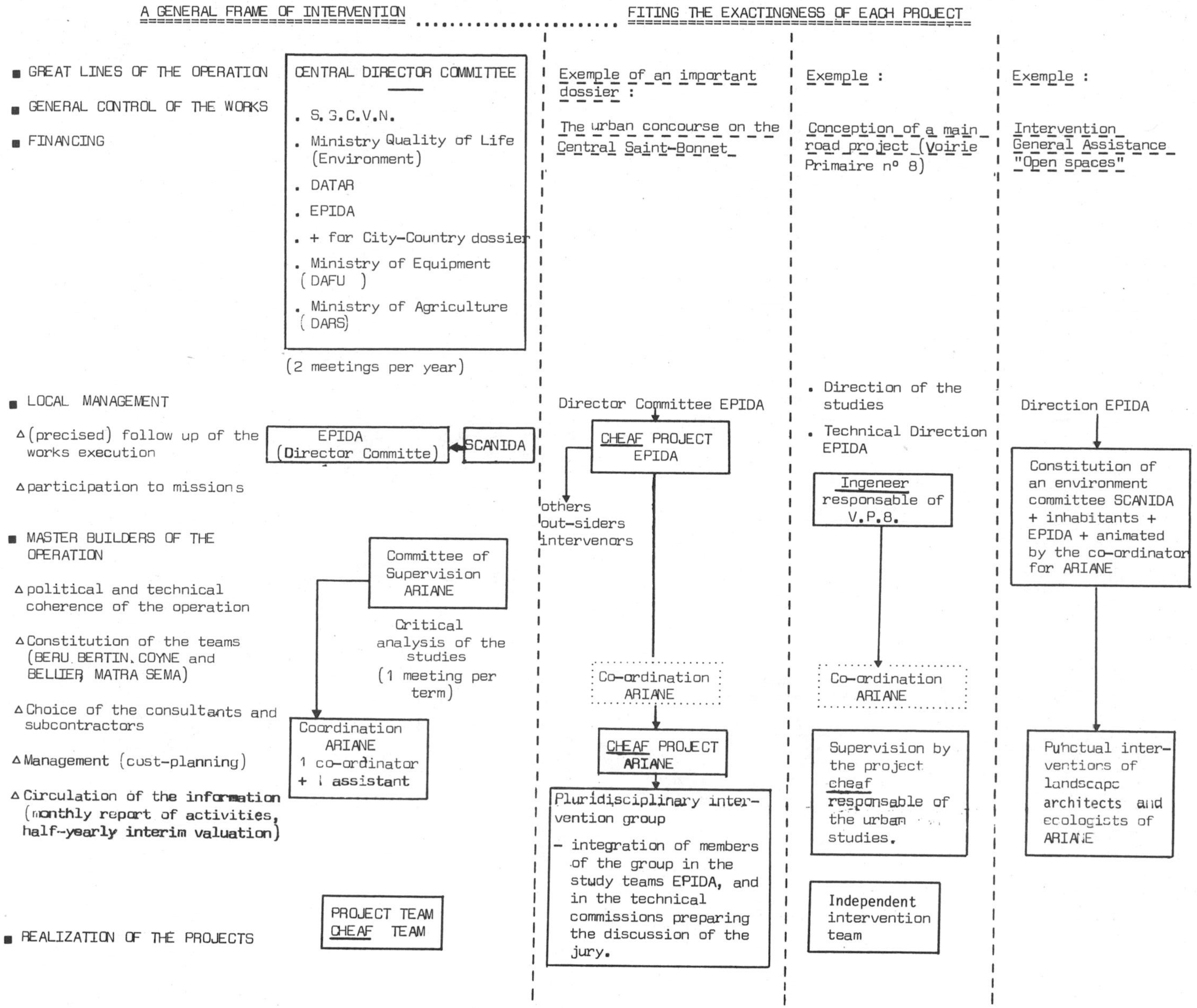
A GENERAL FRAME OF INTERVENTION
FITING THE EXACTINGNESS OF EACH PROJECT
GREAT LINES OF THE OPERATION
GENERAL CONTROL OF THE WORKS
FINANCING
CENTRAL DIRECTOR COMMITTEE
. S.G.C.V.N.
. Ministry Quality of Life (Environment)
. DATAR
. EPIDA
. + for City-Country dossier
. Ministry of Equipment (DAFU)
. Ministry of Agriculture (DARS)
(2 meetings per year)
LOCAL MANAGEMENT
Δ (precised) follow up of the works execution
Δ participation to missions
EPIDA (Director Committe)
SCANIDA
MASTER BUILDERS OF THE OPERATION
Δ political and technical coherence of the operation
Δ Constitution of the teams (BERU BERTIN, COYNE and BELLIER, MATRA SEMA)
Δ Choice of the consultants and subcontractors
Δ Management (cust-planning)
Δ Circulation of the information (monthly report of activities, half-yearly interim valuation)
Committee of Supervision ARIANE
Critical analysis of the studies
(1 meeting per term)
Coordination ARIANE
1 co-ordinator
+ 1 assistant
REALIZATION OF THE PROJECTS
PROJECT TEAM
CHEAF TEAM
Exemple of an important dossier :
The urban concourse on the Central Saint-Bonnet
Director Committee EPIDA
CHEAF PROJECT EPIDA
others out-siders intervenors
Co-ordination ARIANE
CHEAF PROJECT ARIANE
Pluridisciplinary intervention group
- integration of members of the group in the study teams EPIDA, and in the technical commissions preparing the discussion of the jury.
Exemple :
Conception of a main road project (Voirie Primaire n° 8)
. Direction of the studies
. Technical Direction EPIDA
Ingeneer responsable of V.P.8.
Co-ordination ARIANE
Supervision by the project cheaf responsable of the urban studies.
Independent intervention team
Exemple :
Intervention General Assistance "Open spaces"
Direction EPIDA
Constitution of an environment committee SCANIDA + inhabitants + EPIDA + animated by the co-ordinator for ARIANE
Punctual interventions of landscape architects and ecologists of ARIANE

DIFFERENT PHASES OF THE OPERATION "INTEGRATED MANAGEMENT OF THE ENVIRONMENT OF L'ISLE D'ABEAU"

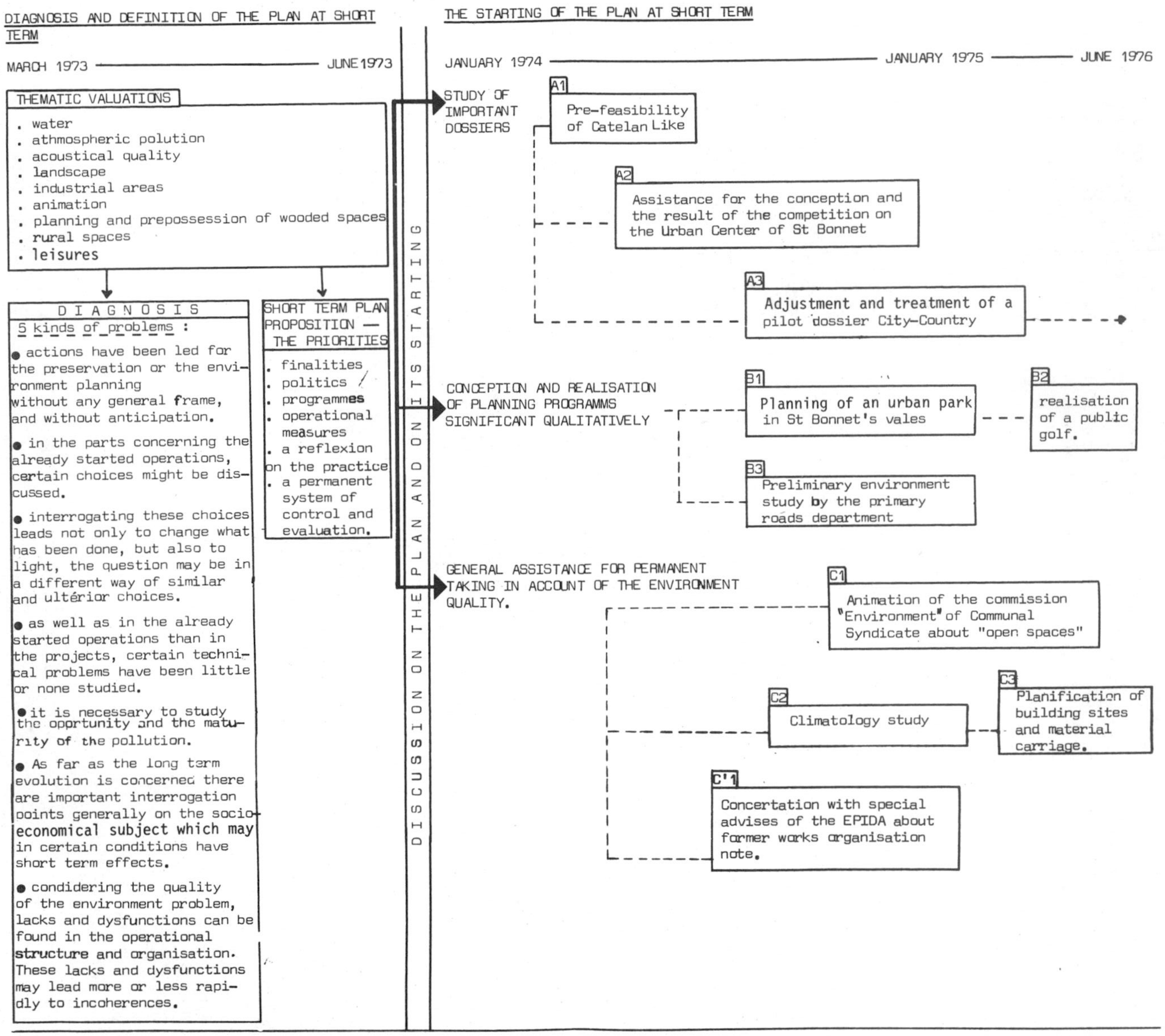

ATTEMPT AT A DETERMINATION OF THE ROLE OF LEGAL MEASURES IN THE ORIENTATION OF URBAN GROWTH*

J.P. Cheylan* F. Desbordes-Cheylan* and L. Farinas Del Cerro**

**Groupe d'Etudes pour l'Application de Méthodes Scientifiques à l'Architecture et l'Urbanisme. Unité Pédagogique de Marseille — Luminy - 13009 Marseille - France*
***Laboratoire d'Informatique pour les Sciences de l'Homme. C.R.N.S. 31, Chemin Joseph Aiguier - 13274 Marseille Cedex 2 — France*

ABSTRACT

By means of formalized observations, which enable us to characterize a certain type of urban growth, we wish to determine precisely the true role played by some orientative measures in urban growth. The method of analysis employed to determine this role is based on the utilization of stochastic processes.

1 — Introduction

The results of the research work described in this paper constitute a methodological step in the development of a more general program. This leads to the implementation of a process of analysis of urban growth mechanisms, which is aimed at producing an explicit understanding of these phenomena. The elaboration of formal and mathematical tools assisting in this step has been effected experimentally for a field of study - the community of Martigues (in the south of France).

2 — Peri - urban growth

We have studied the role played by orientative legal measures in the peri-urban growth in Martigues, a medium-sized town (40,000 inhabitants) in the south of France, which is undergoing rapid expansion. This is partly due to its own dynamism promoted by the industrial employment in the petrochemical and associated industries, and to its role of regional center and also partly due to the influence of an industrial complex of national importance in Fos, the anticipated effects of which have been overestimated. Martigues is sufficiently distant from Marseille, the regional capital, so as not to be influenced. Furthermore, it is governed by a municipality asserting a policy of regional and urban planning. In France, plans for the occupation of land - «Plan d'occupation des sols» - (POS), indicate the building rules applicable in every part of the town area. These plans and the accompanying set of rules define, for homogenous districts, the minimum building surface areas, the maximum building density and for certain areas the restrictions on the authorized usages of land (e. g. industrial zones, regions of urban priority).

*** This research is supported by D.G.R.S.T., under contract number 75 7 0459***

In Martigues, these plans have not yet been adopted. The community however disposes of a plan (Preliminary to the POS), for the land occupation coefficients, which has been in operation since 1970, and which conforms to the same definition.

These measures are put together to form an integral part of a municipal strategy, for the management of town space involving amongst other elements : the previous state of urbanisation, the different opinions of the town council concerning the orientation of urban growth and the pressures of social groups and agents.

The measures may be expressed in two forms :

(1) A spatialised form for the orientations, which have been selected,

(2) A tactical form for concealed or true aims, which is analysable in a certain number of texts.

Peri-urban growth, in the region studied, is marked on the one hand by the creation of estates in rural areas, occupied by town-dwellers and on the other by the appearance, in agricultural spaces, of individual constructions other than estates occupied by town-dwellers. This mode of growth spreads throughout the agricultural space without creating any urban complexes. This phenomenon shall be called «scattering».

There exist several developmental modes of peri-urban growth, which may be characterized by : the nature of construction observed, their temporal mode of appearance, their previous agricultural usuages before construction. Moreover, these characterisations bear a relation with significant regularity to both the preferential localisation of certain types of construction and at the same time to the socio-professional characteristics of the people seeking planning permission.

The municipality has expressed, by its discourse and by means of plans which are a spatial representation of classical orientation, a desire to bring a halt to the «scattering» mode of development, with a view to channelling it towards a zone of development based around two existing villages and hence combatting spatial segregation.

To determine the role played by legal measures, we are led to «compare» the observed evolution after implementation of the orientative measures for the proposed development with that of before.

3 – *Steps and methods involved*

The method of analysis for urban growth elaborated has for objective the production of an understanding of growth mechanisms and conditions.

We would like to show in particular the temporal interactions between the various phenomena studied and variations of the elements assumed to be explanatory of these phenomena. In order to constitute this comprehension of urban phenomena, data will be made up from observations on actual situations.

The steps in this comprehension process may be described as follows :

(a) definition of a problematic : study of the mechanisms of peri - urban growth and in particular mechanisms for the appearance of buildings relating to the previous agricultural land usuage.

(b) constitution of a field of study :
- geographical make-up i.e. the community of Martigues,
- constitution of the objects required for the analysis, i.e. applications for planning permission, representations of buildings on aerial photographs,

(c) constitution of a formal representation of the field of study by the regular description of the objects involved with the help of a descriptive code,

(d) transformation of this field of study to an experimental field (the experimental field is based on a stock of computerised data containing the representations of the phenomenon studied on which may be performed any calculation procedures,

(e) constitution of an interpreting system originating from the problematic and applicable to the experimental field. This interpreting system takes the form of a group of three factors : legal framework, natural milieu, relative localisation of the objects. It is the interdependance of these factors which enables in particular their temporal interactions to be expressed.

(f) definition of mathematical and data-processing tools appropriate to the nature of information available and to the adopted problematic (for the moment, the MARKOV process is used to enable us to translate the evolution of construction in terms of the states of the explanatory factors.),

(g) organisation of hypotheses which are structured in terms of the explanatory factors and decomposable into groups of sub-hypotheses which are interdependant and may be handled by the tools created (we are working presently on a group of sub-hypotheses aimed at isolating, in the community space, the places, moments and modes of determination of construction attributable to the legal framework. Another group of sub - hypotheses aims at discovering the relationships between certain types of constructions and the previous agricultural usuage of the land - parcel on which they stand,

(h) the interpretation of the results : this interpretation is carried out by direct reference to the relationship between the hypothesis considered and the corresponding tool used in the implementation of this hypothesis.

For an example, we shall develop a group of sub-hypotheses originating from the following hypothesis : if the orientative measures governing construction in operation since a given date, play a role in the appearance of consctructions, then different evolutionary mechanisms must be apparent for both observation periods, before and after this date If the evolutions for latter observation period conform to those which the orientative measures aimed at producing then it should be possible to recognise differences in mechanism, implied by the measures taken, by means of the differences in evolution : found for the two periods.

4 – *Foreword on stationary Markov Processes with a finite set of states*

A stationary Markov Process with a finite number of states, $E = \{A, B, C,...\}$ is defined by a semigroup of transition matrices, $\{P^t : t \geq 0\}$ which is in turn defined by :

$$P^t = \exp tG \sum_{n=0}^{\infty} \frac{t^n}{n!} G^n \quad (1)$$

where $G = [G(A,B)]$ is a matrix satisfying the conditions :

$$G(A,B) \geq 0 \quad \text{if } A \neq B$$

and

$$\sum_B G(A,B) = 0 \text{ for } A \in E \quad (2)$$

G is called the infinitesimal operator of the semigroup $\{P^t : t \geq 0\}$.

It must be noted that :

$$\lim_{t \downarrow 0} \frac{1}{t} P^t(A, B) = G(A, B) \text{ for } B \neq A \quad (3)$$

Thus, $G(A,B)\,dt$ describes the evolution of the process in the time interval $(0, dt)$.

The phenomenological description of the Markov process with infinitesimal operator, G, is as follows :

Knowing that the process is in the state, A, at the instant O, it follows that the distribution of its future sojourn time in A is a negative exponential of parameter G (A, A). The distribution for the following state, s, is discrete and defined by :

$$\text{Prob}\ \{s = B\} = -G(A,B)\ /\ G(A,A)\ ,\ B \neq A \quad (4)$$

5 – Description of the model

The evolution of land - usuage is investigated for a group of land - parcels situated in a given region. It is known that the laws governing the evolution of these usuages depend on a certain number of factors, F, G, H, which are defined for each parcel, and are considered as fixed variables varying with time. We wish to use Markov Processes in order to model these evolutions. This is only possible over a time interval during which these factors are constant. The land usuage process, X, will therefore be obtained by pooling together the distinct Markov processes, $X_0, X_1, \ldots, X_g$ defined for the intervals $[t_0\ t_1]$, $[t_1\ t_2]$, ..., $[t_g\ t_{g+1}]$ respectively where for each i $(1 \leq i \leq g)$, t_i is the first instant succeeding t_{i-1} for which at least one of the factors changes value in any one parcel.

Let S^n be the set of states, where $S = \{1, 2, 3 \ldots m\}$ defines the set of possible usuages for each parcel and m is the number of parcels.

Each process X_i will therefore be given by :

$$X_i \quad \bigotimes_{k\ 1}^{n} \quad x_i^k \quad (5)$$

where the x^k are independant stationary Markov processes. The distribution of x_i^k depends only on the value of the factors for the parcel k during the interval $[t_i\ t_{i+1}]$.

6 – Statistical inference problems

There are essentially two problems of statistical inference relevant to our model :

– to test whether a process is a stationary Markov process,

– to test the hypothesis that two stationary Markov processes have the same parameters.

6-1 – Test of the markovian character of the process.

Let us consider an interval of time (O, t) during which the factors remain constant for a set of parcels

$$I = \{i_1\ , i_2\ , \ldots\ , i_k\}$$

Let I_j denote the subset of I formed by the parcels which are in the j - th state at time zero. The well known distribution of sojourn times

$$\tau_1^j\ ,\ \tau_2^j, \ldots, \tau_h^j$$

of these parcels in the j - th state is a negative exponential with unknown parameter, truncated at t.

The Markov hypothesis can thus be verified by performing, for each j, a test of goodness of fit of the observations $\tau_1^j\ \tau_2^j, \ldots, \tau_h^j$. to this distribution. A χ^2 test shall be used to achieve this (see appendix 1).

6-2 – Test of homogeneity

Let us consider two independant stationary Markov processes which have the same finite set of states $\{1, 2, \ldots, m\}$. For $1 \leq j \leq m$ let $Y^j = \{y_1^j, y_2^j, \ldots, y_{n_j}^j\}$ and $Z^j = \{z_1^j\ , z_2^j\ , \ldots z_{m_j}^j\}$ denote samples, of sojourn times in the state j with fixed sizes n_j and m_j arising from the corresponding processes, and likewise

$$L^j = \{l_1^j, l_2^j, \ldots, l_{j-1}^j\ l_{j+1}^j, \ldots, l_m^j\}$$

and

$$K^j = \{k_1^j\ , k_2^j\ , \ldots, k_{j-1}^j\ \ k_{j+1}^j\ , \ldots, k_m^j\}$$

denote the corresponding empirical distributions of the state of exit from j, where :

l_i^j number of jumps from state j to state i in the first sample, $\sum_i l_i^j = n_j$ (6)

and

k_i^j number of jumps from state j to state i in the second sample, $\sum_i k_i^j = m_j$ (7)

We shall divide the problem of testing whether or not these two processes have the same law, into two parts :

(a) verification, for $1 \leq j \leq m$, that the parameters of the exponential distributions, from which Y^j and Z^j originate, are equal. To solve this problem we employ the Neyman-Pearson statistics (see appendix 2),

(b) verification, for $1 \leq j \leq m$, that the samples L^j and K^j belong to the same population. This may be achieved, via classical χ^2 tests. Here again the distinct statistics are independant and can be summed to give an overall test of homogeneity.

7 – Example of a hypothesis

Attention must be drawn firstly to the nature and role of hypotheses used in cognitive processes. It would seem important to mention that the lack of a global theory for urban growth operating as a network of explicit concepts, necessitates strategic choices. These choices consist of postulating that any understanding of urban growth mechanisms may only be arrived at, if it is studied for a group of achievements of this mechanism, and then only if this mechanism is itself of a sufficiently simple nature to be described, in spite of this lack of theory. These considerations lead us to the implementation of apparently simple hypotheses but whose importance may be found within hypotheses concerning several growth modes.

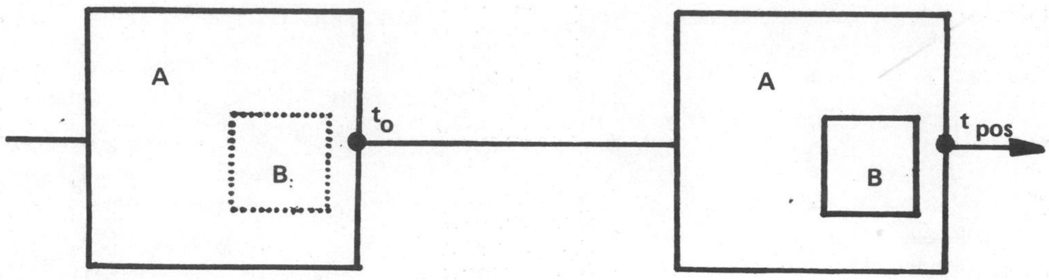

Fig. 1 - POS regions

t_o is the date of the first observation
t_{pos} is the date of implementation of the POS
A_P is the set of parcels homogenous w. r. t. the POS in the region A, not «built on» at the instant t_{pos}
B_p is the set of parcels homogenous w. r. t. the POS in the region B, not «built on» at the instant t_{pos}
A_{p1} is the set of parcels homogenous w. r. t. the POS in the region A, not «built on» at the instant t_o
B_{p1} is the set of parcels homogenous w. r. t. the POS in the region B, not «built on» at the instant t_o

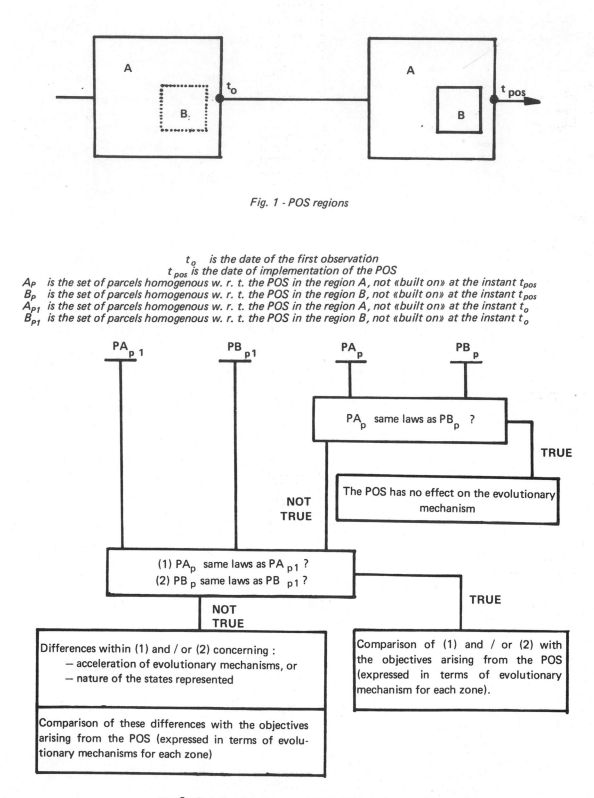

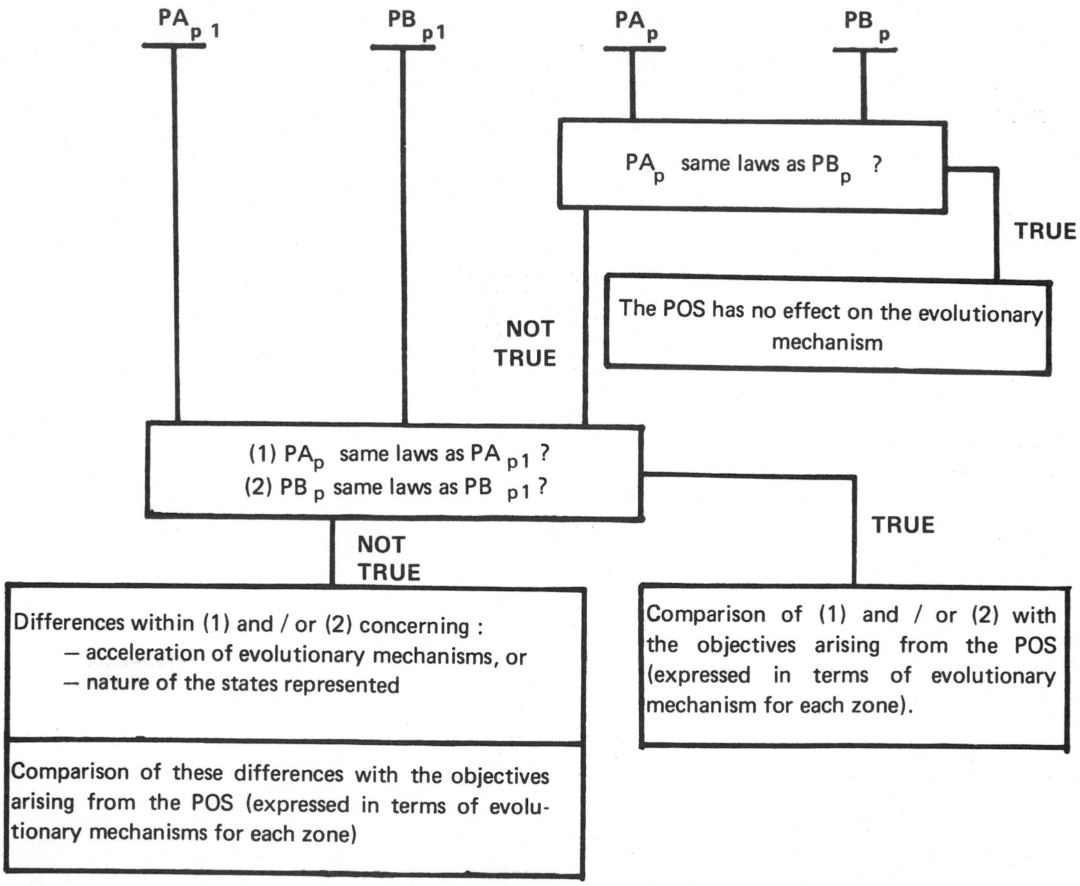

Fig. 2 - Relationship between POS and evolution of land - usage

PA_p is the model for the evolution of land-usage for A_p
PB_p is the model for the evolution of land-usage for B_p
PA_{p1} is the model for the evolution of land-usage for A_{p1}
PB_{p1} is the model for the evolution of land-usage for B_{p1}

The hypothesis considered in(3)will be defined for the following elements :

— A, the space defined for a homogenous zone of the POS,

— B, the space defined for another homogenous zone of the POS,

— PA_{p1}, a mechanism for the diffusion of construction within the time interval (t_o t_{pos}), in the agricultural space («scattering»),

— PB_{p1} ,a mechanism for the diffusion of construction within the time interval (t_{o1} t_{pos}), in the agricultural space («scattering»),

(these constructions are weakly structurised around a nucleus of a few dwellings)

— PA_p is a mechanism for the diffusion of construction after the appearance of the POS, in agricultural space («scattering») indentical to PA_{p1} ,

— PB_p is a mechanism for the construction of detached buildings after the appearance of the POS.

Locally, the desired effect of the application of POS rules may be interpreted as follows :

The constructive rules in zone A define the few possibilities for construction apart from purely agricultural land-usuage. This may be interpreted as an attempt at the reduction of «scattering» construction.

In zone B, the constructive rules define the possibilities for the construction of detached buildings in estates which may be interpreted as being the creation of an «outlet» whose purpose is to recieve the overflow produced by the limitation of «scattering» in A.

The outcome of the implementation of the hypothesis may be interpreted in the light of afore-mentioned elements as a failed attempt at limiting the «scattering» construction (i. e. PA_{p1} identical to PA_p).

The creation of an «outlet» by detached construction is ratified (PB_p different from PB_{p1}) but does not ensure the halting of «scattering», which was its objective.

8 — Conclusion

The study presented in this paper may be interpreted as being the development of tools in an experimentation phase aimed at producing a validation. This validation draws on the one hand on the steps of analysis considered and on the the other on the mathematical tools required for this analysis and relating to the problems tackled.

This work carried out on the community area of Martigues has enabled us to reach an understanding of the relationships existing between urban growth and the legal apparatus of its management.

The use of Markov Processes as the tool for the representation of temporal phenomena has firstly been able to be carried out in accordance with the mathematical hypotheses implied by this type of tool and secondly has enabled the treatment of temporal data having complex structure.

The utilisation of the Markov Process presented, consisted of estimating the changes between two successive evolutionary periods in order to test for any effect of an event which d ivides these two periods. The same tools may be used to test for the similarities or differences between contemporary processes dealing with different classes of objects. It may therefore be verified that either different constructions are brought about by different mechanisms or that different evolutions occur after different types of starting states.

From the point of view of comprehension, the analysis of the role played by orientative legal measures in urban growth has enabled us to show the nature and complexity of the relationships between these measures and the evolutions actually observed. In the example studied, it appears that the intentions contained in the official documents are only partially fulfilled.

In cases where these intentions differ from their preceding mechanisms, only the incitements to develop construction are fully achieved (the attempts at stopping an existing development running up against the inertia of this development).

From the analysis point of view, certain of the difficulties, linked on the one hand to the development of research on scientific reasoning and on the other to the constitution of a stock of theoretical knowledge of urban phenomena will only be raised progressively by various and not always conscious contributions. We believe however that at present it is possible to contribute a few elements whose explanatory content may be relatively limited but whose conditions of explicit and validable constitution indicate however that they may be included in a cumulative process of comprehension acquired. This process might go towards the heuristic elaboration of a theoretical corpus of urban knowledge.

Acknowledgments

We would like to express our thanks to Mr Fernandez de la Vega, for the helpful guidance in the completion of this work, and Mr J. D. Lee for the translation of the French text.

Appendix 1.

We choose an integer p and a partition of the interval (O, t) in p intervals $I_1, I_2, \ldots I_p$, and put :

$$X_j = \sum_{1 \leq i \leq p+1} \frac{[n_i - n_i(\hat{\theta})]^2}{n_i(\hat{\theta})}$$

where :

n_i is, for $1 \leq i \leq p$, the number of observations lying in the interval I_i .

n_{p+1} the number of parcels which are still in state j at time t

$n_i(\hat{\theta})$, $1 \leq i \leq p+1$, is the expected value of n_i , relatively to the estimated value $\hat{\theta}$ of the unknown parameter.

X_j is, under the null hypothesis, distributed as a chi-square with n degrees of freedom.

We can then sum the statistics corresponding to the various initial states j, $1 \leq j \leq m$, since these statistics are clearly independent, to obtain again a χ^2 statistic with m, degrees of freedom which can be used as an overall test for the markovian character of the process.

Appendix 2.

The Neyman-Pearson statistics is in this case :

$$S = 2 \left| \max_{\theta \in \Theta} L_{Y^j}(\theta) + \max_{\theta \in \Theta} L_{Z^j}(\theta) - \max_{\theta \in \Theta} L_{Y^j \cup Z^j}(\theta) \right|$$

where :

$$- L_{Y^j}(\theta) = -n\log(\theta) - 1/\theta \sum_{y_i \in Y^j} y_i - n' t/\theta$$

is the loglikelihood of the observations of the sample Y^j relatively to the negative exponential distribution with parameter θ , truncated at t.

— t is the total time ot observation

— n the number of observation in the sample Y^j falling into the interval (O,t)

— n' the number of observations in the sample Y^j falling outside the interval (O,t)

$L_{Z^j}(\theta)$ and $L_{Y^j \cup Z^j}(\theta)$ have analogous expressions and are respectively the loglikelohood of the sample Y^j and of the pooled sample $Y^j \cup Z^j$

— the Neyman-Peason statistics S is asymptotically distributed as a chi-square with two degrees of freedom (χ^2_2).

References

AMEDO D., GOLLEDGE R. G. — An introduction to scientific reasoning in geography. J. Wiley and Sons, 1975.

BILLINGSLEY D., — Statistical inference for Markov Processes. I. M. S. statistical research monographs, The University of Chicago Press, 1961.

CHEYLAN J.P., CHIAVARI P., DONATI P., DESBORDES — CHEYLAN F. — Vers une explicitation et une formalisation des références spatiales et temporelles dans les systèmes d'informations urbains. Communication. VI European Symposium : urban data management, ed. Dr G. Deprez, Liège — 18 - 22 april 1977.

CHEYLAN M. et Mme, FARIÑAS DEL CERRO L. Essais de constitution de modèles explicatifs partiels de l'évolution des utilisations des sols, march 1977 GAMSAU Bulletin. Ecole d'Architecture Marseille - Luminy.

DAJANI J., REINHARDT M., 1975 — A computer simulation of Urban Growth, Comput. & Urban Soc. vol 1 pp 159 - 168 - Pergamon Press.

DOOB - Stochastics Processes, Wiley New York, 1953

FARIÑAS DEL CERRO L. — Power of some tests for exponential distribution against an alternative of mixture (to appear).

GUENOCHE A. — Présentation d'un système de traitements documentaires et statistiques adapté au calcul en Sciences Humaines. Panorama de la Nouveauté Informatique en France - Tome 1 - pp 181 - 189, AFCET Nov 1966.

LAROUCHE P., 1965 — The simulation of residential growth in the Montreal region, Québec, Québec Department of roads. 1965

SIEGEL S. — Nonparametric statistics for the behavioral sciences, International Student Edition, Mc Graw-Hill - New York. 1956.

SOLID WASTE SYSTEM PLANNING IN CALCUTTA METROPOLITAN DISTRICT

K. J. Nath* and Mrs. S. Nath**

**Assistant Professor, All India Institute of Hygiene & Public Health, 110 Chittaranjan Avenue, Calcutta - 700 073*
***Senior Public Health Engineer, M/s. Atkins Das Private Limited, 21A, Shakespeare Sarani, Calcutta - 700 017*

INTRODUCTION: GENESIS OF THE PROBLEM

A solid waste system is defined to include the generation of waste at source, its collection, transportation and safe disposal causing least nuisance to public health. It is a large expensive and on-going system that is too big, complex and vital to allow actual experimentation without great expense or the potential of great chaos.

Over many years the Calcutta Metropolitan areas has suffered a low standard of service in the collection and disposal of solid wastes. The present condition has put at great risk the health of the whole community. Even though municipal authorities put forward the reason of a lack of technical and financial resources, the root cause is the lack of effort in the past to develop optimal techniques qppropriate to the climate; waste characteristics, transport economics, and the socio-economic structure of the city. Inneffective deployment of limited resources because of poor management has made the system counterproductive. It is ironical that Calcuttans, with perhaps the highest per capita expenditure on solid waste management in South East Asia, has to learn to live with ever-increasing heaps of garbages. The present paper describes the present system of solid waste management in Calcutta Metropolitan District, hereafter referred to as C.M.D., and suggests a system planning for the future.

EXISTING SYSTEM: MUNICIPAL ORGANISATIONS IN C.M.D.

The local Government structure of the C.M.D. is very complex. It consists of two corporations, 33 municipal towns, 37 non-municipal urban centres and 544 rural units covering a total area of 1368 km^2 and a populatio- of about 9 millions (Fig. 1). Even though a centralised planning and development authority known as Calcutta Metropolitan Development Authority has been formed recently, the civic services are looked after by a number of self-governing bodies as given below.

The city proper, with a population of more than 3 million over an area of about 60km^2, is governed by the Calcutta Corporation.

The city of Howrah across the river Hooghly with a population of about 0.5 million and an area of 25 km^2 is under Howrah Municipality.

Thirty four other smaller urban centres with populations ranging from 20 000 to 3 50 00 have got their own municipalities. Together they command a total area of about 450 km^2 and a total population of over 3 millions.

Thirty seven non-municipal urban centres and 544 rural units with a total population of about 3 millions and a total area 800 km^2 are under the jurisdiction of union boards.

The level of conservancy services vary widely while Calcutta Corporation has an elaborate conservancy department as shown in Fig. 2, the smaller municipalities' conservancy services are managed by sanitary inspectors. Excepting Howrah, none of the other municipalities have got any technical personnel in their departments.

Commissioner

Motor Vehicles	Special Deputy Commissioner
Workshop	
Stores	Deputy Chief Engineer
Dumping Ground	District Engineers
and Railway dept.	Supervisors

Fig. 2. Organisational set up for conservancy work in Calcutta Corporation.

QUANTITY AND QUALITY OF REFUSE

It is recognised that the qualitative and quantitative character of the municipal refuse is largely influenced by socio-economic level and cultural heritage of the community. Since within the C.M.D. th level of industrialisation and other social and economic factors vary considerably between the city proper and other suburban towns, a marked difference is noticeable in the refuse characteristics of these areas.

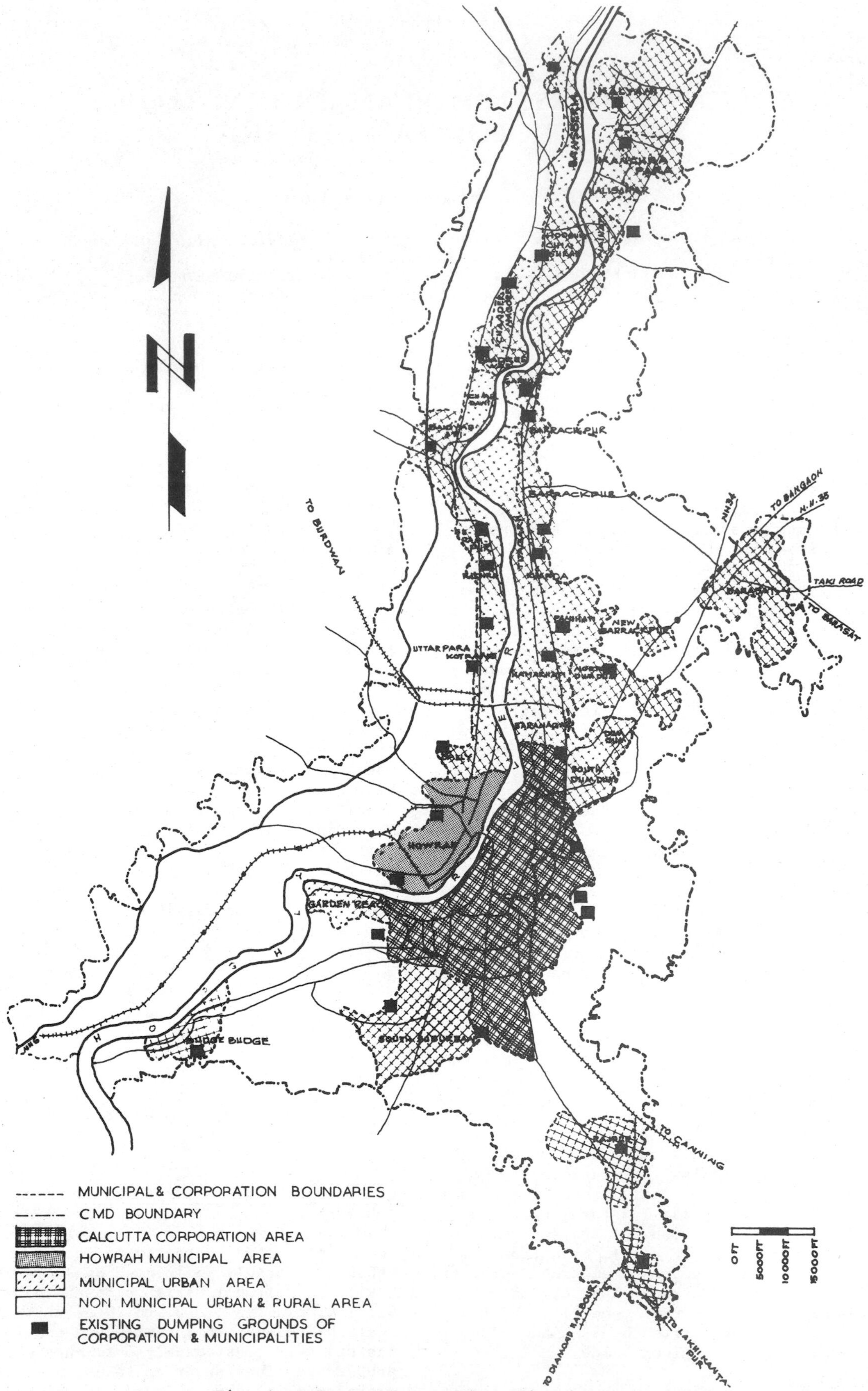

Fig. 1. Calcutta Metropolitan District
Local self-government structure
and locations of disposal sites,

Figures 3 and 4 show the average quality of refuse in Calcutta Corporation area, Howrah Municipal area and other smaller municipalities.

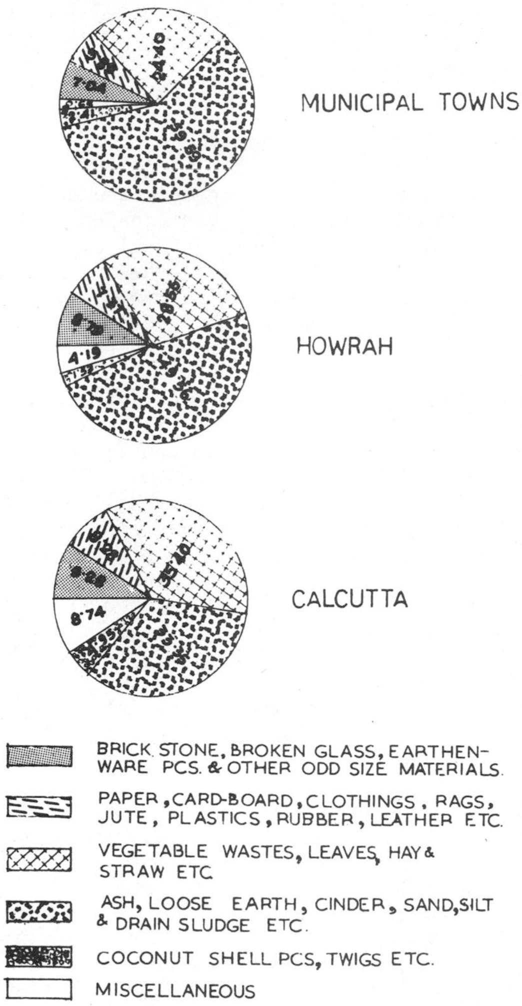

Fig. 3. Physical Characteristics

These are based on the studies conducted by the National Environmental Research Institute and all India Institute of Hygiene and Public Health. Whereas in US cities like Chicago, the major constitutents are paper, synthetics and metals, Calcutta refuse contains large amount of putrefable vegetable matter. The percentage compostible matter is much less in smaller municipal towns compared to the Calcutta Coporation area. The reason is irregular collection and large-scale salvaging by destitutes.

The quantity of refuse collected per capita per day is shown in Table 1. Collection is much less in municipal towns. Presently a total quantity of 2890 tons are collected every day in C.M.D., which is much less than the quantity actually generated.

It should be noted that the areas under union boards have little or no facilities regarding solid waste collection and disposal. No data is available presently as to the qualitative and quantitative character of refuse in those areas which covers the major portion of C.M.D.

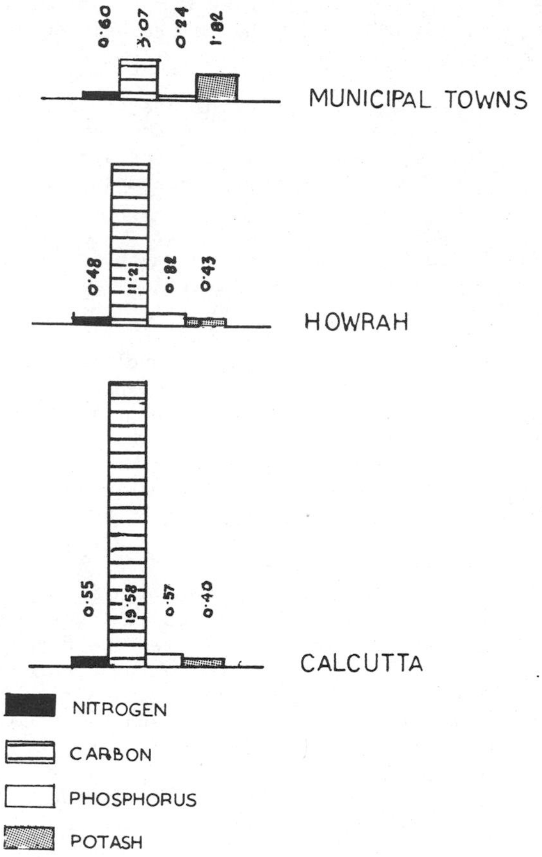

Fig. 4. Chemical Characteristics

Table 1. Total per capita quantity of refuse in C.M.D.

	Per capita collection/ day (kg)	Total collection/day (tons)
Calcutta Corporation	0.51	1800
Howrah Municipality	0.58	340
Smaller Municipalities	0.225	750
Total		2890

The average density of refuse in C.M.D. varies between 500 to 650 kg/m^3 and the average calorific value varies between 1500 and 2500 B.T.U./lb.

MODE OF COLLECTION

Most householder throw their domestic wastes in the streets and about 6500 sweepers using 200 litre hand carts are employed from 5.30 -9.00 a.m. and 2.00 - 5.00 p.m. to remove these waste to about 600/700 Collection points, which are mostly open dumps or vats of poor construction and improper design.

Wastes are removed from these points by open motor trucks having body capacities 5 to 8m^3. Each vehicle is accompanied by 6 loaders who use rakes and baskets. As pointed out by Mr. Frank Flintoff, World Bank Consultant to the Government of India, the major deficiences of the system include:

(i) Street storage dumps are invaded by scavengers and animals which scatter the wastes; rats have access to food and fly larvae can migrate from vats and pupate in the vicinity.

(ii) During rainfall much waste is washed into the gullies and open drains from where it has been removed at ten times the cost.

(iii) The handling process involves collection from strees to hand carts which again dumps them on the ground to be picked up by rake and baskets and put into the trucks. This results in wastage of labour and increases the waiting time for vehicles apart from the great health risk that the workers are exposed to.

The situation in municipalities is worse. In terms of proportion of generated solid waste which are collected and disposed of by municipal staffs, Calcutta Corporation is about 90% efficient, even though time lag between generation at source and their collection creates great environmental problems. In many municipal towns in C.M.D., however, 70 to 80% wastes are never collected. And in areas under union boards collection is less than even 10%.

As discussed earlier, the institutional capacity of the Calcutta Corporation is reasonably good. Most of the municipalities and the union boards under C.M.D., however, are too small to provide effective management of solid waste disposal services.

Calcutta Corporation spends about US $ 2.0/person/year on solid waste management. If spent effectively the sum should not prove inadequate. Expenditure in many municipalities is, however, less than US cents 50 which is grossly inadequate (1).

DISPOSAL FACILITIES

Open dumping on municipal dumping grounds is the existing system of refuse disposal for the Calcutta Corporation area. Filling up private lands is the principal feature in municipal towns. A minor portion of the re fuse in municipalities is manually composted in trenches with night soil. Presently Calcutta Corporation possess about 1750 acres of land in three major dumping grounds (2), the fourth one having been closed down in 1960 due to severe public demonstrations against it. Howrah municipality possess two disposal sites of about 50 acres of land for dumping (3). All other municipalities together posses about 270 acres in 30 disposal grounds. Whereas Calcutta Corporation posseses about 5.5 acres per 10 000 persons, minicipalities possess only 0.8 acre per 10 000 persons (1). Locations of various disposal grounds are shown in Fig. 1. The cost of dumping in the largest disposal grounds of Calcutta Corporation is as high as US $ 1.8 per ton of refuse (2). Even then, the system is technically unsound and has not increased the land value of the reclaimed sites. The practice is unhygienic too.

RATIONAL APPROACH TO PLANNING

It is not surprising that the authorities responsible for our civic problems have failed to achieve the desired level of services. The system that works today is the cumulative effect of point to to point *ad hoc* decisions. At no time in the past has any effort been made to make a long-term planning of the management of solid waste integrated with regional environmental planning. If the various civic bodies within a geo-political region like Calcutta Metropolitan District wish to cooperate in solving their waste management problems, the optimal use of their facilities and personnel has to be found out. A system may not reach optimun level by merely selecting the best components independently, since interactions between components are very significant. The planning of the refuse collection system is essentially the process of evaluating various ways of utilizing men and machines to find out the combination which optimises cost subject to the constraint of a safe and sanitary environment. Figure 5 shows the various areas of decision making that the metropolitan authority must study to find out the most optimum solid waste management system for the area. Alternatives in each component must be examined separately before an optimum system is developed. Deterministic mathematical modeling and computer programming for cost optimisation may be needed to optimise the collection and transportation system, as the options and alternatives are many and varied. But sound disposal system for the C.M.D. area may be developed by judicious consideraion of three aspects, i.e.

i) Refuse characteristics.
ii) Land using planning on regional basis.
iii) Environmental aspects and cost considerations.

Here the options being limited, computer aided studies may not be required.

Solid waste generation	Weight per capita/day	
	Density, physical and chemical characteristics	
	Recycling	Controlled
		Uncontrolled
Storage	Household storage bins	
	Communal storage	
	Point of collection	Communal
		Kerbside
		House to House
Collection system	Frequency of collection.	
	Short range transfer	
	Primary collection vehicles	Animal
		Handcarts
		Motorised
	Method	Crew Manual
		One man Manual
		Mechanical
Transportation system	Type of vehicles	
	Capacity	
	Number of crews	
	No. of trips and haulage	
	Long range transfer stn.	
Disposal	Refuse characteristics	
	Land use planning	
	Environmental aspects	

Fig. 5. Flow chart and decision areas for C.M.D.'s and solid wastes management

MATHEMATICAL MODELING FOR TRANSPORTATION SYSTEM

Deterministic mathematical models incorporating the pertinent fixed and variable parameters may be expressed as follows:

$$C = \frac{C_T}{t} + \frac{C_{T.i} + C_{T.i/t}}{2} + n.h.o + f.l \qquad \times n' \qquad (1)$$

$$f = bq + ade + 15a + 5a \qquad (2)$$

$$f = 480\ a/g \qquad (3)$$

where a = number of collectors per trip

b = pick-up time / ton of refuse

q = average tons of refuse per trip

d = distance to and from the disposal site

e = average haul speed

f = total man-minute/trip

g = total number of trips/day

C_T = initial cost of truck

i = rate of interest on capital

n = total number of trips per year

t = useful life of trucks

o = operation and maintenance cost of trucks / unit run

h = round trip haul distance

c = total running cost per year

l = labour rate/man minute

n' = total number of trucks in operation.

Total man-minute trip has been taken as the sum of pick-up time, haul time, off-route time and at site time. Total running cost per year is the sum of annual depreciation, average annual interest or capital, operation, maintenance and labour charges. d and h should be determined after finding the optimum routing schedule.

Preliminary examination by fitting observed Calcutta Corporation data to this model leads to some interesting observations (4).

It was found that efficiency will increase if the capacity of the present trucks (3 to 5 tons) is increased. Contrary to common belief it was also found that increase in number of trips per vehicle reduces efficiency and increases cost; the reason is perhaps that the average haul of 17 km is too high and makes it imperative to examine the possibility of the introduction of transfer stations. With the available cost parameters and with the addition of rate of interest on the capital cost of transfer stations in equation 1, a series of runs may be carried out with different capacity transfer stations and with different locations. The optimum size of transfer stations was found out to be 1500 tons per week for Baltimore City in USA (5). Reallocation of disposal sites on a rational basis should, however, be the first priority in C.M.D. for optimizing transportation system. As can be seen in Fig. 1, the size and distribution of sites in C.M.D. is haphazard and ill planned, to say the least. There are more than 35 municipal disposal sites scattered all over the area in addition to many private lands which are also being used for dumping. Size of these disposal grounds vary from a few acres to more than 1000 acres. Average haulage for various sites varies between 1.5 km to 17 km. It is felt that disposal sites should be located that at no site will the haulage be more than 10 km. This will make transfer stations unecessary.

VEHICLES DESIGN AND OPERATIONAL CONTROL

Apart from finding out the optimum routing, optimum capacity, crew size and number of trips for vehicles through deterministic models, the area where major decisions has to be taken is the design of vehicles and collecting carts and mode of collection and storage. These should suit the local conditions. Western experience may not be of much help. Refuse density being very high, bulk carriers with compacting arrangement will not be useful. With the level of servicing and maintenance, less mechanisation of the system will be preferable. Introduction of short-range transfer in which the primary non motorised vehicles (hand carts/animal carts/pedal tricycles) will collect and unload directly into long-range secondary transport vehicles, is likely to improve the system. This will also reduce the round trip haul of secondary motorised vehicles to a minimum. The secondary vehicles may be 3 to 5 m^3 trailers fitted with agricultural tractors. Trailers may be stationed in markets and other important places to receive refuse from the primary vehicles. Detachable prime movers will reduce waiting time and wastage of labour. Containerising refuse at all stages of its journey must replace the present system of collection, which is nothing less than an environmental disaster.

It should, however, be mentioned that decisions in the area of xollection and transportation systems must be taken after conducting pilot studies for a sufficiently long period. The Worl Bank has proposed to advance aid to C.M.D.A. for such studies.

RECOMMENDATIONS ON DISPOSAL METHODS

Considering the high density, high organic content and low calorific value of the refuse the theoretical alternatives are between sanitary land filling and composting. Incideration is to be ruled out being too costly and unsuitable for this type of refuse. Whereas sanitary land filling may cost between US $ 0.8 to 1.2, mechanised composting will cost US $ 2.2 to 3.3 and manual or semi-mechanised composting may cost US $ 1.5 to 2. Against this Calcutta Corporation at present is spending about US $ 1.5 for open and insanitary dumping in the existing dumping ground (3). Municipalities are, however, not spending much on disposal since mostly they are filling up private lands.

In C.M.D. area sanitary land filling holds good prospects because of the following reasons:

(i) Lowest cost.

(ii) Existing sites in Calcutta Corporation area may serve for another 20 years and with proper land use planning many potential sites can be located outside the corporation area for smaller municipalities and union board.

(iii) Haulage can be kept below 10 km in most cases.

(iv) Land value will be increased and environmental improvement is possible.

However, it should be kep in mind that by 2001 C.M.D. area is expected to generate about 8000 tons of solid waste per day and sanitary land filling cannot be a permanent solution. Hence pilot scale plants of semi-mechanised composting which require only 2.5 hectars of land for a plant of 100t/day capacity should be taken up immediately, so that thėy can progressively replace sanitary land filling as the pressure on land grows. Compost manure has good demand in the agricultural area adjoining C.M.D.

REGIONAL PLANNING

A look at the map of the C.M.D. will reveal its utterly confusing and chaotic local self-government structure. An optimum solution of the environmental problems is hardly possible is so many agencies (more than 50) try to manage it within their artificial boundaries and varying financial resources. Fragmentation of the entire population into arbiturary and smaller groups has reduced system efficiency. That small municipal organisations are counter-productive in the matter of solid waste management, will be evident from the fact that with even much lesser per capita expenditure the unit cost of collection and disposal of refuse in these municipalities are much higher that that in Calcutta Corporation (1).

Hence it is recommended that the solid waste disposal problems of the whole region must be managed by a unified organisation, which should work in close cooperation with other regional planning bodies like the land use planning organisation and water and air pollution control agencies.

SUMMARY AND CONCLUSION

The complex self-government structrum of the Calcutta Metropolitan District covering a population of 9 millions is discussed. Deficiences in the existing system of solid waste disposal is highlighted. A flow chart for solid waste system planning and the major areas of decision making for C.M.D. is suggested. Mathematical models for transportation planning are discussed. Sanitary land filling and semi-mechanised composting is suggested as a disposal method and reorganisation of the solid waste management system on regional basis is recommended.

REFERENCES:

1. Feasibility studies on refuse and night soil disposal in municipal town in C.M.D., *Report by All India Institute of Hygiene and Public Health*, Calcutta, India, 1977.

2. Feasibility studies for alternate methods of garbage disposal for Calcutta City, *Report by Central Public Health Engineering Research Institute*, Nagpur, India, 1970.

3. Rational methods of refuse disposal from Howrah, *Report by Central Public Health Engineering Research Institute*, Nagpur, India, 1973.

4. S. Neogi *et al.*, Monogram on refuse disposal for Calcutta, *Journal of Institute of Public Health Engineers*, India, 2, 180, 1976.

5. K.J. Nath and M.A. Sampatkumaran, Systems approach to regional solid waste management, Proceedings of the seminar, Institution of Chemical Engineer, India, Calcutta, 1974.

INTEGRATED RESOURCE PLANNING AS A BASE FOR DEVELOPING SINGLE PURPOSE PLANS

Tung Liang* and W. O. Watson Jr.**

**University of Hawaii, Honolulu, Hawaii*
***Dept. of Land and Natural Resources, State of Hawaii*

ABSTRACT

A resource planning model was developed and used to identify the common elements shared by all single purpose plans, to allocate resources to each plan, to designate the responsibility, and to insure the independence of each planning effort. The model serves as a tool for coordinating all single-purpose planning efforts and the basis for resolving the conflicts.

This report describes the planning process, the model structure and some of the model outputs which include economic, resource, social and environmental impacts.

INTRODUCTION

A multitude of plans are simultaneously conducted in almost every nation, state or country. Regardless of the level of the emphasis, land and water are always the most important items which must be carefully considered. Conflicts over the ability to provide adequate land or water for a planned use will jeopardize the chance that the plan will be successfully implemented. In the past, plans were developed for specific projects. Because of lack of coordination, the same piece of land and the same water source were being planned for several uses. It creates a set of plans that could not be implemented because of the conflicts over the use of the water and land resources.

Since nearly every plan involves the demand for water and land, it behooves planners to investigate the possibility of coordinating all the plans into the common resource plan which will assign quantities of water and parcels of land to each single purpose plan with proper impacts displayed. The result of this effort will assure each plan an adequate supply of water and land at specific locations and will allocate the resources in such a manner that the regional goals will be achieved with minimum investment and without conflict. Having thus attained the water and land to be allocated for a specific purpose, the single-purpose plan such as that for agriculture can then be independently completed with the assurance that the resources will be available for its implementation.

THE RESOURCE PLANNING PROCESS

The resource plan formulation process has four principle steps (Fig. 1). First it is necessary to identify and inventory the existing developed resource base with the emphasis on water, land and other related resources. The second step is to evaluate current economic, social and environmental conditions and anticipated changes in these conditions over the planning horizon. The third step involves an examination of future resource demands with respect to the planning considerations and existing plans for future development. The results of this analysis indicate possible areas of resource stress and overload.

The fourth step is the development of alternative plans to overcome problems which have been identified in the preceding investigation. Alternative plans are evaluated on their effectiveness, efficiency and impacts on other factors. Plan selection may be made at this point or it may become necessary to cycle back to step 2 and/or 3 and review planning considerations. The schematic in Fig. 1 illustrates the planning process.

The need for a computer based resource model in the planning process can be found at steps 2 and 3. Here it is necessary to input the vast amount of data concerning the planning considerations and the supply of resources developed to meet the demand placed on water and related land resources by industry and population and determine the impact of those activities on environmental quality. Given this task, a merging of economic planning utilizing the Input-Output model techniques (referred as IO hereafter) and resource planning utilizing the Linear Programming technique (referred hereafter as LP) is required to incorporate all facets of the problem.

Published with the approval of the Director of the Hawaii Agricultural Experiment Station as Journal Series Paper No. 2119.

DEVELOPING THE MODEL

Many planners do not have advanced quantitative modelling training. Decision makers and ordinary citizens are even less skilled. Models stated in mathematical relations are incomprehensible to them. In order to gain their confidence in modelling, a planning model should be started with a set of verbal objectives agreed upon by all concerned. Planners, decision makers and citizens can all equally contribute to the derivation of the verbal objectives which will become binding on everyone once the planning objectives are adopted. This approach is quite different from the manner in which most existing planning models were developed. In a democratic society, this may be the only way of ensuring the acceptability of planning.

Verbal Objectives

The verbal objectives are developed to include the common considerations shared by all planning, which are:

A. Economic

1) Maximize gross regional product with existing resources.

2) Meet projected economic needs based on population projection.

3) Interindustry relation change should be guided when economy is growing.

4) Avoid excessive dominance of any industry to ensure a stable and less recession-prone economy. Assist weak industry to reach competitive size.

B. Resource

5) Avoid water shortage.

6) Avoid land to becoming a limiting factor blocking economic growth.

7) Avoid excessive energy demand which depends on exogenous factors.

8) Avoid excessive harbor load.

c. Social

9) Avoid transferring existing population from one area to another to avoid hardship or social problem.

10) Make sure certain frequently needed services and goods are close to consumer.

11) Avoid commuting patterns which create traffic (energy, etc.) congestion and eventually increase transportation investment.

D. Environmental

12) Economic growth should not pollute the environment excessively.

13) Quality of life should not be adversely affected if possible.

If desired, other objectives can be easily added.

Quantifying Verbal Objectives into the Model

Most of the verbal objectives can be converted into mathematical relations. Some of them were expressed as a set of simultaneous mathematical relations. For easy comparison, each relation or constraint of the model is numbered identical to the number of the corresponding verbal objective. The model can be expressed as:

$$\max_{X_{ijk}} Z = \sum_{ij} (I - A_{ij}) X_{ij} \qquad (1)$$

Subject to:

$$\sum_{ij} (I - A_{ij}) X_{ij} \leqq B_{\mu} \qquad (2)$$

$$\sum_{ij} (I - A_{ij}) X_{ij} \geqq B_{\ell} \qquad (3)$$

$$X_{ijk} \geqq h_{ijk\ell} \text{ for all } i,j \text{ and } k \qquad (4a)$$

$$X_{ijk} \leqq h_{ijk\mu} \text{ for all } i,j \text{ and } k \qquad (4b)$$

$$X_{ijk} = h_{ijk} \text{ for all } i,j \text{ and } k \qquad (4c)$$

$$\sum_{k}^{n+1} w_{k\ell} X_{ijk} \leqq b_{ij\ell} \text{ for all } \ell, i \text{ and } j \qquad (5)$$

$$\sum_{k}^{n} a_{ijkr} X_{ijk} \leqq b_{ijr} \text{ for all } i,j,r \qquad (6)$$

$$\sum_{k} e_k X_{ijk} \leqq E_{ij} \quad \text{for all } i \text{ and } j \qquad (7)$$

$$\sum_{k} t_k X_{ijk} \leqq T_{ij} \quad \text{for all } i \text{ and } j \qquad (8)$$

$$\sum_{k}^{n+1} p_k X_{ijk} \geqq P_{ij\ell} \text{ for all } i \text{ and } j \qquad (9a)$$

$$\sum_{k}^{n+1} p_k X_{ijk} \leqq P_{ij\mu} \text{ for all } i \text{ and } j \qquad (9b)$$

$$P_m X_{ijm} - \sum_{k}^{n+1} p_k X_{ijk} \geqq 0 \text{ for all } i,j,m \qquad (10)$$

$$\sum_{ij c C_I} \left[\sum_{k}^{n} p_k X_{ijk} - P_n + 1\, X_{ijn} + 1\right] = 0.0 \qquad (11)$$

$$\sum_{k}^{n} S_{ijkr} X_{ijk} \leqq s_r b_{ij} \quad (12)$$

$$\sum_{k}^{n+1} q_{ijkr} X_{ijk} \leqq b_{ijr} \text{ for all } i,j,r \quad (13)$$

where:

I : Identity matrix

\$: Base year dollars

A_{ij} : The technical coefficient matrix of the area economy

X_{ij} : A column matrix $X_{ij1}, X_{ij2}, \ldots X_{ijm}$ $\ldots, X_{ijn}$ representing the mth industry output in 10^4\$ (X_{ijn+1} is reserved for representing the jth area resident population)

B_ℓ : A column matrix, $b_{\ell 1}, b_{\ell 2}, \ldots b_{\ell m}$, $\ldots b_{\ell n}$, representing the base year final demand of the mth industry, in 10^4\$

B_μ : A column matrix, $b_{\mu 1}, b_{\mu 2}, \ldots b_{\mu m}$, $\ldots b_{\mu n}$, representing the projected final demand of the mth industry in the last year of the planning period, in 10^4\$

$w_{k\ell}$: Water demand of the kth industry in the ℓth month, in 10^4\$ gallons/ 10^4\$ output

$b_{ij\ell}$: Water supply in the ℓth month and jth area, in 10^4 gallons

S_{ijkr}: The annual discharge of the rth pollutant by the kth industry in ijth area, in tons/10^4\$

s_r : Maximum allowable rth pollutant in the water, in tons/10^4 gallons of water

b_{ij} : The amount of annual surface run-off water in the ijth area, in 10^4 gallons

q_{ijkr}: The amount of the rth resource in ijth area such as urban land, open space, etc., which must be allocated to each unit of the kth industry to ensure a preferred urban density, etc., in acres/ 10^4\$

a_{ijkr}: The amount of rth type of land needed to produce one unit output of the kth industry, in acres/10^4\$

b_{ijr} : Available rth resource, in acres

p_k : Population generated or supported by each unit of the kth industry output, in 10 person/10^4\$

$P_{ij\ell}$: Base year population in ijth area, in 10 persons

$P_{ij\mu}$: Projected population in the last year of the planning period, in 10 persons

$h_{ijk\ell}$: Minimum desirable size of the kth industry in the ijth area, in 10^4\$

$h_{ijk\mu}$: Maximum desirable size of the kth industry in the ijth area, in 10^4\$

P_m : The size of the population whose need for mth industry output is equal to one unit of mth industry output, in 10 persons/10^4\$

C_I : Ith group of areas where industry output generates exactly the employment needed by the resident population

c : Means "included in"

e_k : Energy input required to produce one unit of output of the kth industry, in kwh/10^4\$

E_{ij} : Energy ceiling in the ijth area in kwh

t_k : Shipping requirement to produce one unit of output of the kth industry, in tons/10^4\$

T_{ij} : Shipping capacity in the ijth area in tons

In summary, constraints (2) and (3) are a statement of the interindustry relationships. In a developed economy where technical change is not occurring at a rapid rate, the existing relationships can be utilized in assessing the future. However, if there is rapid technological change and/or the planning time horizon is far in the future, then the technical coefficients will have to be modified in order to reflect any anticipated changes in the relationships. The objective function (1) forces the growth of the regional economy to meet the projected regional demand.

Constraints (4a, 4b and 4c) have been incorporated to override considerations for optimal resource allocation. The effect of these constraints is to direct growth. In other words, the model optimally locates growth but, if desired for some reason, such as avoiding excessive dominance and economic stability, it is possible to limit growth below optimal level and locate growth in less than optimal locations by using these constraints.

Constraint (5) insures that water demand stemming from economic development will not exceed the supply. This segment of the model will limit growth when water supply becomes a bottleneck. The model attempts to achieve the maximum level of growth given the existing water supply. When additional resources such as water in this case are made available, then development will continue. Growth and development will continue and hence the mixture of activity in the economy will change.

Land poses a constraint much in the same way that water does. Land is zoned for specific uses. The availability of land for particular uses is limited. Growth in areas requiring specific land will be stopped when the supply is exhausted. However, in the case of urban use it is possible to continue increasing the intensity of use. Using constraint (6) it is possible to set limits both on the supply of land and the intensity of use. Alternatively, in the case of urban land no constraint need be included but rather the analyst would have to maintain a check of the intensity of use to insure the feasibility of the solution.

Constraints (7) and (8), respectively, consider the capacity for energy and shipping between regions. Bottlenecks preventing growth stemming from these factors can be identified.

In certain instances it may become necessary to minimize the spatial relationship between the population and employment centers. Or it may become necessary to maintain growth in a region in order to keep pace with population growth. Constraints (9a) and (9b) allow for these considerations. The use of (9a) and (9b) directs growth to specific areas in order to create employment for the residents in the area. However, there is specific kinds of growth which must be located in other areas regardless of the need for employment in a given region. This is because industry location is directly related to the availability of resources and other infrastructure.

Constraint (10) insures that service industry location is in fact located in close proximity to the consuming residents. Constraint (11) is included so that daily commuting between subregions can be examined in an effort to minimize traffic when planning the future.

Water quality may also impose a bottleneck of future development if specific standards must be maintained . Constraint (12) limits further development when a predetermined amount of water pollution is attained. Similarly, other standards referencing the quality of life such as air quality can be imposed. Constraint (13) is included to build these into the model.

HOW THE MODEL IS USED*

Resource Planning

The model consists of a set of relations which avoids selecting as the solution an economy or a set of economic activities which together demand more resources than are available in the region. The optimization relation (the objective function (1)) of the model attempts to generate, not exceeding the projected growth, as much output of goods and services as possible, given the existing resource base and the constraints imposed.

In principle, planning should be an interactive process. Needs generated by a projected future population are first identified. Problems such as resource shortage must be detected and tentative remedies developed. Finally, the feasibility and the economics of the developed actions must be evaluated. This procedure may repeat itself many times before a final plan is deemed acceptable. The explicit definition of regional needs in the model reduces ambiguity when planners identify the needs or goals. The model distributes economic activities to where resources are abundant so that the identified goals can be met. If resources are in shortage, the exact type, location, time and quantity will be detected and flagged by the model. The economic impact of such a shortage is also available. The model supplies the information which helps planners and decision makers to identify possible measures to overcome the shortage. The flow chart in Fig. 2 describes the iterative planning procedure with emphasis on the role played by the decision makers and the information flow when the model is used in the planning process.

Model Outputs

Outputs from the model can all be graphically displayed for the use by planners and decision makers in developing the final plan. Some of the graphic displays are illustrated in Figs. 3, 4, 5, 6, 7a, and 7b.

The displays are from a study made of the island of Kauai in the State of Hawaii. Figures 3 and 4 depict the projected goals of population and industry. Figure 4 relates the industrial output in terms of water requirements. The island is divided into hydrographic areas or major drainage basins. Each hydrographic area is designated by a Roman numeral and the resources of each area are analyzed with the intent of providing the resources needed for the projected demand. The graph in Fig. 4 shows that the water

*See "An LP-IO Model for Coordinating Multigroup Inputs in Resource Planning," by Tung Liang, Water Resources Bulletin, Vol. 12, No. 3, June 1976, American Water Resources Association.

supply is limiting the growth patterns in areas II, III, IV, and V.

Figure 5 displays the output in million dollars from the agricultural industry, the visitor industry, and all industries as a result of the limitation placed on them by water supply.

Figure 6 displays the water quality indicators which may be environmental constraints in the plan. The indicators show the amounts of phosphorous, nitrogen, BOD demand and solids in pounds per million gallons of water. The changes are due to the projected industrial growth on the island of Kauai.

Figure 7a displays the social indicators or social constraints. These graphs display the transportation problems which will occur between hydrographic areas II and III. It also shows the number of people that will be employed and an estimate of the resident population in each area.

Figure 7b displays the quality of life indicators. These are also social constraints and the graphs display the density in persons per acre in urban areas and for the number of parks available. The overall density of the hydrographic area is also shown.

There are many other displays that can be obtained from the model as needed to assist the user in the decision-making process for achieving the established goals.

The final result of the resources planning effort will allocate the resources among the projected economic, social and environmental needs. The primary transportation requirements between major river basins will be determined, the major water projects identified, and the other unknowns can then be determined through single-purpose planning.

The following example will explain the relationship between resource planning and single-purpose planning:

Agriculture versus Resource Planning

The purpose of agricultural planning is to develop a set of consistent governmental actions; such as the construction of water and transportation facilities to create an environment conducive to the achievement of a set of agricultural goals using the minimum amount of regional resources.

The basis for any good and acceptable plan is the formulation of operational goals which are specific and quantifiable. For example, the goal to increase agricultural output is not an operational goal. In order to be operational, the goal must specify commodity groups, such as vegetables, meats, etc., and the amounts to be produced. The goals identified above must also be consistent among themselves and with other goals.

The most essential part of the planning process is in the first step of Stage I of the Flow Diagram (Fig. 8). The identification and specification of operational goals must be clear, concise and complete and must be agreed to by decision makers.

Stage I is the resource planning or the long-range portion of the planning process. It contains four steps--step 1, the identification of operational goals; step 2, the determination of adequate land and water to achieve the goals; step 3, the display of social, economic and environmental impacts; and step 4, the recommendations for governmental actions or programs necessary to achieve the goals established in step 1. Having determined the location and the amount of resources and governmental actions designed to achieve the operational goals established, the process moves to Stage II, the development of the agricultural plan, which then determines the individual commodities in the commodity groups to be produced; for example, the tons of lettuce, celery, etc., in the vegetable group required to achieve established goals. If it is found that the economically feasible individual commodities in a group are insufficient to fulfill the goals for that group as established in Stage I, the planning process must be re-examined at appropriate steps to determine whether the goals need to be revised, additional governmental actions are necessary, or new profitable individual commodities can be produced in order to achieve the established agricultural goals.

The major differences between the efforts in Stage I and Stage II are:

1. The goals considered at Stage I are comprehensive. The effort of checking resource adequacy and analyzing impacts is reconnaissance in nature. The emphasis is on the allocation of water and land resources to major human activities within a river basin or between river basins.

2. In Stage II the planning effort emphasizes only agricultural goals after being given specific locations and quantities of resources for the goal implementation by Stage I. Considerations for transfers of resources between river basins is no longer a consideration in the agricultural plan. Careful consideration however is given to the development of a specific source or an infrastructure for the achievement of agricultural goals.

CONCLUSION

The resource planning is a tool used to coordinate all single purpose plans within a region and is used as a basis for resolving conflicts. Once the resources are allocated for the various uses, each use can be planned freely and independently from the other. The relationship that exists between resource planning and the agricultural planning described above can also be applied to recreation planning, city planning, or any other specific purpose planning.

Remember, however, that planning is conditional upon critical assumptions made concerning the future. Many of these assumptions underpin the necessary input data for computer models. The planner must be aware of these assumptions and the input data in order to assess the model's results. In addition, the planner must have control over such assumptions and data in order to evaluate other scenarios of the future and revise the data.

The resource planning model is a tool capable of displaying impacts in all dimensions of concern without a lengthy time delay.

With the use of the model no one dominates, rather the planning staff plays a role of moderator. Decision makers contribute and planning becomes a cooperative process. This is essential as the expertise of many disciplines is required and the model precludes any one discipline from domination.

The resource model facilitates complete and accurate planning, economizes on time and cost, and makes use of the latest generation of computer technology. The model can successfully and efficiently coordinate the input into a meaningful and acceptable plan.

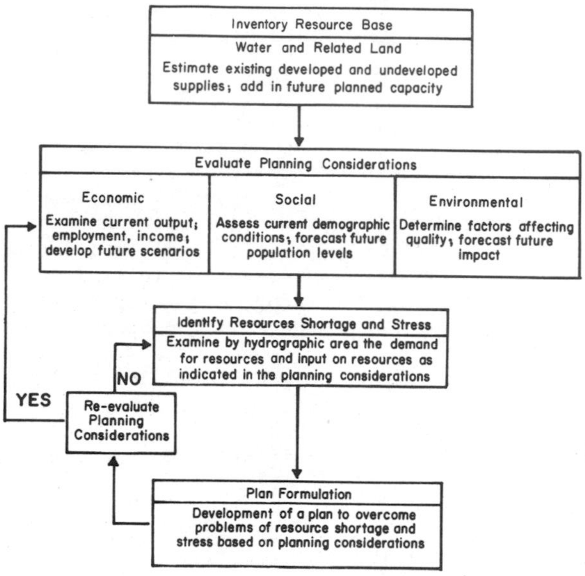

Fig. 1.
Resource planning process.

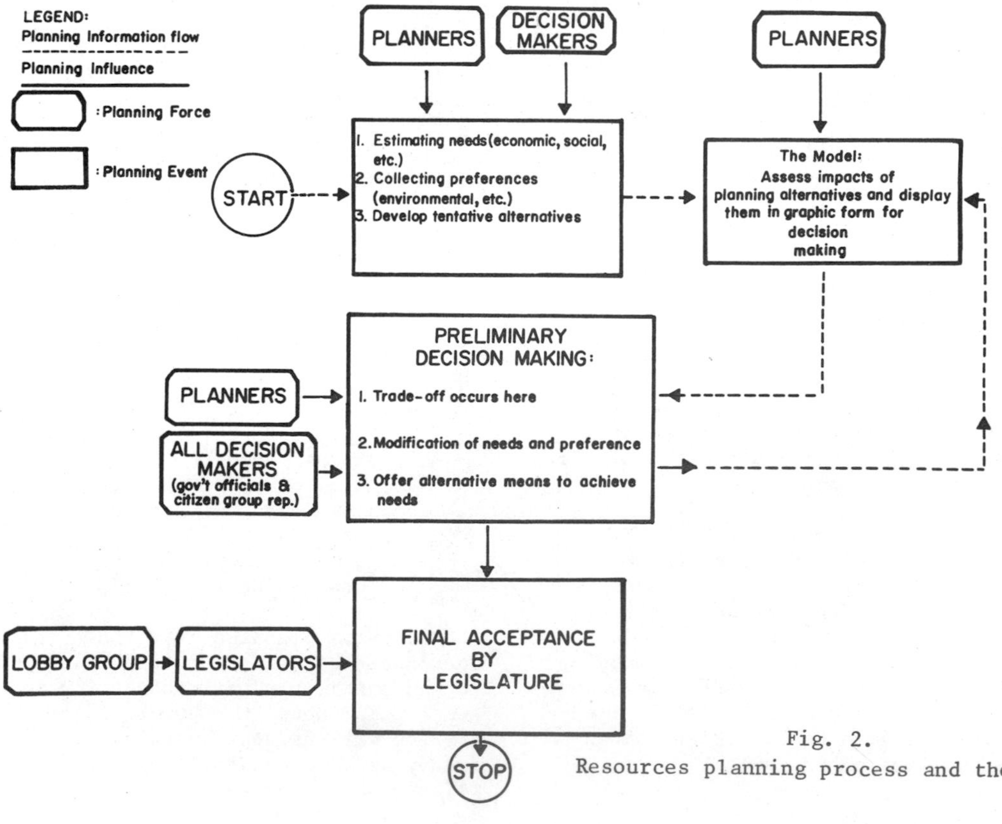

Fig. 2.
Resources planning process and the model

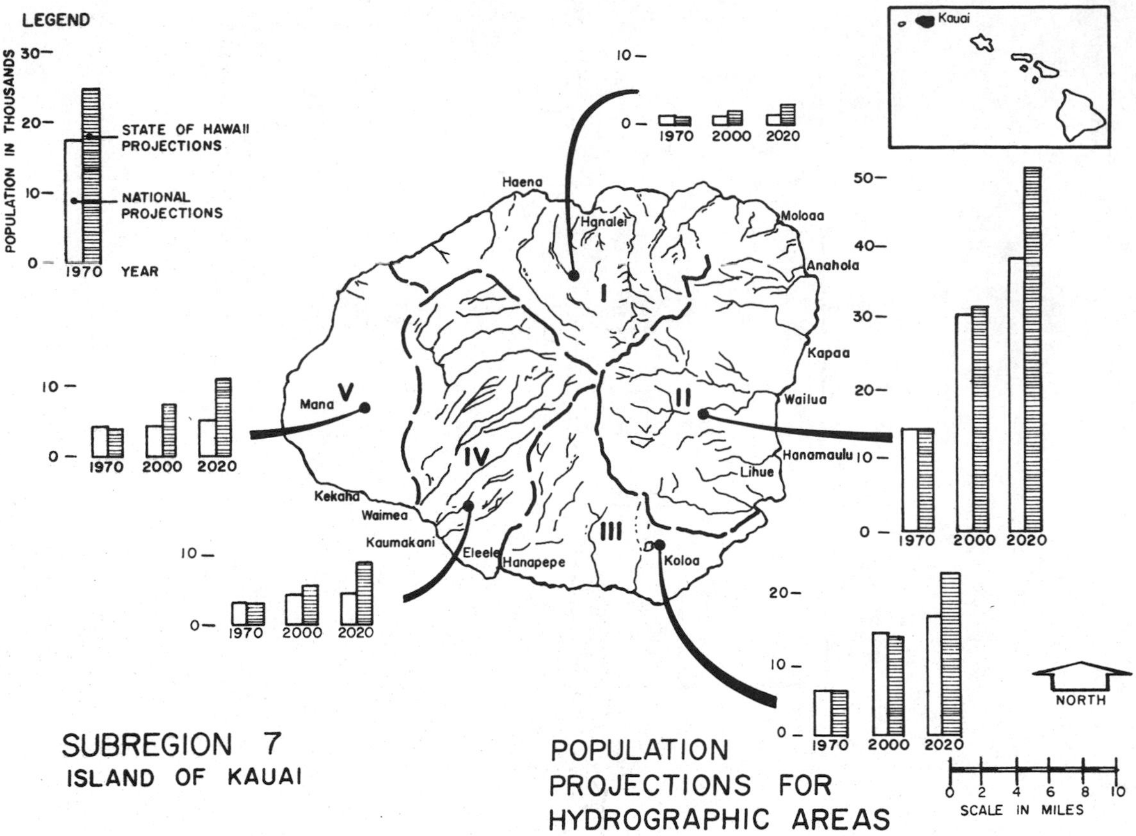

Fig. 3. Kauai County, Hawaii State.

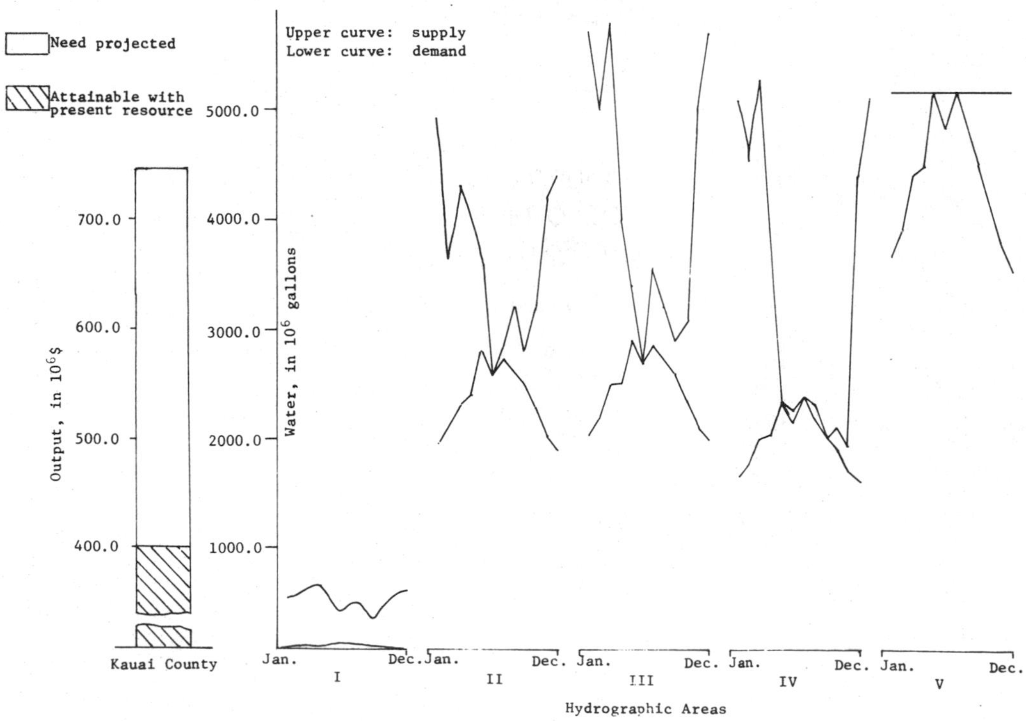

Fig. 4. Developed water supply limiting growth in areas II, III, IV and V.

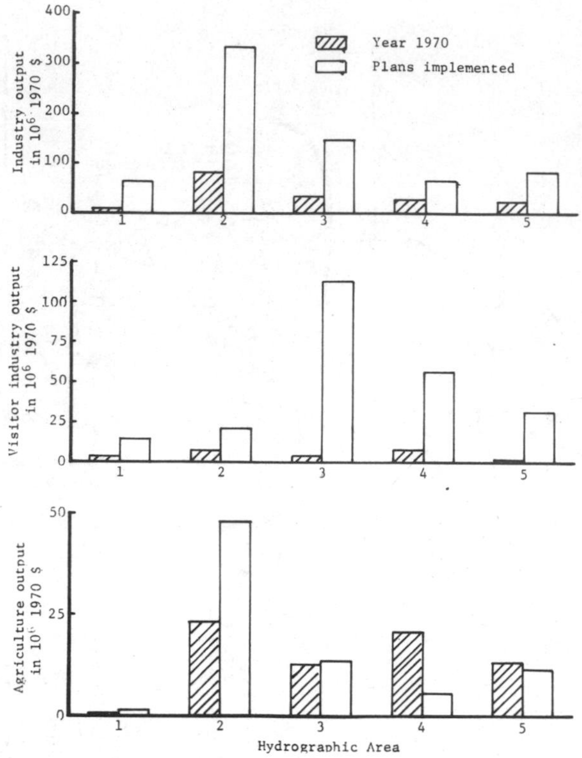

Fig. 5. Economy.

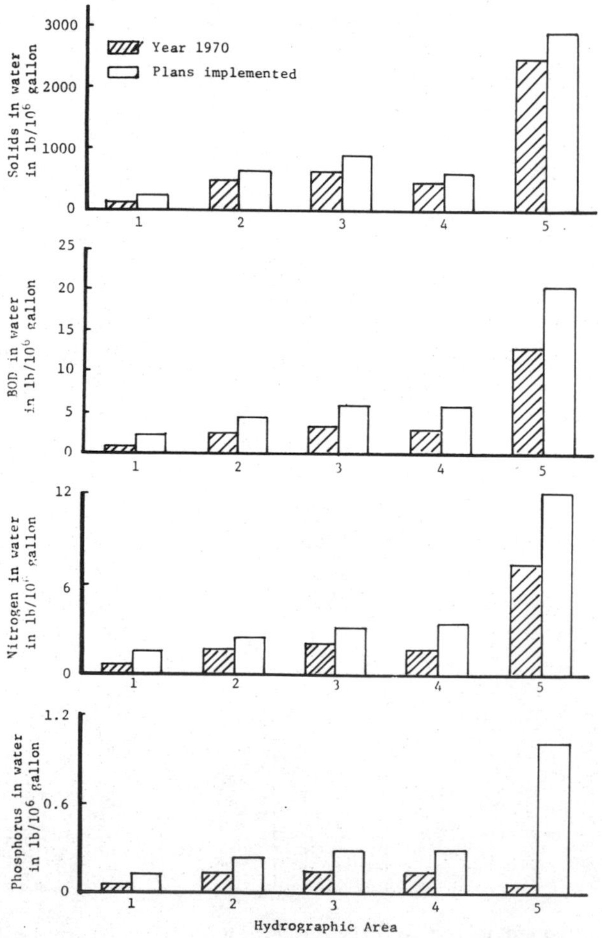

Fig. 6. Water quality indicators.

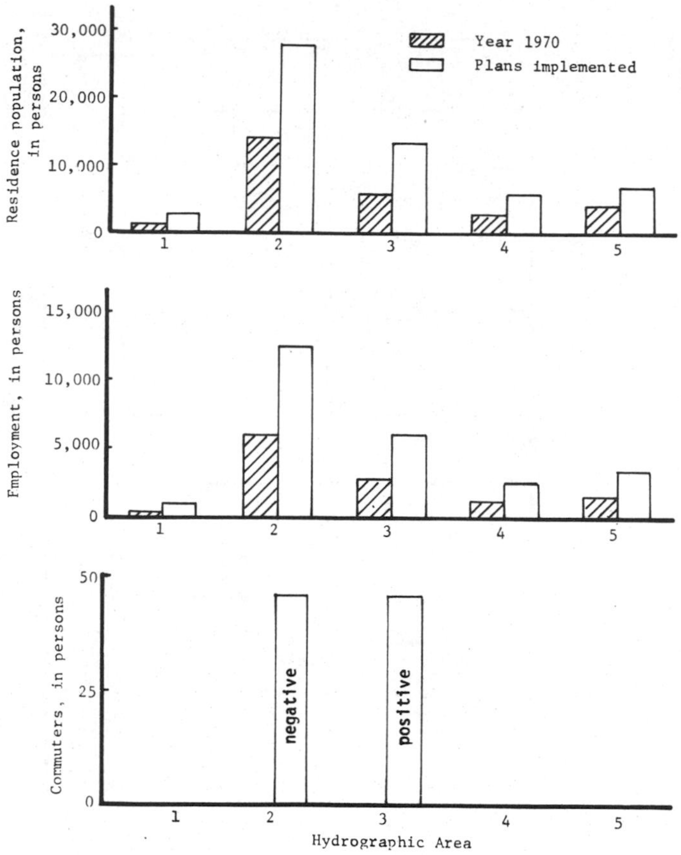

Fig. 7a. Social Indicators.

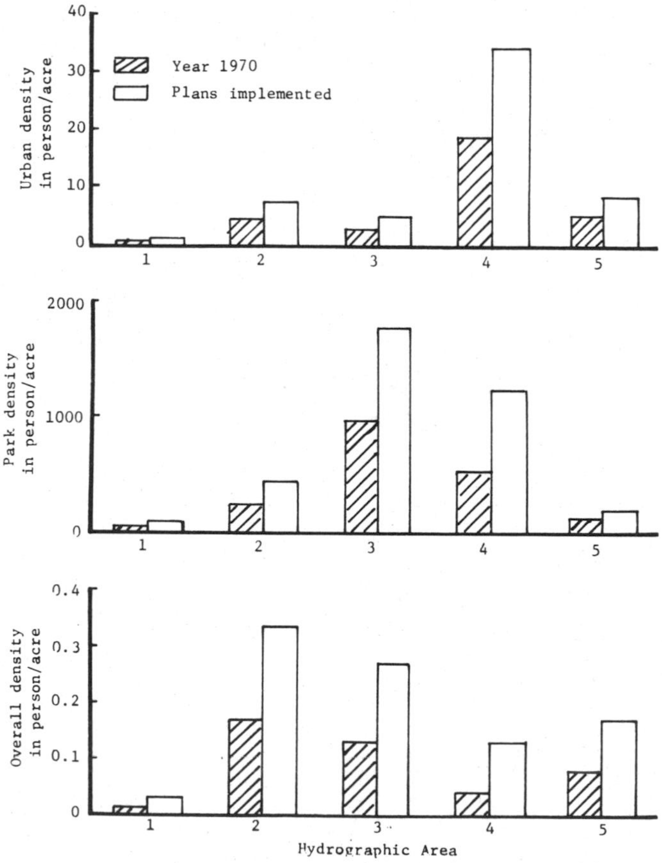

Fig. 7b. Quality of life indicators.

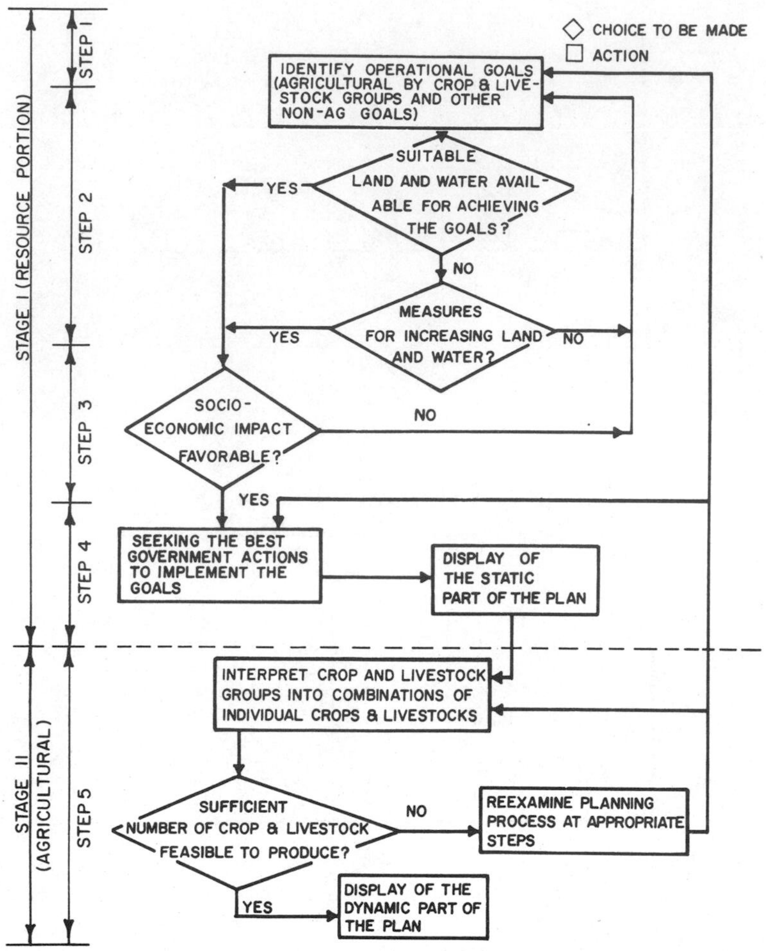

Fig. 8. Flow diagram of the agricultural planning process.

TARGET SETTING BY DELPHI METHOD IN REGIONAL PLANNING

H. Eto

The University of Tsukuba, Ibaraki 300-31, Japan

ABSTRACT

Regional planning often uses the target-achievement framework wherein the target is set to be attained within the planning range. In this process the target setting is a critical issue while the existing analytical method for planning focuses its achievement side for given target. For target setting in socio-economic planning, unlike in economic planning, some subjective opinions are needed and, in fact, the Delphi method was introduced thereto.

Opinion leaders were selected as respondents from various social groups (farmers union, consumers union, workers union, industrial body etc.) and were asked at what level each target is to be set regarding the number of medical doctors in the region, air pollution standard etc. This survey provides the following useful information by a proper statistical analysis. (i) Difference of the preference is measured between different social groups, (ii) balance and tradeoffs are measured between targets for each social group.

The compatibility of targets is examined from the view point of resource constraints in terms of the concepts of degree of feasibility in the associated goal programming problem for given goals determined by the targets. The coordinability between different social groups is measured from the view point of conflict resolution in terms of the distance in the relaxed feasible domain of the associated dynamic goal programming problem. Some concepts of fuzziness are introduced in the course of these measurement.

INTRODUCTION

Mathematical programming model is interpreted in two ways: resource allocation and goal programming. In resource allocation problem, the amounts of available resources are given under which the levels of activities are decided, say, to maximize the utility. In goal programming the levels of targets are given under which the levels of activities are decided to minimize the degree of under-achievement of targets. In formulation the goal programming (G_0) is expressed as follows,

$$\text{minimize} \sum_{i=1}^{n} (w_i^+ y_i^+ + w_i^- y_i^-) \qquad (1)$$

$$\text{subject to} \sum_{j=1}^{n} a_{ij} x_j + y_i^+ - y_i^- = b_i, \quad i = 1, \ldots, m \qquad (2)$$

$$y_i^+, \ y_i^- \geqq 0, \ i = 1, \ldots, m \qquad (3)$$

where b_i denotes the level of target i, y_i^+ and y_i^- denote the level of over- and under-achievement respectively, and w_i^+ and w_i^- denote the weights. Very often $w_i^- \leqq w_i^+$ and possibly $w_i^- = 0$.

The most critical phase in a goal programming process lies not in its calculation but in target setting. In a purely economic planning there may exist an analytical method to determine the proper levels of targets while in a socio-economic planning some subjective evaluation may be needed to do that. A system approach to determining the levels of targets is the Delphi method which was indeed applied thereto in regional planning. Miyazaki prefecture in southern Japan carried it out in mid 1974 (Ref. 1) and Economic Planning Agency carried out the Delphi forecasting (not target setting though) in a similar context in late 1974 (Ref. 2). This work is motivated by these facts, particularly by the former experience but is quite independent of them rather than their description.

In sequel the words of goal and target are almost synonymous and are different only in that the former is a mathematical programming terminology. Namely the use of the former word is strictly associated with goal programming while the use of the latter is rather ambiguous and sometimes denotes a target item.

PROCEDURE OF DELPHI OPINION SURVEY

(i) Respondents are selected from various social groups (leaders of farmers cooperative, workers union, consumers union, welfare organization, industrial body etc.) and from among influential opinion leaders of the press or in educational institutions.
(ii) They are presented some data of existing levels of income, production, public utilities, welfare, eduction, housing admissible standard of pollution etc. and

some of similar data in other regions for a comparison purpose.
(iii) They designate the desired levels of these items as targets or goals in planning range.
(iv) The distribution of the designated levels are shown to the respondents.
(v) The respondents revise their first responses in view of the distribution if they feel it necessary.
(vi) The iteration terminates when the variance of responses becomes small.

The levels of targets designated in this way may well provide a reasonable basis of target setting after some analytical examination and modification.

EXAMINATION OF OPINION GAPS

The Delphi iteration terminates when the opinions converge. Even at this point, however, a between-group variance for social groups may possibly be considerably large in comparison with the total variance. If the variance between any two social groups is small enough, it is to be said that a social convergence or a between-group consensus is attained, or that the opinion gap between groups is small.

For the purpose of evaluating the social convergence or between-group consensus three measuring methods were proposed (Ref. 3). Thanks to these three methods one can quantitatively see whether or not (i) the opinion gap between particular two social groups is significantly large, (ii) a social group is an outlier, (iii) there exist two or three discriminatory clusters of social groups.

If none of the three cases occurs, then the target setting job starts with the obtained responses. If any opinion gap is found, then they must be subject to some modification before a target setting job.

COMPATIBILITY OF TARGETS

If no significant opinion gap is found, then the compatibility of targets can safely be reduced to the feasibility of targets for given technological efficiency and availability of resources. Let (G_1) denote the goal programming problem (G_0) augmented with the conventional resource constraints (4) for given resource level b_i and with informational formulae (5) (6).

$$\sum_{j=1}^{n} a_{ij}x_j + z_i^+ - z_i^- = b_i, \quad i = m+1, \ldots, M, \tag{4}$$

$$z_i^+,\ z_i^- \geqq 0, \quad i = m+1, \ldots, M, \tag{5}$$

$$\sum_{i=m+1}^{M} (u_i^+ z_i^+ + u_i^- z_i^-) - v = 0 \tag{6}$$

where u_i^+ and u_i^- denote the weights. Very often $u_i^- \leqq u_i^+$ and $u_i^- = 0$. The level of v denotes the degree of infeasibility from the view point of resource allocation. A constraint may be put on v for given v^0

$$v \leqq v^0 \tag{7}$$

If the constraint (7) is violated for non-negative v^0, then the levels of goals b_i, $i = 1, \ldots, m$, are reduced to restore the feasibility unless the resource constraints can be relaxed. This raises the problem of tradeoffs between targets.

TRADEOFFS BETWEEN TARGETS

If the goal programming problem is found infeasible for given levels of resources, then the levels of goals b_i, $i = 1, \ldots, m$, must be reduced in a balanced manner. The degree of balance between targets in this reduction process may be measured by the balance among degree of dissatisfaction between targets. The degree of dissatisfaction with the reduced level of a target is measured by the ratio of the number of responses above this level to the total number of responses. If the lower quatile Q_1 is adopted for a target as its goal level, then the degree of dissatisfaction for this target is 0.75 which means 75% of responses is dissatisfied with the level of Q_1. If the degree of dissatisfaction with the reduced level is uniform for every target, then this reduction is said balanced under the assumption of social convergence of opinions. An explicit incorporation of the degree of dissatisfaction into mathematical programming may result in a computational infeasibility and therefore this information is desirably carried by parameters controlled exogeneously from outside. Specifically the operation of (parametric) change of RHS is applied to b_i's, $i = 1, \ldots, m$, in keeping that their dissatisfaction degrees are equal.

Unless a social convergence is attained, the coordinability between social groups must be considered.

COORDINABILITY BETWEEN SOCIAL GROUPS

The balance and tradeoffs can be measured between targets for each social group by the method discussed immediately above. This measure and the aforementioned measure of opinions gap between social groups (Ref. 3) together provide a basis to measure the degree of coordinability between social groups. This degree is measured for a target item in terms of the distance between their optima in the feasible domain of (dynamic) linear programming.

When the goal levels are different, the resulting optima are different though the feasible domains are the same. If lower or upper limits are given on goal levels, the resulting feasible domain are contracted. In any case the optimum point moves in general. The distance between two distinct optima is preferably measured in terms of the structural gap (Ref. 4) rather than the conventional Euclidean distance. This gap which represents the basis exchange number is formally expressed as Card $(B_1 \& B_2)$/ Card B_0 where Card denote the cardinal number of a set, & the conjunction B_i (i = 0, 1, 2) the sets of basic (structural) variables of optimum i. An appropriate definition of B_0 is $B_0 = B_1$ or B_2 which is particularly appropriate when the feasible domain is the same. When the feasible domain is different, another definition of B_0 is given as the basic (structural) variables of the optimum of relaxed feasible domain which is obtained by taking the relaxing (lower limit) constraints. In the latter case the basic variables mean the positive variables.

FUZZINESS IN DELPHI

The Delphi opinions are quite ambiguous and the response behavior in forecasting Delphi may well be modeled in terms of the fuzzy theory (Ref. 5). This model is also applicable to target setting Delphi where a goal level is fuzzy as being dependent on a value judgement. When priority is also asked in Delphi, a transformation from a value judgement to a goal level is assumed linear and is expressed by a matrix whose operations of addition and multiplication are to take maximum and minimum respectively.

$$g = M \times_F v$$

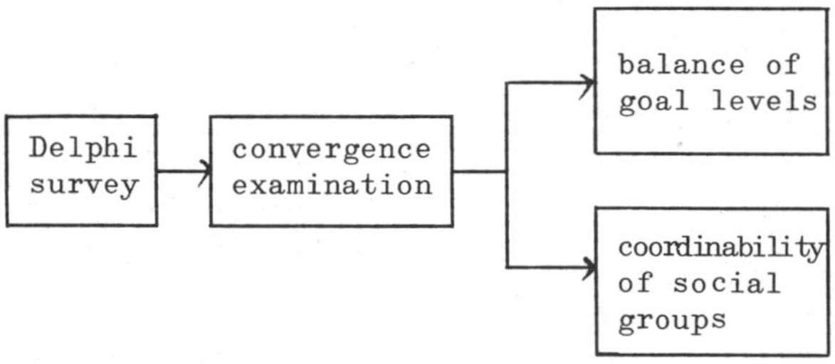

Fig. 1 Flow of Jobs

where g, M, $\times_F$ and v denote vector of goal level, matrix fuzzy operation of multiplication and vector of value. From the obtained data of g and v and under a proper assumption on structure of M, M can be estimated and provides some information of response behavior.

REFERENCES

1. Miyazaki Prfecture, Delphi Surveys on Goals of Development Planning, 1975.

2. Economic Planning Agency, Japan 1974.

3. H. Eto, Statistical Methods to Measure the Consensus of Experts Opinions in Delphi Forecastings and Assessments, Presented at ORSA/TIMS Puerto Rico Meeting, 1974.

4. H. Eto, On Evaluating the Technical Performances of a Computer-Controlled Transportation System, Proceedings of 1st International Conference on Management of Research and Education, 171-175, Poland, 1975.

5. H. Eto, Fuzzy Operational Approach to Analysis of Delphi Forecastings, Proc. 2nd International Conf. Management of R & D, 1977.

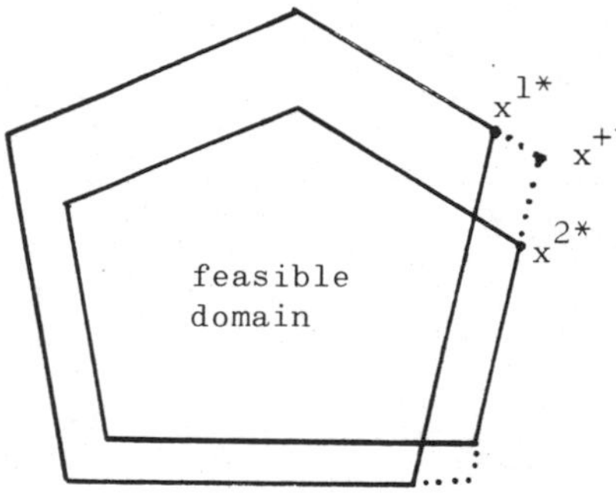

Fig. 2 Movement of Optima according to Goal Levels

SOCIETAL RESPONSE PROFILE ASSESSMENT MATRIX

K. Wada

Group Planning, Shell International Petroleum Co. Ltd. London, SE1 7NA England

1. PURPOSE OF ASSESSMENT

Traditionally, the majority of business organisations have been predominantly concerned about the financial and economic aspects of business activities in planning and achieving the corporate objectives.

However, the consequences of socio-political and cultural changes surrounding business organisations have been increasingly urging us to develop more sensitivity to a variety of societal responses to business activities. Broadening the scope of corporate planning by including such non-quantitative factors as the societal responses seems to be a very significant factor in eventually achieving the corporate objectives.

In this connection, in the hope that it might be of some assistance to managers, we have developed a technique for a systematic and comprehensive assessment of societal responses, the details of which are described in the following sections. The purpose of the proposed method is to identify and examine the nature, potential impacts and consequences of societal responses to a specific set of business activities so that the management could systematically adapt to or interact with such societal feedbacks.

2. STRUCTURE OF ASSESSMENT

2.1 Format and Field of Application

A matrix type of assessment sheet was developed for the purpose of a systematic and comprehensive diagnosis of a variety of societal responses out of which the management or planners could identify the areas of vulnerability for improvement or remedial action.

The matrix (Table 1) has in its column a list of constituents who are classified into three different categories in order of social distance, i.e. stakeholders, closely involved parties, and generally involved parties. On the row, there is a list of concerns which are also classified into three categories, i.e. economic concerns, societal concerns and involvement.

TABLE 1 Societal Response Assessment Matrix

Concerns / Constituents	a. Economic Concerns	b. Societal Concerns	c. Involvement
a. Stakeholders	☐	☐	☐
	☐	☐	☐
b. Closely Involved Parties	☐	☐	☐
	☐	☐	☐
c. Generally Involved Parties	☐	☐	☐
	☐	☐	☐

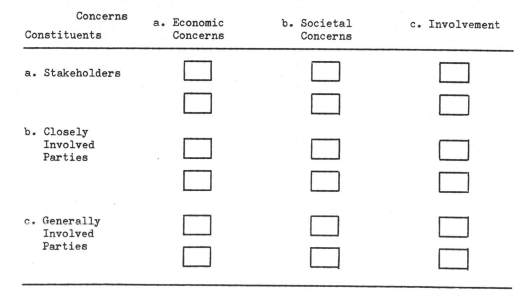

For your ready reference, a general list of constituents and concerns has been prepared as follows :

TABLE 2 Reference List of Constituents

A. Stakeholders

1. Government
1.1 Bureaucrats
- Treasury, MOF
- Ministry of Industry
- SEC, FTC
1.2 Politicians
- Leading Party
- Oppositions
1.3 Local/Municipal Government

2. Shareholders
2.1 Public
2.2 Institutional

3. Employees
3.1 Managers
3.2 Staff
3.3 General Employees

4. Pensioners

B. Closely Involved Parties

5. Banks/Financiers

6. Dealers/Jobbers

7. Competitors

8. Suppliers

9. Consumers
9.1 Industrial
9.2 Mass

10. Labour Unions

11. International Agency
11.1 OECD EEC
11.2 UNCTAD
11.3 OPEC IEA

C. Generally Involved Parties

12. Industry Associations
12.1 General
12.2 Industry

13. Community Leaders

14. Environmentalists

15. Mass Media
15.1 Newspapers, journals
15.2 TV, radio

16. Academics

17. Ethnic Minorities

18. Religious Circles

19. General Public

20. Consumer Unions

The matrix could be used to evaluate societal responses with respect to : -

a) Specific project(s) e.g. large scale crude tanker station construction or coal import terminal etc.

b) New strategic moves, e.g. Diversification, joint ventures etc.

It should be noted that for diagnostic exercises using this matrix, the list of constituents as well as the list of concerns should be specifically prepared for each subject to be assessed since the composition of constituents as well as the types of concerns could significantly vary from one case to another.

The basic characteristic of this matrix assessment is of a static nature which would serve to produce a diagnostic snapshot to visualise societal responses at a point in time.

3. 3. STEPS FOR ASSESSMENT

3.1 Selection of the Subject to be Assessed

First step is to clearly define the subject that is to be assessed through the matrix, e.g. pipeline construction project.

3.2 Identification of the Constituents and Concerns

The next step is to list the relevant constituents who have certain type and magnitude of concerns with regard to the subject chosen. Constituents could be described as external actors (Governments, unions, pressure groups, etc.) who feel they are affected directly or indirectly by the behaviour of the business enterprise. Similarly, make a list of specific concerns that one or more of the constituents have with respect to the subject.

3.3 Construction of Matrix and Rating Method

Using the format illustrated in Table 1, a matrix could be constructed which has in its column the list of constituents and in its row the list of concerns both identified in step 3.2.

The rating method is as follows. The evaluation of societal responses to the selected subject from each one of the constituents for the respective concern is illustrated in the cells contained in the matrix by employing the following coding scheme :

a. 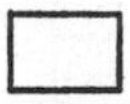 = positive, supportive and favourable state of mind

 = being concerned but staying neutral

 = negative, unsupportive and unfavourable

 = not concerned

This coding is the basic version by which vulnerable areas could be visually located and examined. For diagnostic purposes, this would be sufficient to develop detailed analysis in descriptive part and it is advisable to avoid excessive complication of the coding since it might result in losing its original appeal.

The categorization of constituents is not necessarily based on a rigid definition of each category. It is intended to represent rather loosely the degree of potential impacts of a specific project on a variety of constituents. Therefore, depending on the type of project, any constituent could possibly move from one category to another. For instance, the categorization of Government into Stakeholders as shown in the reference list of constituents is for reference purposes and not a rigid classification. One example which is largely in line with classifying Government as stakeholders would be Shell/Esso joint exploration project of North Sea oil and gas.

3.4 Descriptive Diagnosis

Upon completion of the coding of relevant cells in the matrix it is extremely important to go through the following steps for detailed descriptive assessment.

a) Summarise and record the reasoning for rating key cells in the matrix. This can be effective for further examination of the response and future references and comparison.

b) Identify the key vulnerable areas (cells) and formulate the remedial action points based on reality and feasibility. Where there seems to be no meaningful set of remedial actions available try to assess the consequences of leaving the cell(s) untreated.

c) Wherever possible, try to identify the interrelationship between several cells since, for example, one or two untreated or negative cells could aggravate a number of neutral or supportive cells in a relatively short time span. Conversely, a set of treated cells might improve several other cells without much additional effort. This assessment should be carried out more or less simultaneously with (b) above.

3.5 Management Support and Group Process

A successful application of this method depends to a large extent on the management's awareness and sensitivity toward the external environment. In this connection, a recent speech by Gerrit Wagner, Shell Group Managing Director, clearly highlights the nature of the problem. He said, "There is a wave of social and political pressures that have been gathering strength recently, a problem that is just as critical to any company's future survival as operational and financial problems . . A company must now ensure that while its managers get on with the job, they are also sensitive to changing social attitudes, that they can anticipate the resultant pressures, and that they will be able to cope imaginatively with the unavoidable problems" (from his speech to New York Security Analysts on 29th September 1976).

Assuming that the organisational climate is sufficiently encouraging for the application of this matrix, emphasis should be put on a group process throughout the exercise where a group of managers get together (after completion of individual assessment) and go through a group exercise which would provide an opportunity for an in-depth debate with divergent views on a subject of common interest and thereby stimulate participants' ideas and perceptions to produce rigorous and explicit observations of societal responses.

One of the practical approaches would be to encourage contributions from people who maintain regular contacts with specific sectors of the external environment, i.e. Trade Relations or Public Affairs people with mass media and government ministries; Marketing managers with consumer unions, etc. The synthesis of various contributions and judgments could be processed with the planning function acting as a co-ordinating focal point and then the assessment could be passed on to higher management level for further scrutiny. This, of course, largely depends on the nature and scale of the problem, but the bottom-up two-tier approach would be meaningful for stimulating insights, sensitivities and intuitions.

4. SAMPLE EXERCISE

A sample exercise has been carried out to illustrate the applications of the method (see The Case).

THE CASE : ANGLESEY MARINE TERMINAL

1. The Need for the Terminal

With the progressive expansion of Shell's Stanlow refinery to its present capacity of 18 million tonnes per year, the facilities for discharging supplies of crude oil have become out-moded. This is due both to the refinery's increasing throughput and to the steadily growing size of tankers in world trade, needing larger and deeper berthing.

Over the years, for these reasons, unloading moved first from the Stanlow oil dock to the Queen Elizabeth II dock at the entrance to the Manchester Ship Canal, and then to the Tranmere terminal on the river Mersey itself.

The available depth, width and turning room of the 30 kilometres of the Mersey channel has restricted its use to fully-laden tankers of 90,000 dwt or to tankers of 20,000 dwt capacity carrying 130,000 tonnes. With the eight metre rise and fall of the tide, a tanker entering the Mersey has to make a precisely-timed passage up the channel to ensure adequate under-keel clearance and arrival at Tranmere at the correct state of tide. After berthing at or near high water, tankers of 70,000 dwt and over have to begin to discharge their cargo without delay to avoid grounding on the falling tide.

While these operations are carried out successfully and with precision, it was felt that, with the possible further expansion of Stanlow, this presented an unacceptable environmental risk in the longer term. Additionally, with the completion of the Anglesey Marine Terminal, optimum economic advantage can be taken of the very large crude carriers now in service in world trade.

The site at Amlwch on the north coast of Anglesey, North Wales was chosen because it fulfilled the major requirements for discharging at a single buoy mooring-sheltered location and water up to 37 metres in depth at a short distance from the shore to minimise the length of underwater pipelines. Amlwch is also a reasonable distance from Stanlow - 132 kilometres - which lessened the disturbance to landowners and the agricultural community during construction of the underground pipeline to the refinery.

The main advantage of the single buoy mooring over more conventional types of mooring is that it enables the tanker to swing through 360 degrees around a single point and thus take up a natural position under prevailing conditions of weather and tide. The mooring installed off Amlwch has been designed specifically for the location and will take the largest tankers currently in service (Ref. 1).

2. Development of the Project

The project included three major components mentioned below and each of which had a critical importance to Shell since the terminal would not function unless all the three were completed.

a. Amlwch Single Buoy Mooring/Submarine Pipeline and Shore Station.

b. Rhosgoch Installation.

c. Amlwch - Rhosgoch - Stanlow pipeline of 132 km. stretch.

The development of the project could be chronologically summarised as follows :

1970 - Discussion on pipeline routes with planning departments of Anglesey, Caernarvonshire, Denbighshire, Flintshire and Cheshire.

1971 - Meetings with:

a. Country Landowners Association
b. National Farmers' Union
c. The Farmers' Union of Wales

- Finalised route submitted to Dept. of Trade and Industry.

1972 - Promotion of a Private Bill by the Anglesey County Council.

- A public inquiry. Select Committee hearings and debates in both Houses of Parliament.
- Anglesey Marine Terminal Act received the Royal Assent in October.
- Anglesey County Council (now the Isle of Anglesey Borough Council) was established as the Terminal Authority.
- Anglesey Marine Terminal Committee was organised in which 8 members were nominated by the Council, 3 by Amlwch Community Council, 3 by Shell UK Oil and 1 by Liverpool Pilotage Authority.

1973 - In February, pipeline construction (Amlwch-Rhosgoch-Stanlow) was authorised by the Secretary of State for the Dept. of Trade and Industry under the Pipelines Act 1962.

1975 - Single Buoy Mooring was installed and the pipeline construction was also completed.

3. Societal Response Matrix

From the chronological development described above, it might appear that the project was carried out quite smoothly, but in fact it wasn't. Shell was exposed to a series of severe repercussions from several quarters of the society in mid-1973 which almost brought the entire project to a collapse or at least to a long halt.

These social responses, in retrospect, could have been identified to a large extent and remedial action to avoid or alleviate such harsh repercussions could have been effectively implemented. In this connection a Social Response Assessment Matrix has been constructed assuming the timing of analysis to be in February 1973 when the pipeline construction was officially approved by the Dept. of Trade and Industry but the growing concern among various constituents began to gain momentum (see Attachment).

3.1 Key Areas of Concern

Major concerns at this stage of project development were sharply focused on the concrete and imminent issues and could be identified from the Matrix as follows :

a. Economic Concerns Most of the key constituents showed a keen concern over the adverse effect of the Terminal on the Tourism in north Wales. They were worrying about both the general deterioration of image and visual impacts of the facilities (particularly the Rhosgoch Installation).

b. Societal Concerns There are two concerns expressed quite clearly i.e. safety issues related to the reliability of SBM and the pipeline system (both submarine and land) and visual disamenity of the facility coupled with the fear of noises and smells.

c. Involvement Dominant concerns identifiable here are two-fold, i.e. fear of further industrial development with industry's leadership and plan alterations of the Terminal at the construction stage. Also there is the usual response for more information disclosure.

3.2 Key Constituents

Since all the legal authorisation procedures have already been cleared at this stage, the key constituents we should regard as critical would be as follows :

a. Anglesey residents associations

b. Tourist associations

c. Farmers' Association of Wales

d. Council for Preservation of Rural Wales

e. Mass Media (both national and local news media)

3.3 Action Plans

Based on the close examinations of the nature and magnitude of various concerns held by key constituents as identified from the Matrix, the following set of remedial action plans could be formulated and implemented.

a. Development of more intensive dialogue with the key constituents with regard to the specific concerns they have. For instance, the detailed explanation of Shell's considerations in the construction of Rhosgoch Installation would be instrumental to establish increased understanding by the Tourist Associations and Anglesey residents associations. In fact the Rhosgoch plan included particular attention to careful positioning of tanks, colour, finish of the buildings, siting of fences and choice of lighting. An overall landscaping scheme included the planting of thousands of trees at Rhosgoch and 17 other selected sites in the vicinity and a landscape mound to prevent any visual disamenity. Similar detailed accounts of environmental conservation measures to the members of the Council for Preservation of Rural Wales would serve to mitigate their emotional repercussions to a certain extent.

Certain objectors tend to take a rather extreme stance and indeed one might wish to ask oneself whether private industry should assume any responsibility in the sphere of environmental conservation over and above conscientious and intelligent co-operation with the laws and regulations of central and local government. Nevertheless, efforts to narrow down the gap between the polarized views would have to be exercised at the initiative of the industry.

b. Information Disclosure. More information disclosure on the technical aspects of the Project would facilitate elimination of unnecessary fears and misconceptions with regard to the SBM and pipeline system (both submarine and land). For instance, anxiety about the reliability of SBM would be greatly reduced by providing information with the key constituents that more than 50 SBMs have been installed at many different oil terminals in the world since 1960 out of which Shell operates 16, and there was only one minor spillage recorded at Port Dixon discharging SBM, Malaysia. Therefore, there would not be much reason to fear anything more than, at worst, some small spillages during discharge at the Amlwch SBM. When each tanker is discharging off Amlwch it will be attended throughout by a 75 foot guard launch equipped with 30 tons of dispersant to deal immediately with any spillage, should it occur. In addition, there would be a floating oil fence spread around the tanker to encircle any minor spillage.

c. Clarifying Shell's position with respect to the alteration of plans and further industrial development. For the anxiety expressed over the substantial alteration of the plan at a later stage, Shell gave assurances that they foresaw no alterations of substance to the project and that they would make available, upon request, any reasonable information on the progress of the project.

Also concern has been expressed by conservationists and Tourist associations regarding the possibility of the Terminal leading to refineries being built on Anglesey. For this matter, Shell have given categoric assurances to the Anglesey County Council and to the Select Committee of the House of Lords that they will not build a refinery, a chemical plant or any installation other than the marine terminal and its associated facilities. Probably, it will help to clarify the circumstances at this point in time if Shell try to remind the key constituents that in any case the authorisation of any industrial development in Anglesey is entirely within the discretion of the local authority, representing the local community, who have stated that they are against any such development.

In retrospect, it was rather unfortunate that most of these remedial action plans have not been formulated and implemented in such a systematic and effective manner as may be necessary to complete the follow up process after authorisation.

4. Actual Development in 1973 and its Consequences

The barrage of explicit criticisms were triggered off in July 1973 when an article by Mr. Paul Foot titled "Shell versus Parliament - a Study in Parliamentary Impotence" appeared in the Sunday Times 8 July issue. The key points of the then prevailing criticisms could be best highlighted by quoting a paragraph from the special feature article mentioned above. It said :

a. The total number of permanent jobs brought to Anglesey from the SBM project could not exceed 35.

b. The total net annual revenue from Shell to Anglesey could not exceed £150,000 - a sum equivalent to a 3 per cent reduction in the island's revenue from tourism.

c. The port of Liverpool and the Mersey was not at all congested as was argued and was almost entirely safe from collision or spillage. A Mersey Docks and Harbour Board spokesman told the inquiry that the Board would lose about £1.3 m in revenue each year if the buoy was built.

d. Shell's SBMs throughout the world were constantly liable to oil spillage, and the spillage from the Durban SBM had caused a furore in the South African Parliament. Spillages of similar size at Anglesey would have a catastrophic effect on the island's beaches and on the rich and rare marine and bird life in the area (Ref. 2). In addition, there was an additional allegation claimed later on about

e. Shell misled a public inquiry and a House of Lords Select Committee by not burying about 300 yards of submarine pipeline in the sea bed out of the two-mile pipeline which connects the SBM and the Amlwch shore station.

The situation could be illustrated by the following list of several newspaper headlines which appeared in mid 1973.

23 Sept "Shell breaks promise to bury oil pipeline off unspoilt coast" Sunday Times

24 Sept "Shell deny they misled Lords on Pipeline plan" The Times

25 Sept "Pipe must be buried, say opponents of Shell plan" Daily Telegraph

26 Sept "Unacceptable face of Shell Oil" Western Mail

27 Sept "Part of oil pipeline not to be buried" Liverpool D. Post.

Needless to say, most of these criticisms were based on some misunderstandings or preconceived ideas. For instance, SBMs are a well tried and proven facility for loading and discharging tankers offshore as described earlier in 3.3.

As regards the 300 yards unburied part of the pipeline, the Act authorising the development specified that the pipelines should be buried wherever practicable. The area in question was a comparatively flat and smooth area covered with cobble stones on top of hard rock and Shell's alternative schemes were fully discussed by Dept. of Trade and Industry engineers and approved.

Thus in late October, the Minister for Aerospace and Shipping publicly announced the Dept. of Trade and Industry's approval for Shell to lay the pipeline partly unburied on the seabed off Anglesey.

The most tenacious opposition came from a group called ANDAG (Anglesey Defence Action Group) which consisted of the Council for the Preservation of Rural Wales, tourist associations, Anglesey residents associations, Welsh Nationalists and Bangor University students, etc. They maintained that a trench to take the pipes could be dug over the whole of the two-mile length and appealed to the Advisory Committee on Oil Pollution of the Sea to investigate the technical aspects of the issue.

After two months survey, the Committee concluded in November that they supported Shell's claim not to bury a limited part of the pipeline in the seabed, subject of course to adequate safeguards against the pipes breaking or oil spillages, and indeed that was the end of a series of organised negative societal responses against Shell who had suffered so bitterly to obtain understanding and support from the society for its legally authorised project.

Conclusion

It might be argued that even if the remedial action plans listed earlier had been actually implemented systematically, the project would have experienced the criticisms anyway. However, it should also be recognised that a series of such remedial efforts could have significantly reduced the scope and magnitude of responses based on emotional frustrations, misunderstanding and genuine ignorance.

REFERENCES

1. Shell U.K. Ltd. (1976) Anglesey Marine Terminal, Shell U.K. Ltd., London

2. P. Foot, Shell versus Parliament - a study in Parliamentary Impotence, The Sunday Times Magazine 8th July, pp 8 - 22 (1973)

SELECTED BIBLIOGRAPHY

1. Dickert, T.G. with Domeny, K.R. Ed.(1974) Environmental Impact Assessment - Guidelines and Commentary, University of California, Berkeley, California.

2. T.N. Gladwin and M.G. Royston, An Environmentally-oriented Mode of Industrial Project Planning, Environmental Conservation Vo.2, No.3, pp 189-198 (1975)

3. F.F. Neuhauer and N.B. Solomon, A Managerial Approach to Environmental Assessment, paper presented at the 5th International Conference on Planning in Cleveland, Ohio July 18 - 21 (1976).

4. A.D. Shocker, Sethi, S. Prakash, An Approach to Incorporating Societal Preferences in Developing Corporate Action Strategies, California Management Review Vol. XV, No. 4, pp 97 - 105 (1973).

SOCIETAL RESPONSE PROFILE ASSESSMENT MATRIX

CONCERNS	Economic Concerns				Societal Concerns				Involvement	
CONSTITUENTS	Local Employment Opportunities & Contribution to Revenue	Adverse Effect on Tourism	Adequate Compen-sation	Reliability of SBM	Pipeline Safety (Submarine and Land)	Visual Disamenity & Noises, Smells	Fear for Further Industrial Development	Subsequent Plan Alter-ations	Information Disclosure	Project Legiti-macy
Stakeholders										
Amlwch Community Council	Positive, Supportive	Concerned, but Neutral	Positive, Supportive	Positive, Supportive	Positive, Supportive	Positive, Supportive	Positive, Supportive	Positive, Supportive	Positive, Supportive	Positive, Supportive
Anglesey County Council	Positive, Supportive	Concerned, but Neutral	Positive, Supportive	Positive, Supportive	Positive, Supportive	Positive, Supportive	Positive, Supportive	Positive, Supportive	Positive, Supportive	Positive, Supportive
Anglesey Residents Association	Concerned, but Neutral	Concerned, but Neutral	Concerned, but Neutral	Negative	Negative	Negative	Concerned, but Neutral	Concerned, but Neutral	Negative	Negative
Country landowners Association	Not Concerned	Positive, Supportive	Positive, Supportive	Not Concerned	Concerned, but Neutral	Concerned, but Neutral	Concerned, but Neutral	Positive, Supportive	Concerned, but Neutral	Concerned, but Neutral
Tourists Association	Negative	Negative	Negative	Concerned, but Neutral	Negative	Negative	Negative	Concerned, but Neutral	Negative	Negative
Farmers Union of Wales	Concerned, but Neutral	Concerned, but Neutral	Positive, Supportive	Not Concerned	Concerned, but Neutral	Concerned, but Neutral	Concerned, but Neutral	Positive, Supportive	Concerned, but Neutral	Concerned, but Neutral
Closely Involved Parties										
Dept. of Trade & Industry	Positive, Supportive	Positive, Supportive	Positive, Supportive	Positive, Supportive	Positive, Supportive	Positive, Supportive	Positive, Supportive	Positive, Supportive	Positive, Supportive	Positive, Supportive
The National Farmers' Union	Concerned, but Neutral	Not Concerned	Concerned, but Neutral	Not Concerned	Concerned, but Neutral	Concerned, but Neutral	Concerned, but Neutral	Positive, Supportive	Positive, Supportive	Concerned, but Neutral
Liverpool Pilotage Authority	Negative	Not Concerned	Not Concerned	Concerned, but Neutral	Concerned, but Neutral	Not Concerned	Not Concerned	Not Concerned	Concerned, but Neutral	Not Concerned
Council for Preservation of Rural Wales	Concerned, but Neutral	Negative	Not Concerned	Negative	Negative	Negative	Negative	Concerned, but Neutral	Negative	Negative
Welsh Nationalists	Concerned, but Neutral	Negative	Not Concerned	Concerned, but Neutral	Concerned, but Neutral	Negative	Concerned, but Neutral	Concerned, but Neutral	Concerned, but Neutral	Concerned, but Neutral
Mass Media	Concerned, but Neutral	Negative	Concerned, but Neutral	Negative	Negative	Negative	Concerned, but Neutral	Concerned, but Neutral	Negative	Negative

☐ = Positive, Supportive ▨ = Concerned, but Neutral ■ = Negative ☒ = Not Concerned

EVOLUTION OF ENVIRONMENTAL ASSESSMENT SCALE (E.A.S.) – A TECHNIQUE FOR ENVIRONMENTAL EVALUATION

V. Sulkar and S. Deshpande

Department of Town and Country Planning, Government of Goa, Daman and Diu, Panaji, 403001, Goa, India

ABSTRACT

Efforts of Planners towards "solving" traffic problems in urban areas are generally oriented towards increasing the traffic carrying capacity of the road network to enable faster movement of motor vehicles. This has led to a total disregard towards environment resulting into innumerable environmental problems. It is only since recently that conscious efforts are made in the field of traffic planning giving due consideration to the environmental aspects. The present work attempts to analyse the relationship between traffic and the urban environment and to evolve a methodology to evaluate the impact of traffic on environment in totality through Environmental Assessment Scale.

1. INTRODUCTION

1.1 The phenomenal growth of urban population during the present century has resulted into myriads of environmental problems, such as congestion, pollution and disorder leading to deterioration of the quality of life. The problem has been further aggravated by the stupendous rise in the number of mechanised vehicles, facilitating faster movement of people and goods on the one hand, but, on the other, overburdening the pedestrian-oriented road networks of the cities and causing degradation of environment through traffic congestion, road accidents, noise and air pollution, as well as frustration to the road users.

Unfortunately for a long time the attempts of planners to solve this problem were largely traffic-oriented rather than environment-oriented. As a result, the living environment was often sacrificed for the sake of rapid movement of traffic. It is only lately, that the awareness to safeguard the environment has been felt by the planners. It is obvious that any such attempt needs to be placed firmly on a scientific basis in order to evolve a standard methodology and technique towards solution of this problem.

1.2 The work done in India and abroad in the field of assessing impact of traffic on the urban environment has revealed a strong bias of sectoral approach. This is manifested in the studies of only a few aspects of the phenomenon in isolation, such as traffic noise, air pollution, safety, accessibility. visual intrusion, etc. It is only since the pioneering work by Buchanan Committee (1) that considerable work on the environmental aspects of traffic has been carried out in the developed countries (Hills (2), Antoniou (3). Dark (4). Urban Motorwares Project Team (5)). It is however, since very recently that attempts are made in India to assess the environmental impact of traffic in totality (Deshpande & Thakkar (6)).

2. SCOPE AND METHODOLOGY OF THE STUDY

2.1 The present study aims at filling in the gap in the development of the field of environmental assessment such as the bias towards tangible physical environmental elements vis à vis non-tangible environmental elements, inadequate development of technique for quantification of the quality of the various elements of environment and lack of attempts towards environmental evaluation in totality. In light of this, the scope of the present work includes definition of the domain of environment with respect to the impact of traffic, assessment of impact of traffic on the environment and comprehensive evaluation of the environment through evolution of a suitable assessment scale.

2.2 The methodology adopted is oriented to this comprehensive approach as shown in Figure 1.

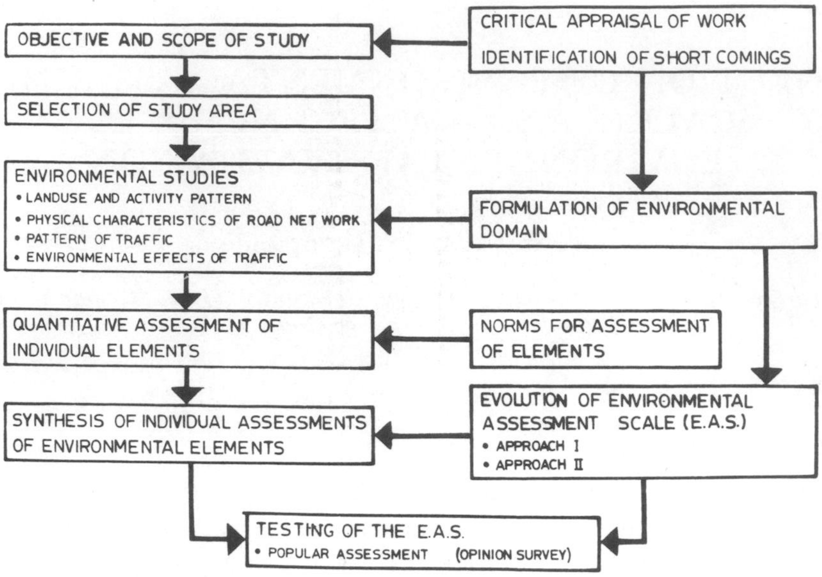

Fig. 1 Methodology of Study

3. SELECTION OF THE STUDY AREA

3.1 A major traffic artery situated in the Central Business District of Ludhiana, Punjab, one of the fastest growing medium-sized industrial cities in India, (population in 1971-4,52,000), has been selected for the study. This study area represents the environmental problems of a typical Indian city infested by hetrogeneous traffic conditions as well as poor management of traffic, leading to a conflict between the traffic and activity pattern with a consequent deterioration of the quality of urban environment in terms of freedom and safety of movement, quiet, air quality, visual quality, etc.

The stretch of the road (Madhya Marg) selected for the study carries a daily traffic of nearly 38.000 vehicles of different types in addition to an enormous traffic of pedestrians generated by this Central Business District which also accomodates the railway station as well as the local bus terminal.

3.2 The road under study was divided into three sections, each about 1/4 km. in lenath, stretching between two major intersections, as shown in Figure 2.

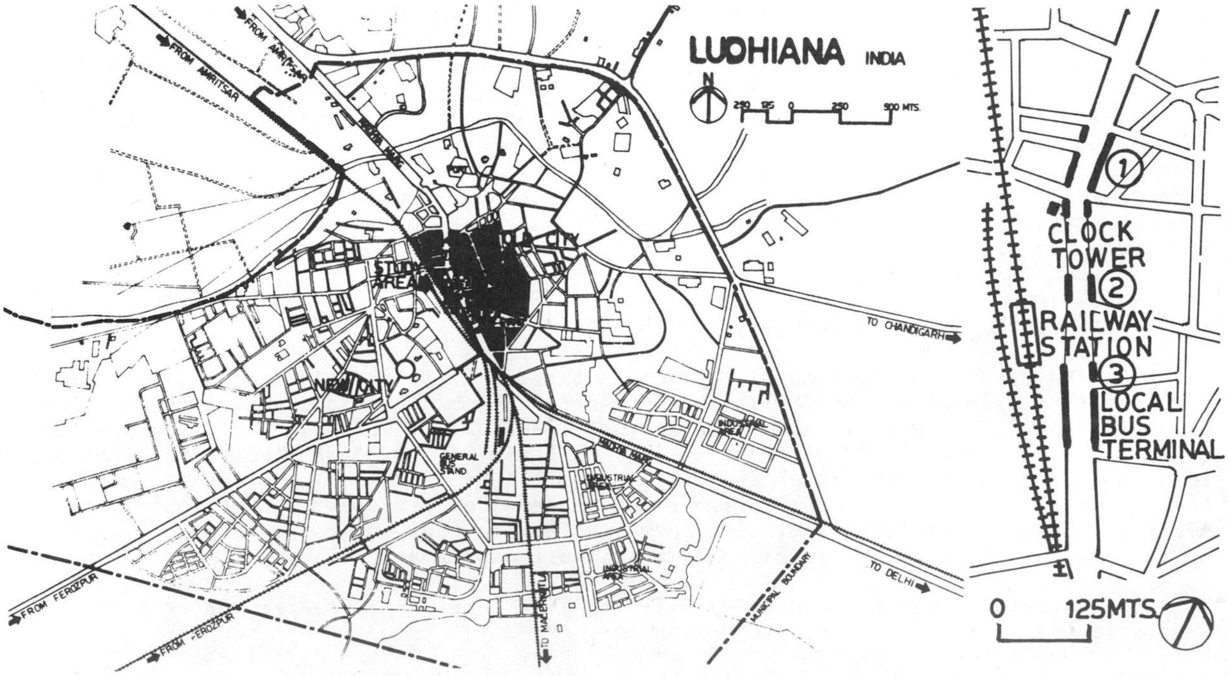

Fig. 2 Location of the Study Area and Road Sections under Study.

Fig. 3 Clock Tower - Landmark in the Visual Environment.

Fig. 4 Heterogenaous Traffic Conditions.

4. STUDIES AND FINDINGS

4.1 Domain of Environment

The elements constituting the domain of the environment under study have been identified as shown in Figure 5, based on an environmental reconnaissance which forms the basis for the design of studies.

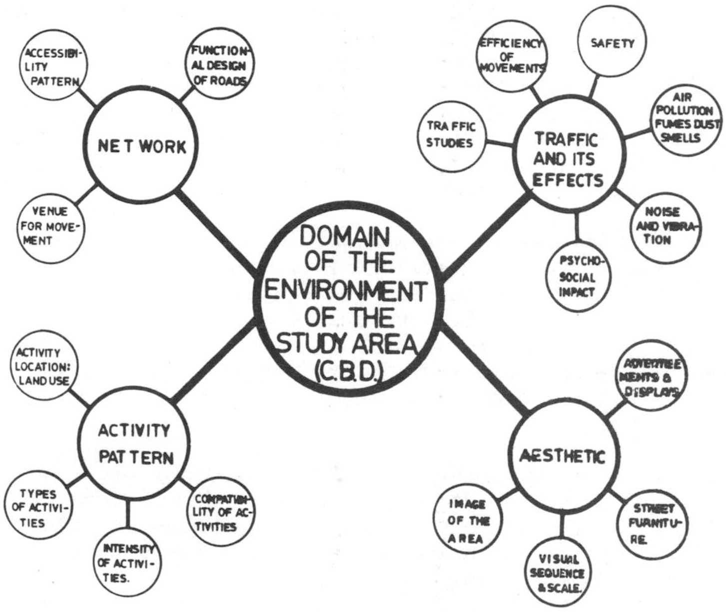

Fig. 5 Domain of Environment.

4.2 The studies carried out cover the entire domain of environment to investigate the constituent elements, viz. landuse and activity pattern, physical characteristics of road network, pattern of traffic and environmental effects of traffic.

4.2.1 The landuse study covered both, the formal sector (commercial, residential. industrial, transportation and recreational use of land) as well as the informal sector (temporary shops, hawkers and vendors, overflow of commercial activity on the right of way in an unauthorised manner) on all the three road sections under study. The road space, whose function is to cater to the traffic, was observed to be itself generating traffic through informal sector. This resulted into a chaos and conflict between the traffic and the activity pattern.

4.2.2 The physical study of the road network revealed that, inspite of the adequate width of right of way (varying between 15 mts. and 50 mts. with an average of 25 mts.). traffic congestion still occured due to defective road network and obsolete road geometrics, wasteful utilisation of road space, heavy encroachment, lack of segregation of movement of different categories of road users, virtual absence of traffic signs and road markings, inadequate traffic amenities works and bad maintenance of pavements of roads and footpaths. As a result, efficiency of road in terms of capacity, road safety and road user comfort was observed to be deteriorated.

4.2.3 The traffic studies included traffic volume survey covering magnitude. composition and directional split of vehicular traffic, pedestrian survey, speed survey and parking survey. Following are the findings of the study:-

a. Total daily traffic on these sections varied between 28,000 and 38,000 vehicles with a peak hourly flow of 3000 to 38000 vehicles.

b. The slow moving vehicles constituted 82% to 90% of the total traffic with an average of 84%.

c. The pedestrian traffic was as high as 2350 pedestrians per hour.

d. Traffic towards the Central Business District (CBD) predominated in the morning peak and vice versa in the evening peak.

e. The excessive traffic congestion resulting from conflicts between various categories of road users had deteriorated the level of service of the road, leading to the lowering of the journey speeds of the motor vehicles to as low as 7 kms. to 9.5 kms. per hour during peak periods, with an average of 16 kms. per hour.

f. The parking index in terms of the ratio of the actual number of vehicles parked along the kerb side to the parking capacity of the kerb side was observed to be as high as 3.12 with obviously an excessive proportion of unauthorised parking not only on the carriage way but also on footpaths along all the three sections.

4.2.4 The study of the environmental effects of traffic covered the environmental elements of road safety, traffic noise and vibration, air pollution and visual intrusion. Following are the findings of the study:-

a. The conflict between the various categories of road users resulted into a severe deterioration of safety and freedom of movement of road users leading to frequent accident occurrence (about three to five accidents per day on each section) as well as psychological frustration to the road users. At the same time, it was also observed that due to low operating speeds of traffic, majority of these accidents were 'damage only' accidents.

b. The traffic noise study revealed that during the peak periods, the average noise level was 71 dBA with an inter-quartile range of 5.5 dBA. The contribution of the heavy vehicles as well as frequent use of horns by all vehicles was observed to be significant in this regard.

c. The vibration effects, positively felt during peak hours in the buildings abutting the road could not be measured. However, in light of the fact that many buildings along the road were structurally weak, the vibration aspect assumes a significant importance.

d. Although chemical analysis of air samples was not conducted, it was found that during peak periods, the air pollution due to the automobile exhaust, dust and smoke created eye irritation, odour and low visibility.

e. The aesthetic studies conducted using sequence technique of photography along the line of movement, revealed that the aesthetic deterioration of the area due to impact of encroachment, indiscriminate and ugly hoardings, lack of landscaping as well as lack of spatial integration of urban landmarks with movement, was significant. It also revealed sub-standard information system available to the road users in form of road signs and road markings.

5. EVOLUTION OF ENVIRONMENTAL ASSESSMENT SCALE (E.A.S.)

5.1 Format of E.A.S.

Based on the domain of the environment defined in 4.1, the inventory of the environmental elements was prepared for their individual assessment. This inventory provided the format for E.A.S. as shown below:-

1. Activity factors - Landuse pattern, intensity of activities in formal and informal sectors, compatibility of landuses.

2. Network factors - Layout of roads, accessibility.

3. Roadway factors - Elements of road geometrics, traffic carrying capacity, traffic amenities, measures of traffic management and control, parking, loading and unloading facilities, pedestrian facilities, etc.

4. Aesthetic factors - Landscaping of roads, advertisement hoardings.

5.2 An assessment scale is based on this format and aims at synthesis of the quality of constituent elements of environment through appropriate weightages. Two approaches have been adopted to arrive at the relative weightages to the above mentioned factors of the environmental domain at macro level.

Approach I - Inter-relationship between the factors of domain of environment and quality of environment.

Each element of the domain was related to the environmental quality defined under the following aspects (effects):-

1. Freedom and efficiency of movement
2. Safety of road users
3. Air quality
4. Quiet
5. Aesthetic quality
6. Psychological impact on road users.

Relative weightages to the elements of environmental domain were worked out as shown in the TABLE 1.

FACTORS \ EFFECTS	EFFICIENCY OF MOVEMENT	SAFETY	AIR POLLUTION	NOISE & VIBRATION	AESTHETIC	PSYCHOLOGICAL	MARKS	INDICES
ACTIVITY PATTERN	O						3	15
NETWORK	O	O					5	25
ROAD WAY	O	O	O	O	O	O	10	50
AESTHETICS					O		2	10
TOTAL MARKS OF EFFECTS	3	2	1	1	2	1	20	100

TABLE 1 Pattern of Weightages - Approach I

Approach II - Value consensus of the professionals in the field of urban planning and development.

Content analysis of the communication in form of exhaustive interviews with the professionals regarding their concept of environment was conducted, which led to the pattern of relative weightages to various factors as given in the TABLE 2.

FACTORS \ EXPERTS	AR TP	P.H. ER	AR	JOURNALIST	EDUCATIONIST	ADM IT	M COMM	CIVIL ER	R H W ER	T T P	MARKS	INDICES
ACTIVITY PATTERN	O	O						O		O	4	16·5
NETWORK	O	O				O		O	O	O	6	26·4
ROAD WAY	O	O	O	O	O	O	O	O	O	O	10	44·6
AESTHETICS			O		O					O	3	10·5
											23	100

TABLE 2 Pattern of Weightages - Approach II

A pattern of relative weightages to the various factors at macro level was arrived at through a comparative analysis of the results obtained through the above mentioned two approaches. Based on these macro level weightages, further weightages to various elements within these factors were arrived at using the inter-relationship between these elements and the various aspects of environmental quality at micro level. The process of evolution of E.A.S. is documented in the TABLE 3.

FACTORS \ EFFECTS	EFFICIENCY OF MOVEMENT	SAFETY	AIR POLLUTION	NOISE & VIBRATION	AESTHETIC	PSYCHOLOGICAL	MARKS	INDICES
• ACTIVITY PATTERN								15
• NETWORK	2	2		1	1	1	10	25
LAYOUT OF THE ROADS	O	O		O		O	6	10
ACCESSIBILITY	O	O					4	15
• ROAD WAY	20	20	7	10	8	15	1223	50
RIGHT OF WAY	O	O	O	O	O	O	80	3·3
CARRIAGE WAY	O	O	O	O	O	O	80	3·3
FOOT PATHS	O	O			O	O	63	2·8
ALIGNMENT	O	O					40	1·6
GRADIENTS	O	O		O	O		65	2·6
SIGHT DISTANCE	O	O		O	O		65	2·6
INTERSECTIONS	O	O	O	O		O	65	2·6
CHANNELISERS	O	O					40	1·6
BUS BAYS	O	O			O		55	2·2
SEGREGATION	O	O	O	O	O		65	2·6
SIGNS	O	O			O		55	2·2
MARKINGS	O	O					40	1·6
INTERSECTION CONT.	O	O	O	O			57	2·4
PED CROSSINGS	O	O				O	48	2·0
PARKING	O	O		O	O	O	73	3·0
LOADING & UNLOADING	O	O					40	1·6
STREET LIGHTING	O	O			O		55	2·2
SURFACE CONDTION	O	O	O	O	O		72	3·0
ENCROACHMENTS	O	O	O	O	O	O	80	3·3
CONVENIENCES					O	O	23	1·2
SURFACE DRAINAGE	O	O			O		55	2·2
• AESTHETICS		4			4		32	10
ADVERTISEMENTS		O			O		8	2·5
LANDSCAPE		O			O		8	2·5
VISUAL SEQUENCE		O			O		8	2·5
IMAGE OF THE AREA		O			O		8	2·5
TOTAL MARKS OF EFFECTS	22	26	7	11	12	16		100

LEGEND
O – RELATIONSHIP

TABLE 3 Evolution of Environmental Assessment Scale.

6. ENVIRONMENTAL EVALUATION

6.1 Quantification of elements of environmental domain.

On the basis of studies carried out, various elements were quantitatively assessed in light of the following:-

a. Wherever quantification of elements was possible (e.g.road factors, traffic factors) the same was compared to the established standards recommended by the Indian Roads Congress and the quality of that factor was evaluated in terms of problem severity using a scalogram technique as shown in TABLE 4.

b. For elements subjective in nature such as visual quality, quantitative evaluation based on the subjective judgement was used.

6.2 Synthesis of assessment of individual elements was then carried out using the E.A.S. individually for each of the three road sections selected for study.

6.3 Based on the environmental index scored by the road section, the environmental quality was defined as shown in TABLE 4.

The study showed that environment of each of the three sections with indices scored between 20 and 40, falls in the 'poor' quality.

FACTORS	NORMS	INDIVIDUAL EVALUATION SECTION-1	SECTION-2	SECTION-3	SYNTHESIZED EVALUATION SECTION-1	SECTION-2	SECTION-3
● ACTIVITY PATTERN	TYPE, CONCENTRATION, COMPATIBILITY	●	●	●	3 00	3 00	3 00
● NETWORK					5 00	5 00	7 00
LAYOUT OF THE ROADS	HIERARCHY, PATTERN, SUITABILITY	●	●	●	3 00	3 00	3 00
ACCESSIBILITY	TYPE, PATTERN, LEVEL	●	●	◑	2 00	2 00	4 00
● FUNCTIONAL DESIGN OF THE ROADS					14 09	12 53	20 63
RIGHT OF WAY	TYPE, STANDARDS	●	●	○	0 66	0 66	3 3
CARRIAGE WAY	VOLUME, SPEED, COMPOSITION	●	●	●	0 66	0 66	0 66
FOOT PATHS	VOLUME, EFFECTIVE WIDTH	●	●	●	0 55	0 55	0 55
ALIGNMENT	TYPE OF ROAD, STANDARDS, SPEED	●	●	●	0 32	0 32	0 32
GRADIENTS	SPEED, COMPOSITION OF TRAFFIC	○	○	○	2 60	2 60	2 60
SIGHT DISTANCE	TYPE OF ROAD, SPEED, STANDARDS	◑	●	○	1 56	0 52	2 60
INTERSECTIONS	TYPE, TURNING TRAFFIC, SPACING, DESIGN FACTORS	◕	○	◑	1 04	0 52	1 56
CHANNELISERS	SPEED, COMOPOSITION OF TRAFFIC, STANDARDS	●	●	●	0 32	0 32	0 32
BUS BAYS AND BUS STOPS	PROVISION, STANDARDS	●	●	●	0 45	0 45	0 45
SEGREGATION	VOLUME, SPEED, COMPOSITION OF TRAFFIC	●	●	●	0 52	0 52	0 52
SIGNS	REQUIREMENT, PROVISION, MAINTENANCE	●	●	●	0 45	0 45	0 45
ROAD WAY MARKINGS	CARRIAGEWAY WIDTH, VOLUME, SPEED	●	●	●	0 32	0 32	0 32
TRAFFIC CONTROL AT INTERSECTIONS	TYPE, VOLUME - VEHICULAR & PEDESTRIAN TRAFFIC	◑	◑	◔	1 50	1 50	2 00
PEDESTRIAN CROSSINGS	VOLUME OF PEDESTRIAN TRAFFIC, LOCATION	●	●	●	0 40	0 40	0 40
PARKING	TYPE, DURATION, ACCUMULATION, EFFECTS	●	●	◑	0 60	0 60	0 60
LOADING AND UNLOADING	TYPE OF VEHICLE, TIME, FREQUENCY, DURTION	●	●	◑	0 32	0 32	0 96
STREET LIGHTING	ISI STANDARDS	●	●	●	0 45	0 45	0 45
ENCROACHMENTS	TYPE, SIZE, LOCATION, EFFECTS	●	●	●	0 68	0 68	0 68
CONVENIECES	PROVISION AND MAINTENANCE	●	●	●	0 24	0 24	0 24
SURFACE DRAINAGE AND SURFACE CONDITION	PROVISION, STANDARDS, MAINTENANCE	●	●	●	0 45	0 45	0 45
● AESTHETICS					2 00	2 00	2 50
ADVERTISEMENTS	LOCATION, SIZE, COLOUR, SHAPE, IMPACT	●	●	●	0 50	0 50	0 50
LANDSCAPE ELEMENTS & STREET FURNITURE	TYPE, PROVISION, IMPACT	●	●	●	0 50	0 50	0 50
VISUAL SEQUENCE	IMPACT	●	●	◕	0 50	0 50	1 00
IMAGE OF THE AREA	TYPE, IMPACT	●	●	●	0 50	0 50	0 50
				INDICES	24 09	22 53	32 13

PROBLEM SEVERITY	INDICES
○ 0% to 20% Adequate	0 to 20 Very Poor
◔ 20% to 40% Tolerable	20 to 40 Poor
◑ 40% to 60% Intolerable	40 to 60 Average
◕ 60% to 80% Positively Undesirable	60 to 80 Good
● 80% to 100% Should be Changed	80 to100 Very Good

TABLE 4 Evaluation of the Environments of the road sections under study.

6.4 Applicability of the environmental assessment scale.

The applicability of E.A.S. was tested by relating the environmental evaluation through E.A.S. to the environmental conception and sensitivity of the people - users of the environment. An opinion survey covering 283 subjects (shoppers, shopkeepers, pedestrians, etc.) of both sexes was conducted using an open-ended questionaire. The analysis of the communication was conducted based on which the evaluation of the environment of Madhya Marg by the subjects was quantified individually. as shown in Figure 6.

CATEGORY OF ENVIRONMENTAL EVALUATION	NUMBER OF SUBJECTS	PERCENTAGE
VERY POOR	148	53.8
POOR	83	28.2
AVERAGE	31	10.2
GOOD	15	5.0
VERY GOOD	8	2.8
TOTAL	283	100.0

OPINION SURVEY

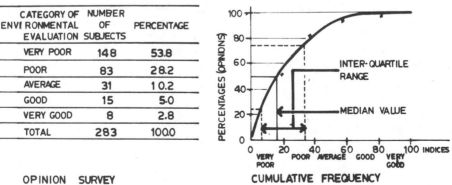

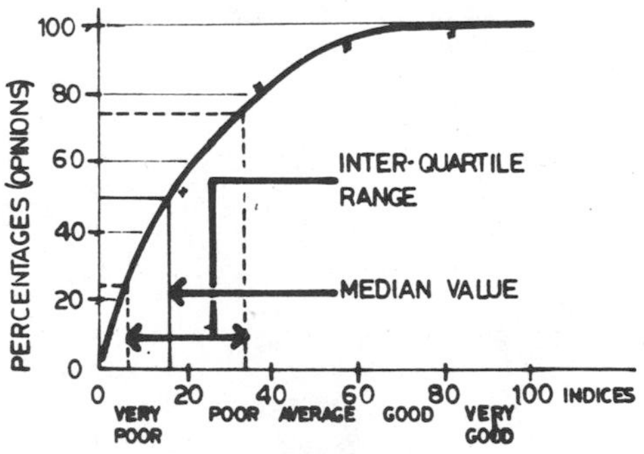

CUMULATIVE FREQUENCY

Fig. 6 Evaluation of Environment by Users.

Note: The evaluation is for entire Madhya Marg passing through the C.B.D. and not for an individual road section under study.

The table reveals that the evaluation of the environment by the subjects falls in categories of 'poor' quality of environment with inter-quartile range spanning over 'poor' and 'very poor' categories. The close agreement between the environmental evaluation using E.A.S. and through opinion survey establishes adequately the applicability of the scale.

7. CONCLUSIONS

1. Although considerable amount of subjective judgement is involved in formulation and use of E.A.S., it does give a rational basis for environmental evaluation.

2. The use of E.A.S. can be extended to prediction of environmental quality likely to be achieved through alternative proposals for improvement and, as such, could be incorporated in the process of decision making to supplement the conventional cost-benefit analysis. Conversely, the E.A.S. can also be used to identify those elements for the improvement on priority basis which would help to maximise the environmental benefits to the community through a proposed investment.

3. Further research work in the field of quantification of environmental elements and establishment of relative weightages to these elements is necessary to make the E.A.S. more realistic and user-oriented and technique fully accepted as an integral part of decision making.

REFERENCES

(1) Buchanan, C.D.(1963) Traffic in Towns H.M.S.O. London.

(2) Dark, J.W.(1964) Computing Buchanan Factors The Chartered Municipal Engineers, Vol.91, London.

(3) Hills, P.J.(1966) Environmental Management The Surveyor and Municipal Engineers. London.

(4) Antoniou, J.(1968) Environmental Management (Planning for Traffic), H.M.S.O. London.

(5) Urban Motorways Project Team (1973) Report of the Urban Motorways Project Team to the Urban Motorways Project Committee, H.M.S.O. London.

(6) Deshpande S.P. and Thakkar S.(1975). The impact of traffic on the quality of a residential environment: A case study of an urban area in Ahmedabad, India. Indian Journal of Ecology Vol.2 No.1.

ENVIRONMENTAL EVALUATION AND ACCESSIBILITY CRITERIA IN PLANNING

F.D. Hobbs

Head of Environmental Modelling and Survey Unit, Chancellor's Court, University of Birmingham, P.O. Box 363, Birmingham B15 2TT, England

1.0 THE OVERALL PROBLEM

1.1 Introduction

Whereas models of process control and monitoring can be entirely self-contained and abstract, in their relationship to the wider implications of environmental planning, this is not the case where human activities are being modelled. Thus, it is necessary to view human activity modelling as one facet of a global system where any input or output, of a sub-model, affects the state of the global process. While these affects have largely been ignored in reaching decisions with an environmental consequence, their exclusion can no longer be tolerated. The limitations of the prospects for growth is now generally recognised by the community at large. As the finite boundaries of growth are approached, diminishing returns are experienced on economic and other grounds which call for a radical review of policies and their implementation. In turn, the direction and emphasis of modelling and forecasting becomes a proper subject for re-examination with major changes required in the formulation of environmental and activity models; particularly those that lie within the ambit of public policy decision making. The assessment of environmental impact studies, and the sensitive monitoring of ongoing processes, are also areas of particular relevance despite the complexities that behavioural studies introduce to evaluation. Existing activity models have now become outdated with the emphases wrongly placed. The objective of this paper is to review the situation, comment on the prevailing uncertainties and illustrate, by way of examples from travel situations, some possible areas for development.

1.2 The Current Situation

The sustained growth in technology, marked in the real world by huge increases in production and consumption since the early 1950's, has failed to ameliorate its adverse consequences when viewed in a context of man's place in the natural order. Further more, the advantages granted by such wealth would have predicated the development and enjoyment of greater self expression coupled to a deeper human satisfaction. This notion has proved largely illusory. Industry has formed immense conglomerates, comprehensively processing an input of raw materials to the output stage of a sophisticated range of products on an international scale. The ability of national and local government to effectively oversee and exercise control of the resulting scale and scope of such operations necessitates understanding complex problems and dealing with conflicting demands. Even a casual review of the statistics reveals the extent of production increases and the nature of the residual conflicts and strains formed in society.

A fundamental difference arises from the tacitly assumed duty of the providers of the wherewithal for modern living to improve the efficiency of their performance, when measured in a context of product costs and employment benefits. This clashes with the poorly integrated objectives of government whose ultimate responsibility however lies in safeguarding and improving the welfare of all their citizens. The dilemma can be illustrated by recourse to an example of the decision of either to provide a number of smaller units or a single large plant. Small plants usually offer more local work, simplify pollution problems, improve locational site choices, preserve communities, provide greater employment, reduce travel needs but usually increase production costs, local goods traffic and require more local infrastructure facilities, which may also represent losses in scale economies. These higher product costs must be offset against the known high costs of operating the sprawling and congested metropolitan regions necessary for the largest producers to satisfy their labour and market demands.

1.3 Environmental Considerations

For many thousands of years philosophers have expressed a common theme for the existence of a bond between man and nature. Its central thesis was that damage to the environment was synonymous with self destruction and that man had to be ever alert to control his propensity to inflict damage to nature. Today, single and combined forces can be unleashed that could bring extinction to the planet, and perhaps beyond. Past generations, noticeably during the development of industrialisation, left technical and economic problems for resolution to future generations when it was anticipated that new skills would have become available. While technology now has untold power to change nature, and exploitation of the environment sometimes becomes an end in itself, an even greater proportion of intractable problems are being left to future generations. Consumption of scarce materials, the failure to prevent waste and pollution, to harness natural energy sources and to install recycling processes are all further illustrations of this situation.

There are many reasons for this state of affairs, but it is partly attributable to the professional stratification of those that deal with the environment. Three major groups can be distinctly identified:
(i) the natural scientists who are principally concerned with the bio-physical systems of the planet, and man's place in the ecological system;
(ii) the planners and builders who provide for man's physical needs by creating the built environment as a place to live, work and enjoy recreation;
(iii) the behavioural scientists whose domain of environmental concern is that of man as a social animal, not only in the built environment but also in a psycho-social system. This system is totally interactive between individuals and communities, and between the physical and metaphysical processes. Because the first two groups only consider psycho-social factors where they impinge directly on their own work, and the latter groups have tended to avoid the close study of the individual in his surroundings, a professional divide has arisen.

Complex psychological questions are posed when related to the cognition of an individual's world in which he has his being. Beyond the explanatory terminology problem, there are other questions which occur about which qualities are distinguishable and heeded, the basis for their assumption, the expectations aroused and what other factors influence the comprehension of the physical environment? Additionally, besides the range of an individual's social attributes lie a host of skills, traits, dispositions and abilities inherent in the observer at a point in time. Because of the scope of both physiological and psychological differences, and the variability of social needs, each individual is likely to use different subsets of environmental elements to conceptualize and record satisfactions for all environmental evaluations. Thus, by determining a quantity for the chosen elements they can be formulated to represent a general measure of an individual's environmental conception. However, a further qualification must be made for each response because a distinctive weighting will be placed on the evaluation of each component so perceived within the frame of reference. Hence, an environmental evaluation will trace a path through the network of perception and manipulatory intellection determined by a threshold sensitivity exhibited by the observer. The process will be dominated by the personal schemata and represents, for each weighted element, a definable measure of environmental sensitivity. Real problems occur where responses are required which lie outside the individual's experience, and his is particularly marked in the time series effects within a servo-environmental situation, where changes are interactive. In general, it is required to measure individual responses to a variety of environmental stimuli by determining a set of all impinging variables that affect this behaviour within the domain of some specified environmental experience. The results of changes in environmental design, or the likely responses by individuals to new environments, is required in order to plan effectively.

2.0 THE TRANSPORT PROBLEM

2.1 The Nature of Movement

The structural organisation of shape, tissue and cell morphology determines locomotor ability in animals; and the human is no exception in possessing this basic attribute of being a mobile organism. Like other animals his structure has evolved to reflect locomotor habits important in all phases of survival, and this attribute can be referred to as mobility. Species' mobility needs not only propulsive ability but also control mechanisms to overcome the two principal physical resistances to motion of gravity and the force reducing movement, known as drag. Unlike other animals man has harnessed energy resources and external control mechanisms to free himself from the restrictions imposed by nature, and while these have taken many thousands of tears to reach advanced levels, the last century has seen the unique conquest of the four environments - terrestrial, aquatic, fossocial and aerial - and more recently the limited ability of escape into the extra-terrestrial reaches. It is perhaps ironic that while some simple animals depend entirely on the environment for their transportation (mobility with passive locomotion) man has now created situations that prevent his own enjoyment of mobility. Thus the ability to reach a given place, necessary for 'ordinary' living or survival, has been removed or reduced, and markedly for some individuals and groups. This is not necessarily a result of an inability to overcome the physical forces of gravity and drag, but the manmade impediments to movement derived from social restraints. These can best be referred to as social and economic forces which form a third and major deterrent to mobility albeit that they occur in a highly mechanised world. Hence, when economic or social conditions preclude the satisfaction of a fundamental movement need through the bad layout of a city, the transport system or some other deprivation of use, then that is a process analogous to precluding passive locomotion.

It is not necessary to trace the developing sources of increased transport availability, ranging from the domestication of animals to the powered exoskeletal machines and through to the mass movement systems, that have created a variety of transport modes. These can be used to overcome the physical resistances of all detected environments. However all known dimensions of movement, including thought processes, consume time. This leads to the situation where basically all transport systems, under a load, operate intrinsically as queueing systems requiring the expenditure of both energy and time to accomplish a movement. The reduction of queueing time invariably involves costs thus providing a further dimension on the ordering of social priorities, referred to above.

Nothing has been said so far about preferences choices or the diversity of behaviour that demarks man from the rest of the animal kingdom; nor of the consequences of power consumption. This entails the conversion of an energy into so called useful product but generates by-products - the latter often seen as a waste product, or a pollutant. When aggregated over time and populations the conversion of energies establishes the conservational needs, while the toxic elements released necessitate pollution controls. Whereas both these are fairly readily identifiable processes the social phenomenon of transport deprivation has only recently become established. It is already clear that many adverse social consequences stem from deprived sections of the community in the face of a perceived abundance around them, and this applies increasingly to transport planning causing changes in the grouping or dispersal of many types of facilities in regional areas.

2.2 The Role and Effect of Transport

Transport is both a basic server and consumer within an economic system. Indeed it is unlikely that the huge increases in material standards of modern industrial societies could have taken place but for the scale economies that modern transport has provided. While superficially increased human interchange has also been fostered the need for more and longer movements is also a direct consequence of mass transit innovations. A significant proportion of the time available to many individuals is expended in travel, often in testing conditions which reduce his life expectancy, but this can then be restored by improved medical care. Other transport disbenefits arise in ecological damage, death and injury, noise and the consumption of scarce resources, which the natural system has produced over millions of years and are now consumed in centuries, if not decades. Future society may thus pay a heavy penalty for the loss of fossilised materials which are required for many other purposes than for use as fuels; productive land is removed from cultivation reducing the eventual food bank; services are dehumanised by packaging and space is required to store vehicles which spend most of their time at rest.

Basically all land uses generate a characteristic pattern of demand and use reproducible in spatial and temporal measurements. Classically, with the exception of participants who enjoy the transport system itself, e.g. spectators at an airport, train spotters etc., and excluding the so-called 'joy' riders who are fulfilling an escapist role from the bounds of their own physiological and psychological make-up, the transport system itself does not generate traffic. It may well encourage more travel by creating new opportunities for interchange, for which there may have been a latent or untapped demand, and reducing 'drag' by allowing easier movement and more time to accomplish journeys between locations.

Obviously the attractiveness of an activity, whether created by economic need, for example work, or for reasons of pleasure is affected by the social characteristics of the population, e.g. levels of education, age, sex, income, type of work, motivational factors, etc.. Thus both psycho-social and socio-economic attributes correlate with differences in behaviour and the desirability of destinations. This attractiveness will affect the intensity of use, partly in terms of activity costs (economic) and partly in relation to the degree of enjoyment conferred (social). While some activities can be foregone others cannot, but there is a degree of flexibility within the decision as alternative times or destinations, although of differing quality, may be available for choice.

It is necessary to note the interactive nature of generation and intensity of use and observe it as a cyclical process. Underuse leads to a least effort and thus a low transport cost but a propensity to attract activity; conversely, overuse situations contain the forces of self destruction in the form of congestion, increased costs and eventually to decay. Thus, any land use system is always encompassed within this cyclical process with events forcing it gradually towards the opposite state. This leads ultimately to redevelopment or replacement to a new set of standards appropriate for some selected time horizon, i.e. generally with an in-built spare capacity.

2.3 Accessibility and Mobility

It should be clear that all pairs of points within the spatial system have a definable quantity and quality of accessibility to each other. One simple index is where accessibility is made directly proportional to the inverse of the movement costs between the points in space. However, comfort, convenience and the opportunity to use not only the terminal activity, but the interconnecting and available modes are essential to a model's discriminatory power.

Accessibility can be viewed as a basic prerequisite for the fuller development of economic and social welfare by the spatial distribution of activity demands with respect to residential locations. It can be seen to operate at far below the satisfaction criteria of an aggregate population; its level of service and optimal state will vary between individuals and identifiable groups. The creation of new modes has led to a corresponding change in the size and shape of cities, the catchment areas for work forces and markets, and the attendant problems of long distance commuting with the relocation of managerial and skilled higher income groups on the urban fringe (or beyond). Opportunities for public transport have decreased as origins, in particular, have become more diffuse and the quality of both public and private transport travel has deteriorated. These are identified by making walking and cycling unpleasant and frequently hazardous, caused congestion on saturated highways and crowded public transport with the attendant high resource consumption and pollution effects creating social deprivation, among the aged or infirm, causing accidents and the overall loss of comfort and quality in living, besides reducing diversity of choice and availability of transport at all in some locations.

2.4 Travel Interactance

Interaction is dependent on both accessibility and mobility; the former can be determined as a measure of the degree of freedom by which a specified destination is approachable from a specified origin and by definition involves effort in overcoming the intervening space. Associated with it are the opportunities which exist and their relationships to the characteristics of the nodal links. Whether or not the accessibility links between disparate origins and destinations can be passed over, in order to enjoy the terminal activities, depends solely on the mobility available to the participant and obviously involves physical, social, economic and transport availability in both temporal and spatial terms. The distribution of facilities can be determined by planning decisions taken by authority by entrepreneural considerations or by combinations of the two.

The term travel impedance thus applies to both accessibility provision and mobility availability and either can determine fully the ability to reach or not to reach a destination, or to provide some minimum value of connectivity greater than zero value. Thus in planning terms these forces increase or contract the influences leading to centralized or decentralized locations.

Different modes between links are invariably in conflict, greater use of one lessening the use or ease of use of another. Because effort in travel to overcome impedance of spatial separation has not been the basic criterion for comparison of longer journeys, by using greater motive power, may lessen time spent on the journey and thus be assumed, in aggregate, to offer improved mobility. However, this proposition ignores many real costs which have not been included in the equation. Basically movement is only desirable to the degree that access requires it and mobility purchased at 'high cost' may be undesirable when included in the overall social costs. Hence the need for balance between spread and diminishing movement choice.

2.5 Accessibility Preferences

The formation of accessibilty preferences is concerned with subjective conceptualisations known as 'images'. Images and objective accessibility coincidence is a complication in measures of maximisation expression. One basic problem of the survey approach to problems is the opportunities imposed by uniformity and limited choices may reflect that situation rather than the preferences-showing system use and not alternatives.

One of the major factors of accessibilty affects land and property values in a relationship which has an overall impact on the land use distribution, affecting not only the size of an urban area, but its structure. Examples of these effects can be seen in advertisements which point out to the prospective consumer that a particular residential location is near shops, schools or accessible to railway stations, nearness to motorway junctions illustrating opportunities for work in city centres, particular factories or at public buildings like hospitals. Accessibility provisions undoubtedly cause important distributional income effects and in general should now be related to individuals rather than the previous use, of a household or car unit model. This creates considerable distortional disturbances in the pattern of opportunity and satisfaction enjoyed by individuals, albeit that their physical location is the same.

The provision of accessibility is a major determinant in controlling the opportunities for developing countries, particularly the growth potential and limiting the influence of natural barriers. Political manipulation or the incorrect determination of transport facilities can lead to severe consequences by dividing a work force from work opportunities, shoppers from a shopping centre, schools from school children, visitors from a patient in hospital - all illustrations of social deprivation. Conversely, if an activity opportunity has access provided but is not desired for enjoyment then it is of no value from zero. The supply side of accessibility equations is determined by the planning authority (or entrepreneur) and the balance of one centre compared to another is determined by the demand side, i,e. the strength of an individual's desire to engage in those activities relative to an evaluation of the disutility of their journey by overcoming the cost/effort requirements on the connecting links, and the terminal rental costs.

2.6 Accessibility Improvements and Deficiencies

Improvement of accessibility can be acheived in two principal ways; first, by reducing spatial separation, i.e. there are diminishing returns to higher rise buildings (even if daylighting factors did not influence the spacing) because vertical travel is equally onerous and energy consuming as horizontal travel; and second, by improved links in the interconnectivity of the network. If a work force wants more choice then distance of work travel is likely to increase, given a mixed distribution of land uses, or congestion may rise if heavily concentrated in an area. Thus, either way, traffic problems emerge. These are not solved in a traditional sense because of the cyclical implications previously referred to above.

Demands change, habits change, therefore balances and optima change in the dynamics of urban planning. Both demands and habits are subject to influence; a society solely directed towards consumption is likely to produce new generations with innovatory ideas devoted to the process of consumption whereas one devoted to conservation is entirely unlikely to expend resources on goods or services likely to lead to shortages, for the next generation. Today most industrialised countries in the world are in the process of foregoing the former state by some tempering of consumer appetites.

Another problem, particularly identified with the diversities of specialisms and locational choices in metropolitan regions, is that of information availability to individuals. Very few can hope for a level of knowledge sufficient to maximise their opportunities of where to go or how to minimise the effort of getting there by selecting the best routeings in terms of the dynamics of a journey yet to be made at the time of selection. Psychological problems also occur, initiated by the fears and anxieties of travel and these may be of particular consequence to the aged and infirm or to parents of younger children. These are due to slow and irregular services, lengthening waits at unprotected bus stops, poor driving or vehicle quality, ticket purchase difficulties, unhelpful crew or other travellers, the necessity of vehicle transfers and the siting of interchange points (e.g. on opposite sides of heavily trafficked junctions), poorly located boarding or alighting points relative to origins and destinations and badly timed return journey services. Choice availability is needed not only locationally but at the right time; thus land use distributions are as affected by the constraints placed by time on an activity as by location.

3.0 ACCESSIBILITY AND MOBILITY MEASUREMENTS

3.1 Introduction

The above discussion has ranged over the perception and response to accessibility and mobility as viewed by different segments of a population. Some of the affects on land use planning have been considered. Summarising the principal measures used in models (and these include the obverse phenomenon of location) have included distance, time, car ownership, household characteristics, employment factors, connectivity of points, attributes of public transport services (regularity, area coverage and modal availability, frequency, suitability of arrival and departure times, duration of route time, destination time available, costs), journey purposes and other ratios such as that of time available at destination to travel time on route or equivalents in terms of monetary or generalised costs. Not many of the modelling processes have included the more difficult psychological variables related to motivation, acceptability, perceived efforts and satisfactions, prejudices, general attitudes and those specific to transport, informational difficulties or the redistributional income effects associated with transport planning decisions. These markedly affect social groups within the community, particularly those that are disadvantaged in some way. Until these areas can be satisfactorily included in some form in the models then their influence tends to be dismissed as unimportant.

A forecasting and calibration problem arises in many models because they are tied to observed behaviour. The formulation of the standard transport modelling process on this basis has resulted in the provision of facilities predicated on current observed use and extrapolated to a selected time horizon on the postulate that changes in household income and car ownership will be reflected in the future by a behaviour derived from matching the new attributes with those of a similar past grouping. However, it is clear that to enjoy accessibility provision an individual level of mobility is a necessity and vice versa. Places on an island, well connected by a network of roads, are no more accessible than if all the islanders owned vehicles, but had no roads on which to drive them. Thus, observations which show that there are more trips per head, where there is higher accessibility and high car ownership, could be considered a dangerous tautology. Greater facility provision and the encouragement of private mobility, despite the fact that about one fifth of most populations could not be licensed to drive in normal circumstances, leads to improved capacity, which is then fully utilised. The result is a self fulfilling prophecy. Other dangers exist in using mass observed behaviour if, for reasons of data simplification, it is fundamentally superficial in character. For instance, if the aged are observed to travel little, or only at paticular times, it is concluded that they do not require or need particular transport services. Therefore, the practice of matching transport facilities to accomodate observed needs usually fail to meet desired needs of large segments of the population.

Other factors to be considered involve creating expectatons in the population at large but only fulfilling them in part, or for certain groups. Desired activity goals (or undesired ones) induce distortion in the reality of elapsed travel time as perceived and influenced by the expectations for enjoyment (or not) at the end of the journey. Another example can be seen in the expectations of villagers currently without a bus service where their expectations, to be derived from the provision of a service, can be measured. Quite opposite results are obtained from a similarly placed group who already enjoy the proposed level and type of service, but will develop arguments and complaints often relating to irregularity of service, high costs and inconsiderate crews. The number of 'available' opportunities for a resident to satisfy his personal demands are self obvious, but availability cannot be separated from desirability, i.e. what to forego or enjoy within one's personal choice situation is subject to a complex of substitutions, often involving carry-over influences from other individuals. There is an additional element, where multiple opportunities occur, related to the grading of those opportunity qualities by the observer. While the zone of travel influence is affected by individual constraints (such as decisions taken outside the transport sector), but usually time of day and day of week are influential as well as the varying perceptions of time, cost and comfort. These are related to the probability of activity availability and the trade-offs in consuming it at a particular time.

3.2 Relationships and Measurements

Most accessibility relationships have used either distance or time as a central index, either in a linear or non-linear form, and sometimes by placing a value on time in some forms of cost function. The idea of a range of opportunities has led to the parallel development of modified forms of the gravity model, applied to the probability of acceptance of destinations within given time bands. Nearly all the forms depend, for their application, on calibration and use with either aggregated or, more recently, disaggregate model formulations. Calibration has normally taken the form of fitting the best 'deterrence' function in the model to satisfy some set of observed data. In conformity with attractor capabilities recognition has been given to models which incorporate differences in potential while others have classified aspects of the network in the form of dispersion of the network, network densities and the accessibility of a vertex, Developments have led to the use of graph theory and the notion of a connectivity index, where route deviousness, or circuity, can also be incorporated as a factor.

Measurements for the current range of models has largely been derived from data banks set up during the period of metropolitan area transport surveys. However, if new types of modelling are to be developed, incorporating the social and psychological nature of the population, then the form of the data required is very different from others, requiring specialised and lengthy techniques. Sampling becomes a major factor because of the costs involved of providing a source basis for the work. The principal techniques include in depth interviews, usually tape-recorded for subsequent content analysis, the development of appropriate attitudinal scales, personality tests, visual display techniques, and invariably the design of games to ascertain the values placed on different 'objects', achievements, and 'choices' relative to socio-economic or psycho-social attributes of the subject. Thereafter, powerful statistical testing is required to attempt to validate the application to existing situations. Because of the overlapping nature of some attributes possessed in common with other individuals it is likely that the finite mathematics of set theory, and the use of probability, will be necessary to establish the likely responses of subjects to sets of environmental stimuli, i.e. the mathematics of the behavioural and social sciences.

The errors of current techniques, exemplified by the process of matching a supply to a conceived demand (not necessarily correctly identified) and extrapolating it, by constraining future behaviour to that presently existing, only compounds the errors of decisions taken as a consequence. Often only the journey to work has been considered in any depth and adds to the dangers when even full time workers only spend, on average, about one fifth of their total time at work. Changes in the pattern of work behaviour are also becoming more pronounced and the availability of time for other pursuits may alone be more constraining in the future. This standard transportation planning process not only fails to meet social and other human needs, but is damaging to the environment and effects resource consumption; both by products which in themselves are interactive with human behaviour. The aim of the planner should not be to educate the population to use and 'enjoy' the system he intends to provide, but to more sensitively identify the basic needs of users, anticipate their aspirations and to use evaluations techniques to formulate public policy decisions that need to meet economic criteria, and safeguard community objectives. Thus the stages of the transportation process are shown below: Fig. 1.

The system shown in Fig. 1 replaces the standard input stages of the current transportation plan, but inventories and forecasts of population, facilities, employment, etc. will be inputs, together with dynamic modelling of trip movements on links, to the Public Policy phase. In order to take effective decisions a degree of local autonomy is required to reflect differences in the population and its infra structures, and the necessity of local budgetary control is obvious if local plan aspirations are to be realised. While it may not be possible to derive and incorporate such a comprehensive technique into planning many of the objectives and tests could already be applied, albeit in a more subjective way than that intended, and there are many possibilities for the use of simulation.

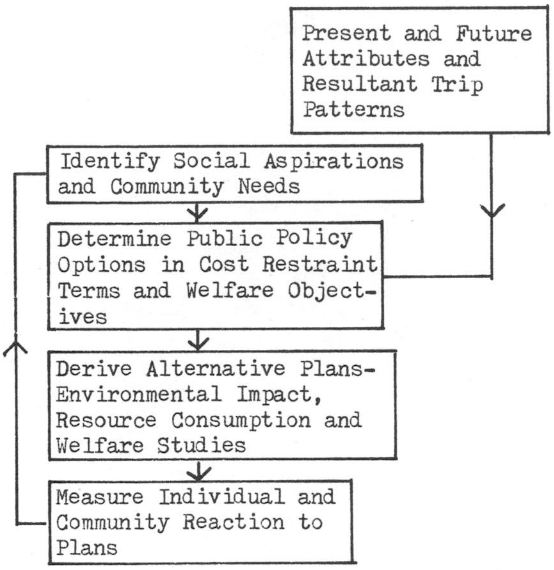

(a)

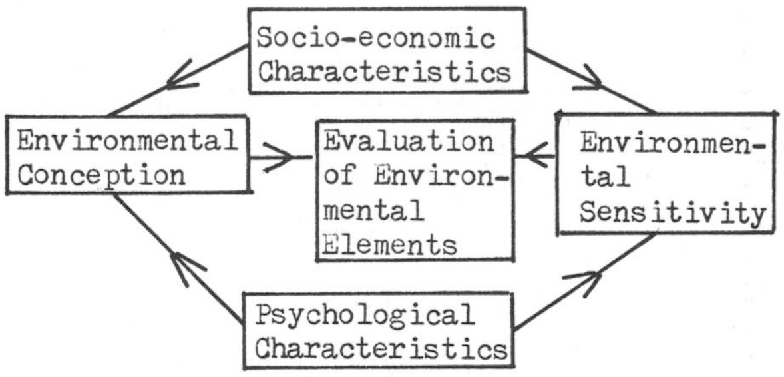

(b)

Fig. 1.(a) The transportation planning process.
(b) Evaluation by individuals of environmental elements.

Appendix: Examples of Techniques

In work undertaken by Allos (i) on modal choice in Birmingham, using discriminant analysis, it was decided to incorporate an index to represent an individual's acceptance of the various modes and his own set of preferences. Individual preferences between private and public transport were indicated by the relative importance attached to selected attributes. The survey resulted in 10 variables of acceptability and 6 variables for the importance of the attributes. Because of their inter-correlation and the difficulty of including 16 additional variables (subsequently reduced to 11) in the discriminant function, the technique of principal component analysis was used to form dummy variates for inclusion in the model as surrogates for their attitudes. Eacg component represented a single indicator, the highest loading component represented a 'bus acceptance' factor, then came 'car acceptance', 'cost importance' and, finally, the lowest loaded component being a measure of 'time importance'. The effects of including the 'attitudinal' factors were marked by significant improvements in the R values, explaining nearly 60% of the variation - a 30% improvement on the best values obtained in the previous models used for the data - and, more important, only misclassifying 8.3% of the observations compared to the previous value of 17.9%.

Work by Mohan (ii), using gaming and other techniques, researched accessibility preferences for Indian and English groups in Birmingham. As an illustration of the respondants' attitudes to 25% less accessibility than currently enjoyed revealed little differences in the rankings for the two ethnic groups for selected common destinations. Table 1 below tabulates the first 6 destinations of the set used. It shows the preferred order for the proximity of desired facilities.

Table 1. Results of Reduced Accessibility

Facility	Indian			English		
	M	R	S	M	R	S
Bus stop	0.11	1	0.16	0.11	1	0.02
Local shops	0.11	2	0.05	0.11	2	0.01
Primary school	0.11	3	0.05	0.10	3	0.05
Doctor's	0.10	4	0.03	0.09	5	0.03
Park	0.09	5	0.04	0.10	4	0.03
Playground	0.08	6	0.05	0.00	16	0.05
Best friend's House	0.05	11	0.03	0.07	6	0.04

M = Median
R = Rank
S = Standard Deviation

(i) A.E. Allos. A study in mode choice for the work trip, Ph.D. Thesis, University of Birmingham (1975).
(ii) S. Mohan. Accessibility considerations in transportation planning, Ph.D. Thesis, University of Birmingham (1975).

OPTIMUM CONTROL CRITERIA FOR POPULATION NUMBER DYNAMICS AND DEGENERATION

Mark T. Anikst and Efim Ya. Frisman

Institute of Automation and Control Processes, Far East Science, Centre of the USSR Academy of Sciences, Vladivostok, USSR

ABSTRACT

The paper presents a multi-criterion approach to the selection of a plan of exploitation of biostock threatened with degradation. The criteria considered are related to preservation of the biostock and its effective exploitation. For a certain class of biostock, possible selections are presented of a plan to ensure a balance between preservation and profitable exploitation. The research uses the Markov random process theory.

INTRODUCTION

The sharp decline in the biostokk of certain valuable species of animals and fish, which has taken place as a result of their excessive exploitation, leads us to the problem of preserving these species. Preservation of the biostock and its profitable exploitation are not incompatible. A compromise between them may be found by selecting an optimal population control plan. Any exploitation plan may be considered as consisting of removing a certain number of stock from some generations. The control criteria may be related either to characteristics in the life cycle of the biostock or to the effectiveness of its exploitation. Apparently a multi-criterion approach is necessary in selecting population number control methods.

Following the example of other authors who have methods involving the thery of random processes in investigating the propagation of biological populations (ref. 1, 2, 3), we have examined a stochastic model of propagation. Among such models, we have found a class of models which reliably predict the highly probable degeneration of a limited biostock (ref. 3). The model we have considered belongs to this class.

METHODS

Let us introduce certain formal structures which we will use in this work. Let M represent a set of functions f(m), m= 0,1,2,..., for which the functional F(f,t)

$$F(f,t) = \sum_{k=0}^{\infty} f(k)t^k e^{-t}/k!$$

exists for any actual t, $t \geqslant 0$. As shown in the Appendix, as M we may select a set of functions f(m) each of which has a nondecreasing concave nonnegative function f(m), such that $|f(m)| \leqslant g(m)$ for all m.

We designate operators G and G_h by the formulas (m = 0,1,2,...):

$$Gf(m) = q(m) + \max_{0 \leqslant s \leqslant m}\left[F(f,v(s))+r(s)\right], \quad s \text{ - integer}, \qquad (1)$$

$$G_h f(m) = q(m) = \begin{cases} F(f,v(m))+r(m), & 0 \leqslant m \leqslant h \\ F(f,v(m))+r(h), & m \geqslant h+1 \end{cases}$$

where $q(m) \in M$, $r(m) \in M$, $v(m) \in M$, $v(m) \geqslant 0$, h - integer, $h \geqslant 0$.

If M is selected as indicated above, then G and G_h map M into itself. The operators will be used to fix the optimality equation.

RESULTS

A limited population with continuous propagation is chosen for investigation. The process of birth and death of this biostock is described as a uniform Markov chain with a transfer matrix: $\{p(i,j)\}$ $i,j=0,1,..$ $p(i,j) = (v(i))^j e^{-v(i)}/j!$, where i is the number of parent stock, j is the number of offspring, v(i) is the mean number of young from i parent stock. One unit of discrete time (step) is taken as the life cycle of one generation. The accepted law of birth and death of the biostock is approximately fulfilled if the cases of 'birth and death of individual stock' are random and unrelated and the probability of each case depends only on the number of parent stock. For complete fulfillment of this law, it is necessary to follow it to the limit, infinitely decreasing the above-mentioned probability and retaining the average number of offspring. In this investigation, we will consider that the average number of offspring v(i) from i parent stock satisfies the following conditions: 1) $v(0) = 0$; 2) $0 \leq v(i) \leq v_o$ with $i = 1,2,...$; 3) v(i) increases strictly concave where $0 \leq i \leq m_o, v(m_o)=v_o$. Condition 1) corresponds to the demands of a limited population. Condition 2) limits the mean number of population in correspondence with the limitations on resources for sustaining life. Condition 3) can be accepted without loss of generality.

Let $\bar{e}^n(m)$ be the mathematical expectation of population number and $\bar{p}^n(m)$ the life expectancy of the nth generation of biostock assuming that the initial number $(n = 0)$ of the generation is equal to m, $m \geq 0$. As shown in (ref. 3), when $n \to \infty$ $\bar{e}^n(m) \to 0$, $\bar{p}^n(m) \to 0$ with more general suppositions concerning the law of birth and death that are assumed here. Therefore, on the average the biostock becomes degenerated. With a probability of 1, the biostock in question most certainly becomes extinct. Let us introduce the criteria for biostock control. The first group of criteria, related to biostock preservation, is as follows: a) average number of offspring in one generation; b) probability of survival of the generation; c) the mean number of generations until the biostock becomes extinct; d) total number of stock for the complete period of existence. The second group of criteria will be represented by e) the whole reward obtained from exploitation of the biostock in a definite time interval. Further, it is demonstrated that strategies optimal with respect to each of these criteria a) – e) have an identical structure, called threshold. It may be described as follows. If the generation count is greater than a certain value h, then m – h stock is removed from that generation. Otherwise, the numerical level of the generation is retained. The value h is termed the threshold. The value of threshold h in optimal control depends on the criteria. For control strategy allowing maximal values for criteria a) – d), the value of threshold is identical and equal to m. For control strategy allowing maximal reward e), the threshold value is less than m. Therefore, control strategy allowing maximum reward is the most extreme plan for exploitation of the biostock. Since we are seeking a compromise between preservation and exploitation, we will select a control strategy which has a threshold with all possible values of h, $0 \leq h \leq \infty$ (h is integer).

Let us consider the problem of two-criterion optimality. As a criterion of biostock preservation, we may select any of the criteria of the first group a) - d), as all of them have identical optimal strategy. Since we desire criteria reflecting the number of the biostock, we select criterion d) (we may take criteria a) - d) together). It is natural to take as the second criterium the total reward obtained from exploitation of the biostock to the point of extinction, that is, criteria e). Then we find a set of threshold values corresponding to the compromise control strategies, that is, strategies which can be improved in one criterion only at the expense of another criterion. We normalize the criteria, extending the values to maximum and employ the optimality principle, which seems to us be the essehce of the problem. This principle (called the maxmin principle (ref.4)) calls for selection of the value of threshold h, maximizing the smallest of the normalized values of the two criteria. Thus, a compromise is effected between preservation of the biostock and its exploitation. Instead of using the optimality principle, we may limit ourselves to finding the compromise control strategy sets.

Let us consider optimal control strategy for criteria a) - d) of the first group. Let a') $e^n(m)$ be the mean number and b') $p^n(m)$ the probability of extinction of the nth generation, if the number of the initial generation is equal to m, the population being controlled for a time interval $\overline{0,n}$ and control strategy optimal. Using the Markov random processes theory with countable sets of states and control strategy (ref.5), we obtain an optimality equation for criteria considered: $e^n = Ae^{n-1}$, $e^o(m) = m$ and $p^n = Bp^{n-1}$, $p^o(m) = \{0 \text{ with } m = 0,\ 1 \text{ with } m \geqslant 1\}$, $m \geqslant 0$, $n \geqslant 1$ (m and n integers), where A = B = G with $q(m) \equiv r(m) \equiv 0$ (see (1)). The results given in Appendix show that with $h = m_o$ and $n \geqslant 1$ $e^n = A_h e^{n-1}$, $p^n = B_h p^{n-1}$, where $A_h = B_h = G_h$ with G = A(= B). Therefore, it follows that the control strategy with threshold structure and threshold $h = m_o$ will be optimal in criteria a) and b) for the time interval $\overline{0,n}$ for all $n \geqslant 1$. As before, $e^n(m) \to 0$, $p^n(m) \to 0$, that is, with this control strategy we are not able to prevent degeneration of the biostock and can only delay it.

Then, let c') $g^n(m)$ be the mean number of generations till degeneration of the biostock and d') $q^n(m)$ the mean number of stock born in the total control period (including the initial number); if in the initial generation there were m stock, the population is controlled in the time interval $\overline{0,n}$ and control is optimal. Let $g'(m)$ and $q'(m)$ be the corresponding values of criteria for optimal control in an unlimited time interval. Optimality equatiom are as follows: $g^n = Cg^{n-1}$, $g^o(m) = \{0 \text{ with } m = 0,\ 1 \text{ with } m \geqslant 1\}$, $g' = Cg'$ and $q^n = Dq^{n-1}$, $q^o(m) = m$, $q' = Dq'$, $m \geqslant 0$, $n \geqslant 1$ (m and n are integers), where C = G with $q(m) = f(m) = g^o(m)$, D = G with $q(m) = f(m) = q^o(m)$, $m \geqslant 0$ (see (1)). From results presented in Appendix, it follows that with $h = m_o$, $n \geqslant 1$, $q^n = C_h g^{n-1}$, $g' = C_h g'$, $q^n = D_h q^{n-1}$, $q' = D_h q'$, where $C_h = G_h$ with G = C and $D_h = G_h$ with G = D. It is clear that control with a threshold structure and with threshold $h = m_o$ will be optimal in criteria c) and d) for a time interval $\overline{0,n}$ for all $n \geqslant 1$

and also for an unlimited time interval. Further, $g^n \uparrow g'$ and $q^n \uparrow q'$ with $n \uparrow \infty$ and convergence is uniform as regards m, for $m \geqslant 0$. The functions $g^n(m)$, $q^n(m)$ with $n \geqslant 0$ and $g'(m)$, $q'(m)$ are increasing and concave with $m \geqslant 0$. Finally, we consider the optimal control strategy for the reward criterion e). Let e') $r^n(m)$ be the mean number of stock removed from the population during the whole control period; if the initial generation count is equal to m, the population is controlled for time interval $\overline{0,n}$ and control strategy is optimal. Let $r'(m)$ be the corresponding reward value during optimal control for an unlimited period. The optimality equations are as follows: $r^n = Er^{n-1}$, $r^0(m) = 0$, $r' = Er'$, $n \geqslant 1$, $m \geqslant 0$ (m and n are integers), where operator $E = G$ when $q(m) = m$, $r(m) = -m$ (see (1)).

The results in the Appendix show the existence of a sequence $\{s^n\}$, $n = 1,2,\ldots$, $s^n \uparrow s'$ when $n \uparrow \infty$, $0 \leqslant s^n \leqslant s' \leqslant m_o$ such that with $h = s^n r^n = E_h r^{n-1}$, $n \geqslant 1$ and with $h = s'$ $r' = E_h r'$ where $E_h = G_h$ when $G = E$. Therefore, it is clear that any $n \geqslant 1$ optimal for criteria e) has a threshold structure. If the control strategy is optimal for the time interval $\overline{0,n}$ then the threshold $h=s^n$, $n \geqslant 1$; if the time interval is unlimited, then the threshold is $h = s'$. Further, $r^n \uparrow r$ with $n \uparrow \infty$ and convergence is uniform with m for $m \geqslant 0$. Functions $r^n(m)$ and $r(m)$ are increasing and concave when $m \geqslant 0$. Since $0 \leqslant s^{n-1} \leqslant s^n \leqslant m_o$ and s^n are integers for all $n \geqslant 0$, there exists $n = n'$ such that with $n \geqslant n'$ $s^n = s'$. Therefore, control which is optimal for criterion e) for the time interval $\overline{0,n}$ has a threshold $h = s'$ for almost all n.

Let us state the problem of optimization for two criteria. As already shown, we wish to select a control strategy optimal for criteria d) and e). Any value may be selected for threshold h, $h \geqslant 0$ (h is integer). In an unlimited time interval, let control strategy with threshold h for criteria d) and e) correspond to functions $q_h(m)$ and $r_h(m)$, when $m \geqslant 0$ (m is the initial population count). Results presented in the Appendix show that the equations $q_h = D_h q_h$, $r_h = E_h r_h$ are applicable. For any $m \geqslant 1$, $q_h(m)$ and $r_h(m)$ are increasing functions of h when $0 \leqslant h \leqslant m_o$ and $0 \leqslant h \leqslant s'$, and they are decreasing functions of h when $h \geqslant m_o+1$ and $h \geqslant s'+1$, respectively. Thus, it is clear that the control strategy with threshold $h < s'$ or $h > m_o$ may be improved for two criteria, d) and e). Therefore, the sets for compromise control strategy corresponds with the threshold values h from the interval $h = \overline{s',m_o}$.

Normalization of criteria d) and e) is achieved by maximizing their values: $Q_h(m) = q_h(m)/q'(m)$, $R_h(m) = r_h(m)/r'(m)$, $m \geqslant 1$. It is clear, that when $m \to \infty$ $Q_h(m) \to 1, R_h(m) \to 1$.

The optimality principle used, called the maxmin principle (of uniformity), consists of the following. By selecting h, $s' \leqslant h \leqslant m_o$ the value $\min_{m \leqslant 1} \min (Q_h(m), R_h(m))$ is maximized. The value $h = h'$, which gives us

$$w = \max_{s' \leqslant h \leqslant m_o} \min_{m \leqslant 1} \min (Q_h(m), R_h(m)),$$

is optimal (it is easy to see that m achieves a minimum). If the compromise which we arrive at through the use of the principle of uniformity cannot be accepted as satisfactory, then the choice of h may be made from the whole interval $h = \overline{s',m_o}$.

APPENDIX

Let us describe the properties of

the operators G and G_h(see (1)).

First let us introduce the needed notation. Let M_1 (M_2) be a set of functions $f = f(m)$, $m = 0,1,2,\ldots$, nondecreasing (increasing) and concave for all m. We designate, as before, M as a set of functions $f=f(m)$, $m = 0,1,2,\ldots$, such that for each f there exists $g\in M_1$: $g(m)\geqslant 0$, $|f(m)| \leqslant g(m)$ for all m. It is clear that $M_2\subset M_1\subset M$. It is easy to show that G and G_h map M into itself. Further, we designate through M (m_1, m_2), a set of function f, $f\in M$, increasing and strictly concave at interval $m = \overline{m_1,m_2}$. Finally, we designate $M_i(m_1,m_2) = M_i \cap M(m_1,m_2), i=1,2.$ The following conditions will be considered fulfilled for functions g,r and v, introduced into expression for the operators G, G_h (see (1)): q M_1, $q(0) = 0$, $q(m) \not\equiv$ const; $r(m)\in M$, r(m) nonincreasing concave function of m, $r(0) = 0$; $v\in M, v(0)=0$, $v(m_o) = v_o$, $0\leqslant v(m)\leqslant v_o$ with $m\geqslant m_o+1$, $v\in M(0,m_o)$. Let $\|f\| = \sup_{m\geqslant 0}|f(m)|$.

The following statements are pertinent.

Theorem 1.

1.1. For $f\in M$ $\|Gf - q\|<\infty$, $\|G_hf - q\| <\infty$.

1.2. let $\overline{M} =\{f: f \;\; M, f(0) = 0\}$. G and G_h are contractions for M with modulus equal to $c=1-e^{-v_o}$

1.3. For $f\in M_1$, $f(m) \not\equiv$ const, there exists $h = s_f$, s_f integer, $0\leqslant s_f\leqslant m_o$ such that $Gf = G_hf$ and $s = s_f$ is minimized from s numbers, with which a maximum expression is attained $F(f,v(s)) + r(s)$, $s = 0,1,2,\ldots$ (see (1)); if $r(m) \equiv 0$, then $s_f = m_o$; further $Gf\in M_1(0,s_f)$ and if $q\in M_2$, then $Gf\in M_2(0,s_f)$.

1.4. For $f\in M_1$, $f(m) \not\equiv$ const, when $0\leqslant h\leqslant s_f$ $G_hf\in M_1(0,h)$ and if $q\in M_2$, then $G_hf\in M_2(0,h)$.

1.5. Let f, $g\in M_1$, $f(m)\geqslant g(m)$, $m = 0,1,2,\ldots$, $f(m) - g(m) \not\equiv$ const, $\Delta f(m)\geqslant \Delta g(m)$, $m = 1,2,\ldots$ (here and further we use the notation $\Delta f(m) = f(m) - f(m-1)$).

Then $Gf(m)> Gg(m)$, $G_hf(m)> G_hg(m)$ ($h\geqslant 1$), $\Delta Gf(m)\geqslant \Delta Gg(m)$, $\Delta G_hf(m)\geqslant \Delta G_hg(m)$, $m = 1,2,\ldots$, and $s_f\geqslant s_g$. For $m = \overline{1,s_g}$ $\Delta Gf(m)\leqslant\Delta Gg(m)$. From Theorem 1, it follows that operators G and G_h have in $\overline{M} = \{f:f\in M, f(0) = 0\}$ the unique fixed points: f', $f_h'\in M$, $f'(0) = f_h'(0) = 0, f'=Gf'$, $f_h' = G_hf_h'$. Let us examine iterative process $f^n = G f^{n-1}$, $f_h^n = G_hf_h^{n-1}$, $n\geqslant 1$, $f^o, f_h^o\in M$, $f^o(0) = f_h^o(0) = 0$. It is clear that $\|f^n - f'\| \to 0$, $\|f_h^n - f_h'\| \to 0$ when $n\to \infty$.

Theorem 2.

2.1. Let $f^o\in M_1$. If $q(m) \equiv r(m) \equiv 0$ (see (1)), then when $h = m_o$ $f^n = G_hf^{n-1}$, $n\geqslant 1$, and $f'(m) \equiv 0$.

2.2. Let $f^o = q$. Then a) - c):

a) $f^n \uparrow f'$, $n\uparrow\infty$ and $f^n(m)> f^{n-1}(m)$, $m\geqslant 1$, $n\geqslant 2$; if $q\in M_2$ then $f^n\in M_2$; $n\geqslant 0$, $f'\in M_2$;

b) there is a sequence of integers $\{s^n\}$, $n\geqslant 1$, such that $0\leqslant s^n\leqslant m_o$, $s^n\uparrow s'$, $n\uparrow\infty$ ($0\leqslant s'\leqslant m_o$), and when $h = s^n$ $f^n = G_hf^{n-1}$, when $h = s'$ $f' = G_hf'$ (adversely, we have n' : $s^n = s'$ when $n\geqslant n'$); if $r(m) \equiv 0$ then $s^n = m_o$ for all $n\geqslant 1$;

c) $f'\in M_1(0,s')$; if $q\in M_2$ then $f'\in M_2(0,s')$.

2.3. For operator G_h (h is integer, $h\geqslant 0$), we have d) - g):

d) function $f_h^o\in M_1$, $h = 0,1,\ldots$,may be selected so that when $0\leqslant h\leqslant s'$ $\Delta f_h^1(m)\geqslant \Delta f_h^o(m)\geqslant \Delta q(m)$ and $\Delta f_h^o(h) > \Delta q(h)$, and when $h\geqslant s'+ 1$ $\Delta f_h^1(m)\leqslant \Delta f_h^o(m)$ and $\Delta f_h^o(h) < \Delta q(h)$, $m = 1,2,\ldots$; then with $0\leqslant h\leqslant s'$ $f_h^n\uparrow f_h'$, $n\uparrow\infty$, $f_h^n(m) > f_h^{n-1}(m)$, $m\geqslant 1$, $n\geqslant 2$ and $f_h^n\in M_1(0,h)$, $n\geqslant 1$, $f_h'\in M_1(0,h)$ (if $q\in M_2$ then f_h^n,

$f'_h \in M_1(0,h)$);

e) if $0 \leqslant u < w \leqslant s'$ ($s' \geqslant 1$, u, w are integers) and $f_u^o = f'_w$ (here $f'_w = G_w f'_w$) then $f_u^1(m) \leqslant f_u^o(m)$, $m \geqslant 1$, and $f_u^1(w) < f_u^o(w)$; if $s' < u < w$ and $f_u^o = f'_w$ then $f_u^1(m) \geqslant f_u^o(m)$, $m \geqslant 1$ and $f_u^1(w) > f_u^o(w)$;

g) with $0 \leqslant h \leqslant s'$, $m \geqslant 0$ $f_h(m)$ increasing function of h; with $h \geqslant s' + 1$, $m \geqslant 0$ $f_h(m)$ decreasing function of h.

REFERENCES

1. Feller, W. Die Grundlagen der Volterraschen Theorie des Kampfes ums Dasein in wahrscheinlichkeintstheoretischen Benhandlung. Acta Biotheoretica, 5 (1933).

2. Karlin, S. A first course in stochastic processes. Academic Press, New-York and London, 1968.

3. Karev, G.P. Degeneration probability in some population models. Kybernetic Problems, 25 (1972).

4. Germeyer, Yu.B. Introduction to operations research theory. "Nauka", Moskow, 1971.

5. Dynkin, E.B., Yushkevitch A.A. Control Markov processes and their applications. "Nauka", Moskow, 1975.

COMPUTER SIMULATION OF ECONOMY MANAGEMENT SYSTEMS

V.V. Tokarev, Yu. M. Fatkin

Institute of Control Sciences, Moscow, USSR

ABSTRACT

The paper discusses the principles underlying dynamic computer simulation of economy management and of the economy itself. Two simulation packages, "Economy" and "Demand-Production", are described and results of numerical experiments are given.

1. SIMULATION PRINCIPLES

To use simulation in development of control systems was an idea that originated and was initially widely applied in technology. Now inroads are made into a new field, economy management systems. Several special-purpose versions of this approach are now in existence.

One version is running one-shot management decisions (management programs), developed heuristically, on a detailed computer model of an economy. It is an everyday tool for forecasting the implications of decisions.

The other version is business games intended for training of executives and for studying the behavioural characteristics of managers in conflict or race situations.

We will concentrate on development of optimal planning and economy management systems in a planned national economy. In terms of control engineering the situation can be described as follows.

The process may be in a number of feasible states and be subjected to sets of control actions and disturbances; the performance can be described in terms of attaining the control objective. If the knowledge of the process (including the disturbances) were complete, the control be programmed in the sense that control actions could be computed in advance as time functions.

The control system is to lead to the control objective under incomplete knowledge of the process. The control system contains a unit for measuring the current process state and a generator of control actions. The control actions are generated on the knowledge of a certain process model. The model, however, contains only the main features of the process description.

Simulation is supposed to determine in advance the performance of the control system, or to determine whether the process model and the algorithm for generating the control actions are workable.

The control system simulation procedure takes several steps. A formalized description of the process and the control system is developed as computer programs. The process is represented by a certain functioning operator $\mathfrak{F}$ which is a rule that determines the current state of the process $x(t)$, on the knowledge of the control action $u(t)$, the initial state x_0 and time t :

$$x(t) = \mathcal{F}(u, x_0, t). \quad (1)$$

That rule can, for instance, be a procedure for solving the Cauchy problem for a system of common differential equations:

$$\dot{x} = f(x, u, t),\ x(0) = x_0. \quad (2)$$

The control objective and performance indices are formalized as conditions for the process phase coordinate vector to belong to a certain set $X(t)$ specified as a time function and a set of functionals J, respectively.

The control system is represented as a control operator $\mathcal{U}$ which determines the control action $u(t)$ on the knowledge of the observed state $x(t)$ of the plant for the specified control objective X :

$$u(t) = \mathcal{U}(x, X). \quad (3)$$

A certain process modes $\tilde{\mathcal{F}}$ (simpler than $\mathcal{F}$) and a certain control performance index $\tilde{J}$ are used. That rule can, for instance, be implemented as a procedure for solving the variational problem:

$$\begin{aligned} & u(t) = \arg \underset{u}{\mathrm{extr}}\ \tilde{J}(\tilde{x}, u) \text{ at:} \\ & \dot{\tilde{x}} = \tilde{f}(\tilde{x}, u, t),\ \tilde{x}(t_0) = x(t_0), \\ & \tilde{x}(t) \in X(t),\ u(t) \in \tilde{U}(\tilde{x}, t) \text{ at } t \in (t_0, T). \end{aligned} \quad (4)$$

Then a closed loop of the process model $\mathcal{F}$ and a control system model $\mathcal{U}$ is made (see Fig. 1).

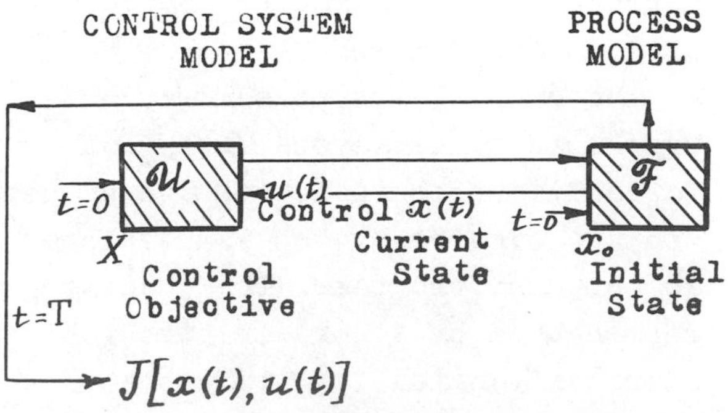

Fig.1. Control System Simulation

The operation of the control system is tested in dynamics. Comparative characteristics can be obtained by testing different control systems in the same plant. To have a relatively full picture, these tests should be staged on a sufficiently representative set of control objectives. Note that for economic systems such a program of tests cannot be carried out in field experiments.

A natural question would be, why not complete the control system with a process model as detailed as $\mathcal{F}$ used for process simulation. If this were done there would be no need in process simulation. At least two circumstances prevent this: (a) the model $\mathcal{F}$ simulates, in particular, the random disturbances which will never be known in advance in selection of the control function: (b) the maximal model dimensional that could be used in today's computers for selection of the control function (e.g. by solving the variational problem (4)) is at least one order of magnitude smaller than the maximal dimension of the model that could be used in the same computers for describing the process behaviour with a specified control function (e.g. by solving the Cauchy problem (2)).

Today's computers can, for instance, integrate, within reasonable time, systems of common differential equations of order $10^2 - 10^3$. This leads to high degree of similarity between the process model $\mathcal{F}$ and the actual plant, but the problem remains unresolved. The latter fact is especially important for economic processes. There are people involved whose behaviour is not easy to describe mathematically. Therefore the control systems should be tested on a set of process models rather than on one model. That set should be such that the characteristics of the actual process be completely covered. Then the performance of the control system can be calculated, for instance, as a guaranteed estimate of functionals for that set of models.

2. THE "ECONOMY" SIMULATING PACKAGE

The package is intended for debugging and obtaining the comparative characteristics of multi-level planning systems and economic regulating mechanisms for a planned national economy. In developing the first stage of the package three questions were posed: (a) Could the packages function automatically as a closed loop system including the process and the control system? (b) How do the ( ) many levels of the control system, inevitable with the high dimensionality of economic problems effect the control performance? (c) How does the inaccuracy in the knowledge of human behavioural characteristics in planning affect the final results of process functioning?

The outline of the simulating package fits the general of Fig. 1 and is shown in more detail in Fig.2. The outline includes units of five types: population functioning $\mathcal{F}_{\pi}$; industry functioning $\mathcal{F}_{\nu}$ ($\nu = 1,\ldots,N$); upper level management $\mathcal{U}_0$; management of final consumption at the lower level $\mathcal{U}_{\pi}$; management of industry at the lower level $\mathcal{U}_{\nu}$ ($\nu = 1,\ldots,N$).

Detailed description of all units involved in the basis version of the package is to be found in (Ref. 1) and one version of the planning system is described in (Ref. 2).

A series of numerical experiments was conducted where an aggregated inter-sectoral model of an economy (Ref. 3) was used. The sectors were divided between two industry functioning units, three sectors in each. The prices of all products were fixed, all random disturbances were assumed zero.

Of the numerous results the three most significant items will be described.

1°. The experiments have shown the feasibility of a closed-loop model of a planned economy. All the experiments stopped once the specified level of capacities was achieved; there were no unexpected stoppages. The yearly stretch of the system's life time amounted to 10 minutes of ICL-4-70 computer time. The maximal path length was five years, or 60 clocking pulses. If the desired final vector of capacities goes approximately as the turnpike does then all industries develop uniformly at about 10% annual growth. The wages grow at the same rate and the stock of cash among the population due to lack of desired products increases annually by an average of 1% of the annual wage. We have now first analytical results on stability of models of a planned economy to various disturbances (Ref.4).

2°. The two-level management system akin to the actual Soviet management system has displayed a performance practically equal to that of an ideal one-level system. There were two planning iterations at the lower level; the plan was recomputed once in a quarter (three clocking pulses) at the lower level and once a year (12 clocking pulses) at the upper level. The deflections of the actual path from the upper level plan amounted to mere 1% in capacities, 1% in supplies to other industries, $\leq$ 3.5% in supplies to the consumer and $\leq$ 3%

in wages. Further increase of the number of iterations and recomputation rate did not result in noticeable improvements.

3°. The simulating package appeared to be a convenient tool for debugging the management systems. Thus two amendments were introduced into the planning system that significantly improved the management performance. By recognizing the existence of bonus payments in upper level planning the amount of cash remaining unused by the population was reduced six-fold and by changing the zero approximation in planning iterations of the lower level the deflections from the plan were reduced approximately three-fold.

3. THE "SUPPLY-PRODUCTION" SIMULATING PACKAGE

In simulating a complex economic system the problem of selecting an optimal policy can be solved in approximate terms. This is exactly the purpose of the "Supply-Production" package which is an illustration of the simulation using the technique described in Section 1 for solving complex optimal control problems.

Let us illustrate this proposition with the problem of consumer demand final product manufacture analysis. The phase variables are: x - stocks of products; S - stocks of cash with the consumers; V - enterprises where the products are manufactured. The control functions u are: c - prices of products; v - the amount of products manufactured per time unit; $\dot{V}$ - rates of industrial expansion. There trade offs of cash stocks, products and prices are specified as constraints Ω incorporating the demand functions. In a general form the optimization problem can be stated as

$$J[x(T), S(T)] \Rightarrow extr,$$
$$\dot{x} = f^x(x,S,u),\ \dot{S} = f^S(x,S,u),\ \dot{V} = f^V(u), \qquad (5)$$
$$\Omega(x,S,u) \le 0,\ t \in [0,T],$$

where the boundary conditions are incorporated into Ω ; $[0,T]$ - the time interval within which the problem is studied; J - the performance function which is the effectiveness criterion whose optimization is the objective of simulation. Were the variational problem (5) analyzable there would be no need in additional simulation of the process. But attempts at finding $u_{opt}(t)$ from solution of the system (5) often even in simple ("low-dimension") cases because of a number of reasons such as discontinuity of the right-hand parts of differential equations, simultaneous constaints on phase coordinates and contrao functions, etc.

Let us assume that the differential equations and the constraints in (5) permit each time the solution of the Cauchy problem if the control function $u(t)$ is specified. Consequently, eliminating $J \Rightarrow$ extre we obtain from (5) a simulation model of the economic problem of "Demand-Production" for consumer goods.

The number of equations in the model that can be solved simultaneously on an ICL-4-70 computer is estimated (Ref. 5) as about 10^3. Under these circumstances for one man or even a group to obtain the best decision on the process, the amounts to be produced and industry expansion seems out of the question.

To handle this situation reduce the initial problem to a new one with special rules. Then we have

$$\tilde{J}[\tilde{x}(T), \tilde{S}(T)] \Rightarrow extr,$$
$$\dot{\tilde{x}} = \tilde{f}^x(\tilde{x},\tilde{S},\tilde{u}),\ \dot{\tilde{S}} = \tilde{f}^S(\tilde{x},\tilde{S},\tilde{u}),\ \dot{\tilde{V}} = \tilde{f}^V(\tilde{u}),$$
$$\tilde{\Omega}(\tilde{x},\tilde{S},\tilde{u}) \le 0,\ t \in [t_0, T]. \qquad (6)$$

The notation is understandable from (5). The performance criterion $\tilde{J}$ corresponds to J in (5). Their association can be different; moreover, the exact formalization of the functional J may be unknown therefore the correspondence may be purely intuitive.

One important requirement to the problem (6) is the possibility of obtaining a solution $u_{opt}(t) = \arg \operatorname{extr} \tilde{J}(\tilde{u})$. This requirement may be met, for instance, if the reduction rule includes the aggregation of the variables in the initial problem. Then to obtain $u(t)$ one should desaggregate $\tilde{u}_{opt}(t)$. Substituting the resultant $u(t)$ into (5) we obtain, from solution of the Cauchy problem, the value of the performance function $J[x(T), S(T)]$ and $x(t)$, $S(t)$, $V(t)$ which can be regarded as the sample and then compute $\tilde{x}_{opt}$, $\tilde{S}(t)$, $\tilde{V}(t)$. Their difference from the precomputed $\tilde{x}_{opt}(t), \tilde{S}_{opt}(t), \tilde{V}_{opt}(t)$ can be regarded as misalignment. If the misalignment exceeds a specified value, the optimization problem (6) can be resolved, etc.

The rules for reduction of (5) into (6), desaggregation of $\tilde{u}_{opt}(t)$ into $u(t)$, determination of misalignment etc. form a set P. If the rule $\mathcal{P}$ is selected from P, then the monitoring functional J of the problem has been found unambiguously. It is obvious that from a specified set one can, generally speaking, find

$$\mathcal{P}_{opt} = \arg \operatorname*{extr}_{\mathcal{P} \in P} J(\mathcal{P}). \qquad (7)$$

To solve (7), the problems (5) and (6) have to be solved repeatedly, therefore the best result could be comparison of a limited amount of rules $\mathcal{P}$. It would be natural to select the rules $\mathcal{P}$ simular to the practical rules

In developing the algorithm for solution of the above problem a multi-level description of the demand (consumers) and products was introduced with different classes of consumers and categories of products that were, in their turn, divided into types. Thus in equations (5) a hierarchical structure was introduced (Ref.6). On the other hand, the categories of products may be associated with the existing industries. In other words, decomposition into categories (components of x) make it possible to divide the components of V into categories). Prices of consumer goods can be changed in a centralized fashion and the amounts manufacture, in each industry with due regard for the constraints. Numerical solution of the problem with the use of model information has led to the relation of the total product stocks $x(t)$ and of cash $S(t)$ with the population. For comparison the case was considered where the problem (6) was not solved and the zero path $\tilde{x}(t) \equiv 0, \tilde{S}(t) \equiv 0 \; (t \in [t_0, T])$ was "tracked" instead.

Despite the approximate nature of the information used in the computation a conclusion can be made that there is a zone where the solution is stable (the stocks tend to zero) and that the solution of the optimization problem can be effectively used. This effect may be expected to increase with the dimensionality of the problem.

REFERENCES

(1) A.N. Dyukalov, Yu.N. Ivanov, V.V. Tokarev, Essentials of computer simulation in economic management systems. I,II, Automatica i Telemechanika, No.12, 76 (1973), No.1, 93 (1974); Engl.

transl.- Automation and Remote Control 34, 1927 (1974); 35,84 (1974).

(2) A.N. Dyukalov, Yu.N. Ivanov, V.V. Tokarev, Control theory and economic systems. II, Avtomatika i Telemechanika, No.6,69 (1974); Engl. transl.- Automation and Remote Control, 35, No.6, Part 1 (November, 1974).

(3) Yu.P. Ivanilov, A.A. Petrov, Computation of an optimal plan for production expansion using a dynamic -model. In Control Engineering at the Service of Communism, vol.6, Energya, Moscow (1971) - in Russian.

(4) I.P. Boglaev, On stability of a model of a planned economy, Avtomatica i telemechanika, No.9, 80 (1975); Engl. transl.- Automation and Remote Control, 36, 1454 (1975).

(5) L.N. Bleskina, G.N. Dmitrieva, Dubovsky S.V., V.A. Leont'ev, S. Lukasik, A.A. Makarov, Yu.M. Fatkin, Yu.A. Shalaev, Hierarchical limitative demand-production model, VI IFAC Congr., Boston, 1975.

(6) Yu.M. Fatkin, Optimal control in dynamic systems described by differential equations of a hierarhical structure, Avtomatika i telemechanika, No.10, 169 (1973); Engl. transl.- Automation and Remote Control, 34, 1685 (1973).

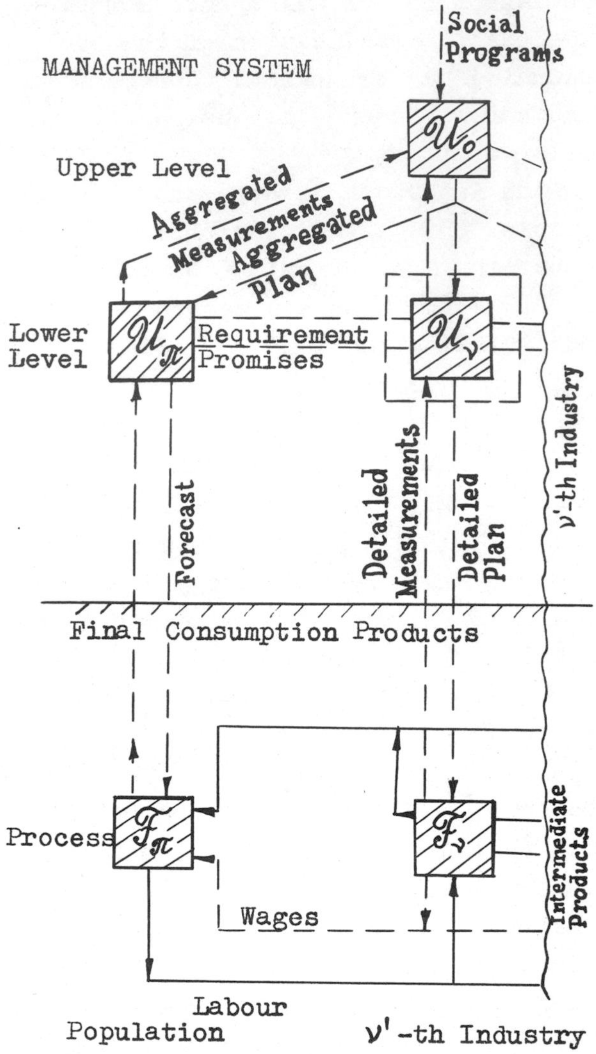

Fig. 2. Simulating Package "Economy"

A SIMULATION MODEL ON URBAN LAND USE IN A METROPOLITAN AREA—WITH ENVIRONMENTAL REFLECTIONS

A. Ando, K. Amano and M. Kashiwadani

Department of Transportation Engineering, Kyoto University, Kyoto, Japan

ABSTRACT

The purpose of this study is to develop a long-run and over-all simulation model which makes it possible to forecast the spatial transformation of each activity in a metropolitan area under a given set of environmental standards. As the major output of the model, the transition of quantities of residential, industrial, and other urban facilities is obtained in each subdivided district in the object region. Quantities of pollutants and pollution eliminating facilities required are also obtained at the same time.

To improve applicability of the model, it is composed as a recursive dynamic model, considering both stock and flow aspects of various activities. Since the model treats many subdivided districts as well as many sectors of activities, it should be a large-scale one. Concepts of hierarchical structure are introduced into the model for assuring its operationability.

INTRODUCTION

Various kinds of environmental standards have been established in order to maintain the life and natural environment required in urban areas. Since environmental and other urban problems of today have appeared as the results of complicated interactions of various urban activities, a precise description of these connections becomes necessary for urban analyses. As well as these interactions among activities, an inter-regional prospect should also be considered, since effects of each individual activity do not end in a restricted territory such as a city, but spread over the border.

Judging from this viewpoint, a practical urban analysis scheme should pay respects to inter-sectoral and inter-regional relations among activities explicitly, and which should be able to focus on each subdivided districts in addition to the whole object region. To develop such a global metropolitan simulation system is the purpose of this study.

OUTLINE OF THE MODEL

The model which is applicable to long-run forecasts must not fail to consider dynamic aspects of activities. In this study, the total system is composed as a recursive dynamic model, which consists of three sub-models. The first one is called "Activity sub-model", which is to analyze the flow aspects of activities. The second one: "Location sub-model" is to analyze the stock aspects of them. As shown in Fig. 1, these two sub-models are executed by turns under the control of the third one: "Control sub-model", which determines the quantitative frame for the whole object region performing adjustments to the outer-object area.

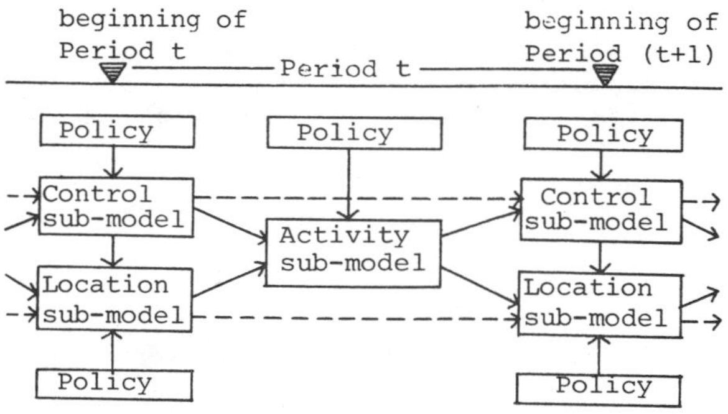

Fig. 1. The outline of the recursive simulation model.

CLASSIFICATION OF ACTIVITIES

To analyze various activities indiscriminately for many subdivided districts would crucially lose operationability which is required in such a practical model. It might be said that to classify these activities into a few groups in accordance with their characteristics and to handle each group adequately are reasonable, at least from the viewpoint of operationability. And in this sense, too, it might be useful to classify activities in terms of market ranges where their supplies meet their demands, as Christaller (1) did.

The break down of the activities in the larger number of levels would lead the analysis to the more exact one. However, it might not be desirable, since it makes operationability decrease. This is particularly the case with such a model that treats a macroscopic description of a metropolitan area. The minimal unit of space handled in the model should be small enough to be distinguished by its properties, while the largest one corresponds to the object region as a whole. It is proper to regard each prefecture, which possesses rather closed function, as the medium unit for data bases as well. The defined hierarchy is of three levels as shown in Fig. 2.

a) Region: the largest unit of space, i.e. the whole object region.
b) Locale: the medium unit supposing each prefecture.
c) District: the smallest unit consists of several cities, wards, towns and/or villages.

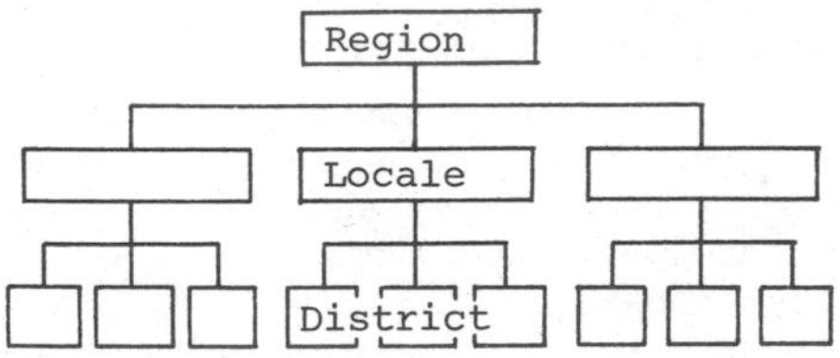

Fig. 2. Hierarchy of regions.

Corresponding to the regional hierarchy, all activities are classified into three levels.

a) Regional activities: activities whose products meet their demands in the whole object region or even a wider area.
b) Local activities: activities whose products balance in each Locale.
c) District activities: daily activities whose products are consumed in respective Districts.

Products of these levels of activities are called R-goods, L-goods, and D-goods respectively. It is impossible to consider that actual activities are completely separable into three groups. Nevertheless, the hierarchical structure of urban activities can be clarified in this way. The formulations are made to be in conformity with this concept. For instance, Leontief's Balanced Input-Output Analysis Model (2) is employed as the basic method in Activity sub-model.

In this study, all activities are classified into 31 sectors as shown in Table.

GENERAL FRAMEWORK OF THE MODEL

The outlines of respective sub-models are summarized as follows.

Control Sub-model

This sub-model is to estimate various characteristics of economy held in the object region during each time period. Three sectors are contained.

Population and employee sector. Population and numbers of employees of respective sectors are estimated for the object region.

Final demand sector. Regional final demands are estimated for each final demand item.

Income sector. Net products of respective activities and personal incomes are calculated as the results of activities held in the particular period. This sector is executed at the end of each period, and gives basic data for the estimations of the next period.

Location Sub-model

Regional population, employees, capital formations, etc. are distributed to each District through this sub-model, which consists of the following sectors.

Land value sector. This sector forecasts the land value of the present period for each District.

Demolition sector. Vacant land and annexed relocation demands derived from usage conversion or urban renewal are estimated in each District.

Industrial sector. Regional employees and industrial capital formations are distributed to each District.

Table The Classification of Activities

Regional activities

01	Agriculture, forestory, and fishery products
02	Mining
03	Foods and drinks
04	Textile products
05	Wooden products, pulp, and paper articles
06	Printing and publishing
07	Chemicals
08	Metal products and machinery
09	Miscellaneous industrial products
10	Electric power and gas supply
11	Non-residential building construction
12	Far-flung transportation
13	Wholesale trade
14	Public construction of R-level
15	Community services of R-level
16	Government service of R-level
17	Clerical business

Local activities

18	Water supply and sanitary services
19	Residential building construction
20	Urban transportation
21	Communication
22	Financial, insurance, and real estate business
23	Business services
24	Recreation services
25	Public construction of L-level
26	Community services of L-level
27	Government service of L-level

District activities

28	Retail trade and personal services
29	Public construction of D-level
30	Community services of D-level
31	Government service of D-level

Residential sector. Increases of employees obtained in places of work from Industrial sector are distributed to places of residence. Population of each District is also obtained.

Adjustment sector. This sector calculates quantities of land required from both Industrial and Residential sectors. In Districts where land constraints are violated, it performs adjustments among respective location demands. Then the land use structures of the present period are forecasted.

Activity Sub-model

Upon the employees and industrial assets obtained from Location sub-model, Activity sub-model is to estimate respective activity levels in each District. Corresponding to the hierarchy of activities, this sub-model is composed as a three-level system called "3-level Input-Output Analysis", and which consists of Input-Output Analyses of R-, L-, and D-level. Extensions to include some investigations on environmental reflections and trading patterns can be made.

Combining these three sub-models organically, the simulation is to be executed. Figure 3 shows the general flows of the simulation in each time period.

CONTROL SUB-MODEL

The major outputs of this sub-model are summarized in Fig. 4. From results of previous periods, regional population and numbers of employees are estimated at the beginning of each period. Then respective final demand items on which economic activities are held are estimated. Finally, net products and personal incomes are calculated for each level of regions at the end of that period, and these values are to be used as the major inputs to this sub-model of the following period.

Most formulations are based on exogenously given standard values and to estimate derivations from them. Since the purpose of this model is to analyze relative differences among Districts within the Region, the absolute values are not necessarily required. In this case, regional standard values can be obtained from other adequate econometric models.

When the basic formulation of y is given as

$$y = f(x_1, x_2, \ldots x_n) \qquad (1)$$

and a point $(x_1, \ldots x_n, y)$ exists in the neighborhood of the point $(x_1^\circ, \ldots x_n^\circ, y^\circ)$, y can be expanded.

$$y = y^\circ + (x_1 - x_1^\circ)\frac{\partial f(x_1^\circ \cdots x_n^\circ)}{\partial x_1} + (x_n - x_n^\circ)\frac{\partial f(x_1^\circ \cdots x_n^\circ)}{\partial x_n} + O(\Delta^2) \qquad (2)$$

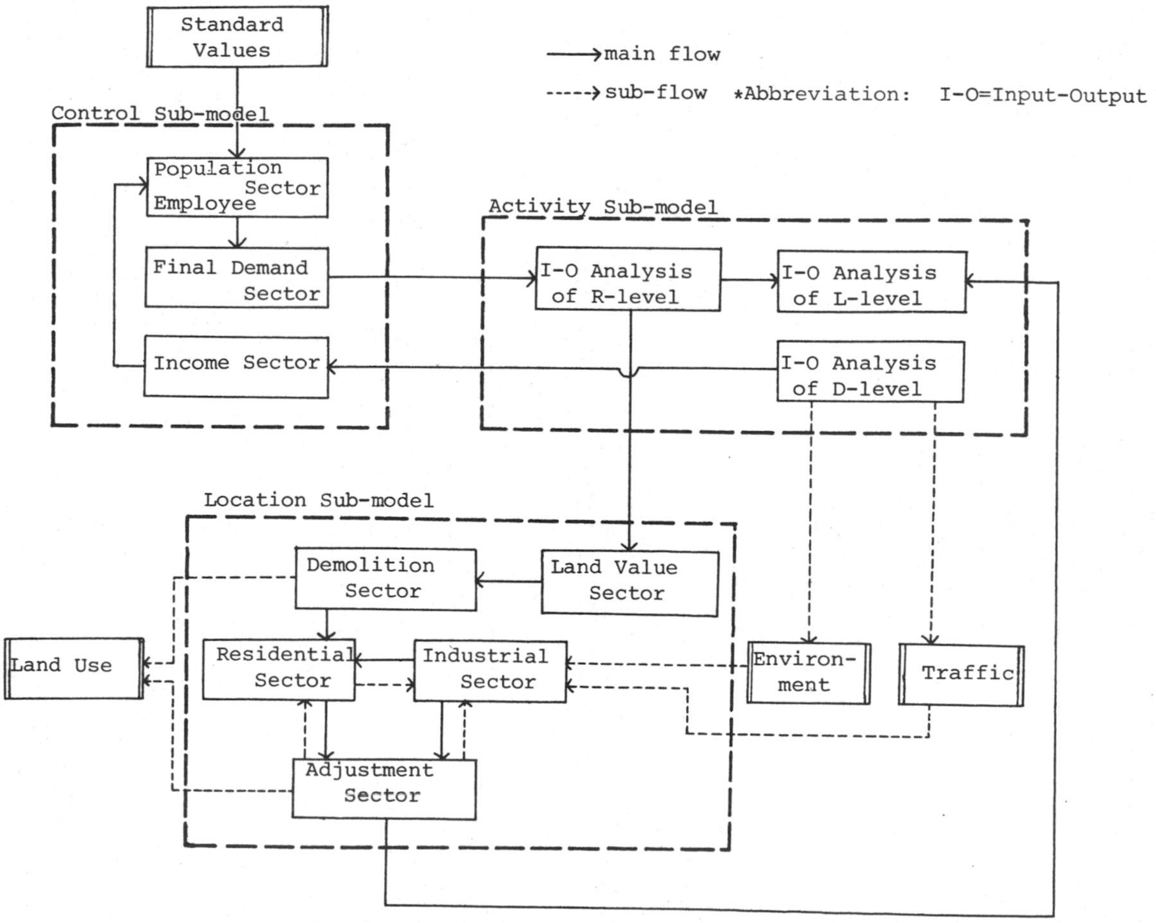

Fig. 3. The general flow-chart of the model.

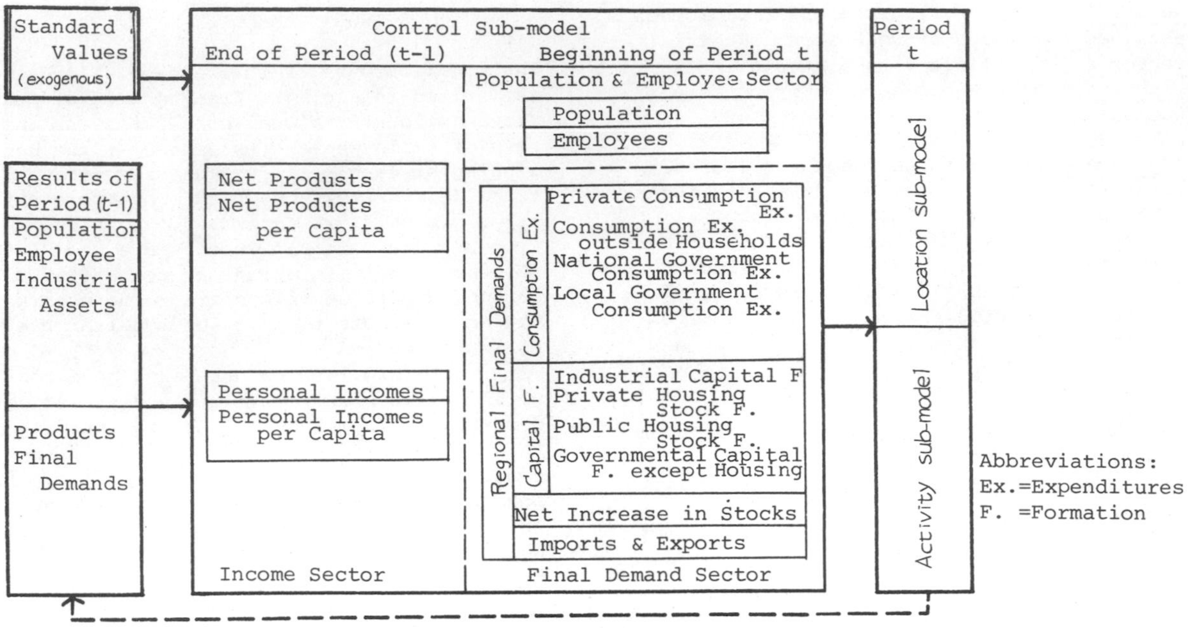

Fig. 4. The outline of Control sub-model.

Supposing a case where y is given as a linear function:

$$y = a_0 + a_1x_1 + \ldots + a_nx_n \qquad (1')$$

eq.(2) can be rewritten ignoring $O(\Delta^2)$ as

$$y = y^\circ + a_1(x_1 - x_1^\circ) + \ldots + a_n(x_n - x_n^\circ) \qquad (2')$$

When $(x_1^\circ, \ldots x_n^\circ, y^\circ)$ is known as a set of standard values, to estimate y with this information would be more accurate than to estimate it directly.

For example, national government consumption expenditures; C3 and local ones; C4 are estimated with parameters $\varphi..$ by

$$\left.\begin{array}{l} C3(t) = C3^\circ(t) + \varphi_{31}(YA(t-1) - YA^\circ(t-1)) + \varphi_{32}(N(t-1) - N^\circ(t-1)) \\ C4(t) = C4^\circ(t) + \varphi_{41}(YA(t-1) - YA^\circ(t-1)) + \varphi_{42}(N(t-1) - N^\circ(t-1)) \end{array}\right\} (3)$$

where YA means regional net products, N is regional population, and t indicates time period.

LOCATION SUB-MODEL

This sub-model is to estimate quantities of stocks (i.e. land, industrial assets, employees, population, etc.) in each District. In most of activities, changes in stocks occurred in the present period are estimated first. Quantities of stocks are obtained from adding those changes to quantities in the previous period. Since total changes in the Region are given by Control sub-model, the most crucial problem is how to distribute them to each District.

The outline of Location sub-model is shown in Fig. 5. The subjects to be distributed are "location demands" which consist of regional capital formations; $\Delta K_i(t)$, numbers of employees; $E_i(t)$, population; $N(t)$, etc. obtained from Control sub-model. Distributions are performed with the results of Location and Activity sub-models in previous periods, and should satisfy constraints of land and pollutants in all Districts.

Fundamental Formulations for Distributions

Industrial sector is one of the most important part in this sub-model. The basic formulation of stock distributions is deduced as follows.

When the quantity of stocks in locale ℓ in Period t; $S^\ell(t)$ is given as a function of informations obtained from analyses of Period (t-1) or before:

$$S^\ell(t) = f^\ell(t-1) \qquad (4)$$

regional quantity is distributed to each Locale as

$$S^\ell(t) = \frac{f^\ell(t-1)}{\sum_\ell f^\ell(t-1)} \cdot \sum_\ell S^\ell(t) \qquad (5)$$

Taking backward difference of eq.(5), the distribution rate of regional changes in stocks; $\sum_\ell \Delta S^\ell(t)$ is deduced.

$$\frac{\Delta S^\ell(t)}{\sum_\ell \Delta S^\ell(t)} = \frac{f^\ell(t-1)}{\sum_\ell f^\ell(t-1)} + \left(\frac{f^\ell(t-1)}{\sum_\ell f^\ell(t-1)} - \frac{f^\ell(t-2)}{\sum_\ell f^\ell(t-2)}\right)\frac{\sum_\ell S^\ell(t)}{\sum_\ell \Delta S^\ell(t)} \qquad (6)$$

The results of distributions by eq.(6) permits coexistence of Locales where quantities of stocks increase or decrease. When quantities of stocks can be sufficiently explained by eq.(4), the results are supposed to be more stable in a long-term than formulating changes directly. (However, eq.(6) is invalid when $\sum_\ell \Delta S^\ell(t) = 0$.)

Distributions are made in two stages, i.e. distributions from Region to each Locale and from Locale to each District included in the particular Locale. They are called local and district distributions respectively. In this case, since results of local distributions, act as control totals for district distributions, the stability of district distributions would be improved. In addition, in a practical sense, it would be easier to obtain certified data in the prefecture basis than in the city or county basis.

Corresponding to the hierarchy of activities, the following premises are adopted.

a) Since demands for D-goods are supplied from respective Districts, district activities should be located within Districts where demands exist without selection.

b) Demands for L-goods are supplied from respective Locales. Then there is no selectability of location in local distributions. In district distributions, however, selectability would not be excluded, and all Districts within that Locale should be regarded.

c) Regional activities can be located in all Districts. Selectability would not be excluded both in local and district distributions.

Therefore, formulations of local and district distributions may be different even in the same activity, and two-stage distributions would be suitable to the hierarchy of activities.

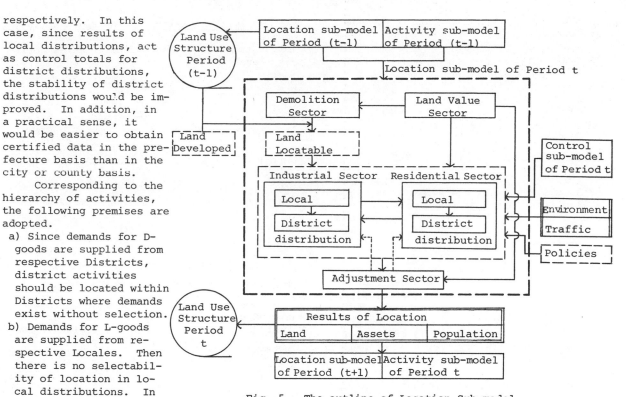

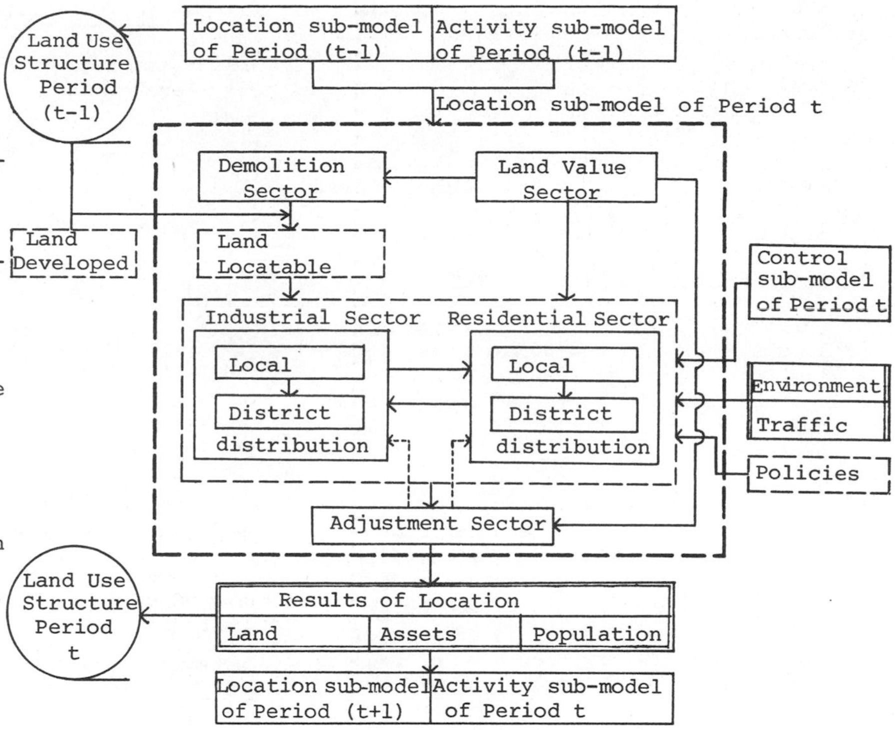

Fig. 5. The outline of Location Sub-model.

Industrial Sector

This sector is divided into three parts. The first one is to distribute capital formations of manufacturing industries, and the second one is to distribute numbers of employees of activities belonging to the tertiary industry. The third one aims at agricultural, mining, and construction activities. This part is executed after all other activities including residential ones have been located.

In manufacturing industry, environmental aspects should be considered. In this study, it is assumed that location can be made only in Districts where environmental standard of pollutant p; P_p^d is not violated in the flow analysis of the previous period. The set of locatable Districts is defined for activities with $a_{pj}>0$ as

$$\mathcal{Q}_p^{\ell}(t) = \left\{ d\in\ell \mid Y_p^d(t-1)<P_p^d \right\} \tag{7}$$

where $Y_p^d(t-1)$ is the quantity of pollutant p discharged in Period (t-1) and a_{pj} is the polluting coefficient of sector j. In case regarding plural pollutants, the set:

$$\mathcal{Q}^{\ell}(t) = \bigcap_p \mathcal{Q}_p^{\ell}(t) \tag{8}$$

would be considered. Moreover, if $\mathcal{Q}^{\ell}(t) = \phi$, Locale ℓ need not be regarded in local distributions. (Only the set: $\mathcal{L}(t)=\{\ell \mid \mathcal{Q}^{\ell}(t)\neq\phi\}$ should be considered.)

When the distribution rate of regional capital formations; $\kappa_i^{\ell}(t)$ is estimated, local capital formations; $\Delta K_i^{\ell}(t)$ is obtained.

$$\Delta K_i^{\ell}(t) = \kappa_i^{\ell}(t)(\Delta K_i(t)-\Delta KP_i(t))+\Delta KP_i^{\ell}(t) \tag{9}$$

where $\Delta KP_i^{\ell}(t)$ is politically predetermined formations. For district capital formations; $\Delta K_i^d(t)$ obtained from district distributions similarly as local ones, the quantities of land required are calculated by Adjustment sector. If land constraints are violated, some necessary adjustments are performed. Consequently, district industrial assets are given by

$$K_i^d(t) = (1-\rho_i)(K_i^d(t-1)-\nabla K_i^d(t))+\Delta K_i^d(t) \tag{10}$$

where ρ_i is the rate of depreciation and $\nabla K_i^d(t)$ is the quantity of assets eliminated in Demolition sector.

Tertiary industries are divided into 6 types, and the numbers of employees are distributed regarding the hierarchy of activities.

In this article, Industrial sector was taken as an example, and where environment is described as the degree of pollution especially in the manufacturing industries. However, concerning residential activities, other environmental measures, e.g. population density, ought to be regarded.

ACTIVITY SUB-MODEL

This sub-model is to analyze the flow aspects of activities and based on the 3-level Input-Output Analysis Model.

3-level Input-Output Analysis Model

The purpose of this model is to obtain products or activity levels in each District from regional final demands estimated in Control sub-model. The methodology is summarized in Fig. 6. (For convenience' sake, "Input-Output" will be abbreviated as "I-O" hereafter.)

Initially, regional products are obtained from given final demands through "I-O Analysis of R-level". After dividing regional outputs of R-goods into each Locale, local outputs of L- and D-goods are obtained through "I-O Analysis of L-level". In the same way, district outputs of D-goods are obtained through "I-O Analysis of D-level".

The fundamental assumptions of the model are described as follows.

Assumption 1 Hierarchy of activities are defined as three levels.

Assumption 2 Each good is produced by only one activity. This means that activities and goods are in one-to-one correspondence.

Assumption 3 Input coefficients in each Locale and District can be identified, which also coincide with regional ones.

Assumption 4 Trading is competitive, i.e. goods are never identified by the places of production.

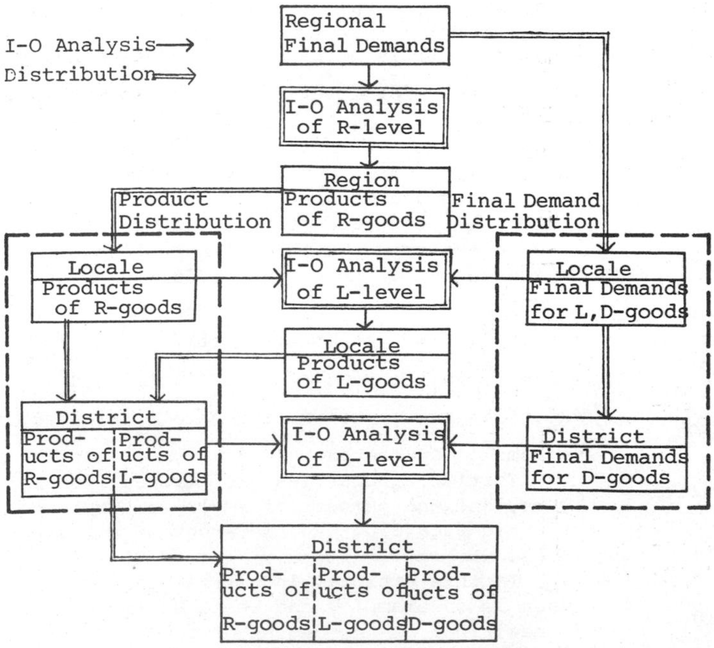

Fig. 6. 3-level I-O Analysis Model.

I-O analysis of R-level. The regional input coefficient matrix is divided into 9 minor matrices corresponding to three activity levels.

$$A = (a_{ij}) = \begin{pmatrix} A_{RR} & A_{RL} & A_{RD} \\ A_{LR} & A_{LL} & A_{LD} \\ A_{DR} & A_{DL} & A_{DD} \end{pmatrix} \qquad (11)$$

The balance equation for the whole region is

$$\begin{pmatrix} X_R \\ X_L \\ X_D \end{pmatrix} = \begin{pmatrix} A_{RR} & A_{RL} & A_{RD} \\ A_{LR} & A_{LL} & A_{LD} \\ A_{DR} & A_{DL} & A_{DD} \end{pmatrix} \begin{pmatrix} X_R \\ X_L \\ X_D \end{pmatrix} + \begin{pmatrix} \hat{Y}_R + J_R + F_R - M_R \\ \hat{Y}_L + J_L \\ \hat{Y}_D + J_D \end{pmatrix} \qquad (12)$$

where X is the regional output vector, $\hat{Y}$, the net regional final demand vector, J, the net increase vector in stocks, $F(M)$, the export vector to (import vector from) the outer-object area, with suffixes R, L, D which indicate levels of activity. Besides F_L, M_L, F_D, and M_D are fixed to 0 for Assumption 1.

For specified values assigned for the second term in the right hand together with unit matrices I_R, I_L, and I_D, regional products are obtained.

$$\begin{pmatrix} X_R \\ X_L \\ X_D \end{pmatrix} = \begin{pmatrix} I_R - A_{RR} & -A_{RL} & -A_{RD} \\ -A_{LR} & I_L - A_{LL} & -A_{LD} \\ -A_{DR} & -A_{DL} & I_D - A_{DD} \end{pmatrix}^{-1} \begin{pmatrix} \hat{Y}_R + J_R + F_R - M_R \\ \hat{Y}_L + J_L \\ \hat{Y}_D + J_D \end{pmatrix} \qquad (13)$$

I-O analysis of L-level. The balance equation for local and district activities in Locale ℓ is

$$\begin{pmatrix} X_L^\ell \\ X_D^\ell \end{pmatrix} = \begin{pmatrix} A_{LL} & A_{LD} \\ A_{DL} & A_{DD} \end{pmatrix} \begin{pmatrix} X_L^\ell \\ X_D^\ell \end{pmatrix} + \begin{pmatrix} A_{LR} X_R^\ell + \hat{Y}_L^\ell + J_L^\ell \\ A_{DR} X_R^\ell + \hat{Y}_D^\ell + J_D^\ell \end{pmatrix} \qquad (14)$$

The local output vector X_R^ℓ is derived with a diagonal matrix R_R^ℓ, which would be given a priori in the model.

$$X_R^\ell = R_R^\ell X_R \qquad (15)$$

where $\sum_\ell R_R^\ell = I_R$.

Therefore, the local products of each level are obtained from local final demand vectors of L- and D-goods, i.e. $(\hat{Y}_L^\ell + J_L^\ell)$ and $(\hat{Y}_D^\ell + J_D^\ell)$.

$$\begin{pmatrix} X_L^\ell \\ X_D^\ell \end{pmatrix} = \begin{pmatrix} I_L - A_{LL} & -A_{LD} \\ -A_{DL} & I_D - A_{DD} \end{pmatrix}^{-1} \begin{pmatrix} A_{LR} X_R^\ell + \hat{Y}_L^\ell + J_L^\ell \\ A_{DR} X_R^\ell + \hat{Y}_D^\ell + J_D^\ell \end{pmatrix} \qquad (16)$$

The property that the sum of X_L^ℓ or X_D^ℓ in eq.(16) coincides with X_L or X_D in eq.(13) is sufficiently secured.

I-O analysis of D-level. The balance equation of district activities in District d is

$$X_D^d = A_{DD} X_D^d + (A_{DR} X_R^d + A_{DL} X_L^d + \hat{Y}_D^d + J_D^d) \qquad (17)$$

As done in the I-O analysis of L-level, the district products of regional and local activities are derived with given diagonal matrices

R^d_R and R^d_L.

$$\left.\begin{aligned} X^d_R &= R^d_R X^\ell_R = R^d_R R^\ell_R X_R \\ X^d_L &= R^d_L X^\ell_L \end{aligned}\right\} (d \in \ell) \quad (18)$$

where $\sum_{d\in\ell} R^d_R = I_R$ and $\sum_{d\in\ell} R^d_L = I_L$.

Then the district products of district activities are obtained.

$$X^d_D = (I_D - A_{DD})^{-1}(A_{DR}X^d_R + A_{DL}X^d_L + \widehat{Y}^d_D + J^d_D) \quad (19)$$

Consequently, products of all activities: (X^d_R, X^d_L, X^d_D) are obtained in each District.

With the 3-level I-O Analysis Model, calculations are executed from upper to lower levels irreversibly. Since the model's consistency is secured, a limited application to a particular District is also possible. The second merit of the model is operationability. Therefore, this model is thought eligible in case analyzing many subdivided districts.

The Distribution Models

The following variables should be predetermined to the 3-level I-O Analysis Model.

a) regional input coefficients; a_{ij}.

b) regional net final demands; $\widehat{Y}_i$.

c) regional net increase in stocks; J_i.

d) regional exports and imports; F_i, M_i. (only for R-goods.)

Using those variables, the I-O analysis of R-level can be executed. However, to execute analyses of lower levels, the following variables should be distributed in advance.

X^ℓ_R, $\widehat{Y}^\ell_L$, $\widehat{Y}^\ell_D$, J^ℓ_L, and J^ℓ_D for the local level,

X^d_R, X^d_L, $\widehat{Y}^d_D$, and J^d_D for the district level.

Therefore, the first subject is to determine product distribution coefficients R^ℓ_R, R^d_R, and R^d_L. Their values are hardly supposed to be stable, since regional distributions of producing factors vary with time. That is why the product distribution model is required.

In this study, every final demand item is estimated in Control sub-model. To convert it into goods bases, unit converters; c_{ij} are used, where subscript i indicates goods and j indicates final demand items. Then regional net final demands in goods bases; $\widehat{Y}_i$ are obtained from those in item bases; Y_j.

$$\widehat{Y}_i = c_{ij}Y_j \quad \text{or} \quad \widehat{Y} = CY \quad (20)$$

where C is the unit converter matrix constituted from c_{ij}. Concerning unit converters, the following assumption is added.

Assumption 3a Unit converters are the same throughout the Region.

Although the 3-level I-O Analysis Model just requires $\widetilde{Y}^\ell_L$, $\widetilde{Y}^\ell_D$, and $\widetilde{Y}^d_D$, distributions of net final demands for all goods are determined at the same time from eq.(20). Since those distributions are supposed to depend on income distributions, capital formations, etc., which are also unstable, the final demand distribution model becomes necessary.

Activity sub-model is to be executed with Location sub-model. Therefore, distributions of investimental items are to be given in the latter sub-model, and the distribution models for consumption items are required to be formulated here.

An Extension to the Environmental Analysis

Since activity levels have been estimated only from their products, a scheme which makes it possible to estimate non-productive activities, such as pollution eliminating activities within firms, should be developed.

Leontief's model (3) is an early work of this kind, where all activity levels including pollution eliminating ones are determined simultaneously from environmental standards exogenously given. On the other hand, the model adopted by the Ministry of International Trade and Industry of Japan (4) is to estimate products of goods, quantities of pollutants, pollutants eliminated, and pollutants discharged under the given self-eliminating rates. Since pollutant elimination much depends on environmental policies, the latter model is adopted here for the extension. (See Fig. 7.)

The extension is summarized as follows.

a) Pollutions handled here is what originated from fixed sources and measured in quantity.

b) Eliminating activities within firms are the object of the analysis. Regardless of diffusion, these activities are completed in each District.

c) Sanitary services as public utilities are handled in Sector 18.

The following assumptions are added.

Assumption 3b Polluting coefficient; a_{pj} and input coefficient to anti-pollution activities; a_{ip} are the same throughout the Region, where $a_{pj} = X_{pj}/X_j$ and $a_{ip} = X_{ip}/X_p$.

Assumption 5 Self-eliminating rate; q_p is

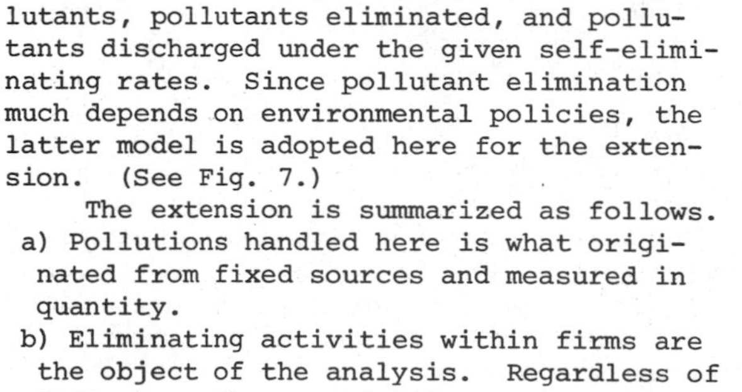

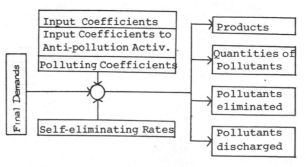

Fig. 7. An I-O model for environmental analysis.

the same throughout the Region and common to all activities, where $q_p = X_p/U_p$.

Note that X_p is pollutant p eliminated and U_p is quantity of pollutant p before elimination ($U_p = \sum_j X_{pj}$).

Assumption 6 There is no secondary pollution caused by pollution eliminating activities, i.e. $X_{pp} = 0$.

The balance equation (12) is extended as follows.

$$\begin{pmatrix} X_R \\ X_L \\ X_D \\ X_P \end{pmatrix} = \begin{pmatrix} A_{RR} & A_{RL} & A_{RD} & A_{RP} \\ A_{LR} & A_{LL} & A_{LD} & A_{LP} \\ A_{DR} & A_{DL} & A_{DD} & A_{DP} \\ A_{PR} & A_{PL} & A_{PD} & 0 \end{pmatrix} \begin{pmatrix} X_R \\ X_L \\ X_D \\ X_P \end{pmatrix} + \begin{pmatrix} \tilde{Y}_R + J_R + F_R - M_R \\ \tilde{Y}_L + J_L \\ \tilde{Y}_D + J_D \\ -Y_P \end{pmatrix} \quad (21)$$

where Y_P is a vector consists of pollutants discharged.

The bottom line of eq.(21) is rewritten as

$$X_P = Q_P (A_{PR}\ A_{PL}\ A_{PD}) \begin{pmatrix} X_R \\ X_L \\ X_D \end{pmatrix} \quad (22)$$

where Q_p is a diagonal matrix consists of q_p.

When the minor matrices of eq.(11) are substituted by

$$A^*_{MN} = A_{MN} + A_{MP} Q_P A_{PN} \quad (M,N=R,L,D) \quad (23)$$

eq.(21) can be simplified.

$$\begin{pmatrix} X_R \\ X_L \\ X_D \end{pmatrix} = \begin{pmatrix} A^*_{RR} & A^*_{RL} & A^*_{RD} \\ A^*_{LR} & A^*_{LL} & A^*_{LD} \\ A^*_{DR} & A^*_{DL} & A^*_{DD} \end{pmatrix} \begin{pmatrix} X_R \\ X_L \\ X_D \end{pmatrix} + \begin{pmatrix} \tilde{Y}_R + J_R + F_R - M_R \\ \tilde{Y}_L + J_L \\ \tilde{Y}_D + J_D \end{pmatrix} \quad (24)$$

This is the same in form as eq.(12), where input coefficients are substituted. When this equation is adopted in the I-O analysis of R-level, 3-level I-O Analysis concerning environmental reflections can be executed in the same way.

From X^d_R, X^d_L, and X^d_D obtained in the I-O analysis of D-level, gross quantities of pollutants, pollutants eliminated, and pollutants discharged are obtained in each District.

$$U^d_P = (A_{PR}\ A_{PL}\ A_{PD}) \begin{pmatrix} X^d_R \\ X^d_L \\ X^d_D \end{pmatrix} \quad (25)$$

$$X^d_P = Q_P U^d_P \quad (26)$$

$$Y^d_P = U^d_P - X^d_P \quad (27)$$

The frame of the 3-level I-O Analysis is shown to be unchangeable whether environmental analysis is incorporated into it. The size of input coefficient matrix is also the same on account of Assumption 6. Therefore, the extension is made without harming operationability of the model.

CONCLUSION

The features of the model are summarized as follows.

a) Considering both stock and flow aspects of activities, the total model is composed as a recursive dynamic model.
b) The model can analyze each subdivided district as well as the metropolitan area as a whole.
c) Activities which characterize urbanization, such as city services and retail trade, are handled positively in addition to producing industries.
d) Sectoral and spatial interactions among activities are considered explicitly. Environmental aspects can also be considered within the model.
e) The model would be a large-scale one in nature. In this study, an attempt to make the model to be compatible with operationability is made through introducing hierarchical concepts into the model.

For empirical studies, Kanto Region of Japan, which consists of Tokyo Metropolis and 6 surrounding prefectures, are taken as the object region. Results of some numerical investigations will be presented in the session.

REFERENCES

(1) Christaller, W.(1933), Die Zentralen Orte in Süddeutschland, Verlag von Gustav Fischer, Jena.
(2) W. Leontief, et.al., The economic impact ---industrial and regional---of an arm cut, R. of Eco. & Statistics, 47, 217 (1965).
(3) W. Leontief, Environmental repercussion and the economic structure: An Input-Output approach, R. of Eco. & Statistics, 52, 262(1970).
(4) Ministry of International Trade and Industry (1976), About the Input-Output Table for Environmental Analysis (in Japanese), Tokyo.

INTERFACING SIMULATION MODELS FOR NEARSHORE ENVIRONMENT SYSTEMS OF LARGE LAKES

D.C.L. Lam and C.R. Murthy

Applied Research Division, Canada Centre for Inland Waters, Burlington, Ontario, Canada

ABSTRACT

Several program modules have been developed for predicting thermal plumes, waste effluent and patches in the coastal zone. Some efforts have been made to link up these models as well as biochemical models. These are part of an integrated study to develop a general program package with greater flexibility and versatility in the prediciton of the movements of waste effluents and, in particular, thermal discharges. The requirements for developing the package and its use for the control, planning and assessment of impacts on the environmental systems will be discussed.

INTRODUCTION

Recently, the emphasis of many oceanographic and limnological studies have been shifted to areas closer to the shore. These nearshore areas are increasingly used for recreation and resource development, particularly the siting of nuclear power plants and waste discharge systems. In terms of the ecology of the coastal environment, the biological system is strongly influenced by the water movements, the thermal structures and the environment's capacity to disperse pollutants. For the plant designers, the sitings of outfalls and intakes are important considerations to minimize undesirable feedbacks to the cooling water control system.

It is feasible to relate the physical aspects to the overall system by means of simulation models. We have developed at the Canada Centre for Inland Waters (CCIW) a number of program modules of thermal plume models, advection-diffusion transport models, oil and toxicant spill models and radioactive waste models. These computer models have been used individually in the studies of particular problems. However, much has to be done to integrate these efforts to produce an overall general program package, which may provide broader and more objective results for management and planning purposes in the coastal areas of large lakes. One of the expected performances from the package is, e.g., to predict the movement of some waste materials which may be mixed in a heated effluent emitted from a submerged diffuser. This will require the interfacing of many of the program modules.

Fundamental in the success of interfacing the various program modules is the reliability and compatibility of the individual submodels. This paper concerns the necessary requirements in the construction of the package, by examining the data base, the existing individual submodels, and the prospects of interfacing them.

OBSERVATION DATA BASE

Recent studies, e.g., Murthy and Blanton (1), have shown that the dynamics of the coastal zone are distinctly different from the offshore zone. An array of complexities has been observed in coastal currents which vary in magnitude from place to place and from time to time. Thus, deterministic predictions often used in large-scale lake models (e.g., Simons (2)) are not feasible at present for nearshore environment systems. Nearshore simulation models, therefore, must still draw upon existing data for information on the complicated flow fields. At CCIW, a vast volume of climatological and limnological data have been collected and analyzed. In spite of the complexities of the physics involved, it is possible to determine the frequency of occurrence of certain characteristic episodes that appear to repeat themselves at any given location. Typical elements of a current climatology in the coastal zones include: (i) extremely low, almost stagnant, current flows; (ii) strong longshore flow lasting 24 hours or longer and accompanied by upwelling or downwelling episodes; and, (iii) reversal currents usually occurring between the periods of upwelling and downwelling and generating large shear-diffusion. By referring to the frequency of occurrence of these three flow regimes, in a given time and location, it is possible to supply typical values of the mean currents into the various submodels. The idea here is to produce at least the output response from the simulation model under different possible flow regimes. In the case of a thermal plume, for example, for stagnant flows, the recirculation of heated water into nearby cooling intakes may occur more often.

Figure 1 shows the complexities of the flow field by looking at the dye-plume behaviour in coastal currents during a typical diffusion experiment. In the experiment, fluorescent rhodamine B liquid dye was released continuously for several days from an anchored source about 1 km from the shore and the concentrations were measured by fluorometers. In the region about 1 km from the source, the dye plume conformed to a thin strip and showed little meandering. However, beyond this region, large-scale lateral meandering occurred. Thus, it is not possible to incorporate these time variations in the model without proper statistical treatment of randomness. Only the mean flow is used, and the prediction is made on the ensemble-mean concentration. The dye plume and patch data serve mainly for deriving the "relative diffusion" characteristics (3), and are also used for verification purposes. Similarly, observed data of thermal plume have been analyzed. Thus, the data bank contains information on the flow conditions, ambient temperatures, wind speeds, thermal plumes, dye plume and patch concentrations. Although these experiments have not been designed particularly for modeling purposes, they form a very powerful basis in the course of model development.

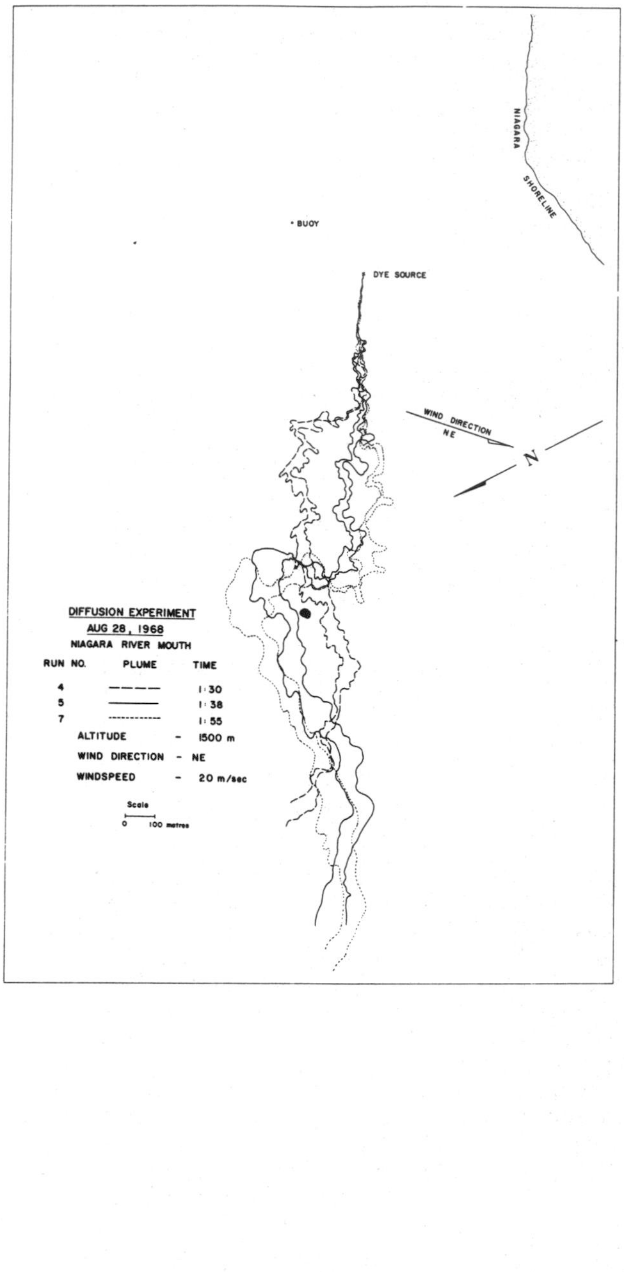

Fig. 1. Dye plume behaviour in coastal currents.

ADVECTION-DIFFUSION MODELS FOR WASTE EFFLUENTS

The purpose of an advection-diffusion transport model is to predict the movements involved, namely (i) the advective motions due to the mean current transports and (ii) the subgrid turbulent dispersion due to random fluctuations. More precisely, to avoid the variations (Fig. 1) in the instantaneous current velocity v and concentration c, it is necessary to look at them as $v = \overline{v} + v'$ and $c = \overline{c} + c'$, where the bar (—) notation indicates the mean taken over some time and space and the prime (') notation is for the fluctuating quantities. The mean transport, $\overline{v \cdot c}$, is then given by $\overline{v \cdot c} = \overline{v} \cdot \overline{c} + \overline{v'c'}$, in which the first term is called the mean advection, and the second term the mean turbulent fluctuation in terms of the mean quantities. The most commonly used is the gradient hypothesis which states that the turbulent exchange is proportional to the concentration gradient, i.e., $\overline{v'c'} = - K\, \partial\overline{c}/\partial n$, where K is an effective eddy diffusion coefficient and n is the normal to the surface through which the exchange takes place (4). Thus, it is possible to write the time rate of change of concentration in terms of the mass balance of the mean advection and the mean eddy diffusion:

$$\partial\overline{c}/\partial t = - \nabla\cdot (\overline{v}\ \overline{c}) + \nabla\cdot (K\nabla\overline{c}) \qquad (1)$$

where t is time and ∇ is the ordinary gradient operator. Equation (1) is the well known advection-diffusion equation which can be solved numerically.

Many experimental sutdies (3) - (6) have been conducted to determine the formulation of the eddy diffusivity K in the coastal waters of oceans and lakes. These studies, which are based on the statistical analysis, show that K is not a constant, but rather grows with the scale of the diffusion. In the case of a continuous release, a convenient measure of the scale of the plume is the cross-plume width L_y, whereas in the case of an instantaneous release, the scale can be measured by the radius r of the patch. The manner in which K grows with the length scale L_y or r has been investigated theoretically for a number of flow conditions. For example, for the case of shear-diffusion, which may be caused by reversal currents as discussed earlier in this paper, K grows linearly with the length scale. In inertial subrange diffusion, however, K is proportional to the 4/3 power of the length scale. It is possible that several types of diffusion exist in the coastal environment and these theoretical laws may not hold at all times for any location. A simpler approach is to define the diffusivity by using the lumped data collected at many locations with different flow conditions. Such empirical relationships have been found (3) - (6) for a number of diffusivities in the cross-flow or flow directions. Two typical relationships are the following:

for the cross-plume diffusivity (5),

$$K_y = 0.02\, L_y^{1.2} \qquad (2)$$

and for the diffusivity in a radially symmetrical patch (6),

$$K_r = 0.15 r^{1.1} \qquad (3)$$

Figures (2) and (3) show the results of applying these length-scale dependent diffusivities in the advection-diffusion model for a continuously released plume and an instantaneously released patch, respectively. The results of using a constant diffusivity are also included. Thus, in the case of the plume, the constant diffusivity tends to produce slower diffusion, resulting in a higher maximum concentration at the centre of the plume. The concentration tends to disperse faster with constant diffusivity, however, in the case of the patch, resulting in a lower maximum concentration. In both cases, the length-scale dependent diffusivity appears to follow the dispersion mechanism very closely and produces better simulated results.

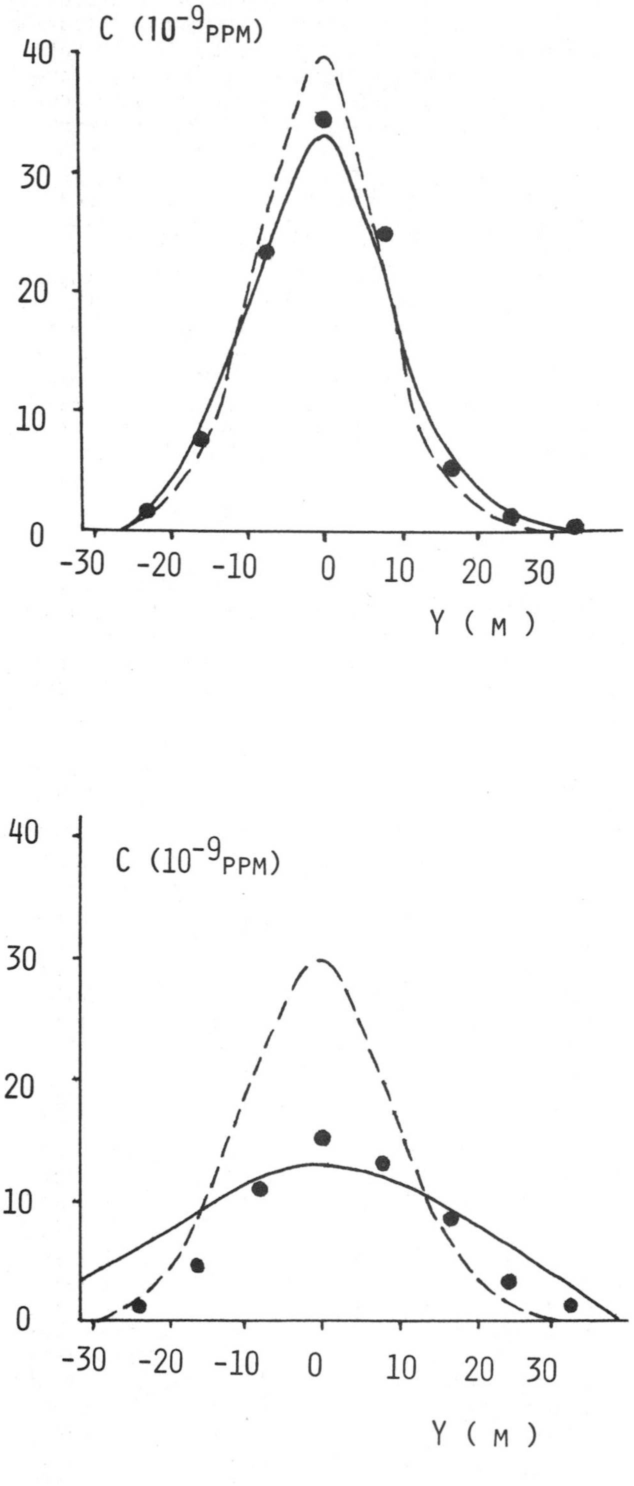

Fig. 2. Cross-plume concentrations : (i) observed (dot); (ii) computed, using variable diffusivity (Eq. 2) (solid line); (iii) computed, using constant diffusivity, K_y = 40 cm^2/s., (dotted line). Upper figure at 1200m from source; lower figure at 2000m.

THERMAL POLLUTION MODELS

The waste heat discharged from energy generating plants may float or sink, depending on the ambient temperature. It may be swept away by longshore current, or stay near the outfall during stagnant periods. The dynamics involved are rather complicated, since it involves temperature changes, pressure redistribution, and buoyancy forces. Moreover, the diffusivity for temperature is different from the diffusivity for mass, not only in the sense that the mean fluctuations $\overline{v'T'}$ and $\overline{v'c'}$ differ from each other, but also the dynamic regimes in the nearfield (0 - ½ km) and in the farfield (½ - 2 km) are different. It is not surprising, therefore, that the success of a thermal effluent model depends strongly on the choice of the thermal eddy diffusivity. While relations (2) and (3) are shown to be valid for the dispersion of dissolved materials in the far-field, thermal discharges appear to behave differently in the nearfield. To allow for the testing of various models of diffusivity, the thermal plume model (7) developed by Raithby of the University of Waterloo at CCIW has been programmed modularly. At present, it uses a set of two coupled partial differential equations relating the thermal diffusivity to the turbulent kinetic energy, k, and the dissipation rate, ε. In this so-called K-ε model (8), (9), the Richardson number (10) is used in the vertical diffusivity to regulate the stratification process. The overall model involves the numerical solution of the three-dimensional momentum and energy equations.

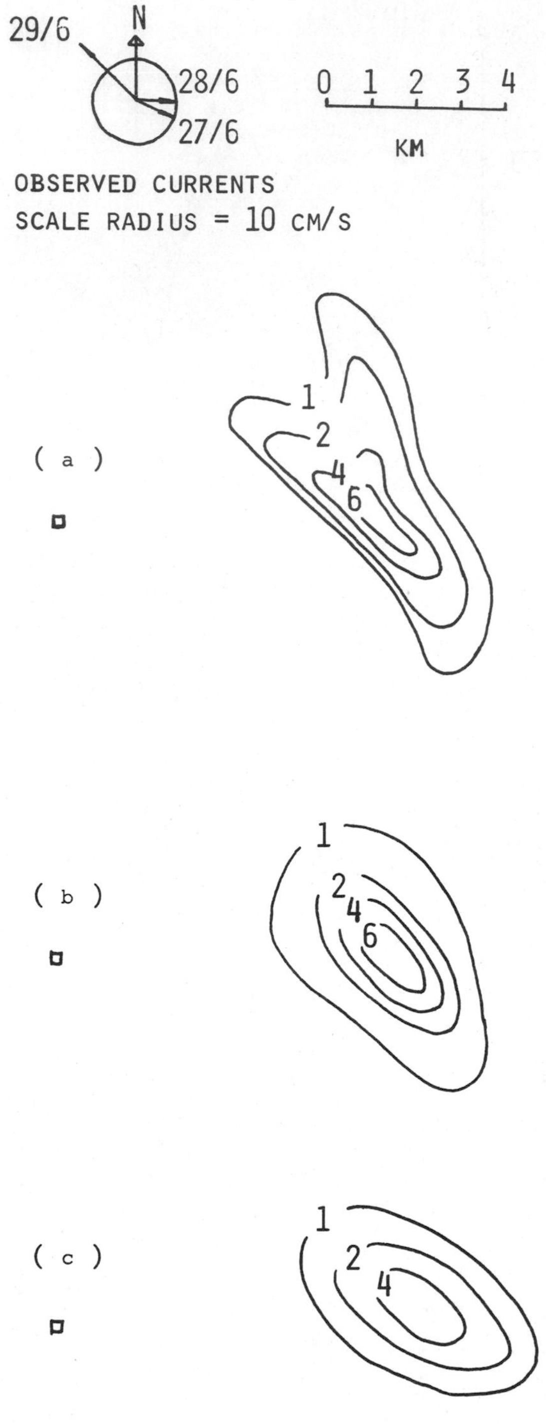

Fig. 3. (a) Observed concentration 53 hrs. after release (◘ is location of release at 1400 GMT, 26/6/72); (b) computed conc. with variable diffusivity (Eq. 3); (c) computed conc. with constant diffusivity, $K_r = 5 \times 10^4 \, cm^2/s$.

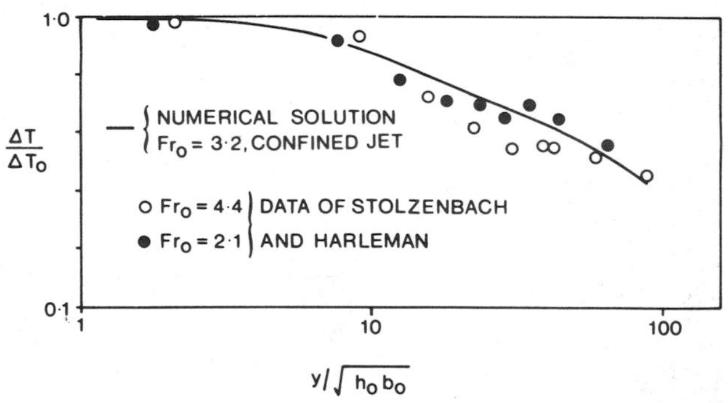

Fig. 4. Decay in centreline temperature in a thermal jet. $\Delta T/\Delta T_o$ and $y/\sqrt{h_o b_o}$ are the dimensionless temperature and distance from outlet respectively. Fr_o is the Froude number at the outlet. (Raithby (7)).

Figure (4) shows the computed and observed results (7) of the decay of temperature at the centreline of a thermal plume, under a stagnant flow condition. In this run, the original temperature of the jet is 30°C, and the ambient temperature is assumed to be at

$20^{o}C$. These conditions are quite typical of the outfall environments at a power plant. The calculated velocities and the pressure fields can also be included in the output. In the case of a buoyant jet as shown in Fig. (4), the velocities are large near the surface, spreading the heated effluent to either side of the centreline. Return flows occur at the sides of the jet beneath the warmer water, so that the nearby water is entrained by the jet to compensate for the lateral spreading. On the other hand, the model predicts a sinking jet, when an effluent at $10^{o}C$ is injected into a receiving body of water at $0^{o}C$. In the periphery of the jet, a region of high density water occurs at $4^{o}C$, causing this water to sink and 'warm' up the underlying waters. Some of these results have been observed in thermal plume experiments (11).

TOXICANT AND BIOCHEMICAL MODELS

The biochemical models mainly concern the temporal kinetic changes in the ecosystem and the toxicant models refer to mostly chemical reactions of toxic substances and their effects on the ecosystem. Since the ecosystem in the coastal waters is very complicated, model development in these areas is still in the early stages (12), (13). The fundamental difficulties are the prescription of the boundary conditions with the offshore waters, and the general lack of knowledge in the littoral zones very close to the shore. Nevertheless, the common approach is to represent the kinetic interactions between chemical and biological system variables by a system of coupled ordinary differential equations:

$$\frac{d\vec{c}}{dt} = A\vec{c} \qquad (4)$$

where t is time; $\vec{c}$ is a vector consisting of the concentrations of c_i, the biochemical variables; and A is the coefficient matrix. The coefficient, A_{ij}, will be non-zero only if there is an interaction between c_i and c_j. The interactions include growth, grazing, mortality, respiration, uptake, and regeneration (13), and the coefficients may be functions of temperature, light, or the concentrations themselves.

In the case of the toxicant model (14), most of the interactions are chemical reactions. These are very fast reactions in comparison to the biological processes. In order to establish the impact on the biological communities, chemical equilibrium must be assumed in the model. This can be obtained from the steady state solution of equation (4) for the chemical kinetics. An example of such reactions is the chemical equilibrium of soluble and insoluble lead compounds in natural lake environment.

INTERFACING OF NEARSHORE SIMULATION MODELS

Two main types of interfacing must be considered in the development of the general package. One is to maintain the proper interface between the nearshore thermal plume model and the farfield advection-diffusion model; and the other is to link the combined physical models to the biochemical models. Figure (5) shows a scheme of the possible interfacing links. In terms of the physical models, the transition from the nearfield to the farfield must at least include the transition of the diffusivities; i.e., the length-scale dependent diffusivity must be incorporated beyond a transition point between the two regimes. This will allow a spatially continuous simulation of the advective and diffusive movements of the effluents, which may be originated from a nearfield source. The source may be associated with a surface discharger or a submerged diffuser. One potential use of the coupled physical model is to examine the cooling water system in a series of coastal outfalls and intakes, such as in the case of a chain of nuclear reactor plants. The data base will provide the information on the frequencies of typical current climatological elements. Thus, the model results can be used as a feedback to the optimal control design in the cooling system. On the other hand, the dispersion of the effluents to the offshore zone can be handled by interfacing the farfield model (½ - 2 km) to a lake-wide transport model (2 km and over) (2). Again, the continuity of the physical processes must be maintained. In this way, the influence of the lake-wide circulation can be brought into the simulation through observed or computed currents.

It is essential that the physical models can simulate the movements of both conservative and non-conservative materials, or a mixture of several of them. In any case, Eq. (1) can be generalized to a system of P. D. E.'s to deal with a multi-component system. Furthermore, it is possible to augment the right-hand side of such a system by that of Eq. (4), i.e.,

$$\partial\vec{c}/\partial t = -\nabla\cdot(\overline{v}\,\vec{c}) + \nabla\cdot(K\nabla\vec{c}) + A\,\vec{c} \qquad (5)$$

Equation (5) shows the interfacing between the farfield advection-diffusion model and the biochemical model so that the kinetic changes occur as the effluents move along (14). Another type of interfacing is that between the thermal plume model and the biochemical model, dealing with thermal pollution problems. Here, the coefficients in A in Eq. (4) may depend on the temperature, and, hence, the thermal impact on the ecological system can be evaluated. However, the formulation of the effect of temperatures, for instance, on such coefficients as growth rates of phytoplankton still remains to be established.

The development of the general package will depend upon the advancement of individual models. At the present stage, it appears

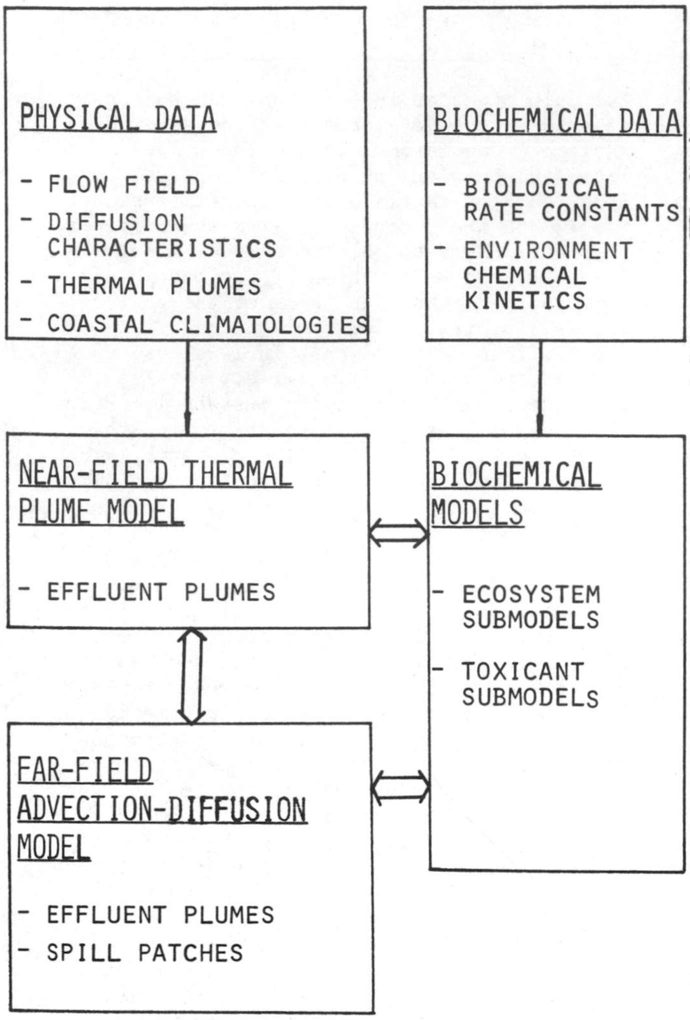

Fig. 5. A scheme for interfacing physical and biochemical models.

that the linkage of nearfield and farfield models should be first attempted, since the general advection-diffusion model as described by Eq. (5) forms the computational framework for most of the interfacing (2). It is found (15) that, because of the difference in the length scales between the models, the variable grid finite-difference or finite element techniques compatible with these scales offer better computational aspects, particularly for relations like Eqs. (2) and (3). Subsequent linkage to the biochemical models can be made, if more data are available for calibration and verification.

REFERENCES

(1) C. R. Murthy, and J. O. Blanton, Coastal Zone Climatological Studies of the Laurentian Great Lakes, Proc. 2nd World Congress, Int. Water Resources, Assoc., vol. V, p. 431 - 448, (1975).

(2) T. J. Simons, Interfacing physical and biochemical models of large lakes, Proc. IFAC World Congress, 61.3, (1975).

(3) C. R. Murthy, and G. T. Csanady, Experimental studies of relative diffusion in Lake Huron, J. Phys. Ocean., 1, p. 17 - 24, (1975).

(4) A. Okubo, Horizontal and vertical mixing in the sea, in D. W. Wood (ed.) Impingement of man on the oceans, J. Wiley Publ., N. Y., p. 89 - 168, (1971).

(5) C. R. Murthy, and B. C. Kenney, Diffusion in coastal currents of large lakes, Rapp. P. - v. Reun, Const. int. Explor. Mer, 167, p. 111 - 120, (1974).

(6) C. R. Murthy, Horizontal diffusion characteristics in Lake Ontario, J. Phys. Ocean., p. 76 - 84, (1976).

(7) G. D. Raithby, Prediction of dispersion of surface discharge, unpublished CCIW contract report, (1976).

(8) B. E. Launder, D. B. Spalding, The numerical computation of turbulent flows, Comp. Meth. in Appl. Mech. Engg, 3, p. 269 - 289, (1974).

(9) W. E. Dunn, A. J. Poliscastro, R. A. Paddock, Surface thermal plumes: evaluation of mathematical models for the near and complete field, Argonne Nat. Lab. Rep. ANL/WR-75-3, pt. 2, 531 p., (1975).

(10) G. H. Jirka, G. Abraham, D. R. F. Harleman, An assessment of techniques for hydrothermal prediction, M. I. T., R. M. Parson Lab. Rep. 203, (1975).

(11) G. K. Sato, C. H. Mortimer, Lake currents and temperatures near the western shore of Lake Michigan, Special Rep. 22, Ctr. Great Lakes Studies, U. Wisconsin, (1975).

(12) J. T. Leendertze, S.-K. Liu, A water-quality simulation model for well mixed estuaries and coastal seas, vol. VI, N. Y. Rand Inst. Rep. R-1586-NYC, (1974).

(13) C. W. Chen, M. Lorenzen, D. J. Smith, A comprehensive water quality ecological model for Lake Ontario, Tetra Tech Rep., Lafayette, Calif., (1975).

(14) D. C. L. Lam *et al.*, Computer model for toxicant spills in Lake Ontario, Environmental Biogeochemistry, Vol. 2, Ann Arbor Sci. Publ., Michigan, p. 743 - 761, (1976).

(15) R. B. Simpson, The irregular rectangular mesh package, CCIW unpublished contract report, (1977).

A SIMULATION MODEL OF DISTRICT HEATING SYSTEM

Nakaji Honda* and I. Hayakawa**

**University of Electro-Communications, Chofu-shi Tokyo 182, Japan*
***Tokyo Institute of Technology, Meguro-ku Tokyo 152, Japan*

ABSTRACT

This paper describes about modeling and simulation of district heating system (DHS), which is important for the protection against air pollution, the effective use of energy and the improvement of the condition of our living, for the purpose of grasping the dynamical behavior and the structure from the macroscopic point of view. This model is built by means of System Dynamics (SD), which is useful to analyse a complicated social system.

1. Introduction

District heating system (DHS) has some advantages of the followings; 1) Avoidances of air pollution, 2) Use of cheaper fuels, 3) Avoidances of fire risks, 4) Lower cost of heat to the consumer. However, it is generally difficult to estimate the prospect of the utilization of DHS and the future heating load because these factors are significantly influenced by social and economical environment. DHS has also managerial risk as it needs a large initial investment for the construction of plant system and pipeline laying. It is, therefore, necessary to analyse and evaluate the dynamical behavior of DHS as social system, based on a long term forecast.[1],[2]

The computer simulation by means of System Dynamics (SD) is an efficient method for the analysis of such a system with nonlinear multifeedback loops as social one.[3] Thus, we try to assess the dynamical behavior of DHS including environment and energy problems by the simulation of SD model.

2. Simulation Model[4],[5]

2.1 Conditions of the model

We make a model of DHS by using SD. The conditions for our model of DHS are described as follows.

The model should

1) be able to grasp the dynamical relations of the macroscopic factors (for example, energy and air pollution, the unit price of heat, etc.) of DHS.
2) be considered the characteristics of economical and social factors (for example, population dynamics, individual income, etc.) surrounding DHS.
3) be able to predict the long term dynamical behaviors of heat demand, plant scale, management factors, etc. which are important in the planning of DHS.
4) include some decision making mechanisms.
5) be able to deal with the influences of regional characteristics (for example, climate, building use, etc.) on DHS.

2.2 Structure of the model

This model is composed of seven sectors, of which essential contents are shown as follows;

1) Heat supply and demand sector

The total amounts of heat supply, heat demand and heat losses are evaluated from the number of houses supplied with district heating, from the average amount of heat consumption per a house which depends on individual income and the unit price of heat, and from the parameter of heat losses.

2) Population and houses sector

The total number of houses is calculated by dividing regional population by the number of persons per a house. The number of houses supplied with district heating is also calculated by multiplying the total number of houses by the utilization rate of DHS which depends on individual income and protecting policy against air pollution.

3) Heating load sector

Total heating load is calculated by multiplying the number of houses supplied with district heating by average heating load per a house. Necessary plant scale is obtained from the table function which represents the relation of total heating load and plant scale.

4) Fuel sector

The quantity of fuel consumption for district heating is calculated by multiplying the amount of heat supply by the quantity of fuel consumption per unit calorie. And fuel cost is also calculated by multiplying fuel consumption by the unit price of heat.

5) Management sector

Sale of heat is calculated by multiplying the amount of heat demand by the unit price of heat. And both running and fixed costs are obtained from respective table functions which represent the relations of plant scale and both costs. Nominal profit is obtained by subtracting the sum of running, fixed and fuel costs from sale of heat.

6) Air pollution sector

The quantities of air pollutant (Sulphur oxides (SO_X)) from district heating and from individual heating are calculated by multiplying each amount of fuel consumption by each emission factor of SO_X respectively.

7) Exogenous variables sector

Regional population, individual income, price index and the unit price of fuel are set up as table functions of time series data.

The relations among these sectors are shown in Fig.1. In Fig.1, a dashed line expresses the boundary of the model, and the arrows indicate the direction of relations. Fig.2 shows the structure of the model as a flow diagram which is the method for the representation of SD. The names of factors and their meanings are summarized in Table 1. Factors underlined in Fig.2 mean table functions, which are divided into three types as follows;

1) Exogenous factors —— which are set up by any predicted values as time series data, so that the responses of the model can be investigated through simulation. (Table 1,2, 3,4)

2) Policy factors —— which take policy data for studying how to make the manegerial decisions of DHS. (Table 8,12,13)

3) System chatacteristics —— which are determined based on actual data and the results of analysis of district heating. (Table 5,6,7, 9,10,11)

2.3 Feedback loops

Feedback loops of the model are shown in Fig.3, in which plus and minus signs indicate positive and negative relations respectively. Several feedback loops are formed by these relations. For example, the loop, profit——(-)——▶the unit price of heat——(-)——▶heat demand——(+)——▶sale of heat——(+)——▶profit, is a positive loop.

3. Simulation[4]

3.1 Conditions of simulation

The model of DHS is programmed by DYANAMO language and simulated by computer. In this simulation, the simulation interval is 25 years, and each factor of the model is calculated every one year. Here, simulated region is A-regidential district, and constants are set up as follows;

initial plant scale: 25Gcal/h
emission factor of SO_X from district heating: 17.6 g/l or 8.8 g/l
emission factor of SO_X from district heating: 17.6 g/l
average heating load per a house: 4800 Kcal/h
initial unit price of fuel: 15 Yen/l
used fuel quantity per unit calorie: 10^{-4} l/Kcal.

Four exogenous factors are given as predicted values of A-regidential district in Fig.4. And, it is assumed that three policy factors are shown in Fig.5. Here, Fig.5-(a) shows the encouraging policy of utilization of DHS for the protection against air pollution. Fig.5-(b) also shows the decision making of the enlargement of plant scale corresponding to the increase of heating load. In this simulation, the unit price of heat is assumed to be always constant as shown in Fig.5-(c) because it is easy to investigate the trends of each cost, revenue and profits.

3.2 Simulation results

Simulation results are shown in Fig.6(a)-----(h).

1) Fig.6-(a) shows that the total number of houses increases as population increases, and

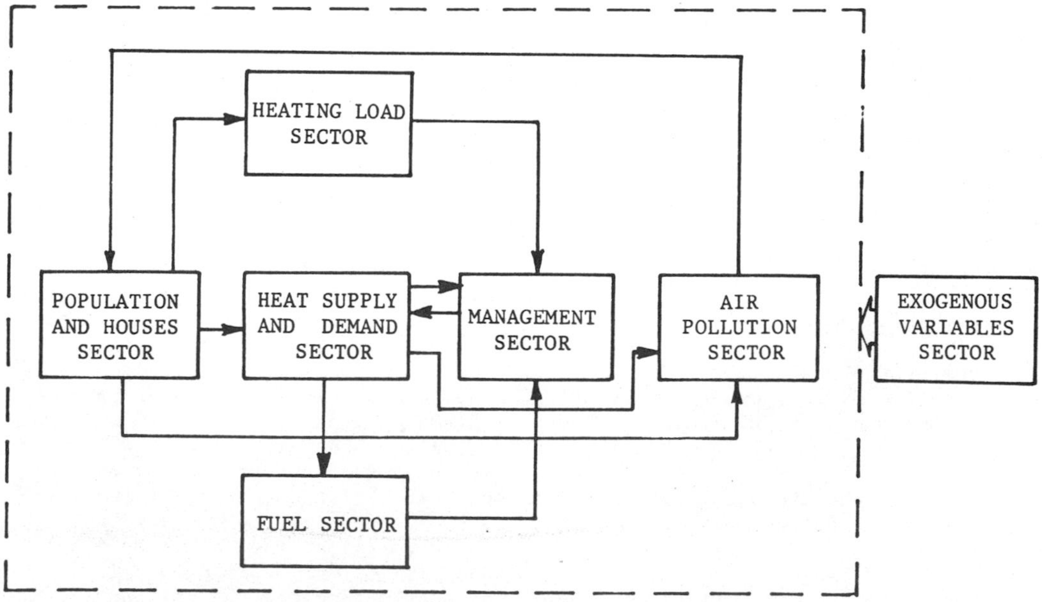

Fig.1 The Structure of the Model

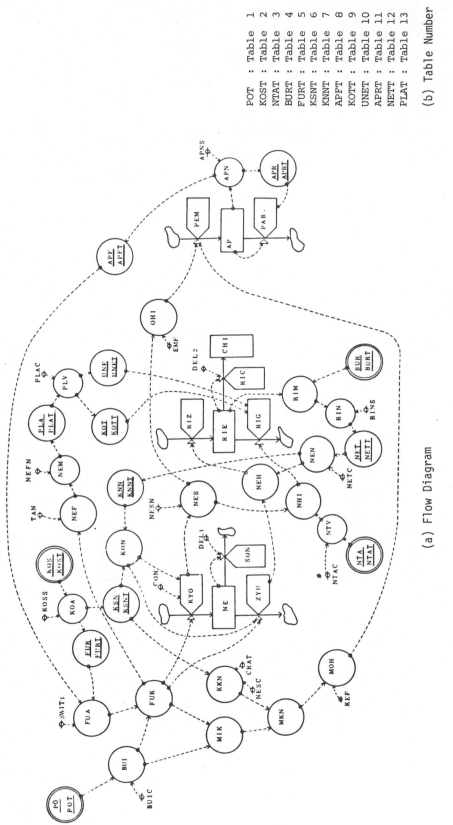

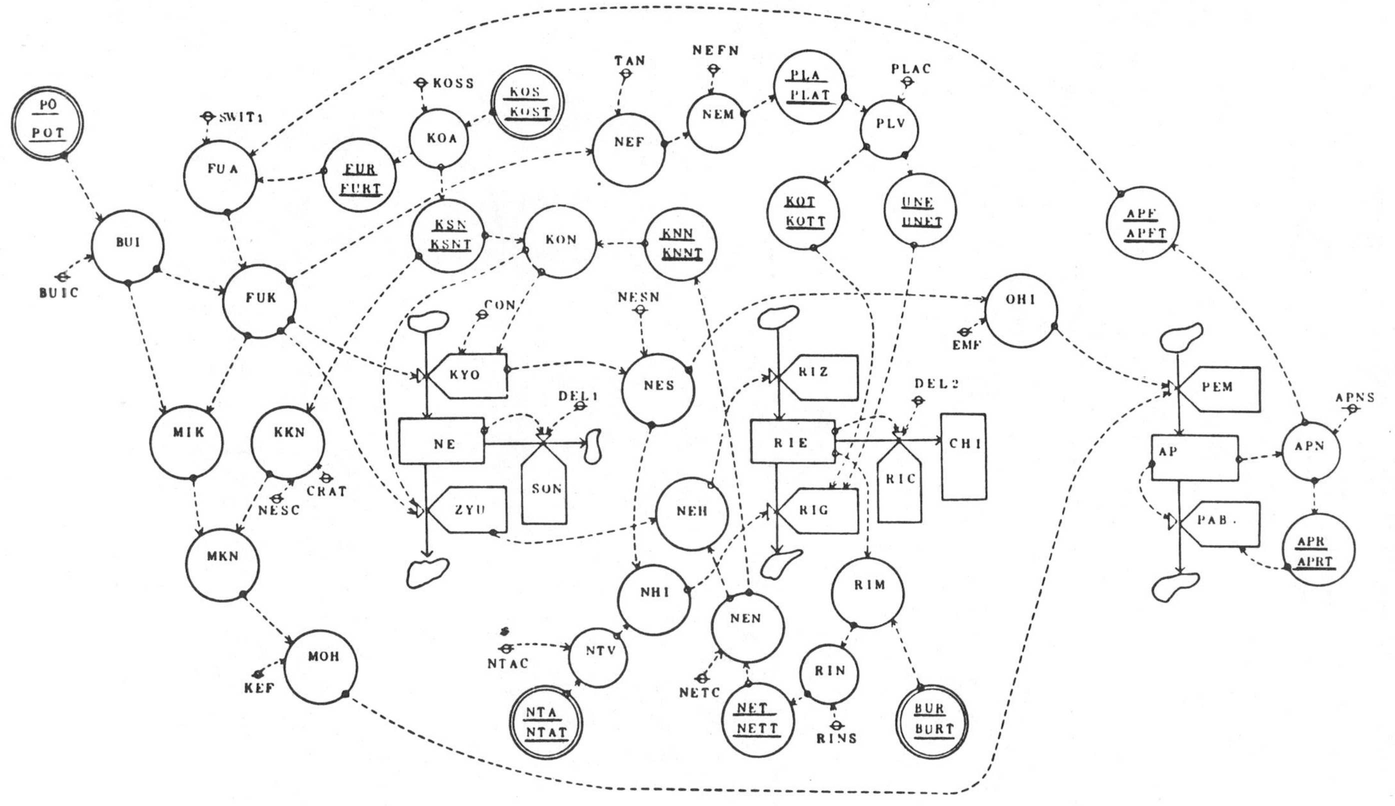

(a) Flow Diagram

POT : Table 1
KOST : Table 2
NTAT : Table 3
BURT : Table 4
FURT : Table 5
KSNT : Table 6
KNNT : Table 7
APFT : Table 8
KOTT : Table 9
UNET : Table 10
APRT : Table 11
NETT : Table 12
PLAT : Table 13

(b) Table Number

Fig.2 Flow Diagram and Table Number

Table 1 The Factors of DHS Model

PO	regional population (table function)
BUI	the number of houses
FUK	the number of houses which are supplied with district heating
MIK	the number of houses which are equipped with individual heating
FUA	the utilization rate of district heating
KOS	individual income (table function)
NEF	total heating load
PLA	total heating load - plant scale index (table function)
PLV	plant scale
KYO	the annual amount of heat supply
ZYO	the annual amount of heat demand
NE	the amount of heat losses
KON	the average amount of heat consumption per a house by district heating
KNN	the unit price of heat - the average amount of heat consumption per a house (table function)
KSN	individual income - heat consumption index
NTA	the unit price of fuel (table function)
NHI	fuel cost
NES	the quantity of fuel consumption by district heating
KKN	the average quantity of fuel consumption per a house by individual heating
MKN	the total quantity of fuel consumption by individual heating
RIZ	annual revenue
RIG	annual expenditure (table function)
RIE	annual nominal profit
CHI	profit accumulation
RIM	annual real profit
BUR	price index (table function)
NET	annual real profit - the unit price of heat
NEN	the unit price of heat
NEH	sale of heat
KOT	plant scale - fixed cost (table function)
ONE	plant scale - running cost (table function)
OHI	the emitted quantity of air pollutant from district heating
MOH	the emitted quantity of air pollutant from individual heating
PEM	total quantity of air pollutant
AP	the magnitude of air pollution
PAB	pollution absorption
APR	the magnitude of air pollution - pollution absorption (table function)
APF	the magnitude of air pollution - the utilization rate of DHS (table function)

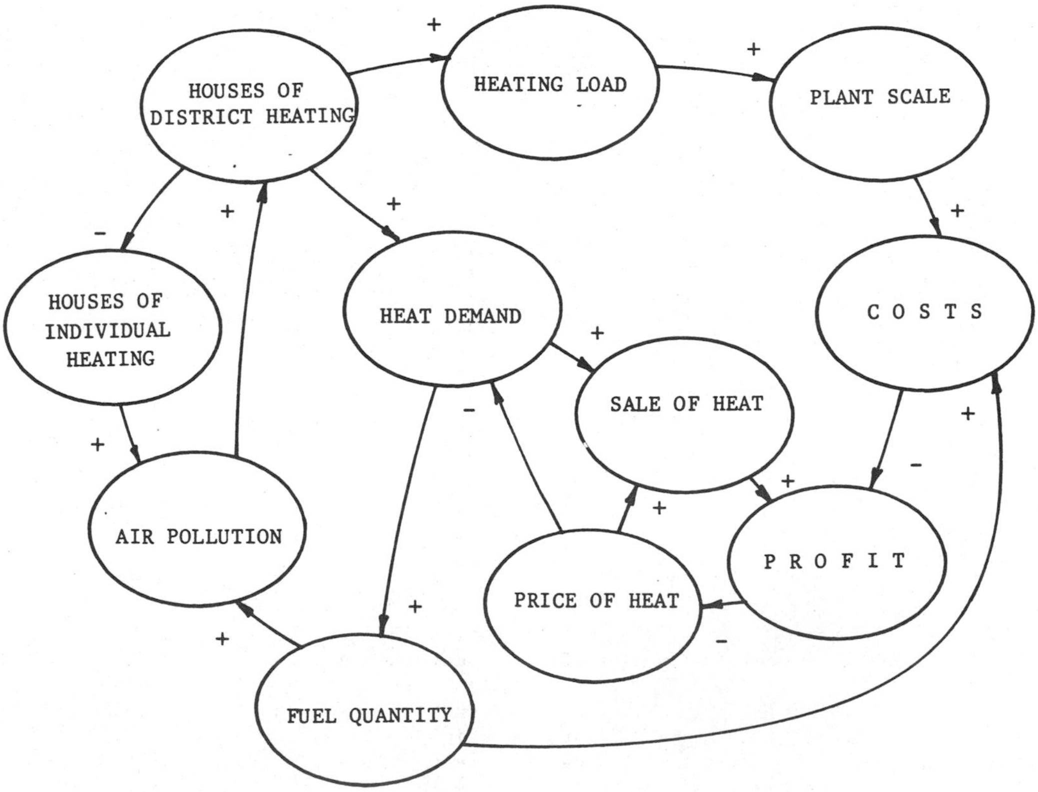

Fig.3 Feedback Loops

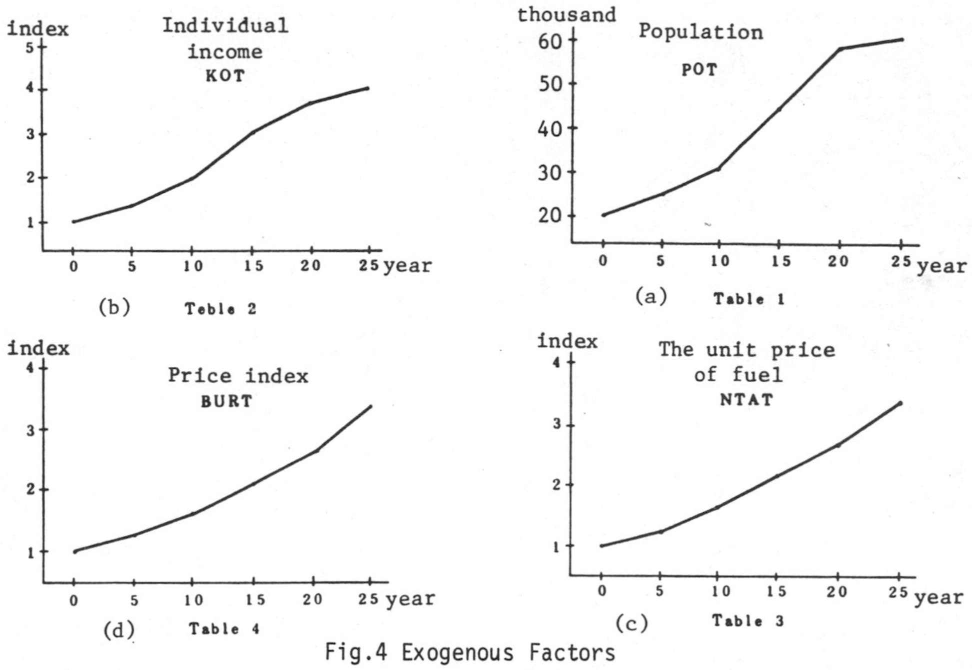

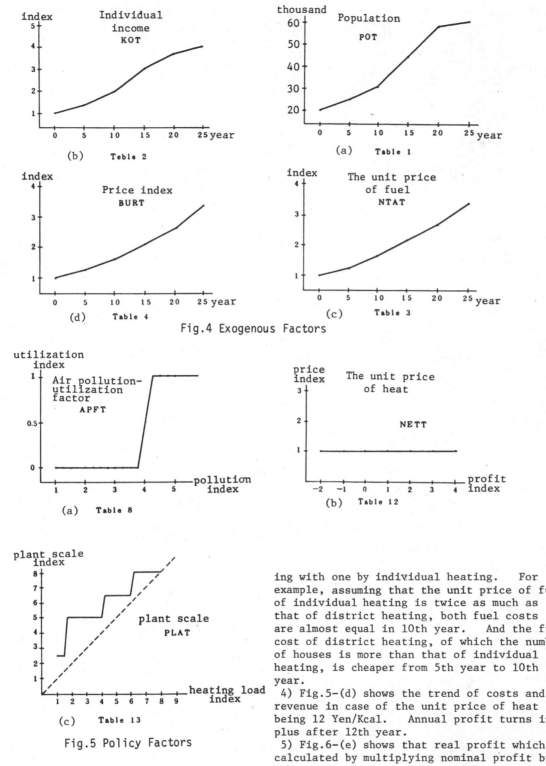

Fig.4 Exogenous Factors

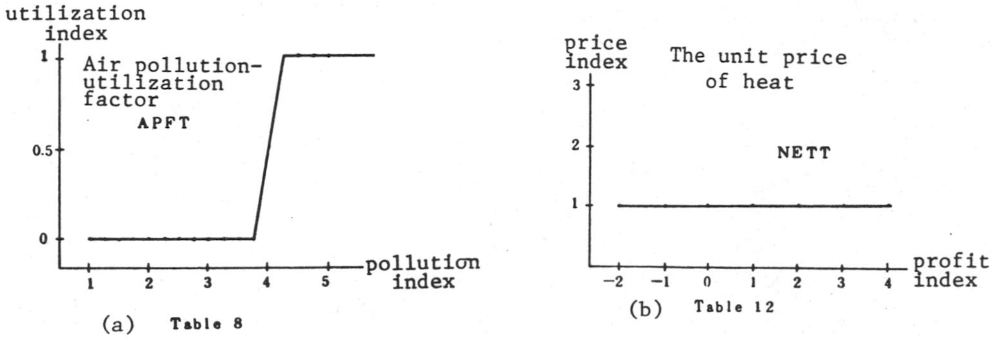

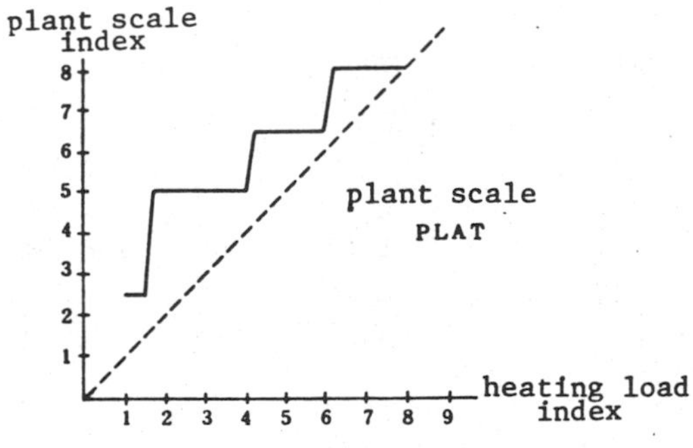

Fig.5 Policy Factors

the relation between the number of houses of district heating and of individual heating changes.

2) In Fig.6-(b), the dynamical behaviors of heat supply, heat demand and heat losses are shown. Heat demand increases rapidly from 7th year to 14th year.

3) Fig.6-(c) shows the enlargement of plant scale for the increase of total heating load. Economy of both fuel costs can be studied by comparing fuel consumption by district heating with one by individual heating. For example, assuming that the unit price of fuel of individual heating is twice as much as that of district heating, both fuel costs are almost equal in 10th year. And the fuel cost of district heating, of which the number of houses is more than that of individual heating, is cheaper from 5th year to 10th year.

4) Fig.5-(d) shows the trend of costs and revenue in case of the unit price of heat being 12 Yen/Kcal. Annual profit turns into plus after 12th year.

5) Fig.6-(e) shows that real profit which is calculated by multiplying nominal profit by price index is less than nominal. Profit accumulation turns into plus after 19th year. In case of the unit price of heat being 15 Yen/Kcal, each result is shown in Fig.6-(f). This shows that profit is rather less for the reason of the decrease of heat demand.

6) In Fig.6-(g), it is possible to compare the emitted air pollutant quantity from district heating with that from individual heating in case of both emission factors being equal (= 17.6 g/l). The emitted quantity from district heating being regulated half

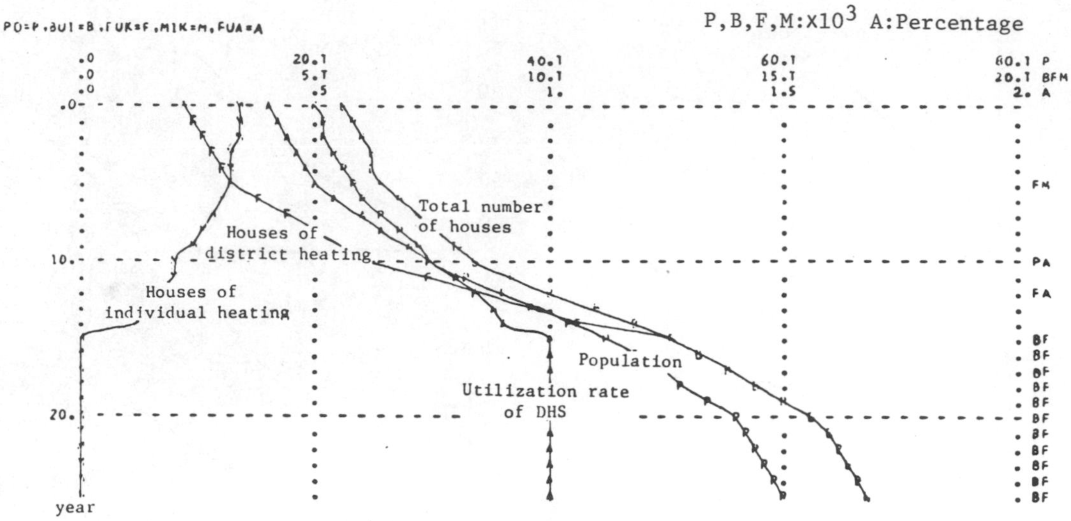

(a) Population and Houses

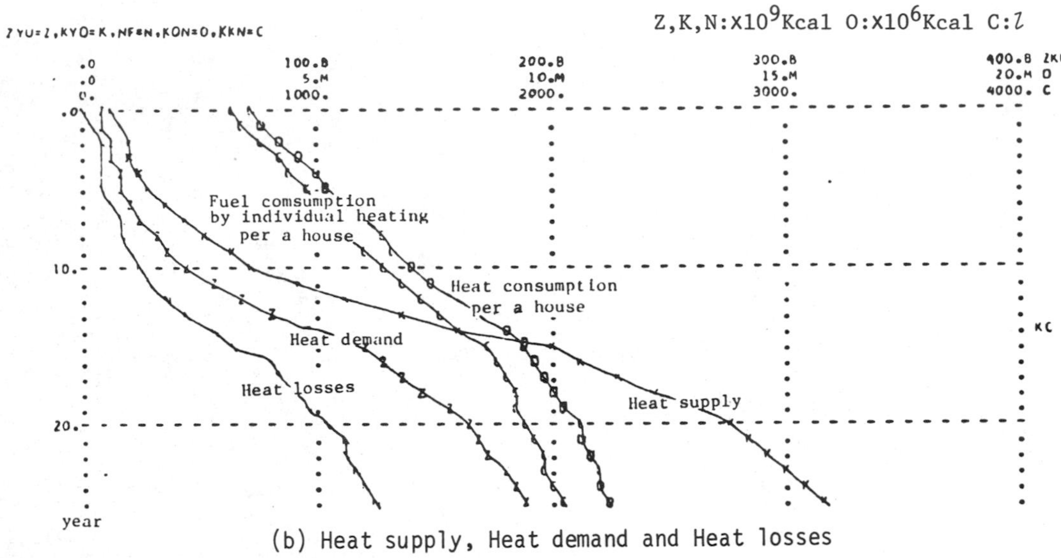

(b) Heat supply, Heat demand and Heat losses

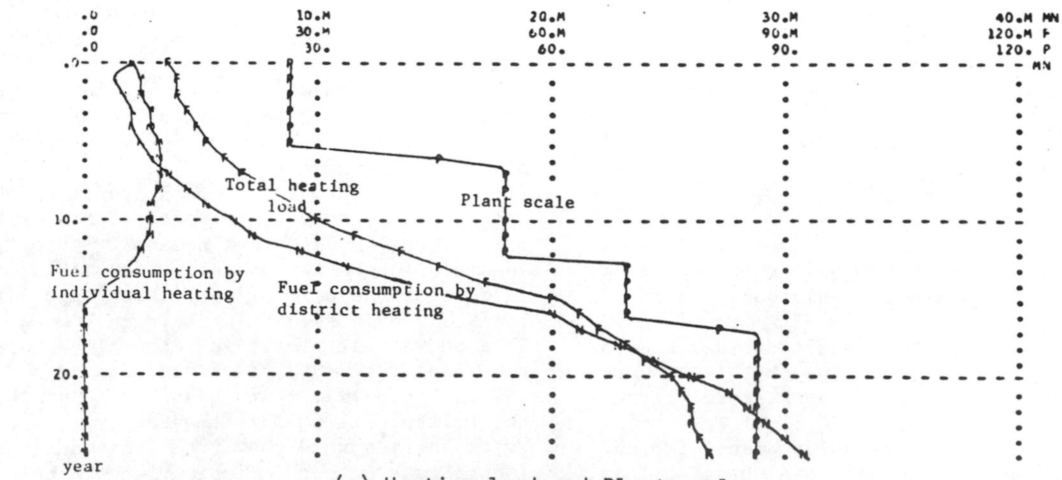

(c) Heating load and Plant scale

Fig.6 Simulation Results (1)

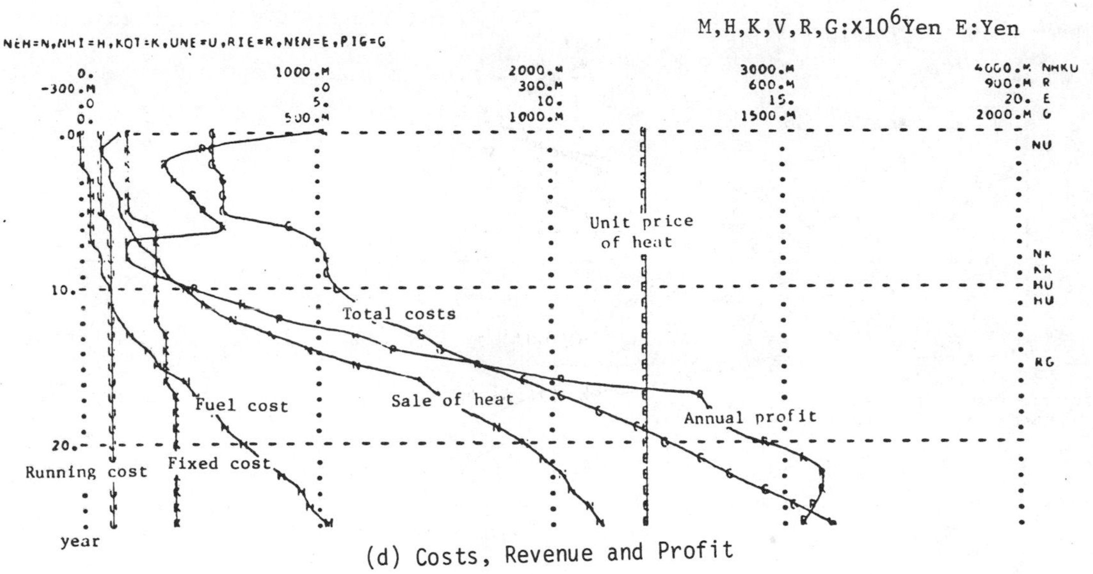

(d) Costs, Revenue and Profit

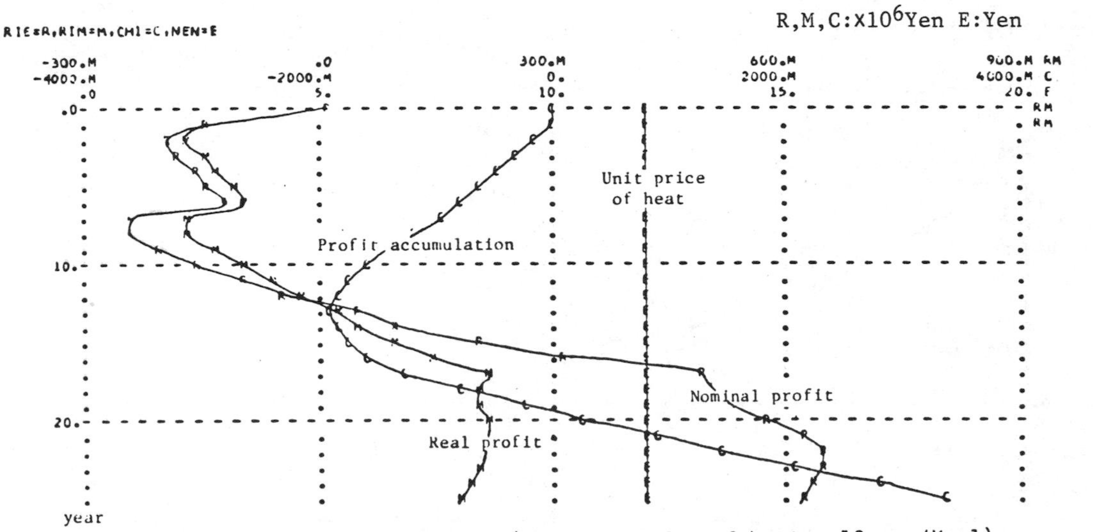

(e) Nominal and Real Profits (the unit price of heat = 12 yen/Kcal)

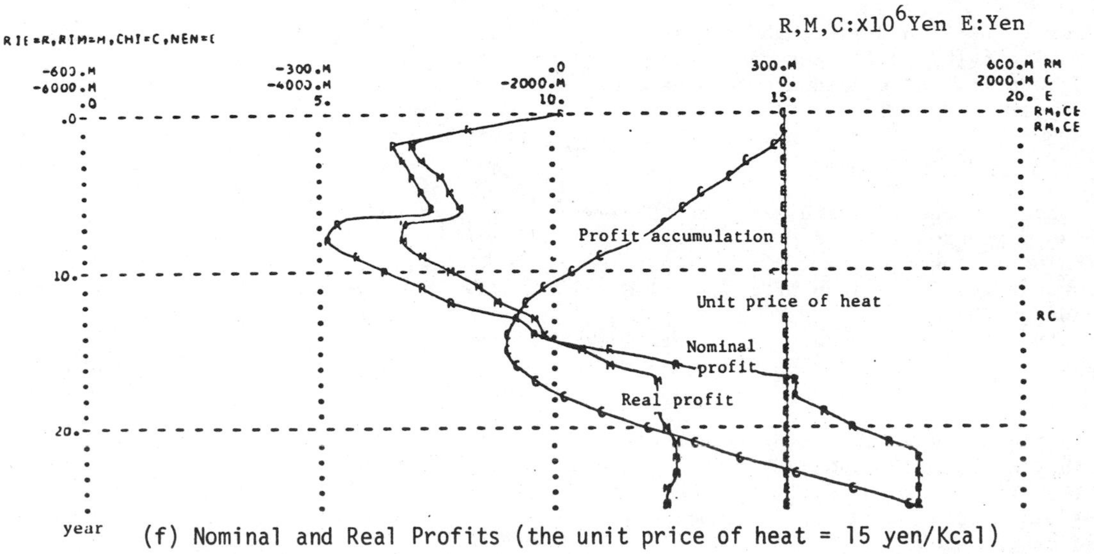

(f) Nominal and Real Profits (the unit price of heat = 15 yen/Kcal)

Fig.6 Simulation Results (2)

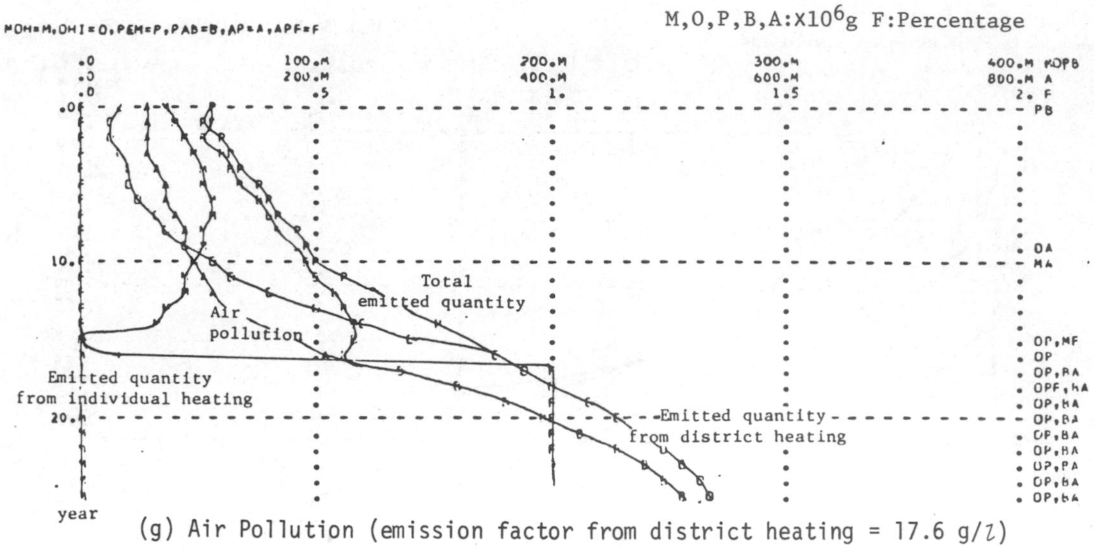

(g) Air Pollution (emission factor from district heating = 17.6 g/l)

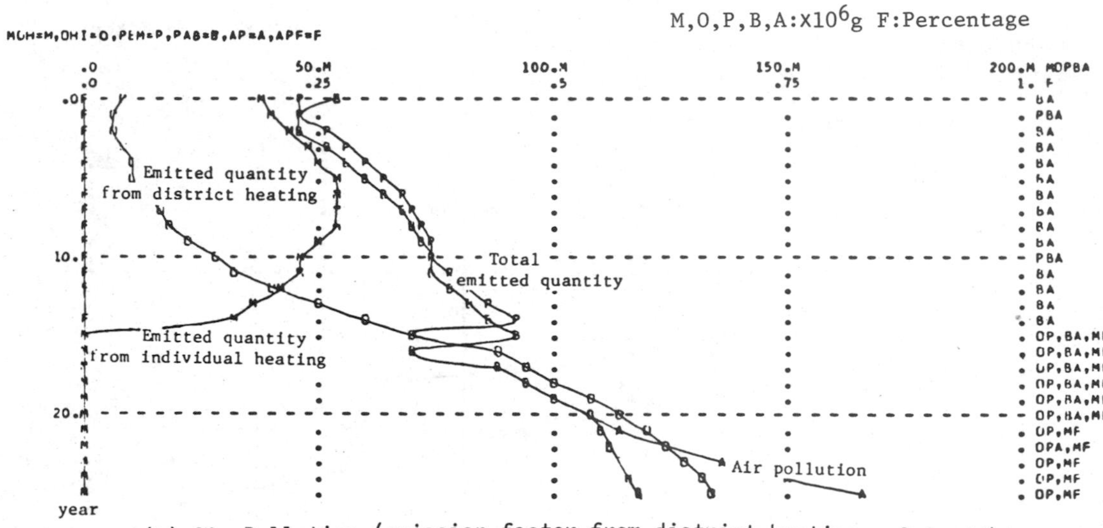

(h) Air Pollution (emission factor from district heating = 8.8 g/l)

Fig.6 Simulation Results (3)

(emission factor = 8.8 g/l), the results are shown in Fig.6-(h). In this case, total emitted quantity is reduced about 25 percent in 10th year.

4. Concluding Remarks

The modeling and the simulation of DHS have been discussed in this paper. This model is built based on relatively simplified structure as the first step of the model development of DHS.

Hereafter, it is necessary to further investigate the structure of the model and the validation of simulation.

The authors would like to express their appreciations to Prof.S.Aida (UEC), Dr.T.Kubo (TIT) and Dr.M.Kaneshima (TIT) for their helpful discussions, and Mr.F.Sugimoto (UEC) for his assistances.

REFERENCES

1. Hayakawa I., "The Planning of District Heating and Cooling", Maruzen press, 1973.
2. Diamant R.M.E. and MacGarry J., "Space and District Heating", London Iliffe Books 1968.
3. Forrester J.W., "Urban Dynamics", MIT press, 1969.
4. Hayakawa Lab., Tokyo Institute of Technology, "A Dynamic Model of District Heating and Cooling", Unpublished Report, 1974.
5. Hayakawa Lab., Tokyo Institute of Technology, "The Foundamental Reserches of District Heating and Cooling (2)", Unpublished Report, 1974.

SIMULATION OF SOME PLANNING AND CONTROL PROCESSES IN PUBLIC PASSENGER TRANSPORT (ENVIRONMENTAL ASPECTS)

A.A. Voronov, A.P. Artynov, V.V. Skaletsky and A.I. Vasilchenko

Institute of Automation and Control Processes, Far East Science Centre, USSR Academy of Sciences, Vladivostok, USSR

ABSTRACT

In this work we pose the problem of decreasing the harmful influence of city transport systems on the environment through the use of decision making computer simulation for stages of long-term, current and opporational planning and control.
For this purpose, we have isolated the basic factors of the effect of public transportation systems on the environment and have suggested methods of taking them into account.
In solving problems pertaining to long-term planning, we have suggested the use of effectivity criteria, taking into account such factors of transport effect on the environment as atmospheric pollution, transport noise, transport fatigue of passengers etc. in unified cost terms.
We show that problems concerning current and operational planning and also problems of operational control should be solved by methods of vector optimication, since at such stages as planning and control, it is usually impossible to express the values of optimality criteria representing the transport effect on the environment in unified cost terms. Possible approaches to the solution of problems of planning and controlling public passenger lines of large cities have been indicated, taking into account environmental aspects, using computer methods.

INTRODUCTION

The passenger transport lines in operation in large cities have a considerable effect on the environment. The main aspects are:
- pollution of the atmosphere by exhaust fumes and dust;
- transport noise;
- traffic accidents;
- use of city real estate for transport communication lines.

The intensity of environmental effect depends on the number of passengers carried and the number of vehicles on the route, and so the problem of protecting the city environment has been intensified by the rapid increase in passenger transport traffic.

At present, a decrease in the effect of public transport on the environment may be achieved by use of the following measures.

Engineering measures: improvements in vehicles with regard to reducing noise level and decreasing exhaust fumes, the designing of motors which ensure complete combustion of the fuel used cars and buses, automation of traffic regulation, automation of public transport control in large cities and so forth.

City planning and construction measures: the use of freeways for automobile traffic and special roads for heavy truck traffic, the concentration of suburban regions near subway stations, the planned organization of suburbs as isolated units, the effective use of open and closed areas, green belts, the construction of special structures and facilities to localize and decrease noise and environmental pollution (tunnels, the construction of clover leaves and division of traffic streams on different levels, and underground passageways for automobile traffic).

Organizational measures: the reduction of norms for toxic particles and gases released into the atmosphere and the organization of a system of control of technical inspection of transport vehicles, and the optimization of the functional parameters of metropolitan transport systems.

A complex approach to the gradual transformation of cities and their transport systems by social planning, constructional and organizational measures in defense of urban man's environment aids in ensuring a high level of economic, social, ecological and architectural planning effect in this transformation.

The economic effect is conditioned by the selection of the most rational transport system, which not only provides the population with comfortable and high speed communication but ensures effective environmental control measures.

The social effect is expressed in improved living and commuting conditions for the population, in a reduction of traffic fatigue.

The ecological effect is concerned with providing means of preserving the natural environment, in defending urban man from harmful effects of transport and also with reducing the population density on individual segments of the public way by the provision of comfortable fast trsnsport systems.

The architectural planning effect consists of projecting a design structure for suburban units near existing transportation lines so as to more effectively use the available areas, to decrease pollution of the atmosphere, to reduce the noise level and the number of traffic accidents (1).

In this work an evaluation is offered of the effectiveness of some of these measures, however the methods of calculation offered are based on traditional technical economic comparisons of variants, which do not allow one to select the optimal solution with regard to various factors involved. Moreover, the work does not include evaluations of city areas occupied in various ways by transport systems. Also the possibilities of decreasing the harmful effects of transport on the environment by means of optimization of functional parameters of the transport system are not included. A detailed calculation of these factors is apparently possible only with the use of computer simulation methods. Therefore the aim of the present work is use of simulation methods for calculating the interrelation of transport systems and the environment in the solution of a broad class of problems in planning and controlling public passenger transport in order to reduce the harmful effects of transport on the environment.

COMPLEX EVALUATION OF MEASURES FOR REDUCING TRANSPORT EFFECT ON THE ENVIRONMENT IN PROBLEMS OF LONG-TERM PLANNING

Computer simulation of transport systems gives us the possibility of using criteria of any complexity, taking into account the quality of service offered to passengers, the technical and economic parameters of public transport operation and its interaction with the environment and so forth. In determining the numerical values of the criteria, cost evaluation of economic, social, ecological and architectural planning effects are difficult to achieve, though these effects have considerable influence on the type of transport system selected. Taking into consideration losses entailed with certain measures, a complex evaluation of the effectivity of various transport systems may be made with the aid of the following criteria:

$$E = (K_1 + K_2 + K_3 + K_4 + K_5 + K_6 + K_7)\, E_h + K_8$$

where E is the annual operation expenses of the existing transport system in thousands of rubles;

K_1 is the cost of measures for reducing pollution of the environment, in thousands of rubles;

K_2 is the cost of measures to reduce noise, in thousands of rubles;

K_3 is the sum of economic losses from traffic accidents, in thousands of rubles;

K_4 is the cost estimate of measures taken to improve traffic conditions for transport units, in thousands of rubles;

K_5 is the cost estimate of city real estate areas occupied by transport lines of various types in thousands of rubles;

K_6 is the total capital expended on rolling stock, in thousands of rubles;

K_7 is the total capital invested in construction of transport facilities, in thousands of rubles.

K_8 is the sum of economic losses caused by loss of time by passengers en route and transport fatigue of passengers, in thousands of rubles.

E_h is mean capital investment return coefficient for the economy.

As a rule, the direct cost estimate of various factors is difficult to determine because it is obtained indirectly through the cost of environment protection measures.

A unified method of evaluation of

the effects of the factors in a cost expression allows us to determine the effect of transport on the environment in solving such problems of long-term planning, as:

- planned distribution of transportation loads among types of transport;
- planning the quantity of rolling stock and rational selection of types of transport;
- distribution of rolling stock among the various routes;
- prediction of the development of the route lines of various types of transport etc.

Transport system parameters are introduced into each complex criterion. For example, the intensity of motor vehicle traffic affects the noise level, the number of traffic accidents and the loss of passenger time en route. Moreover, the noise level depends on the types and operational characteristics of the transport units.

The evaluation of the estimated loss connected with use of city real estate areas occupied by the transport system is made on the basis of data on the necessary length and breadth of transportation lines for various types of transport, on the various values of land tracts etc.

In conducting measures related to the improvement of traffic conditions, for instance, in comparing highways having all traffic on one level with freeways having separated streams of traffic on several levels and so forth, it is necessary to calculate the effect in terms of changes in such factors as the increase of traffic speed, time lost at stop lights, reduction in the number of speed-ups and slow-downs, all of which aid in lowering the noise level, air pollution and number of trips.

In the computer simulated model (2) the criteria are detailed into the runs and stops of the route network of individual transport units, so the measures related to environment protection are accounted for by means of introduction of pertinent initial information about the transport system. Such information for the simulation model may be facts concerning the route network, operational characteristics of the means of transport and information about passenger loads. For instance, the use of such engineering measures for lowering the noise level as the use of baffles to absorb noise, recesses and tunnels on transport lines, in the model changes only the noise characteristic of those segments and stops of the transport network where these measures were taken.

Such measures as improvement of the equipment of the vehicles, using rubberized components in construction to lower the noise level etc., change the technical operational characteristics of transport means.

The model takes such construction projects as speedways, special roads and city areas of various values (suburban zones) into account by changing the initial information about the characteristics of the route network. For example, the use of speedways shortens the trip time of transport units in runs on these segments, while changes in the transport network are included as descriptions of new routes or corrections of those already included in the model, when in the group of runs and stops, new elements are added with descriptions of their parameters.

Measures of the organization plan, related to approval of the norm for toxic particles in exhaust fumes sent into the air, the allowable noise level etc., are simulated by introducing the allowed levels into the initial information concerning the runs and stops of the network. Thus, by varying the initial information on passenger loads, structure of the transport system and characteristics of the transport units, we may evaluate the effectivity of the various technical, contructional and organizational measures.

EVALUATION OF THE EFFECT OF TRANSPORT ON THE ENVIRONMENT IN THE SOLUTION OF PROBLEMS OF CURRENT PLANNING

The marked difference in problems of this class from the aforementioned is in the more detailed information concerning passenger loads and in more strict demands for the accuracy of the solution. As a rule, selection of the type of transport at the long-term planning stage is based on factors such as the number of passengers involved and the length of the trip. As all types of transport are compared, the most promising win out, that is, the ones best able to handle the passenger loads with allowable limits for other factors. From the promising types of transport available, one or a combination of two is selected which shows the lowest values in the aforementioned criteria, taking into account the size of the investment needed, the operational expenses required and the effect of the transport on environment.

In the development of the existing transport system in an existing city or in the case of extending lines to a new suburb, selection of the type of transport is practically reduced to a solution of problems about the preferred development of one of the existing types of transport.

In selecting the type of transport, as in solving other problems, it is important to take into consideration not only the effect of transport on the environment, but also the demands which the environment makes on transport. For instance, the climate and the local relief greatly affect the selection of the means of transport. It is well known that in regions of the Far North, electric transport is considerably more dependable and convenient than automobile transport. At the present time, the influence of the environment on the selection of means of transport is considered a secondary factor and is practically not considered.

Moreover, obtaining the cost estimate of various factors during the stage of current planning is extremely difficult.

If for problems of long-term planning this cost estimate may be obtained at least indirectly through the cost of related measures, for current planning this method of evaluating factors affecting the environment is not satisfactory. Therefore, it is necessary to use criteria having different units of measurement.

One of the methods allowing us to overcome this difficulty, is the multi-criterion approach, enabling one to find the optimal solution when these solutions are characterized by not one but several criteria. For example, solution of problems of optimal distribution of transport units on routes for vector criteria $N = (N_1, N_2, N_3, N_4, N_5, N_6)$ may be solved by an ordinary extremum problem (3). Here

- N_1 is expenses connected with the organization of traffic, in rubles;
- N_2 is losses of passenger time in waiting for transport units and in travel time, in hours;
- N_3 is the difference between existing and allowable noise level, in decibels;
- N_4 is the level of atmospheric pollution, in mg/m^3;
- N_5 is losses in passenger productivity related to transport fatigue, in per cent;
- N_6 is the number of traffic accidents.

In optimization of parameters of the functioning of city transport facilities for simulation models, the interaction between transport units on the routes is taken into consideration. Moreover, it is possible to simulate the interaction between public carriers and the city's automobile transport system. For instance, the intensity of traffic streams may be simulated by changing the parameters characterizing runs on segments of the routes.

Simulating the interaction of individual units on the routes enables us to calculate the waiting time of units approaching the stops, the increase in the number of runs and stops, all of which leads to an increase in the noise level and pollution of the atmosphere.

PROBLEMS OF OPERATIONAL PLANNING AND CONTROL

In solving problems of operational planning and control, it is necessary to take into account even more detailed information, on the basis of which a decision is taken. This applies to information about the condition of the rail and road network, of the depoe of rolling stock and buses, of the passenger loads as well as information about factors influencing the level of transport effect on the environment. Such factors might include, for instance, the weather forecast for the next few days (hours) and so forth. Direct calculation of these factors gives us the most accurate solution to problems of operational control.

This approach demands a close scrutiny of factors influencing the level of transport effect on the environment. At the present time, the list of such factors has not been sufficiently studied.

As with current planning, all problems of an operational type must be solved as multi-criterion problems, since to express all optimality criteria in a cost expression is, as a rule, not possible. These problems may be solved by means of computer simulation control as described above and by means of Markov chain processes (4,5). For instance, the method of Markov chain processes allows us to find optimal operation control of transport with several criteria, explicitely a set of control strategies where one can improve a control strategy in one criterion only at the expense of another criterion.

CONCLUSION

In this work methods were investigated for determining the effect of public passenger transport facilities on the environment and for determining the criteria of this effect, such as transport noise, pollution of the environment, traffic accidents, the degree to which the city area is taken up by transport lines and so forth. The possibility of decreasing the effect of passenger lines on the environment is demonstrated with the aid of simulation processes of making appropriate control strategy decisions at the various stages of long-term, current and operational planning and control. The necessity of posing all problems at the stages of current and operational planning and control in the form of multicriterial problems is explained. Possible methods of solving these problems are given.

REFERENCES

1. Bolonenkov, G.V., Laperye, S.I. Evaluation of the Effectivity of a Public Transport System With Regard to Its Effect on the Environment. Review of Problems of Large Cities, Gosinti, edition 35, 1975 (In Russian).

2. Artynov, A.P., Vasilchenko, A.I., Skaletsky, V.V. Simulation of Train Traffic in the Public Passenger Transport Network. Coll.: Methods of Optimal City Planning and Control (Passenger Transport), pp 106-114. 1976, Vladivostok (In Russian).

3. Podinovsky, V.V. The Solution of Multi-Criterial Problems as Optimization Problems with One Criterion in Indeterminant Conditions. Avtomatika i vychislitelnaya tekhnika, N° 2, pp 45-47, 1976 (In Russian).

4. Artynov, A.P., Voronov, A.A., Skaletskaya, E.I., Skaletsky, V.V. Formalization of Certain Methods for Public Transport Control. Coll.: Methods of Optimal City Planning (Passenger Transport), N° 2, pp 3-13, 1976 (In Russian).

5. Voronov, A.A., Artynov, A.P., Skaletsky, V.V. Simulation and Optimization of Transport Control Systems. Proceedings of the VII International Synposium on Transportation and Traffic Theory. August 14-17, 1977, Kyoto, Japan.

A MODEL FOR REDUCTION AND CONTROL OF POLLUTION

H. Mine* and K. Yoshida**

**Dept. of Applied Math. & Phys., Faculty of Engineering, Kyoto Univ., Kyoto, Japan 606*
***The Ministry of Finance, Tokyo, Japan*

INTRODUCTION

This paper discusses an optimization model for reduction and control of pollution generated by enterprises. In the previous report (1), the model has been formulated as the problem of finding the optimal allocation of available resources which maximizes the social welfare function. In this paper, the model is expanded to cover intermediate goods. First, several notations are introduced for the purpose of formulation.

NOTATIONS AND ASSUMPTIONS

R^k : k dimensional Euclidian Space
s : number of individuals
ℓ : number of enterprises
n : number of goods and services
Also, n means the number of products made by all enterprises.
m : number of types of pollution
W : social welfare function, $W \in R^1$
u : individual utility, $u \in R^s$
U : individual utility function, $U \in R^s$
$\bar{x}^i$: goods (including services) consumed by i-th individual, $\bar{x}^i \in R^n$
x^i : goods (including services) possessed by i-th individual, $x^i \in R^n$
P : price vectore of goods
E : enviromental level, e.g. purity of water or air, $E \in R^m$
$\bar{E}$: enviromental level in case all production activities are stopped, $\bar{E} \in R^m$
y^j : outputs of j-th enterprise, $y^j \in R^n$
$\bar{y}^j$: inputs for production by j-th enterprise, $\bar{y}^j \in R^n$
$\tilde{y}^j$: inputs for reduction of pollution by j-th enterprise, $\tilde{y}^j \in R^n$
F^j : production function of j-th enterprise, $F^j \in R^n$
B^j : level of pollution discharged by j-th enterprise, $B^j \in R^m$
D^j : level of pollution generated by j-th enterprise, $D^j \in R^m$
A^j : level of pollution reduced by j-th enterprise, $A^j \in R^m$

With respect to these notations, the following assumptions are made:

a) Social welfare function W is a monotone increasing and concave function of individual utilities $u=(u_1,u_2,\ldots,u_s)$. That is,

$$W=W(u), \quad \frac{\partial W}{\partial u_i} > 0, \quad \frac{\partial^2 W}{\partial u_i^2} < 0 .$$

b) Environmental level decreases according as amount of pollution discharged by enterprises becomes large. That is,

$$E = \bar{E} - \sum_j B^j .$$

c) Level of individual utility is determined by amount of goods (including services) consumed by each individual and pollution level around him. That is,

$$U=(U_1,U_2,\ldots,U_s), \quad u_i=U_i(\bar{x}^i,E),$$

$$\frac{\partial U_i}{\partial \bar{x}^i_k} >0, \quad \frac{\partial U_i}{\partial (\bar{x}^i_k)^2} <0, \quad \frac{\partial U_i}{\partial E_t} >0, \quad \frac{\partial U_i}{\partial E_t^2} <0.$$

d) Each enterprise uses inputs to produce its outputs. Production function is "well-behaved", e.g. twice differentiable, continuous, monotone, increasing and concave. That is,

$$y^j=F^j(\bar{y}^j), \quad \frac{\partial F^j}{\partial \bar{y}^j_k} >0, \quad \frac{\partial^2 F^j}{\partial (\bar{y}^j_k)^2} <0.$$

e) Level of discharged pollution is equal to the difference between level of generated pollution and level of reduced pollution by the enterprises. Amount of generated pollution of the enterprise is expressed as a function of its inputs for production. The function form is considered to be monotone increasing and convex. Reduction of pollution requires some input resources, of which effects are considered to be monotone increasing and concave. That is,

$$B^j=D^j(\bar{y}^j)-A^j(\tilde{y}^j), \quad \frac{\partial D^j}{\partial \bar{y}^j} >0,$$

$$\frac{\partial^2 D^j}{\partial (\bar{y}^j)^2} >0, \quad \frac{\partial A^j}{\partial \tilde{y}^j} >0, \quad \frac{\partial^2 A^j}{\partial (\tilde{y}^j)^2} <0.$$

OPTIMIZATION PROBLEM OF ENVIRONMENT CONTOL

The aim of this paper is to maximize the social welfare function under the above assumptions. The problem is expressed as follows:

$$\begin{aligned} \text{maximize} \quad & W=W(u), \\ \text{subject to} \quad & u_i=U_i(x^i,E), \quad i=1,2,\ldots,s, \\ & \sum_i \bar{x}^i=\sum\{y^j-\bar{y}^j-\tilde{y}^j\}+\sum_i \bar{x}^i, \\ & y^j=F^j(\bar{y}^j), \quad j=1,2,\ldots,\ell, \end{aligned}$$

$$E = \bar{E} - \sum_j B^j,$$

where

$$B^j = D^j(\bar{y}^j) - A^j(\tilde{y}^j), \quad j=1,2,\ldots,\ell.$$

The problem can be solved by Lagrange's multiplier method. Let α (ϵR^s), β (ϵR^n), γ^j (ϵR^ℓ), $j=1,2,\ldots,\ell$) and δ (ϵR^m) be Lagrange's multipliers. Then the following Lagrangean is derived:

$$L = W + \alpha(U-u) + \beta\left(\sum_j \{y^j - \bar{y}^j - \tilde{y}^j\} + \sum_i x^i - \sum_i \bar{x}^i\right) + \sum_j \gamma^i (F^j - y^j) + \delta\left(\bar{E} - \sum_j (D^j - A^j) - E\right)$$

By Kuhn-Tucker Theorem, the following necessary conditions for maximization are derived:

$$\frac{\partial L}{\partial u_i} = \frac{\partial W}{\partial u_i} - \alpha_i = 0; \quad \frac{\partial W}{\partial u_i} = \alpha_i \tag{1}$$

$$\frac{\partial L}{\partial \bar{x}_k^i} = \alpha_i \frac{\partial U_i}{\partial \bar{x}_k^i} - \beta_k = 0; \quad \alpha_i \frac{\partial U_i}{\partial \bar{x}_k^i} = \beta_k \tag{2}$$

$$\frac{\partial L}{\partial E_t} = \alpha\left(\frac{\partial U}{\partial E_t}\right) - \delta_t = 0; \quad \frac{\partial U}{\partial E_t} = \delta_t \tag{3}$$

$$\frac{\partial L}{\partial y_h^j} = \beta_h - \gamma_h^j = 0; \quad \beta = \gamma^j \tag{4}$$

$$\frac{\partial L}{\partial \bar{y}_k^j} = -\beta_k + \gamma^j\left(\frac{\partial F^j}{\partial \bar{y}_k^j}\right) - \delta\left(\frac{\partial D^j}{\partial \bar{y}_k^j}\right) = 0; \tag{5}$$

$$\frac{\partial L}{\partial \tilde{y}_\ell^j} = -\beta_\ell + \delta\left(\frac{\partial A^j}{\partial \tilde{y}_\ell^j}\right) = 0; \quad \beta_\ell = \delta\left(\frac{\partial A^j}{\partial \tilde{y}_\ell^j}\right) \tag{6}$$

$$\frac{\partial L}{\partial \alpha} = U - u; \quad u = U \tag{7}$$

$$\frac{\partial L}{\partial \beta} = \sum\{y^j - \bar{y}^j - \tilde{y}^j\} + \sum x^i - \sum \bar{x}^i = 0;$$

$$\sum_i \bar{x}^i = \sum_j y^j - \sum_j \bar{y}^j - \sum_j \tilde{y}^j + \sum_i x^i \tag{8}$$

$$\frac{\partial L}{\partial \gamma^i} = F^j - y^j = 0; \quad y^j = F^j(\bar{y}^j) \tag{9}$$

$$\frac{\partial L}{\partial \delta} = \bar{E} - \sum(D^j - A^j) - E = 0;$$

$$E = \bar{E} - \sum_j \{D^j(\bar{y}^j) - A^j(\tilde{y}^j)\} \tag{10}$$

DISCUSSION ON THE NECESSARY CONDITIONS

Equations (7)~(10) reflect the constraints of the problem. The other necessary conditions are considered as follows:

In Equation (1), $\partial W/\partial u_i$ means the marginal social significance of i-th individual. The value of this quantity is considered to be determined from historical viewpoints, political reasons, philosophical concept, public morality and soon. α means the shadow price of income for each individual. β is the shadow price of the goods which is equal to the price P in the free market, Equation (2) shows that α is inversely proportional to the to the marginal utility of income. This means that bigger income is to be assigned to the individuals who have greater social significance, (that is, their marginal utility of income assume smaller value), while smaller income is to be assigned to those who have less social significance.

Equation (1) shows the balance condition between the marginal social significance of an individual and the shadow price of his income, and gives the optimal condition for comsuption of the goods under the maximization of the social welfare function.

In Equation (3), δ_t is the shadow price of the environment which is to be equal to the weighted sum of marginal individual utilities for the environment with the marginal social significance of each individual. This implies that the price of the environment should be determined so as to be equal to total sum of the marginal substitution rate of the income for the environment.

Equation (4) and (5) gives the optimal condition for the production activities. For one input $\bar{y}_k^j$ and one output y_k^j, Equations (4) and (5) are expressed as follows;

$$\gamma_h^j = \beta_h \tag{4'}$$

$$-\beta_k + \sum_h \gamma_h^j \left(\frac{\partial F_h^j}{\partial \bar{y}_h^j}\right) - \sum_t \delta_t \frac{\partial D_t^j}{\partial \bar{y}_k^j} = 0 \tag{5'}$$

Then the substitution of (4)' for (5)' yields

$$\sum_h \beta_h \left(\frac{\partial F_h^j}{\partial \bar{y}_k^j}\right) = \beta_k + \sum_t \delta_t \frac{\partial D_t^j}{\partial \bar{y}_k^j}. \tag{11}$$

This equation shows that the marginal product due to input in terms of output shadow prices should be equal to the private cost (i.e. input shadow price) plus the social cost of the marginal generated pollution due to the same input.

Equation (6) implies that the shadow price of the input goods for the reduction of the pollution should balance the marginal effect of the improvement of the environment in terms of the shadow price of the environment.

It is noted, that the optimization in the about discussion is achieved in the sense of Pareto's optimum, and can be expressed by a flow diagram as shown in Fig. 1. If the influence of the pollution is assumed to be disregarded, then the economic optimization can be achieved as the Pareto's optimum in the free market with the principle of perfect competition. In these circumstances, each individual decides to consume goods so as to maximize his utility within his income. Let P be the price vector of the goods. Then, the optimization problem of the i-th individual is defined as follows;

$$\text{maximize} \quad U^i(\bar{x}^i)$$
$$\text{subject to} \quad P\bar{x}^i = Px^i.$$

For the purpose of maximization, Lagrange's multiplier ε_i and the corresponding Lagrangean L^i are introduced, where

$$L^i = U^i + \varepsilon_i P(x^i - \bar{x}^i).$$

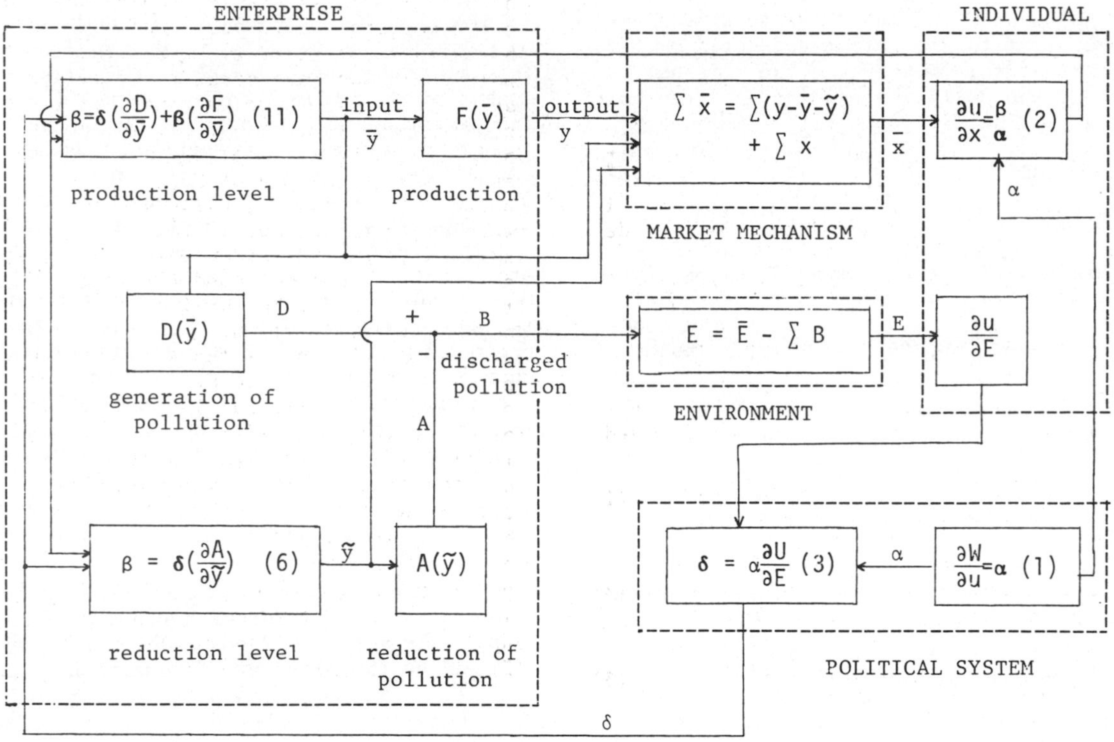

Fig. 1. Flow Diagram of the Model

Then the following necessary condition for optimization is derived;

$$\frac{\partial U^i}{\partial \bar{x}^i} = \varepsilon_i P. \qquad (12)$$

On the other hand, it is natural for each enterprise to have the maximal net profit. This optimization problem is expressed as follows:

$$\text{maximize} \quad Py^j - P\bar{y}^j,$$
$$\text{subject to} \quad y^j = F^j(\bar{y}^j).$$

In the same way as the above case, Lagrange's multiplier ϕ^j and Lagrangean L^j are intoduced, where

$$L^j = P(y^j - \bar{y}^j) + \phi^j(F^j(\bar{y}^j) - y^j).$$

The necessary conditions for optimization are

$$\phi^j_h = p_h, \qquad (13)$$

$$-p_k + \phi^j\left(\frac{\partial F^j}{\partial \bar{y}^j_k}\right) = 0. \qquad (14)$$

From the substitution of Equation (13) for Equation (14), it holds that

$$p_k = \sum_t p_h \frac{\partial F^j_h}{\partial \bar{y}^j_k}. \qquad (15)$$

Equation (12), (13), (14) and (15) correspond to Equation (2), (4), (5) and (11), respectively, in case $\delta_t=0$; that is, the environmental conditions are disregarded. This implies that, under the optimal conditions, the equilibrium point shifts by the distance corresponding to $\delta(\partial D^j/\partial y^j)$. It is noted, however, that there is no mechanism which makes the equibibium point shift in such a way, because the existing principle of capitalistic economy allows the enterprises to disregard the social cost arising from their production activities.

Thus, it is necessary to find some incentive mechanism which reduces the input level for production from the existing value $\bar{y}^j$ determined in the market to the preferable value $\bar{y}^{j*}$ in consideration of the social costs as shows in Fig. 2.

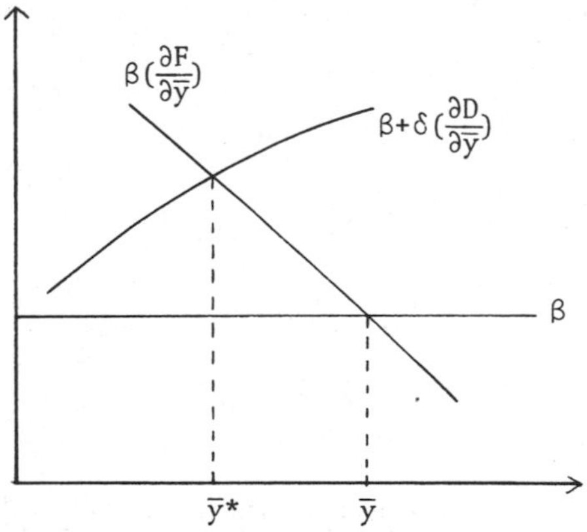

Fig. 2. Shift of Optimal Level

Therefore, if the private enterprise itself reduces the pollution level, then it has to impose the additional cost for the reduction of the pollution upon the consumers. Then the Pareto's optimum is attained by pricing the goods of the enterprise as

$$\beta' = (\beta + \delta(\partial D^j_h/\partial \bar{y}^j_k))(\partial F^j_h/\partial \bar{y}^j_k)^{-1}. \qquad (16)$$

SOCIAL COST AND REDUCTION COST

It is noted that δD^j means the total equivalent value of the pollution generated by the j-th enterprise. Let dD^j be the marginal amount of the pollution generated by the unit input $d\bar{y}^j$. That is,

$$\delta dD^j = \delta \frac{\partial D^j}{\partial \bar{y}^j} d\bar{y}^j \qquad (17)$$

Since $\delta(\partial D^j/\partial \bar{y}^j)$ is the marginal social cost of the generated pollution, the above relation implies that the equivalent value of the generated pollution is equal to the social cost to be imputed to the price of the goods. From equations (4), (5) and (17), it holds

$$\delta dD^j = (-\delta + \gamma^j \frac{\partial F^j}{\partial \bar{y}^j}) d\bar{y}^j$$

$$= -\beta d\bar{y}^j + \beta dy^j .$$

Integral of this relation yields

$$\delta D^j = \beta y^j - \beta \bar{y}^j \qquad (18)$$

This equation shows that the total equivalent value of the generated pollution is equal to the difference between the total price of the output and the total price of the input.

On the other hand, $\beta d\tilde{y}$ means the cost for the reduction of the pollution. From Equation (6), it holds

$$\beta d\tilde{y}^j = (\delta \frac{\partial A^j}{\partial \tilde{y}^j}) d\tilde{y}^j = \delta dA^j .$$

Integral of this relation yields

$$\delta A^j = \beta \tilde{y}^j \qquad (19)$$

This implies that the equivalent value of the reduced pollution is equal to the total input cost for the reduction of the pollution.

CONCLUDING REMARK

In the case where private enterprises reduce the pollution by themselves for environment control, they have to impose the social cost for pollution reduction upon the consumers by pricing the goods as

$$\beta' = (\beta + \delta \frac{\partial D}{\partial \bar{y}})(\frac{\partial y}{\partial \bar{y}})^{-1}$$

in order to attain Pareto's optimum.

This policy has been derived from the viewpoint of finding the optimal allocation of available resources which maximizes the social welfare function. The optimal conditions can be expressed by the flow diagram of Fig. 1. This diagram shows that $\partial W/\partial u = \alpha$ is the most essential part of the optimal conditions.

The exat form of the social welfare function cannot necessarily be identified. It is noted, however, that the problem can be solved if Lagrange multiplier α is known. The value of α has to be estimated from fistorical viewpoints, political reasons, public opinion, etc.

One of the incentive mechanisms which make the equilibium point sift to achieve Pareto's optimum is to introduce a criteria of discharge level of the pollution. Let B^{j*} be the specified level of the discharged pollution for the j-th enterprise. If $B^j > B^{j*}$, the j-th enterprise should be impose a heavy penalty equivalent to the social cost.

REFERENCES

(1) H. Mine, Reduction and Control of Pollution, Special Research Program of Methodology of Environmental Control suported by the Ministry of Education, Japan.

(2) P. A. Samuelson, Aspects of Public Expenciture, The Review of Economics and Statistics.

(3) P. A. Samuelson, The Pure Theory of Public Expenditure, ibid.

(4) J. R. Hickes, The Foundation of Welfare Economics, The Economic Journal.

(5) J. R. Hickes, The Rehabilitation of conmer's surplus, Readings in Welfare Economics.

(6) F. M. Bator, The Simple Analytics of Welfare Maximization, The American Economic Review.

(7) O. Lange, The Foundation of Economic Welfare, The Economic Journal.

(8) J. E. Mead, External Economics and Diseconomics in a Competitive situation, Readings in Welfare Economics.

(9) K. J. Arrow and M. Kurs, Public Investment, the Rate of Return, Fiscal Policy.

(10) G. Debreu, Valuation Equilibrium and Pareto Optimum, Readings in Welfare Economics.

(11) L. Hurwicz, Optimality and informational Efficiency in Resource Allocation Processes, ibid.

(12) T. K. Kumar, The Existence of an Optimal Economic Policy, Econometrica.

OPTIMAL CONTROL MODELS OF REGIONAL ECONOMIES

R.J. Bennett

Department of Geography, University College, London

Summary - Control of socio-economic systems which are partitioned into a set of N spatial regions presents some new and fascinating problems in optimal control. Most existing developments of optimal control theory for spatially distributed systems are based on models described by partial differential and difference equations (see for example (1)). For such models it must be assumed that the space is continuously differentiable or at least regularly partitioned (e.g. on a Cartesian lattice) and that interaction between locations is controlled by a pattern of distance decay. In addition it is usually assumed that at least the structure (but not necessarily the parameters) of the model is known a priori. Spatial models described by partial differential equations are of little utility for developing control models of regional economies, and this paper is concerned with extending the results of optimal control theory to situations in which the spatial domain of interest (e.g. a national economy) is partitioned into N regions which interact arbitrarily such that no distance metric is necessarily involved. In the first section a suitable mathematical representation of regional systems is developed. In section two the results of control theory are extended to this system description for T-stage strategies under uncertainty. Section three treats some of the major research problems that remain to be answered, especially the interaction between parameter estimation and the derivation of optimal controllers.

1. MATHEMATICAL REPRESENTATION

Most models which represent the dynamics of urban or regional economies have been built on the basis of the Lowry (2) and Wilson (3) interaction-allocation framework. These have often been comparative-static, and the TOMM and EMPIRIC models are examples (4). Other developments have sought to allocate changes to regional distributions of population and economic activity introduced via forecasts of changes in the levels of basic and exogenously determined employment. The resulting changes in population and service industry are then often allocated using an entropy-maximising approach. Other approaches to dynamic modelling of regional dynamics have been based on four themes: simulation, econometric estimation, accounting frameworks, and time series identification. Simulation models have evolved mostly around the Forrester (5) urban dynamics framework (see Batty (6)). Econometric models also permit simulations to be undertaken but use estimates of the magnitude of parametric relations determined from time series data. Most of these models have been designed to be linked to national econometric models such as the Brookings and SSRC, and Wharton models in the United States of the H.M. Treasury model in the U.K. (see 7,8,9). These models are aspatial in basis but attempts at simple disaggregation e.g. into central city and suburbs have been made by Glickman (10). This approach is useful as it provides connections with national management objectives and permits derivation of statistical forecasts and confidence intervals. The accounting approach has been developed by Rees and Wilson (11) for the analysis of population cohorts, but the method has more general applications to urban and regional modelling(Wilson (3)chapter 11). Time series identification methods have been developed mainly for the determination of relative cyclical sensitivity of different regions to changes in overall macro-economic indicators. Because of data availability, unemployment levels have been the main indicators examined. A number of studies have sought to evidence the regional variety of lag, lead, magnitude and turning-point differences using spectral, cross-spectral and lagged correlation functions as diagnostics (see 12 to 16). Such models allow the representation of spatial dynamics and inter-regional multipliers and are extremely useful in forecasting. A summary of this area of work and the identification methods that can be utilised is given by Bennett (17).

Despite this breadth of interest in models of regional economies, little attention has been given as yet to models which permit the development of optimal control solutions in regional systems. In order to develop models which do permit this development, a system representation is given below.

Most of the models of regional economies discussed above have been developed for mathematical systems defined in structural form (17):

$$(A_o+A_1z+\dots A_pz^p)y_t=(B_o+B_1z+\dots+B_qz^q)u_t \tag{1.1}$$

in which y_t is a (Nx1) vector of system endogenous variables, u_t is a (Nx1) vector of system control variables, A_i and B_i are each (NxN) matrices of parameters, z^i is the unit shift operator $zy_t=y_{t-1}$. The dimension N of the vectors refers to the N regions of a given national economy such that there is one endogenous and one control variable for each region. This univariate representation is retained for simplicity below, but all results hold equally when the input-output data are multivariate.

The structural form (1.1) describes the combined autoregressive and distributed lag structure of the regional system as the ratio of two matrix polynomials. It is for this representation of spatial systems that most specification and estimation methods have been developed, but for most control purposes it is more convenient to place (1.1) in a reduced form (Chow (18), Pindyck (19)).

$$Y_t=AY_{t-1}+BU_{t-1}+v_{t-1} \quad (1.2)$$

where

$$A=(A_o^{-1}A_1 \mid A_o^{-1}A_2 \mid \dots \mid A_o^{-1}A_p)$$

$$B=(A_o^{-1}B_o \mid A_o^{-1}B_1 \mid \dots \mid A_o^{-1}B_q)$$

$$Y'_{t-1}=(-y_{t-1} \mid -y_{t-2} \mid \dots \mid -y_{t-p})$$

$$U'_{t-1}=(u_{t-1} \mid u_{t-2} \mid \dots \mid u_{t-q})$$

The (Nx1) vector v_t is a random sequence for which there may be correlation between regions, i.e. $cov(v_{ti},v_{tj})\neq 0$ in some cases. This arises when A_o is non-diagonal; however it is assumed throughout the discussion below that A_o is diagonal and hence there will be no correlation in residuals between equations.

If (1.1) is identifiable then so will be (1.2). When the coefficients in (1.1) are not known _a priori_ and must be estimated from statistical records, there may be difficulty in developing control strategies based on (1.2). This problem is discussed in section three.

2. OPTIMAL CONTROL MODELS

Control models of regional economies are not well developed but Bennett and Chorley (20) have recognised four possible approaches. First, dynamic control is concerned with regional economies such as (1.2) but which are aggregated to an overall lumped form as in national macroeconomic planning. Second, spatial control is concerned with regional economies which are disaggregated but in which no account is taken of temporal evolution. This latter approach characterises many decisions on the optimal layout of service facilities (e.g. schools, hospitals) and also electoral and administrative districting. A third approach is by separation of space and time variables in which regional economic control with (1.2) is separated into two functions, one depending only on time, and the other depending only on space (1). Fourier expansion and the Galerkin technique are examples of this method. The final approach is concerned with development of complete regulatory and servomechanism control solutions in which full account is taken of spatial and temporal dependence, and in which redesign and adaptation of system coefficients can also be included. It is clear that the first three approaches provide only approximate solutions appropriate to special cases.

For regulator and servomechanism problems we require control based upon some criterion of loss. A frequently used criterion, and that adopted below, is the quadratic objective (loss) function W:

$$E(W)=\sum_t^T (Y_t-r_t)'M(Y_t-r_t) \quad (2.1)$$

The E(W) term is the expectation of the objective function in which r_t is a (Nx1) vector of targets one for each region, and M is a (NxN) symmetric, positive semi-definite matrix of weights which is assumed _known_. When $r_t=r$ for all t, i.e. a constant, we have a regulator problem, and when r_t is a changing set of targets there is a regional servomechanism problem. When T=1 we have a one-stage control problem. But in regional economic control we must almost always take T 1: first, because regional economies are sluggish, the response time to control is usually slow; industrial inertia and the length of learning time required in social systems limits the magnitude and rapidity of changes such that control is not socially or politically disruptive. Secondly, regional economic control is cost-limited in that the financial resources available are usually insufficient to achieve a one-term controller given the marginal return to control and the opportunity costs on capital. Thirdly, our understanding of most regional economies is limited to broad ranges of behaviour which can be predicted with reasonable accuracy and it may not be possible to apply the magnitude of control input necessary to achieve the desired final state in one step. This limits the choice of controls to an admissable set determined by stability and other criteria.

Given the model of regional economies (1.2) and initial conditions Y_o, the optimal control problem is to choose that set of N spatial and T temporal controls $U_1,\dots,U_T$ to minimise the welfare funtion. The regional model (1.2) is identical in structure to multivariate models of lumped systems and is subject to the same observability and controllability criteria. Using this symmetry property, we may write the optimal control solution directly. Using the results of Chow (18) for example the optimal control is given by:

$$U_t^o=-(B'H_tB)^{-1}B'H_tAY_{t-1} + (B'H_tB)^{-1}B'h_t \quad (2.2)$$

where H_t is a (NxN) matrix and h_t is a (Nx1) vector and both satisfy the matrix Ricatti equations given by:

$$H_{t-1}=M+A'H_t(A-B(B'H_tB)^{-1}B'H_tA)$$
$$H_T = M \tag{2.3}$$

and

$$h_{t-1}=Mr_{t-1}+A'h_t-A'H_tB(B'H_tB)^{-1}B'h_t$$
$$h_T = Mr_T \tag{2.4}$$

Provided that we specify the data on the initial conditions Y_o to match the (Nx1) vector of targets r_o for each region, we may integrate (2.3) and (2.4) forwards in time from these specified initial conditions to determine the optimal control setting U^o_t at each intermediate time point over the T stages of control. The facility with which optimal quadratic controllers for regional economies can be developed in the form (2.2) to (2.4) above exposes a number of outstanding research problems which are discussed in the next section.

A simple example of a two-region economy will exhibit the use of (2.2) to (2.4). Consider a model (1.2) of a two-region economy in reduced form and described by:

$$\begin{bmatrix} Y_{t,1} \\ Y_{t,2} \end{bmatrix} = \begin{bmatrix} 1 & 2 \\ 3 & 1 \end{bmatrix} \begin{bmatrix} Y_{t-1,1} \\ Y_{t-1,2} \end{bmatrix} + \begin{bmatrix} 2 & 1 \\ 4 & 2 \end{bmatrix} \begin{bmatrix} U_{t-1,1} \\ U_{t-1,2} \end{bmatrix} \tag{2.5}$$

It is desired to move the endogenous variable vector Y_t form its intial values to a final value Y_T according to an optimal control equation (2.2) using quadratic costs (2.1). If we assume for simplicity that we have a one stage problem, the control solution reduces to a simple calculation. If we let

$$r_T = \begin{bmatrix} 10 \\ 5 \end{bmatrix} \quad ; \quad Y_o = \begin{bmatrix} 1 \\ 4 \end{bmatrix} \quad ;$$
$$M = \begin{bmatrix} 1 & 0 \\ 0 & 1 \end{bmatrix} \tag{2.6}$$

Then the optimal control rule is given by the vector equation for feedback from stage T to stage one:

$$\begin{matrix} U^o_{t,1} \\ U^o_{t,2} \end{matrix} = \begin{bmatrix} -13.6 \\ 2 \end{bmatrix} \tag{2.7}$$

This is the one-stage regulator for the achievement of the targets r_T for the given initial conditions. A typical example of such a policy might be the disposition of regional labour subsidies as control instruments to achieve given employment targets. Another example is the use of the control variable as a financial or fiscal instrument with targets specified in terms of cash needs measured against a number of social indicators (such as social service, health, education and welfare needs)in each region. In each of these examples the flow of resources required is from central to local areas as in federal systems such as the U.S. and Canada, or as with the devolved system of local authority finance in the U.K. under the Rate Support Grant. In such cases it is often necessary to impose constraints such that total central government expenditure do not exceed a predetermined figure. The problems surrounding the imposition of such limits as either equality or inequality constraints are discussed in the next section.

3. PROBLEMS IN REGIONAL ECONOMIC CONTROL

The quadratic controller (2.2) to (2.4) above is extremely attractive for use in regional economic control, not least because all of the classical results of mathematical control theory for multivariate systems will apply directly. But before it can be utilised, it will be necessary in most instances to overcome a number of major problems, the most important of which are discussed below.

One major problem concerns the use of the quadratic cost criterion (2.1). This has the advantage of simplicity and of permitting simple mathematical manipulation. However, these advantages should not blind us to the difficulties associated with assuming quadratic costs: the arbitrariness in treating both positive and negative deviations from targets with equal weight. For example, increases or decreases from a target level of employment, or of a target for satisfaction of social welfare needs, are not equally tolerable. Moreover we would not expect positive and negative deviations to be equally tolerable over all regions; some regions (the more developed) might be able to tolerate positive deviations from employment levels (reducing over-heating) but might be less able to tolerate negative deviations (which generate excessive wage-push inflation). In less developed regions characterised by predominant patterns of labour surplus, the tolerance would be reversed. Such patterns require that we allow the weighting matrix M to be non-diagonal. Long-term research is required in order to determine with greater precision objective spatial welfare functions alternative to the quadratic; although Livesey (21) questions whether more complicated welfare functions will be any less arbitrary or more determinate.

A second problem concerns the interaction of regional and national control models. In federal systems and in centralised states with devolved agencies there are great difficulties in reconciling regional control optima with national control objectives. Practical attempts to integrate these various levels have not been overwhelmingly successful (22). Two main mathematical approaches are possible based upon either multilevel control or the determination of optima under constraints. Multilevel control treats the integration problem as a hierachical joint optimisation of both regional and national control targets which creates a number of difficulties in practice. The joint optimisation problem is usually of large dimension and there will be the frequent appearance of near-equivalent local optima. One approach to the dimensionality problem in practice, of course, is that many economic systems employ decentralisation to the federal or devolved decision units. A number of workers have considered control of systems which are completely decentralised, i.e. decoupled (see ref.(23)). When the regional system is not constitutionally decoupled it is necessary to adopt a number of mathematical devices to reduce the system dimensions. Three forms of such mathematical decomposition can be adopted (23,20). The first, structural decomposition, involves partitioning the system into separate subsets one for each region, each with independent targets and controls which are then coordinated. A second method, influence decomposition, partitions the controls into levels based upon which levels set preemptive target values for the others, i.e. splitting the economy into executive (policy-determining) and subordinate regions. Control decomposition provides a third method which uses any of the special structural properties of the mathematics of the control solution itself to simplify to independent optimisation problems. The advantages and disadvantages of the decomposition approaches are well illustrated by the difficulties of coordinating the controls in the decomposed models. One dual-feasible method given by Schoeffler (24) uses a dissagregation of the objective function (2.1) into N parts for each region. The interaction between the N regions is taken into a set of (NxN) slack variables Z_t which allow complete decoupling with the real interaction effects set equal to the slack variables. For the resulting two levels the control problem at level 1 is solved for the decoupled set of N independent systems, then at level 2, the first level solution is forced to satisfy an interaction-balance principle. The difference between the true system interactions X_t and the slack variables Z_t is used to define a set of Langrangian multipliers λ for which a necessary condition for a minimum is determined when the derivative equals zero. Hence for a two-region system, optimisation is carried out over the modified cost function:

$$E(W)=E(W_1(U_{t1},Y_{t1},X_{t1})) + E(W_2(U_{t2},Y_{t2},X_{t2}))+\lambda'(X_t-Z_t) \qquad (3.1)$$

In practice this optimum must often be determined iteratively.

The introduction of constraints often allows many of the dimensionality problems of multilevel control to be overcome by designing control systems incorporating specific constraints on the interaction of the various levels of economic management. In the central allocation of the Rate Support Grant in the U.K. for example, Tan (25) has shown that the imposition of linear equality constraints can produce regional optima in line with national government spending limits. The control variables are subject to a set of $q < N$ independent linear constraints:

$$F_t U_t = f_t \qquad (3.2)$$

in which f_t is a (qx1) vector of specified central spending targets and F_t is a (qxN) matrix of known constants. The optimal control rule is then given following (25) by:

$$U_t^o=-D_t^{-1}B'H_tAY_{t-1}-D_t^{-1}F_tP_t^{-1}F_t +D_t^{-1}B'h_t-D_t^{-1}F_{t-}'P_t^{-1}F_tD_t^{-1}B'h_t +D_t^{-1}F_t'P_t^{-1}f_t \qquad (3.3)$$

where

$$D_t = B'H_tB \qquad P_t = F_tD_t^{-1}F_t' \qquad (3.4)$$

which is a modified form of (2.2) with H_t and h_t defined in (2.3) and (2.4). Equation (3.3) is identical in the deterministic and stochastic cases, i.e. certainty-equivalence applies when the controls are subject to linear equality constraints.

In the U.K. allocation of the resources element of the Rate Support Grant and in U.S. revenue-sharing it is usually politically necessary to include inequality constraints. These prevent inequalities in local tax bases from being used to precept taxation income away from better-off regions to give to other regions, i.e. all equalisation between regional expenditure needs and the necessary financial resources is achieved by allocation from central government, regions with an excess of local revenue will have control flows set to zero. Tan (26) has shown that in this case a similar modification of the control rule (2.2) results after the introduction of a slackness condition into (3.2) but new difficulties arise because of the need to consider the generalised inverse. The new control solution is given by choosing the optimal control settings subject to (2.1) and the inequality constraint:

$$F_t U_{t-1} \leqslant f_{t-1} \qquad (3.5)$$

which is a modification of (3.2). The problem of the generalised inverse arises from the introduction of (3.5) into the system equation (1.2). Using the slack variables S_t we may rewrite (3.5) as:

$$F_t U_{t-1} - S_t = f_t \qquad (3.6)$$

which gives a modified system equation:

$$Y_t = AY_{t-1} + \underline{B}\underline{U}_t + v_t \qquad (3.7)$$

where

$$\underline{B} = [B \mid C]$$
$$\underline{U}_t' = [U_t \mid S_t] \qquad (3.8)$$

in which C is a null matrix of appropriate dimension. The control rule for the T-stage case is then given by:

$$\underline{U}_t^o = -(\underline{D}_t^{-1}\underline{B}'H_t A + \underline{D}_t^{-1}F'\underline{P}_t^{-1}F_t\underline{D}_t^{-1}\underline{B}'H_t A)Y_{t-1}$$
$$+\underline{D}_t^{-1}\underline{B}'h_t - \underline{D}_t^{-1}F_t'\underline{P}_t^{-1}F_t\underline{D}_t^{-1}\underline{B}'h_t$$
$$+\underline{D}_t^{-1}F_t'\underline{P}_t^{-1}f_t \qquad (3.9)$$

where the matrices H_t and h_t are defined in (2.4) with the same initial conditions, and:

$$\underline{D}_t = G'H_t G$$
$$\underline{P}_t = F_t\underline{D}_t^{-1}F_t' \qquad (3.10)$$

Further discussion is given by Tan (26).

A third problem in regional economic control concerns the fact the the system model (1.2) is usually not known with certainty but is derived from parameter estimates using time series or other data. The important consequence is that a separation principle usually does not hold between parameter estimation and control (27). Attempts at separate treatment of the two problems will not yield a global minimum of the objective funtion (2.1),(see ref.(20)). In response to this problem we may adopt the Åstrom and Wittenmark 'self-tuning regulator' which gives recursive estimates of the parameters and optimal control at each step as a special form of Kalman filter. Although this solution gives optimal estimation and control, it has not been found possible to extend the results to multivariate or regional systems. In the multivariate and regional cases we are thrown back on suboptimal solutions, the most useful of which is the learning algorithm given by Chow (18, ch.11). Further developments of this method for regional systems are still required.

A fourth problem is how to make allowance for changes in coefficients and structure of the system model (1.2). Most economic and regional systems are dominated by evolution and shifts in coefficients in their describing models. There has been growing awareness of this problem (e.g.(18)), and it is relatively simple to extend the structure of the control solutions given above to systems with parameter dynamics. What is lacking as yet is a satisfactory method of identifying the parameter models and learning that occurs when these are not known *a priori*. Evaluation of a number of the available methods (17,28, 29) does not give unequivocal support to the universal efficiency of any of the presently available techniques. Some window function, bounding techniques and adaptive estimation methods may perform very adequately in specific instances, but the method which will be of most utility in any specific case cannot usually be predicted in advance. Again, when both the system model and any model of change in the coefficients are both unknown, the self-tuning regulator (27) or Chow (18) learning method must be modified in regional economic control systems. These problems are being currently investigated at University College.

A final outstanding problem of the control approach taken in (1.2) and (2.2) is that it is well known that regional economies are unusually open systems with many cross-flows between regions arising from high levels of migration, journey-to-work, and trade and product flows. This makes the system model complex and undermines the assumption of (1.2) that the control instruments are independent of each other between regions. Dependence enters from the constitutional structure of regional economic systems (as distinct from separate nation states) which limits the degrees of freedom of economic control even in federal situations. If we require to specify goals independently for each region, new ways of thinking with regard to economic regulators will be required. In almost all decentralised states macroeconomic regulation is maintained as a central government function but we know from the controllability conditions that govern (2.2) that we cannot achieve optimal regional targets without independent control instruments. We are drawn to accept, therefore, that some measure of disaggregation of macroeconomic regulators is required.

4. CONCLUSION

There has been little application of the methods of optimal control theory to the management of regional economic systems. This is suprising since, as briefly sketched in sections 1 and 2, all of the results of the mathematical control theory of multivariate systems apply provided that we do not attempt to impose any distance metric on the system. Despite the simplicity of representing regional systems as multivariate control models a number of important research problems arise which have been discussed in section 3. These problems concern the way in which we design control systems to satisfy controllability criteria, the manner in which decentralised (decoupled) systems can be realised, and the need for developments of regional control theory which can handle uncertain models with uncertain adaptive coefficients with linear relations between the control instruments.

5. REFERENCES

(1) Butkovskii, A. G. (1969) Distributed Control Systems, Elsevier, New York.

(2) Lowry, I. S. (1964) A Model of Metropolis, RM-4125-RC, Rand Corp., Santa Monica.

(3) Wilson, A. G. (1974) Urban and Regional Models in Geography and Planning, Wiley, Chichester.

(4) Lowry, I. S. (1967) Seven Models of Metropolitan Development: A Structural Comparison, Rand Corp., Santa Monica.

(5) Forrester, J.W. (1968) Urban Dynamics, MIT Press, Cambridge, Mass.

(6) M. Batty, Modelling Cities as Dynamic Systems, Nature, 231, 425-428 (1971).

(7) F. W. Bell, An Econometric Forecasting Model for a Region, J. Regional Science, 7, 109-128 (1967).

(8) S. Czmanski, A Method of Forecasting Metropolitan Growth by Means of Distributed Lag Analysis, J. Regional Science, 6, 33-49 (1965).

(9) J. Paelinck, Dynamic Urban Models, Papers Regional Science Assoc., 14, 25-37 (1970)

(10) N. J. Glickman, An Area-Stratified Regional Econometric Model, Reg. Sci. Res. Instit., Discussion Paper.

(11) Rees, P.H. and Wilson, A.G. (1977) Spatial Population Analysis, Arnold, London.

(12) L. King, E. Casetti, and D. Jeffrey, Economic Impulses in a Regional System of Cities: A Study of Spatial Interactions, Regional Studies, 3, 213-218 (1969).

(13) P. Haggett, Leads and Lags in Inter-Regional Systems: A Study of Cyclical Fluctuations in the South West Economy, in Chisholm, M. and Manners, G., Spatial Policy Problems of the British Economy, University Press, Cambridge, (1971).

(14) Sant, M. (1973) The Geography of Business Cycles: A Case Study of Economic Fluctuations in East Anglia, London School of Economics, London.

(15) R. J. Bennett, Dynamic Systems Modelling of the North West Region, Environment and Planning, Series A, 7, 525-538, 539-566, 617-636, 887-898 (1975).

(16) L. W. Hepple, Spectral Techniques and the Study of Interregional Economic Cycles, in Peel, R., Chisholm, M. and Haggett, P. (1975) Processes in Physical and Human Geography, Butterworth, London.

(17) Bennett, R.J. (1978) The Analysis of Space-Time Systems, Pion Press, London.

(18) Chow, G. C. (1975) Analysis and Control of Dynamic Economic Systems, Wiley, New York.

(19) Pindyck, R. (1973) Optimal Planning for Economic Stabilisation, North Holland, Amsterdam.

(20) Bennett, R. J. and Chorley, R. J. (1977) Environmental Systems: Philosophy, Analysis and Control, Methuen, London.

(21) D. Livesey, Can Macro-Economic Policy Problems Ever be Treated as Quadratic Regulator Problems?, Conference Publ. 101, Inst. Elec. Engrs., London (1973).

(22) Klaasen, L.H. and Paelinck, J. H. P. (1974) Integration of Socio-Economic and Physical Planning, University Press, Rotterdam.

(23) J. D. Schoeffler, On-Line Multilevel Systems, in Wismer, D. A. (1971) Optimisation Methods for Large Scale Systems, With Applications, McGraw-Hill, New York.

(24) Aoki, M. (1976) Optimal Control and System Theory in Dynamic Economic Analysis, North Holland, Amsterdam.

(25) K. C. Tan, Optimal Control of Linear Econometric Systems with Linear Equality Constraints on the Control Variables, forthcoming (1977).

(26) K. C. Tan, Optimal Control of Linear Econometric Systems with Linear Inequality Constraints on the Control Variables, forthcoming (1977).

(27) K. J. Åstrom and B. Wittenmark, Problems of Identification and Control, J. Math. Anal. and Applications, 34, 90-113 (1977)

(28) R. J. Bennett, Nonstationary Parameter Estimation for Small Sample Situations: A Comparison of Methods, Int. J. Systems Sci., 7, 257-275 (1975).

(29) R. J. Bennett, Consistent Estimation of Nonstationary Parameters for Small Sample Situations - A Monte Carlo Study, Int. Econ. Review, 18, forthcoming (1977).

WATER-RESOURCES SYSTEM OPTIMAL CONTROL

V. Priazhinskaya and Iosif Khranovich

Institute of Water Problems, the USSR Academy of Sciences

ABSTRACTS

Quantity and quality control in a water-resources system is considered to be an optimization problem on a graph with retarded controls, a nonconvex biseparable objective functional, and bilinear constraints of the type of equalities. Based on the branch and bound scheme, the solution of the problem with the given error is reduced to a finite series of convex estimating problems.

THE PROBLEM

Water-resources system is a whole complex of interacting water sources, reservoirs and customers interconnected by a net of streams. A river stream flow, ground water, and water from fresheners serve as water sources. The sources supply the system with water which is of quality and in quantities within the given limits. The main water customers are different agricultural and industrial enterprises, municipal water-supply, energetic, fisheries, water transport, and recreation. The water is used either without being returned or some part (or the whole) of it is returned into the system. The process of water utilization is followed by the change of its quality, regulated within the given limits by treatment. Reservoirs play the role of accumulators thus allowing the coordination of the water inflow and utilization in the system. Besides, the reservoirs from a single whole with such customers as fisheries, water transport, and recreation using the water without withdrawing it. On the reservoirs and streams natural processes of water quality changing and those occasioned by anthropogenetic influence are taking place. The quantity of the water running through the streams is limited by their efficiency.

Utilization of the water resources is characterized by economic effects depending on the quality and quantity of the water withdrawn from as well as returned to the system. The optimal functioning consists in distributing the water in such a manner and in setting such a degree of water treatment that the summary investment (including the efficiency of water utilization) would be reduced to a minimum.

While dealing with a complex problem of optimal utilization of water resources, the aspects of quantity and quality are usually studied separately [1]. That is - either the distribution of given quality is investigated or the water quality parameters are determined on the assumption that some water quantity is given. Suitable mathematical models are constructed in accordance with that division. However qualitative and quantitative water properties are closely interconnected and must be considered jointly which is done in this paper.

A mathematical model of water resources control is based on the description of the water-resources system as a dynamical lumped-parameter one. The water-resources system in the model is represented by a graph $\Gamma(I,S)$. The geometrical configuration of the graph corresponds to the schematic image of the system. A set of graph nodes I corresponds to sources, reservoirs, locations of water intake and return, etc. A set of links S is identified with the streams and the customers, including also links, introduced to represent water-sources on the graph $\Gamma(I,S)$.

A distinctive feature of $\Gamma(I,S)$ is the introduction of storages, representing reservoirs in conjunction with customers that utilize the water of the reservoirs without withdrawing it. The storages are located in the graph nodes, their stock being bounded above and below.

$$\bar{W}_i \geq W_i \geq \underline{W}_i, \quad i \in I \qquad (1)$$

by absolute continuous time functions $\underline{W}_i(t) > 0$ and $\bar{W}_i(t) \geq \underline{W}_i(t)$.

The flows move along the graph links with some retardation and amplification, the value of the amplification factor k_s being between 1 and 0. The flow Z_s out of the link is related with the flow V_s into the link by an equality

$$Z_s(t) = K_s V_s(t - \theta_s). \qquad (2)$$

Introducing into (2) and operator ϑ_s of the constant retardation θ_s (2) becomes

$$Z_s = K_s \vartheta_s V_s. \qquad (2')$$

$\Gamma(S,I)$ link flows have upper and lower limits in the form of piecewise continuous functions $\underline{V}_s(t) \geq 0$ and $\bar{V}_s(t) \geq \underline{V}_s(t)$ so

$$\bar{V}_s \geq V_s \geq \underline{V}_s, \quad s \in S. \qquad (3)$$

The water sources are represented by nodes, each connected by means of two links S_1 and S_2 (with the amplification factors $K_{S1} = 1$ and $K_{S2} = 0$) leading this node to the node through which the water enters the system. The flow into the link S_1 simulates the intensity of the source water inflow into the system; the flow into the link S_2 corresponds to the unutilized part of the source intensity. In accordance with the part, played by the flows of the links S_1, S_2, we set the value of retardation $\theta_{S2} = 0$ and the retardation θ_{S1} will be the time interval between the moments when the water is withdrawn from the source and when it enters the system. The sources are characterized by flow intensity $b_i(t) \geq 0$, which is the maximum water quantity that can be obtained from the source per unit of time. The flow V_{S1}, corresponding to the intensity of the water entering the system, is limited, its lower boundary being the minimal flow $\underline{V}_{S1} \geq 0$ and its upper boundary being the maximal flow $\bar{V}_{S1} = b_i(t)$. The flow V_{S2} of utilized source intensity must be between $\underline{V}_{S2} = 0$ and $\bar{V}_{S2} = \bar{V}_{S1} - \underline{V}_{S1}$.

The water quality in the system is characterized by a vector of a pollutant concentration C. The set of different kinds of pollutants P may be divided into subsets $P_q (q \in Q, \bigcup_{q \in Q} P_q = P)$ in accordance with an index of pollution. For example pollutants may be separated into such groups: sanitary-toxicological, general sanitary, and organoleptical. The pollutant concentration of each set P_q must meet the conditions:

$$\sum_{p \in P_q} C^{\alpha}_{zp} [\bar{C}^{\alpha}_{zp}]^{-1} \leq 1, \qquad (4)$$

where $\bar{C}^{\alpha}_{zp}$ are the maximum acceptable concentrations, $z \in R = S \cup I$. If $z \in S$ then index α will be H and K corresponding to the beginning or the end of a link. Besides, the values of pollutant concentrations are limited by

$$C^{\alpha}_{zp} \geq \underline{C}^{\alpha}_{zp}. \qquad (5)$$

Physically the values $\underline{C}^{\alpha}_{zp}$ are nonnegative, in particular for the dissolved oxygen $\underline{C}^{\alpha}_{zp}(t) > 0$. Being nonnegative the concentrations C^{α}_{zp} in accordance with (4) are limited by the maximum acceptable values of $\bar{C}^{\alpha}_{zp}$. For $z \in S$ functions $\bar{C}^{\alpha}_{zp}(t)$ and $\underline{C}^{\alpha}_{zp}(t)$ are piecewise continuous, for $z \in I$ they are absolute continuous.

The set of links is divided into subsets S_I, and S_{II}. S_I corresponds to stream and to customers who do not treat water, and S_{II} - to customers using treatment plants. And so we have links $s_2 \in S_I$ and links $s_1 \in S_I$ or $s_1 \in S_{II}$.

The change of the pollutant concentrations along the links $s \in S_I$ and in reservoirs is supposed to be described by a system of linear differential equations with constant coefficients. By solving this system one obtains pollutant concentrations c_v of flows into the links $s \in S_I$ as $C^H_{vs} = \{C^H_{vsp}, p \in P\}$ and from the links as $C^K_{vs} = \{C^K_{vsp}, p \in P\}$ these concentrations being connected with a nonsingular matrix of interaction a_s and with a constant vector of the effect of nonconsidered components β_s in a following expression:

$$C^K_{vs} = a_s \vartheta_s C^H_{vs} + \beta_s \quad (6)$$

The change of the concentrations C_w for the storages is:

$$W_i \dot{C}_{wi} = -\alpha_i \circ W_i [C_{wi} - \beta_i] + a_i \dot{W}_i [C_{yi} - C_{wi}] \quad (7)$$

where W_i is the stock in the storage i; C_{wi} is a vector of storage i pollutant concentrations, C_{yi} is a vector of pollutant concentrations in a flow into the storage or out of it; α_i is a vector of pollutant abatement intensity; a_i and β_i correspond to a_s and β_s ; the point over the function means that time derivatives of the function are taken; o is a symbol of the weak vector multiplication which for vectors of the same dimension $a = \{a_r\}$ and $b = \{b_r\}$ gives the vector $d = a \circ b$ with coordinates $d_r = a_r b_r$.

The pollutant concentration of flows from the links $s \in S_{II}$ is determined by the waste treatment plant efficiency, therefore a relation of the type (6) between C^K_{vs} and C^H_{vs} for these links is absent. Not effecting the common character of the problem the retardation values of these link flows are assumed to be zero.

The quality of flows into the system out of the nodes-sources is described by a pollutant concentration vector C_{bi}.

The efficiency of water-resources system elements is characterized by the functionals of expenditures for the planning period $[T_0, T_1]$

$$F_z(x_z, c_z) = \int_{T_0}^{T_1} f_z(x_z, c_z, t)\,dt, \ z \in R, \quad (8)$$

where $x_z = V_z$ if $z \in S$ and $x_z = W_z$ if $z \in I$; $C_z = C^H_{vz}$ if $z \in S_I$, $C_z = C^H_{vz}, C^K_{vz}$ if $z \in S_{II}$ and $C_z = C_{Wz}$ if $z \in I$. The integrand f_z characterizes the efficiency of the water-resources system element and includes both direct expenditures and the losses due to the deviation of the water parameters from the optimal ones. f_z is a nonnegative piecewise continuous time function in which the effect of expenditures made at different times is taken into account. Note, that f_z for links $z \in S_{II}$ depends upon the pollutant concentrations of flows into and out of the links; f_z for links $z \in S_I$ depends upon the concentrations of flows only into these links; for the streams $f_z = 0$ on the set, given by constraints (1), (3), (5).

For every fixed moment of time f_z is supposed to be a biseparable function, i.e., f_z is a sum of functions, each being depended on two scalar variables x_z and C^α_{zp} forming a block of separability.

$$f_z(x_z(t), C_z(t), t) = \sum_{\alpha} \sum_{p \in P} f^\alpha_{zp}(x_z(t), C^\alpha_{zp}(t), t). \quad (9)$$

Each function f^α_{zp} due to the law of diminishing returns is continuous and convex for each variable x_z and C^α_{zp} and is unlimitedly increasing for $x_z, C^\alpha_{zp} \to \infty$. But for the variables x_z and C^α_{zp} taken together the functions f^α_{zp} generally speaking are nonconvex, therefore both the function f_z (9) and the functional F_z are nonconvex.

The water and pollutant distribution in the water-resources system is subjected to the law of flow continuity, in accordance with that, the flow and pollutant values in the nodes of $\Gamma(I,S)$ are related by the mass water balance equations

$$\dot{W}_i = \sum_{s\in S_i^+} Z_s - \sum_{s\in S_i^-} V_s + b_i,\ i\in I \qquad (10)$$

and pollutions

$$\dot{W}_i C_{yip} = \sum_{s\in S_i^+} Z_s C^{K}_{vsp} - C^{H}_{vsp}\sum_{s\in S_i^-} V_s + b_i C_{bip},\ i\in I, p\in P, \qquad (11)$$

where S_i^+ is a set of links leading into a node i, S_i^- is a set of links leading from the node i. Owing to the physical features of the spread of the pollutants contained in the equation (11) the input concentrations of all the links leading from the same node are equal, i.e. $C^H_{vsp} = C^H_{vrp}$ for $s, r \in S_i^-, i\in I$.

The problem of the optimal control of the water-resources system is formulated as a problem of finding such link flows V storage stocks W and their pollutant concentrations C_v, C_w that minimize the total expenditures for all the elements of $\Gamma(I,S)$ for the planning period on a set, defined by constraints (1)-(7) and (10),(11). Let us express this problem in a vector form: find a vector $X^o = W^o, V^o, C^o$ which minizes the expenditure functional

$$F(x) = \sum_{z\in R} F_z(X_z, C_z) \qquad (13)$$

on a permissible set G. This set is defined by constraints of the type of equalities

$$\dot{W} - HV - b = 0, \qquad (14a)$$

$$\dot{W}\circ C_{yp} - B_p(V, C_v) - b\circ C_{bp} = 0,\ p\in P, \qquad (14b)$$

$$W\circ\dot{C}_w + E(W, C_w) + a_w W\circ[C_y - C_w] = 0, \qquad (14c)$$

$$C^K_{vI} - a_I\vartheta_I C^H_{vI} - \beta_I = 0 \qquad (14d)$$

and of the type of inequalities

$$\bar{V} \geq V \geq \underline{V},\ \bar{W} \geq W \geq \underline{W},\ C \geq \underline{C}, \qquad (15a)$$

$$\sum_{p\in P_q} C_p \circ [\bar{C}_p]^{-1} \leq 1,\ q\in Q, \bigcup_{q\in Q} P_q = P \qquad (15b)$$

and by the initial conditions

$$V(t) = V^o(t),\ C^H_v(t) = C^{Ho}_v(t),\ t\in[T_o-\theta, T_o), \qquad (16a)$$

$$W(0) = W^o(0),\ C_w(0) = C^o_w(0). \qquad (16b)$$

Constraints (14a) and (14b) are mass balance equations (10) and (11) written in a vector form. Constraints (14c) and (14d) are equations (7) and (6) accordingly, and constraints (15) correspond to (3), (1), (4) and (5). Besides the evident matrix and vector symbols in (13)-(16), the following designations are used. The difference between the matrix H and the incidence matrix of $\Gamma(I,S)$ is as follows: instead of +1 in the incidence matrix a linear operator $K_s\vartheta_s$ is placed into H. The elements of H are

$$H_{is} = \begin{cases} -1, & \text{if the link } s \text{ leads from the node i,} \\ K_s\vartheta_s & \text{if the link } s \text{ leads to the node i,} \\ 0, & \text{for the link } s \text{ being non-incident to the node i.} \end{cases}$$

Bilinear forms are $B_p = H^+ K\circ\vartheta V\circ C^K_{vp} - C^H_{vp}\circ H^- V$, $E = \alpha_w\circ W\circ[C_w - \beta_w]$, where the matrix H^- is constructed from H by means of changing the operators $K_s\vartheta_s$ into zero; the matrix H^+ is constructed from H by means of converting $K_s\vartheta_s$ into +1 and changing all -1 into 0.

In the problem of the optimal control (13)-(16) the stocks W and their pollutant concentrations C_w play the role of phase variables, the link flows V and their pollutant concentrations C_v are controls. The problem (13)-(16) simulates a system with retarding control therefore besides the initial conditions on the phase variables one must know the values of the controls on a semi-interval of the initial retardation.

The problem of the optimal control (13)-(16) is Lagrange's problem with a nonconvex biseparable objective functional, a free right endpoint, and fixed time; this problem corresponds to the real situation of a functioning water-resources system. In this problem the constraints for the phase variables and controls of the type of inequalities (15) are linear; the constraints of the type of equalities in a solved form (14a) and (14d) are also linear. The constraints of the type of equalities in unsolved form (14b) and (14c), containing the controls, the phase variables, and their derivatives, are bilinear.

To apply directly well-known results of the optimal control theory to the study of the problem (13)-(16) with the retarding control, the nonlinear constraints of the type of equalities and the nonconvex objectional functional is difficult. However, distinctive features of the considered problem make it possible to investigate whether a solution exists, to obtain the conditions of the optimality, and to construct a method of its solution.

As the system of equations (14d) determines the vector which is included only in system (14c), the vector w in accordance with (15) is separated from 0, the matrix a_I is nonsingular in accordance with its construction, the retardation in the controls of the problem (13)-(16) with a free right endpoint does not effect upon our application of the theorem of the existence and the extremal principle to locally convex problems [2]. From the theorem of the existence it follows that there exists a vector x^o in a nonempty set G, vector components V^o, C_V^o being limited measurable vector-functions, vector components W^o, C_W^o being absolute continuous vector-functions with limited measurable derivatives. The necessary conditions of the optimality, described by the relation between the vector of the solution x^o and the vector of dual optimal variables of the problem y^o are the result of the extremal principle. The components of y^o, corresponding to the constraints of the type of equalities (14), have the meaning of shadow values which are optimal differential estimations of the water used in the system in the best manner. The components of y^o corresponding to the constraints of the type of inequalities (15), are interpreted as optimal estimations of the demands of the water-resources system elements from the water quality and quantities. For two main special cases of the problem (13)-(16) corresponding to the optimal distribution of the water of given quality and to the optimal treatment of the prescribed water amount the conditions of the optimality are also sufficient ones, as these cases can be considered as Lagrange's problems with convex integrands and linear constraints.

THE METHOD OF SOLUTION

The multiextremal problem (13)-(16) with the nonlinear constraints of the type of equalities is solved in assumption of two simplifying suppositions.

1. The discrete time is introduced. The dynamics of the system consists in the possibility to change to regime of the system functioning in the predetermined moment of time. Between that moments the system is a stationary one.

2. An approximate solution of the problem is found. Such a vector is taken as a solution that ensures an objective functional optimum with the sufficient accuracy and does not differ from the permissible set of vectors more than on prescribed error.

While constructing the optimal vector, the bilinearity of the constraints of the type of equalities and the biseparability of the objective functional are essentially used.

The planning period $[T_0, T_1]$ is divided into N segments by means of points $T_0 = t_0 < t_1 < \dots t_N = T_1$. Generally speaking the segments $[t_n, t_{n+1}]$ can be of different length $\rho_n = t_{n+1} - t_n$. In the intervals (t_n, t_{n+1}) all the variables of the problem (13)-(16) are considered as constants, the integrals are approximated by sums, the derivatives are approximated by the relations of finite differences. The finite-dimensional analog of the problem (13)-(16) in discrete time comes to finding a vector $x^0 = W^0, V^0, C^0,$ which minimizes the functional

$$\Phi(x) = \sum_{n=0}^{N-1} \sum_{z \in R} \sum_{p \in P} \sum_{\alpha} \varphi^{\alpha}_{zpn}(x_{zn}, C^{\alpha}_{zpn}) \quad (17)$$

on the permissible set $\bar{G}$ given by the constraints of the type of equalities including the mass balance equations

$$h_1(x) = W_{n+1} - W_n - \rho_n [H V_n + b_n] = 0, \quad (18a)$$

$$h_{2p}(x) = [W_{n+1} - W_n] \circ C_{ypn} - \rho_n [B_{pn} + b_n \circ C_{bpn}] = 0, \; p \in P \quad (18b)$$

and the laws of pollutant concentration transformation

$$h_3(x) = W_n \circ [C_{w,n+1} - C_{wn}] - \rho_n E_n + a_w [W_{n+1} - W_n] \circ [C_{yn} - C_{wn}] = 0, \quad (18c)$$

$$h_4(x) = C^{K}_{vIn} - a_I C^{H}_{vI,n-\theta} - \beta_I = 0 \quad (18d)$$

of the type of inequalities

$$\bar{V} \geq V \geq \underline{V}, \quad \bar{W} \geq W \geq \underline{W}, \quad C \geq \underline{C}, \quad (19a)$$

$$\sum_{p \in P_q} C_p \circ [\bar{C}_p]^{-1} \leq 1, \; q \in Q, \; \bigcup_{q \in Q} P_q = P \quad (19b)$$

and by the initial conditions

$$V_n = V_n^0, \; C_v = C_v^0, \; t \in [T_0 - \theta, T_0); \; W_0 = W_0^0, \; C_{w0} = C^0_{w0}. \quad (20)$$

In the problem (17)-(20) the values of θ are discrete and in accordance with ρ_n.

The error of the objective functional optimum must not be more than prescribed one $\varepsilon_0 > 0$ the difference between the approximate solution x^* and the permissible set $\bar{G}$ is estimated by a vector δ_0 which dimensionality coincides with the member of constraints defining $\bar{G}$. Not effecting the common character of this problem, the vector δ_0 coordinates $\delta^2_{0p} > 0$ and $\delta^3_0 > 0$ corresponding to the constraints (18b) and (18c), are supposed to differ from zero. And so the vector x^* must possess the property.

$$\Phi(x^*) - \min_{x \in \bar{G}} \Phi(x) \leq \varepsilon_0 \quad (21)$$

and belong to a set G^*_A which is described by the constraints (18a), (18d), (19), (20) and by the conditions

$$|h_{2p}(x^*)| \leq \delta^2_{0p}, \quad |h_3(x^*)| \leq \delta^3_0. \quad (22)$$

The solution of the multiextremal problem (17)-(20) is reduced to finding the optimal vectors of a series of convex estimating problems. The construction of this series is made by means of the branch and bound scheme. The application of this scheme to the solution of the problem (17)-(20) is possible because the convex envelope of the biseparable function on a rectangular set is the sum of the convex envelopes of the function with two variables on two-dimensional rectangles. In this case the complex problem of constructing the convex envelope of a function of many variables is reduced to a finite member of simplier problems of constructing the convex envelope of functions of two variables. This procedure was described and can be realized by means of a computer. The forming of the convex envelopes of bilinear forms on the rectangular sets was described and programmed.

On the stage j the aggregate of the convex estimating problems constitutes a set $\{A_{jl}\}$. The union of the permissible sets G^{jl}_A of these problems contains the permissible set $\bar{G}$ of an original problem.

(a) $\bigcup_l G^{jl}_A \supset \bar{G}$.

The objective functionals $\Phi^{jl}(x)$ of the estimating problems are constructed as minorants of the objective functional of the original problem $\Phi(x)$ on the permissible sets G^{jl}_A

(b) $\Phi^{jl}(x) \leq \Phi(x),\ x \in G_A^{jl}$.

The estimating problems A_{jl} are so constructed to ensure the existence of the aggregate of the problems $\{A^\nu\}$ which union of permissible sets contains $\bar{G}$ and is contained in G_A^*. The difference between the optimal values of $\Phi(x)$ on G_A^ν and of $\Phi^\nu(x)$ is not more than ε_0, i.e.

(c) $\min_{x \in G_A^\nu} \Phi(x) - \min_{x \in G_A^\nu} \Phi^\nu(x) \leq \varepsilon_0, \bar{G} \subset \bigcup_\nu G_A^\nu \subset G_A^*$.

The optimal value of each estimating problem $\omega_{jl} = \min_{x \in G_A^{jl}} \Phi^{jl}(x)$ according to (b) can be a lower boundary of the original functional $\Phi(x)$ on the set G_A^{jl}.

The value $\omega_j = \min_l \omega_{jl}$ in accordance with (a) can be a lower estimation of the optimal value of the original problem $M = \min_{x \in \bar{G}} \Phi(x)$ on the stage j, i.e. $\omega_j \leq M$. The value $\Omega_j = \Phi(\bar{x}^j) = \min_{i \leq j} \min_{l_i} \Phi(x^{il})$ is an upper estimation of M on the stage j. Thus on the every stage the estimation of the error, obtained due to the vector $\bar{x}^j$ of the state j taken as an optimal vector, is $\Delta^j = \Omega_j - \omega_j \geq \Omega_j - M$. Therefore, if $\bar{x}^j \in G_A^*$ and $\Delta^j \leq \varepsilon_0$, the vector $\bar{x}^j$ meets the conditions (21), (22) and can be considered as one we sought for.

The transition from the stage j to the stage $j+1$ may be made, if at least one of the conditions (21),(22) is broken, and this transitions in replacing the problem A_j, where the lower estimation ω_j was achieved by two problems. The permissible set G_A^j of the problem A_j is substituted by two subsets $G_A^{j+1,1}$ and $G_A^{j+1,2}$. The union of $G_A^{j+1,1}$ and $G_A^{j+1,2}$ is contained in G_A^j and contains the subsets $\bar{G} \cap G_A^j$. On these sets one forms the convex problems $A_{j+1,1}$ and $A_{j+1,2}$ that are included into the aggregate of the estimating problems in return for the excluded one A_j. In result one has the aggregate of problems $\{A_{j+1,l}\}$ of the stage $j+1$.

To conduct the convex estimating problems $\{A_{jl}\}$ one must construct the objective functionals $\Phi^{jl}(x)$ the permissible sets G_A^{jl} and the rules of the transition from the problem A_j to $A_{j+1,1}$ and $A_{j+1,2}$. The convex envelope $co_{\pi^{jl}} \Phi(x)$ of the objective functional of the problem (17)-(20) on the rectangular set π^{jl} given by a system of constraints

$$\bar{V}^{jl} \geq V \geq \underline{V}^{jl},\ \bar{W}^{jl} \geq W \geq \underline{W}^{jl},\ \bar{C}^{jl} \geq C \geq \underline{C}^{jl}; \quad (23)$$

serves as an objective functional of the estimating problem A_{jl}. The bounds of the permissible set π^1 of the problem A_1 solved on the first stage coincide with the system of constraints (19a) together with the conditions $C \leq \bar{C}^1 = \bar{C}$. For the transition from π^1 to the sets π^{jl} considered on the next stages one divides as follows

The permissible set G_A^{jl} of the problem A_{jl} is constructed as an intersection of convex sets D_{jl} and M_{jl}. The set D_{jl} is given by the constraints of the type of equalities (18a), (18d),(20) and by the inequalities of the type of (19a) and (19b) where upper and lower bounds are replaced by the bounds of the set π^{jl}. The set M_{jl} is a convex envelope of a set given by the constraints (18b) and (18c), if $x \in \pi^{jl}$ The construction of M_{jl} is an equivalent transition from these constraints of the type of equalities to two systems of the constraints of the type of inequalities where operators $h_{2p}, -h_{2p}, h_3$ and $-h_3$ are replaced by their convex envelopes

$$co_{\pi^{jl}} h_{2p}(X) \leq 0,\quad co_{\pi^{jl}}[-h_{2p}(X)] \leq 0, \quad (24)$$
$$co_{\pi^{jl}} h_3(X) \leq 0,\quad co_{\pi^{jl}}[-h_3(X)] \leq 0,$$

The problems $A_{j+1,1}$ and $A_{j+1,2}$ are formed from A_j as followed. If $x^j \in G_A^*$, one chooses such a block of separability of the vector x^j, where the maximal difference between the value φ^{α}_{zpn} of the component of the price functional of the original problem and the convex envelope of this problem $co_{\Pi^j} \varphi^{\alpha}_{zpn}$ is achieved.

If $\Delta^j \leq \varepsilon_o$, one chooses such an equation from the systems of the constraints (18b) and (18c) where in a point X^j a maximal deviation from the given error δ_o is achieved. In this equation the block of separability of the vector X^j is chosen where a maximal difference between the original operator and its convex envelope is achieved. If $\Delta^j > \varepsilon_o$ and $X^j \bar{\in} G^*_A$ one of these blocks of separability is chosen.

The separation of the set Π^j into $\Pi^{j+1,1}$ and $\Pi^{j+1,2}$ is made in accordance with such a coordinate from the chosen block of separability where one achieves

$$max\{min[\bar{X}^j_{zn} - X^j_{zn}, X^j_{zn} - \underline{X}^j_{zn}], min[\bar{C}_{zpn} - C_{zpn}, C_{zpn} - \underline{C}_{zpn}]\}.$$

In the sets Π^j, $\Pi^{j+1,1}$ and $\Pi^{j+1,2}$ all the constraints (23) coincide except the constraints for the coordinate of separation. The value of this coordinate on the stage j is the upper bound of the corresponding unequality in the constraints of the set $\Pi^{j+1,1}$ and the lower bound of $\Pi^{j+1,2}$. I.e., if X_{zn} is this coordinate

$$\bar{X}^{j+1,1}_{zn} = X^j_{zn}, \quad \underline{X}^{j+1,1}_{zn} = \underline{X}^j_{zn}; \quad \bar{X}^{j+1,2}_{zn} = \bar{X}^j_{zn}, \quad \underline{X}^{j+1,2}_{zn} = X^j_{zn}. \tag{25}$$

A described series of the estimating problems has the properties (a)-(c) and results in the solution in a finite number of stages. The demonstration of this statement is generalization of the results of [3] for separable functions.

The method of solving the problem (17)-(20) worked out in this paper may be used in combination with a method improving the upper estimation Ω_j of each stage. The following two-stage relaxation procedure is considered as an example. On the first stage fixing the vector of the permissible pollutant concentrations C^1, one finds an optimal vector V^1, W^1 of the problem of the optimal distribution of the water of given quality. On the second stage the obtained vector V^1, W^1 is fixed, and the vector C is considered as a variable one. The problem of optimal treatment of the water in given quantities is solved. The optimal vector C^2 received on the second stage, is used as an initial one to repeat the solution of the first stage problem and so on.

The method of the problem solution described above can be used as an approximate one with the estimation of the error, if one interrupts the solution on any stage.

REFERENCES

I. В.Г.Пряжинская. Методы системного анализа при планировании водных ресурсов. "Природные условия Западной Сибири и переброска стока рек в Среднюю Азию", "Наука", Новосибирск, 1975.
2. А.Д.Иоффе, В.М.Тихомиров. Теория экстремальных задач. "Наука", Москва, 1974.
3. В.Н.Бурков, А.И.Лазебник, И.Л.Хранович. Метод ветвей и границ как регулярный метод решения нерегулярных задач математического программирования. "Автоматика и телемеханика" №7 и №10, 1972.

DECENTRALIZED STABILIZATION AND REGULATION IN LARGE-SCALE MACROECONOMIC-ENVIRONMENTAL MODELS, AND CONFLICTING OBJECTIVES

H. Myoken*, H. Sadamichi and Y. Uchida****

**Faculty of Economics, Nagoya City University, Mizuhoku, Nagoya 467, Japan*
***Research Institute for Economics and Business Administration, Kobe University, Rokko, Kobe 657, Japan*

ABSTRACT - This paper is concerned with methodology and applicability of hierarchical multilevel approach to large-scale econometric models in which environmental aspects are introduced. A simulation study of stabilization and regulation problems will be made for large interconnected dynamical systems under hierarchical decentralized control. Conflicting objectives as seen in such systems will be also investigated by considering renewals of weights for performance criteria. An evaluation of the method proposed is shown by a numerical example.

1 INTRODUCTION

There have recently appeared various applications of optimal control theory to national policy and planning implemented by the use of macroeconometric models on the assumption that there is a single controller (See Kendrick[1], for instance). However, dynamic large-scale systems including macroeconomic policy models primarly is the product of informationally decentralized control process, in which different agencies control different sets of policy instruments. A number of researchers in studies along these lines have attempted to attack the decentralized formulations of three categories from (i) team theory (Marschak and Radner[2], Ho and Chu [3]), (ii) competitive organizational forms (Arrow and Hurwicz[4]) and (iii) hierarchical organizational forms (Mesarovic et al[5])(See Varaiya[6], also). To our knowledge, there is still not a unified theory for dynamic large-scale systems with emphasis on decentralized control strategies.

In this paper, we adopt the viewpoint of analyzing some sort of hierarchical multilevel decentralized system and deal with decentralized stabilization and regulation of large-scale macroeconomic-environmental models. Fig. 1 illustrates one of the simplest possible cases of hierarchical multilevel decentralized systems. Conceptually speaking, a hierarchical multilevel system is a decentralized system where a given controlled system is controlled by a group of goal seeking systems in a hierarchic arrangement (Mesarovic et al[5]). Presented in Section 2 of this paper is the simplest possible case involving a two-level structure of large-scale interconnected econometric models. Section 3 treats the simulation method of optimal control paths and its practical computation. Section 2 and Section 3 follow by the results which slightly modify the procedures given by Myoken and Uchida[7] and Uchida[8]. Macroeconometric approach to the environmental problem under consideration is described and the experimental examples are numerically presented to illustrate the proposed procedures in Section 4 and Section 5, respectively. Last section gives some conclusions about future research.

Fig. 1. Two-Level Structure

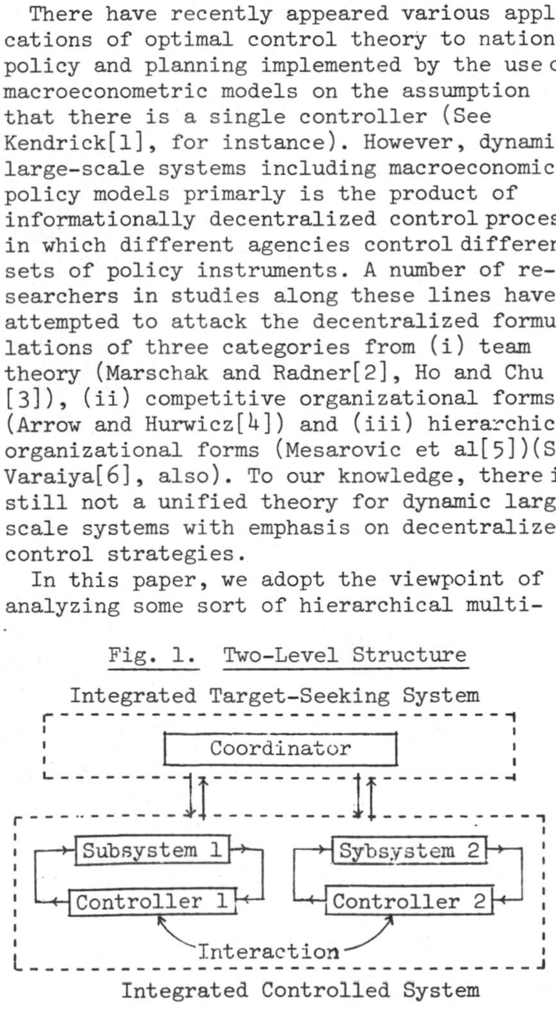

2 THE BASIC MODEL AND THE OPTIMAL CONTROL POLICY

Consider a general stochastic non-linear dynamic system governed by

$$y(t) = \tilde{\alpha}(y(t), \tilde{s}(t-1)) + \tilde{u}(t) \qquad (1)$$

where $y(t)$ is an NY-vector of the current endogenous variables, $\tilde{s}(t-1)$ is an $N\tilde{S}$-vector of the predetermined variables which, for most statistical purposes, are classified as

predetermined variables:
- lagged endogenous variables
- exogenous variables:
  - control(instrument)* variables
  - deta-interaction variables

*
- current control variabels
- lagged control variables

and $\tilde{u}(t)$ is an NY-vector of random disturbances.

By introducing the new state variables, the system of high-order (1) will be ended up with first-order nonlinear difference equation system as follows:

$$s(t)=\alpha(s(t),s(t-1),x(t),z(t))+u(t) \quad (2)$$

where s(t) is the state variable vector of NS-order; x(t), the control variable vector of NX-order; z(t), the data-interaction variable vector of Nz-order; u(t), the random disturbance vector of NS-order. (One possible porcedure for putting the system (1) into the system (2) refers to Uchida[8].) s(t) contains all of the current endogenous and control variables, which play an important role in analyzing the choice of targets-instruments. Furthermore notice that $NS \geq NX+NY$.

Some of endogenous variables will be selected as policy targets, and there are also the desired policy sequences for control variables. Let targets and instruments be brought up together for p(t), and let the desired values for p(t) be denoted by d(t). Without loss of generality, we can assume that

$$p(t) = Hs(t) \quad (3)$$

where many elements of the matrix H may be supposed to be zero or to be unity. The choice of targets-instruments can be freely selected by establishing reasonable matrix H. When p(t) is not expressed as linearly combination of the state vector, the new state vector should be defined in the form of the system (2).

Suppose the performance index is specified as

$$\phi = \Sigma_{t=1}^{NT}\phi(t)$$

$$\phi(t) = \|p(t)-d(t)\|^2_{W(t)} + \|s(t)-s(t-1)\|^2_{wI} \quad (4.2)$$

where $\|p(t)\|^2_{W(t)}=p(t)'W(t)p(t)$; W(t) is the symmetric and positive definite matrix and w is the positive scalar. [Refer to [9]]

To perform the control of large-scale econometric models we will emphasize on the practical computation rather than pursuing the theoretical aspects. In addition, contemporary analysis of policy decision is oriented towards the short run. We can approximate the system (2) about nominal paths indicating superscript "^" as follows:

$$s(t) = A(t)s(t-1) + B(t)x(t) + e(t) \quad (5.1)$$

where

$$[A(t)\vdots B(t)]=(I-\frac{\partial\hat{\alpha}}{\partial s(t)})^{-1}\left[\frac{\partial\hat{\alpha}}{\partial s(t-1)}\vdots\frac{\partial\hat{\alpha}}{\partial x(t)}\right] \quad (5.2)$$

$$e(t) = \hat{s}(t) - A(t)\hat{s}(t-1) - B(t)\hat{x}(t) \quad (5.3)$$

The optimal control problem is to find the solution x(t) so as to minimize (4) subject to (5). By the principle of optimality [10], the optimal feedback control solution is

$$x(t)^* = F(t)s(t-1) + g(t) \quad (6.1)$$

where

$$[F(t)\vdots g(t)] = (B(t)'R(t)B(t))^{-1}B(t)'[wI-R(t)A(t)\vdots g(t)-R(t)e(t)] \quad (6.2)$$

$$\hat{A}(t) = A(t)-B(t)F(t) \quad (6.3)$$

$$\hat{e}(t) = e(t)+B(t)g(t) \quad (6.4)$$

$$q(t-1) = H'W(t-1)d(t-1)+\hat{A}(t)'q(t) +(wI-R(t)\hat{A}(t))'\hat{e}(t) \quad (6.5)$$

$$R(t-1) = H'W(t-1)H+w[2I-\hat{A}(t)-\hat{A}(t)'] +\hat{A}(t)'R(t)\hat{A}(t) \quad (6.6)$$

and

$$q(NT) = H'W(NT)d(NT) \quad (6.7)$$

$$R(NT) = H'W(NT)H+wI \quad (6.8)$$

It should be noted that the estimation of state variables is unnecessary, since all the previous state variables in (6.1) are defined by observable economic variables.

3 THE SIMULATION METHOD OF OPTIMAL PATHS AND ITS COMPUTATION

Suppose optimal paths indicating superscript "*" are given using the above method as

$$\hat{s}(0),\ s^*(1),\ s^*(2),\ \ldots,\ s^*(NT)$$

Such optimal paths "*" are final values if they satisfy a given convergent condition. However, we use the optimal path "*" as nominal value "^" at the next step, when the convergent condition is not satisfied: The above procedure is used to compute linearized approximations, optimal control solutions and optimal paths.

Two possible criteria for finding the convergence may be considered. One is

$$\text{(C1)} \quad \left|\frac{\phi^*_l-\phi^*_{l+1}}{\phi^*_l}\right| < EPS_1 \quad (7)$$

where subscript l denotes iterative step;

$$\phi^*_l = \Sigma_{i=1}^{NT}\phi^*(t)_l \quad (8)$$

$$\phi^*(t)_l=\|p^*(t)_l-d(t)\|^2_{W(t)}+\|s^*(t)_l-s^*(t-1)_l\|^2_{wI} \quad (9)$$

This implies that the iterative commutation of nominal values and optimal paths are performed until ϕ is minimized. The other is

$$\text{(C2)} \quad \left|\frac{WMAX_l - WMAX_{l+1}}{WMAX_l}\right| < EPS_2 \quad (10)$$

where

$$WMAX_l = \max_{\substack{t=1,2,\ldots,NT\\ j=1,2,\ldots,NP}}\{W_j(t)_0(p^*(t)_l-d_j(t))^2\} \quad (11)$$

where NW stands for the dimension of W(t); $W_j(t)_0$, the j-th component of W(t). The second condition implies that such commutation is carried on until the error ratio between the optimal paths and desired paths in policy targets are equal to given weights. In this case it is assumed that the weights are revised by the following procedure:

$$W_j(t)_{l+1} = W_j(t)_l \cdot \frac{W_j(t)(p_j^*(t)_l - d_j(t))^2}{m_l} \quad (12)$$

$$m_l = \frac{1}{NP \cdot NT} \Sigma_{i=1}^{NT} \|p^*(t)_l - d(t)\|^2_{W(t)_0} \quad (13)$$

In such case, it is interesting to observe that the above two convergent criteria will be also applied to adjust conflicting objectives in the policy problem.

By using either (C1) or (C2) presented above, such iterative step will be repeated until the optimal paths converge. The converged value is the best optimal path under the forecasting sequence for one data-interaction variable. Next we use the optimal path to perform the operation of coordinative forecasts for data-interaction variables among other subsystems. Let the data-interaction variable vector be denoted by

$$z(t) = \beta(v(t), v_G(t)) \quad (14)$$

where v(t) stands for the state variable vector contained in the system except the subsystem under consideration; $v_G(t)$, the data or dummy variable vector for the whole subsystem.

The desired optimal path for each individual subsystem will be obtained under the forecasting value for data-interaction variable. Then we use the value for optimal path to find the new forecasting value for data-interaction variable. Such iterative step is repeated, and the operation of coordinative forecasts for data-interaction variables is continued until the differentials between forecasting values for the new and old data-interaction variables are within admissible domain. (See Fig.2)

Suppose optimal paths are given using the above simulation method as s*(t), x*(t), z*(t), t=1,2,...,NT. In what follows we provide one possible practical method for computing optimal control solutions. The linearized approximation of (2) in the neighborhood of optimal paths "*" is given as:

$$\begin{aligned} s(t)-s^*(t) &= A(t)[s(t-1)-s^*(t-1)] \\ &+ B(t)[x(t)-x^*(t)] \\ &+ C(t)[z(t)-z^*(t)] \end{aligned} \quad (15)$$

where

$$[A(t)\vdots B(t)\vdots C(t)] = (I - \frac{\partial f^*}{\partial s(t)})^{-1}[\frac{\partial \alpha^*}{\partial s(t-1)} \vdots \frac{\partial \alpha^*}{\partial x(t)} \vdots \frac{\partial \alpha^*}{\partial z(t)}] \quad (16)$$

In practice, target path for policy is given by optimal path obtained from the simulation of optimal control policy, and the solution should be obtained every period when implementing the optimal control policy.

Now let the performance index be measured by

$$\psi = \Sigma_{t=MT}^{NT} \psi(t) \quad (17.1)$$

$$\psi(t) = \|s(t)-s^*(t)\|^2_{H'W(t)H+\sigma I} + \|x(t)-x^*(t)\|^2_{\sigma I} \quad (17.2)$$

where σ is the positive scalar. Also, let the forecasting value for data-interaction variable be

$$z(t) = z^*(t), \quad t=MT+1, \ldots, NT \quad (18)$$

Thus the policy at period MT will be shown by

$$x(MT) = x^*(MT) - K(MT)(s(MT-1)-s^*(MT-1) + J(MT)(z(t)-z^*(t)) \quad (19)$$

where

$$[K(t), J(t)] = (B(t)'\Pi(t)B(t)+\sigma I)^{-1} B(t)'\Pi(t)[A(t)\vdots C(t)] \quad (20)$$

$$\Pi(t-1) = H'W(t-1)H + \sigma I + \sigma K(t)'K(t) + (A(t)-B(t)K(t))'\Pi(t) (A(t)-B(t)K(t)) \quad (t=MT, MT+1, \ldots, NT) \quad (21.1)$$

$$\Pi(NT) = H'W(NT)H + \sigma I \quad (21.2)$$

s(MT-1) on the right-side of (19) indicates the state variable vector at period (MT-1), which is similar to the predetermined variables vector at period MT. If, for example, the policy implementation at period MT reaches a decision at the first half of the period (MT-1), a part of s(MT-1) (which perhaps consists of y(MT-1) and x(MT-1)) may be unobserved variables. Therefore we substitute the forecasting values for unobserved variables. When the compensatory policy is implemented at the latter half of the period MT, we must make up for the forecasting errors at the first half of the period. Furthermore z(MT) is not always consistent with the optimal path z*(t), if the up-to-date value of forecasting is used at both the first half of the period. Now let superscript "o" indicate the forecasting values and let subscripts "I" and "II" indicate the forecasting policy at the first half of the period and the compensatory policy at the latter half of the period, respectively. Then the above results can be expressed as:

$$x(MT)_I = x^*(MT)-K(MT)(\overset{o}{s}(MT-1)-s^*(MT-1) -J(MT)(\overset{o}{z}(MT)_I-z^*(MT)) \quad (22.1)$$

$$x(MT)_{II} = x^*(MT)-K(MT)(s(MT-1)-s^*(MT-1)$$

Fig. 2: Simulation of Optimal Paths

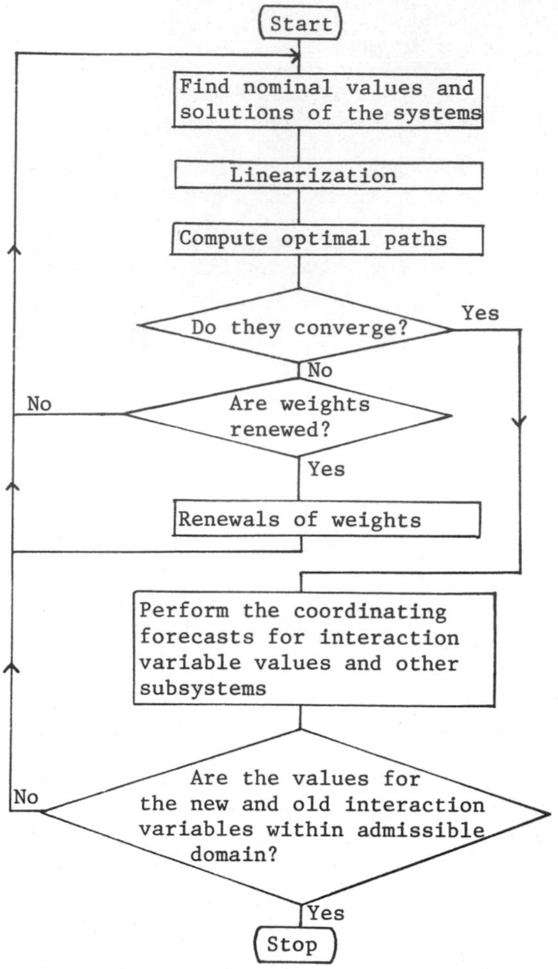

$$x(MT)_{II} = x^*(MT) - K(MT)(s(MT-1) - s^*(MT-1)) - J(MT)(\mathring{z}(MT)_{II} - z^*(MT)) - x(MT)_I \tag{22.2}$$

4 MACROECONOMETRIC APPROACH TO ENVIRONMENTAL PROBLEM

An econometric model tries to relate various aggregative variables of an economy in question, such as gross national product, consumption, investment, exports and imports by means of a system of regression equations. In the present paper we will consider environmental problem approached by the use of such model whose parameters could, conceivably, be estimated from empirical data, and which could be used as a basis for forecast or decision-making. This approach must be one of the first attempts to discuss decentralized stabilization and regulation in connection with environmental questions.

For the purpose of the approach, the system of environmental sector is linked in the existing macroeconometric system as follows:

(a) non-environmental system (the existing econometric system):

$$s(t)_a = \alpha_a(s(t-1)_a,\ x(t)_a,\ z(t)_a)$$

$$z(t)_a = \beta_a(s(t)_b,\ v_G(t)_a)$$

(b) environmental system:

$$s(t)_b = \alpha_b(s(t-1)_b,\ x(t)_b,\ z(t)_b)$$

$$z(t)_b = \beta_b(s(t)_a,\ v_G(t)_b)$$

where subscripts "a" and "b" indicate the vectors of variables contained in non-environmental and environmental systems, respectively; it is assumed that $s(t)_a$ and $s(t)_b$ are not overlapped, and that $x(t)_a$ and $x(t)_b$, also are not overlapped. Then, macroeconometric system has been represented by two subsystems. By the application of the proposed simulation method in this paper to subsystems, we will obtain the optimal paths of the whole economic system in which environmental aspects are incorporated.

The greatest difficulty in construction of such system is the unavailability of data. The model builder in socio-economics is concerned with nonexperimental data, unlike the physical and natural scientists, who can generate experimental data through controlled experiments. On the other hand, adequate data regarding environmental variables are not sufficiently available and are strictly unreliable, which are also different from aggregative economic variables specified in national accounting. Therefore the up-to-dating estimation should be performed about means and variances of parameters in environmental system. After that, the policy simulation proposed should be then implemented by incorporating the estimated equation into the second subsystem of environmental system.

5 A NUMERICAL EXAMPLE

In the first place, the following system is empirically used to evaluate the algorithm for the policy simulation method in Section 3.

System: NS = 7; NX = 3; NVG = 2

$$s_1(t) = 0.7\frac{s_1(t-1)}{s_2(t-1)} + 0.3\frac{x_1(t)}{s_3(t-1)} + 0.1\frac{s_4(t)}{s_6(t)}$$

$$s_2(t) = s_1(t-1)$$

$$s_3(t) = x_1(t)$$

$$s_4(t) = 0.7\frac{s_5(t)}{x_2(t)} + 0.4s_4(t-1)s_7(t-1)(s_1(t) + 0.1v_{G_1}(t)$$

$$s_5(t) = 0.3s_4(t)x_3(t) + 0.7\frac{s_5(t-1)}{s_6(t-1)} + 0.2(s_2(t)s_3(t) + 0.02v_{G_2}(t))$$

$$s_6(t) = x_2(t)$$

$$s_7(t) = x_3(t)$$

Table 1: Optimal Paths and Policy Decisions

item	period	desired value: d(t)	computed value: p(t)		
			policy simulation		policy decision
		weight: W(t)	g h	i j	k l
a	1	1.100 1.0	1.105 1.071	1.090 1.137	
a	2	1.200 2.0	1.201 1.166	1.189 1.233	
a	3	1.300 3.0	1.202 1.219	1.199 1.171	
b	1	1.000 0.5	1.038 0.9337	0.9956 1.095	
b	2	1.200 1.0	1.161 1.036	1.125 1.219	
b	3	1.400 1.5	1.335 1.276	1.277 1.345	
c	1	1.000 2.0	1.153 1.127	1.141 1.214	1.153 1.127
c	2	1.000 2.0	1.161 1.101	1.153 1.154	1.265 1.251
c	3	1.000 2.0	1.297 1.281	1.298 1.039	1.375 1.407
d	1	1.200 2.0	1.196 1.156	1.189 1.153	1.196 1.156
d	2	1.400 2.0	1.237 1.184	1.224 1.182	1.354 1.328
d	3	1.600 2.0	1.400 1.370	1.383 1.319	1.476 1.475
e	1	1.000 1.0	1.248 1.229	1.252 1.122	1.248 1.229
e	2	1.000 1.0	1.326 1.298	1.327 1.122	1.335 1.309
e	3	1.000 1.0	1.368 1.358	1.364 1.291	1.383 1.369
f	1	1.100 1.0	0.7872 0.7504	0.8001 0.5988	0.7872 0.7504
f	2	1.200 1.0	0.8324 0.8595	0.8507 0.4774	0.8273 0.8595
f	3	1.300 1.0	1.034 1.066	1.052 0.7243	1.021 1.049

Notes:

a: $p_1(t)$ in the system = $p_1(t)$ in the subsystem 1
b: $p_2(t)$ in the system = $p_2(t)$ in the subsystem 1
c: $p_3(t)$ in the system = $p_1(t)$ in the subsystem 2
d: $p_4(t)$ in the system = $p_2(t)$ in the subsystem 2
e: $p_5(t)$ in the system = $p_3(t)$ in the subsystem 2
f: $p_6(t)$ in the system = $p_4(t)$ in the subsystem 2
g: policy simulation results based on the proposed method, where weights are kept unchanged.
h: policy simulation results based on the proposed method, where weights are renewed.
i: policy simulation results based on a single system, where weights are kept unchanged.
j: policy simulation results based on a single system, where weights are renewed.
k: policy decision by the proposed method, where g is used for optimal path.
l: policy decision by the proposed method, where h is used for optimal path.

$$\underset{6\times7}{H} = \begin{pmatrix} 1 & 0 & 0 & 0 & 0 & 0 & 0 \\ 0 & 0 & 1 & 0 & 0 & 0 & 0 \\ 0 & 0 & 0 & 1 & 0 & 0 & 0 \\ 0 & 0 & 0 & 0 & 1 & 0 & 0 \\ 0 & 0 & 0 & 0 & 0 & 1 & 0 \\ 0 & 0 & 0 & 0 & 0 & 0 & 1 \end{pmatrix}$$

Initial condition: $s(0)=(1,1,1,1,1,1,1)'$

data variables:

$$v_G(1) = \begin{pmatrix} 1 \\ 4 \end{pmatrix}, \quad v_G(2) = \begin{pmatrix} 2 \\ 5 \end{pmatrix}, \quad v_G(3) = \begin{pmatrix} 3 \\ 6 \end{pmatrix}$$

And

$$w = 1.0; \; EPS_1 = EPS_2 = 0.1$$

Next, the system is decomposed into two subsystems, and the optimal paths then are computed.

Subsystem 1: NS = 3; NX = 1; Nz = 1; NV = 2; NVG = 0

$$s_1(t) = 0.7\frac{s_1(t-1)}{s_2(t-1)} + 0.3\frac{x(t)}{s_3(t-1)} + 0.2z(t)$$

$$s_2(t) = s_1(t-1)$$

$$s_3(t) = x(t)$$

$$z(t) = 0.5\frac{v_1(t)}{v_2(t)}$$

$v_1(t) = s_1(t)$ in the subsystem 2

$v_2(t) = s_3(t)$ in the subsystem 2

$$\underset{2\times3}{H} = \begin{pmatrix} 1 & 0 & 0 \\ 0 & 0 & 1 \end{pmatrix}$$

Initial condition: $s(0) = (1, 1, 1)'$

Subsystem 2: NS = 4; NX = 2; Nz = 2; NV = 3; NVG = 2

$$s_1(t) = 0.7\frac{s_2(t)}{x_1(t)} + 0.4s_1(t-1)s_4(t-1)z_1(t)$$

$$s_2(t) = 0.3s_1(t)x_2(t) + 0.7\frac{s_2(t-1)}{s_3(t-1)} + 0.2z_2(t)$$

$s_3(t) = x_1(t)$

$s_4(t) = x_2(t)$

$z_1(t) = v_1(t) + 0.1v_{G_1}(t)$

$z_2(t) = v_2(t)v_3(t) + 0.02v_{G_2}(t)$

$v_1(t) = s_1(t)$ in the subsystem 1

$v_2(t) = s_2(t)$ in the subsystem 1

$v_3(t) = s_3(t)$ in the subsystem 1

$$\underset{4\times4}{H} = \begin{bmatrix} 1 & 0 & 0 & 0 \\ 0 & 1 & 0 & 0 \\ 0 & 0 & 1 & 0 \\ 0 & 0 & 0 & 1 \end{bmatrix}$$

Initial condition: $s(0) = (1, 1, 1, 1)'$

data variables:

$$v_G(1) = \begin{bmatrix} 1 \\ 4 \end{bmatrix};\ v_G(2) = \begin{bmatrix} 2 \\ 5 \end{bmatrix};\ v_G(3) = \begin{bmatrix} 3 \\ 6 \end{bmatrix}$$

Moreover, when MT=2, policy decision will be implemented, where notice that policy decision is performed when forecasting the state variable vector in the subsystem 2 as

$$s(1) = (1.1, 1.2, 1.1, 0.9)'$$

but that the optimal paths obtained by the policy simulation remain the same in the subsystem 1. Table 1 describes the experimental results obtained.

6 RESULTS AND DISCUSSIONS

The algorithms for policy simulation can be evaluated by using an illustrative example of numerical computation in Section 5 as follows:

(i) When weights are kept unchanged, we can observe that any of optimal paths based on a single system and subsystems, respectively are about the same values. (Refer to g and i in Table 1.)

(ii) As is shown in h and j of Table 1, however, values for optimal paths based on two subsystems are close to the desired values rather than ones obtained by a single system. Compare in particular the case where $p_6(t)$ in the system is equal to $p_4(t)$ in the system, and one will admittedly see the difference.

(iii) From the numerical example, it may be difficult to evaluate the algorithms for policy decisions.

We now performed experiments of policy simulation by decomposing a single system into subsystems. In view of optimization problems of large-scale systems, however, such computation procedure does not necessarily follow that it is a routine practice. The primary objective of policy simulation for subsystems have been so far achieved under forecasting values for a number of data variables. Thus, without performing policy simulations independently, they should be implemented under coordinative forecasting for interaction variables. In doing so, policy simulation results obtained are somewhat more desirable rather than these obtained from individual system.

The numerical example is merely a preliminary analysis and further concrete research is empirically required*. In addition, more work needs to be done developing some extended methods. For example, alternative convergent conditions must be clearly investigated by analysing forecasting results for interaction variables in the nonlinear subsystems case.

* Simulation results of practical large-scale macroeconomic-environmental policy will be furnished on request addressed to the authors.

REFERENCES

[1] D. Kendrick, Applications of Control Theory to Macroeconomics, Ann. Econ. & Soc. Measurement 5(1976), 171-190.

[2] J. Marschak and R. Radner, The Economic Theory of Teams, Yale Univ. Press, 1971.

[3] W. C. Ho and K. C. Chu, Team Decision Theory and Information Structure in Optimal Control Problems-Part I, IEEE Trans. on Aut. Control, AC-17(1972), 15-22.

[4] K. J. Arrow and L. Hurwicz, Decentralization and Computation in Resource Allocation, in R. W. Pfout(ed.), Essays in Economics and Econometrics, Univ. of North Carolina Press, 1960, 34-104.

[5] M. D. Mesarovic, D. Macko and Y. Takahara, Theory of Hierarchical Multilevel Systems, Academic Press, 1970.

[6] P. P. Varaiya, Trends in the Theory of Decision-Making in Large Systems, Ann. Econ. & Soc. Measurement 1(1972), 493-500.

[7] H. Myoken and Y. Uchida, Stabilization and Regulation for Large-Scale Econometric Models, (in Japanese) the 6th SICE Symposium on Control Theory, Tokyo, 1977.

[8] Y. Uchida, A Hierarchical Multilevel Approach to Environmental Planning in a System of Regions, Working paper 7702, Nagoya City Univ., 1977.

[9] H. Myoken, Controllability and Observability in Optimal Control of Linear Econometric Models, Working paper 7501, Nagoya City Univ., 1975.

[10] R. Bellman, Dynamic Programming, Princeton Univ. Press, 1957.

SOME POSSIBILITIES TO CONSIDER ENVIRONMENTAL ASPECTS IN URBAN PLANNING MODELS

H. K. Aben

Institute of Cybernetics, Academy of Sciences of the Estonian SSR, 200 104 Tallinn, Estonian SSR

ABSTRACT

Urban planning is considered as a closed loop automatic control problem in welfare space. Limitation of natural resources and pollution control change the structure of this space and introduce new coordinates into it. Therefore, environmental aspects deform the welfare space and change the trajectory of the development of the society, i.e. the way of life of the society changes.

Optimization of the settlement pattern is considered as an iterative optimization problem. At one stage socio-economically optimal numbers of inhabitants of the cities are determined by the aid of dynamic programming model; at the other optimal allocation of factories is found by the aid of non-linear model with constraints for the pollution.

It is shown that with certain assumptions urban land market (capitalist economy) and central planning (socialist economy) lead to the same urban structure.

An economic method of pollution control is presented. The territory polluted by a factory above the allowed standard is considered to be belonging to this factory with payment of the price of land, even when all the territory is actually not used by this factory. To diminish pollution, factories have to make additional investments into technology that is compensated by decreasing the territory they have to pay for.

Optimization of the city structure with regard to the environmental factors is considered. Some simple rules for choosing optimal allocation of a factory and its optimal technology from the point of view of pollution control are formulated.

QUALITY OF LIFE AND URBAN PLANNING

In recent years, improvement of the quality of life has become a primary goal in the more advanced industrial countries. That is due to the realization that economic growth, as it is conceived and measured by traditional national accounting methods, is no longer considered as an adequate indicator of real well-being. Various sets of factors, named social indicators, which characterize the quality of life, have been elaborated (1,2,3).

As an example we list the factors which are considered to be most important for the quality of life in (2):

1) personal security
2) physical and mental well-being
3) work satisfaction
4) education and culture
5) research and innovation
6) leisure time and recreation
7) natural environment
8) housing and urban environment
9) transportation and communication
10) political participation

Social indicators are to a great extent determined by planning decisions taken by various municipal agencies. However, social indicators are partly determined also by the behaviour of the citizens and by their reaction to the planning decisions of the municipal agencies (4). E.g. the services level in the city depends partly on the citizens' preferences to certain transport facilities, shopping centres, etc.

In Fig. 1 the process of formation of social welfare is schematically shown. The municipal agencies make

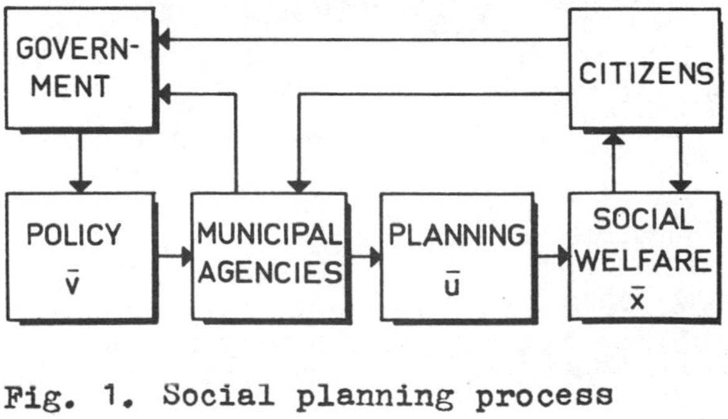

Fig. 1. Social planning process

their planning decisions (vector $\bar{u}$ on the basis of the policy vector $\bar{v}$ elaborated by the government. The vector of social indicators $\bar{x}$ is a consequence of the planning vector $\bar{u}$, but it is also influenced by the citizens' behaviour. Existence of several feedbacks in social policy diagram is one of its essential features (5).

Urban planning in a narrower sense is only part of social planning, i.e. certain components of the vector $\bar{u}$ are determined by urban planning. However, for urban inhabitants social and urban planning almost coincide.

URBAN PLANNING AS CLOSED-LOOP CONTROL PROBLEM

The aim of social planning is to maximize the discounted integral of the community welfare over a certain time period (6). Let $W(\bar{x},\bar{u},t)$ denote the community welfare function which corresponds to the vector $\bar{x}$ of social indicators at the time moment t and depends also on the planning vector $\bar{u}$, and let $Q(t)$ be the discount function which compares welfare of different periods. The goal of social planning can now be expressed as

$$\max \int_0^\infty W(\bar{x},\bar{u},t)Q(t)dt \qquad (1)$$

The existence of a community welfare function can be proved, at least when using certain assumptions about the distribution of utilities between the individuals (7,8).

Let $\bar{x}$ be the phase vector which determines the location of a point in the n-dimensional Euclidean space E^n of social indicators

$$\bar{x}(t) \in E^n \qquad (2)$$

The vector $\bar{x}(t)$ determines the social welfare at the time moment t. From the geometric point of view social development is determined by the trajectory of the end of the vector $\bar{x}(t)$ in the phase space E^n.

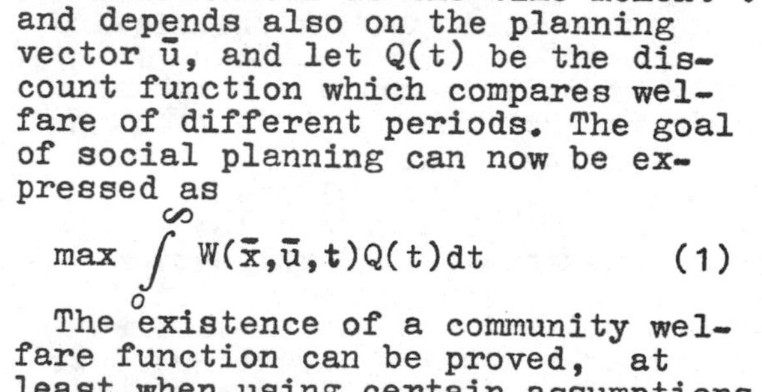

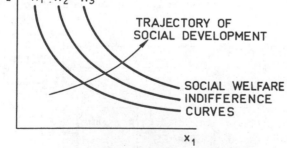

Fig. 2. Social development determines a trajectory in the space of social indicators

For two-dimensional case it is illustrated in Fig. 2 where indifference curves correspond to the loci in the space of social indicators in which the welfare is the same.

The aim of social planning is to choose the planning vector $\bar{u}(t)$ (the vector of control variables) so as to maximize the goal function (1). The planning vector $\bar{u}(t)$ may be interpreted as a point in r-dimensional Euclidean space

$$\bar{u}(t) \in E^r \qquad (3)$$

The choice of $\bar{u}(t)$ is subject to certain restrictions which are determined by the economic and social structure of the society and by its technological possibilities, i.e. $\bar{u}(t)$ has to belong to the set U of possible planning decisions

$$\bar{u}(t) \in U \in E^r \qquad (4)$$

The vector $\bar{u}(t)$ is determined by all the planning decisions including social, economic, territorial, etc. decisions. Part of its components are determined by urban planning decisions. Therefore, the aim of urban planning is to help to optimize the trajectory of the society in the phase space of social indicators which determine the quality of life of the society.

Some authors (9) suggest to fix the end of the planning period T and the desirable welfare $\bar{x}_0(T)$ for that time. In this case the goal function is

$$\min \| \bar{x}(T) - \bar{x}_0(T)\| \qquad (5)$$

where $\bar{x}(T)$ is the actual welfare at time T and $\|\cdot\|$ denotes norm of a vector in space E^n. That is a classical control problem.

However, in social planning the final state of welfare cannot be predetermined. That is due to the fact that the welfare function $W(\bar{x},\bar{u},t)$ is time-dependent. Forecasting of social preferences for a longer period is actually impossible. Therefore in comparison with (5) the goal function (1) is more flexible and takes into account the dynamic character of social values.

The discount function $Q(t)$ in (1) takes into account the decreasing value of future welfare for the present well-being as well as the lack of exact information about the future welfare function. It follows that urban planning should be considered as a closed-loop control problem (10) since on the basis of the present value of $W(\bar{x},\bar{u},t)$ and on the constraints on $\bar{u}(t)$ the future expression of W and the control vector $\bar{u}(t)$ are to be determined.

Urban planning is strongly dependent on the general social planning. E.g. if in the welfare function W free time has a great weight, then correspondingly in urban planning stress could be laid upon the optimal allocation of employment, housing and services as well as upon the development of transport facilities and highways. If in the welfare function stress is laid upon higher consumption, then primary objectives are developing production and economy in urban development.

In this way society's preferences determine the social welfare function W, on the basis of which the urban planning decisions $\bar{u}(t)$ should be taken in order to maximize the quality of life.

INFLUENCE OF ENVIRONMENTAL FACTORS

Let us consider in greater detail social planning in the two-dimensional welfare space. In Fig. 3 the point O_0 denotes the present state of the society welfare, x_1 and x_2 are two social indicators (e.g. consumption of commodities 1 and 2). The line AB gives the budget constraint. I.e. during the next period one of the states on the line AB can be reached. Optimal movement of the society is to the point O_1 where the highest welfare with the given budget restraint can be reached.

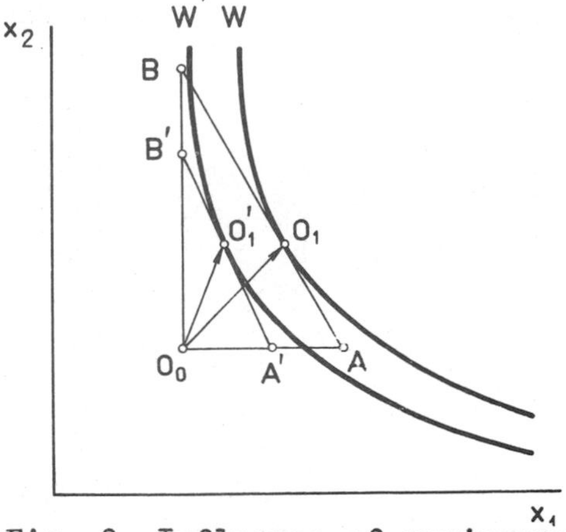

Fig. 3. Influence of environmental factors on the vector of social development

Assume now that restrictions to the environment pollution are installed. Abatement of the pollution demands additional costs and therefore with the same resources the society cannot reach a state on the line AB any more. Let the budget constraint line be A'B'. The lines AB and A'B' are not parallel because costs for the abatement of pollution are different for different products and commodities. Some authors estimate that environment protection costs from 2 to 5 per cent of the production depending on the branch of society (11).

The highest welfare which can be reached with the new budget constraint A'B' is at point O_1' where an indifference curve W' is tangent to the line A'B'.

Two simple but important conclusions can be drawn from the foregoing analysis. First, with pollution abatement consumption diminishes. Second, with pollution abatement the structure of the consumption changes in favour of these commodities whose production is connected with smaller pollution. Therefore, consideration of environmental factors changes the trajectory of social development and, consequently, the way of life of the society.

However, for diminishing consumption society gets a compensation - an environment of better quality, cleaner air, water, soil, etc. In the present consideration environment forms a new coordinate (or several coordinates) in the space of social indicators.

The dilemma between higher consumption and higher environment quality is illustrated in Fig. 4. With fixed costs c_i $(c_1 < c_2 < c_3)$ higher environment quality demands reduction in consumption. Since costs for preserving environment quality rise nonlinearly, determination of optimum environment quality is of primary importance.

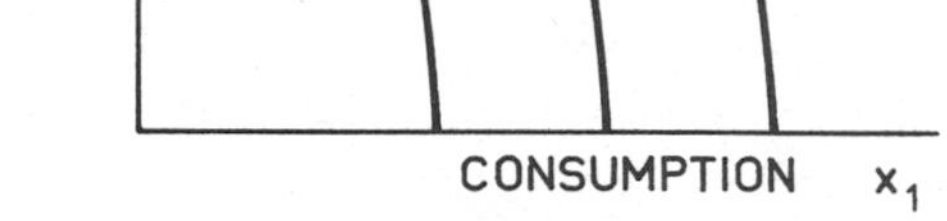

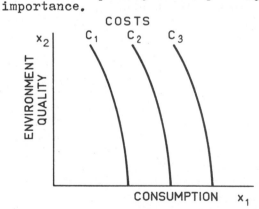

Fig. 4. Dilemma between consumption and environment quality

REGIONAL PLANNING AND OPTIMAL CITY SIZE

The city size strongly influences the well-being of its inhabitants. On the one hand, in larger cities production is more economic and effective, the salaries are higher, there are wider possibilities for education, etc. On the other hand, in large cities inhabitants spend more time on trips and, as a rule, the environment is worse (air pollution, noise), crime rate is higher, etc. However, since in larger cities technology is more advanced, in small industrial cities pollution is sometimes even higher. Determination of an optimal settlement pattern is a complicated problem of socio-economic optimization.

Traditionally formation of the settlement pattern is considered either from the point of view of the transport factor (12), or it is considered as a purely economic allocation and growth problem (13,14). If the primary goal is the growth of community welfare, main attention in regional planning should be paid to the optimization of the settlement pattern and of the size of the cities from the social point of view, bearing in mind also environmental factors as social indicators (15).

Let us define the utility of a city as a quantity which expresses its socio-economic effectiveness. It should take into account the effectiveness of production as well as the well-being of the inhabitants, including quality of the environment. To a certain extent the utility of a city is analogous to the utility of dwelling space, used in another model of social optimization (16). The utility function of a city $U(n)$ shows the dependence of its utility on its size, e.g. on the number of inhabitants n. We assume as usual in the welfare economics (10) that the function $U(n)$ is twice differenciable, and that the following conditions hold:

$$\frac{dU(n)}{dn} > 0, \quad \frac{d^2U(n)}{dn^2} < 0 \tag{6}$$

for all n.

Different cities have different utility functions due to the differences in natural resources, environmental conditions, established city structure, location and accessibility

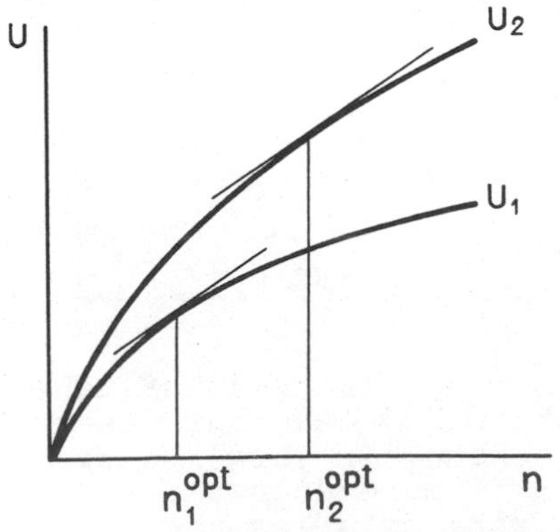

Fig. 5. Utility functions of two cities

for other cities, level of public services, etc. E.g. the utility of a city, located in the centre of a region, is higher from the transport aspect, since the medium loss of time for visiting it by the inhabitants of other cities is lower than for a city on the border of the region. At the same time, the utility of the latter may be higher from the point of view of environment quality. In Fig. 5 utility functions of two cities are shown for illustration.

Development of the settlement pattern may be considered as a change in the number of inhabitants n_i in various cities i. These changes are due to the building of new plants and factories and to their reconstruction or to the closing of old ones, to the development of services centres, to the foundation or relocation of educational and scientific establishments, to the growth or decline of the population, etc. If the change in the number of inhabitants of a city due to a single planning decision (e.g. building of a factory) may be considered to be comparatively small, then optimization of the settlement pattern consists of the numbers of inhabitants n_i.

Optimal settlement pattern can be determined by the aid of the model

$$\left.\begin{aligned} &\max \sum_{i=1}^{m} U_i(n_i) \\ &\sum_{i=1}^{m} n_i = N \\ &p_i \leq n_i \leq q_i \end{aligned}\right\} \tag{7}$$

where m is the number of cities in the region considered, N is the total number of inhabitants in the region at the end of the planning period, p_i and q_i are lower and upper bounds for the number of inhabitants of the i-th city which may be determined by political, social and economic considerations. Model (7) maximizes the total utility of the settlements.

Model (7) can be solved by the methods of dynamic programming. If the order of developing different cities is of importance, a specific dynamic programming procedure can be used (17).

After the determination of the socially optimal settlement pattern, economically and environmentally most effective allocation of plants and institutions is to be found. By solving this problem the optimal numbers of inhabitants of different cities n_i should be taken as constraints.

If for a certain branch of industry optimal allocation and sizes of the plants are to be determined, one has to solve a problem with discontinuous goal function

$$\left.\begin{aligned} &\min \sum_{i=1}^{r} \left[a_i x_i + b_i(x_i) + \right. \\ &\qquad \left. + \sum_{j=1}^{m} c_{ij} y_{ij} \right] \\ &b_i(x_i) = 0 \text{ when } x_i = 0 \\ &b_i(x_i) = b_i \text{ when } x_i > 0 \\ &\sum_{i=1}^{r} x_i = A \end{aligned}\right\} \quad (8)$$

In this model x_i is the plant capacity in the city i, y_{ij} are production flows, c_{ij} are transportation costs, A is the needed total production in the region. Model (8) takes into account the dependence of the production costs on the capacity of the plant.

To take into account the environment quality, restrictions to the maximal amount of pollution should be added to model (8)

$$\sum_{i=1}^{r} x_i p_i \leqslant P \qquad (9)$$

In the latter inequality p_i is pollution due to unity of production and P is the upper limit for pollution in the region.

Model (8),(9) can be solved by various approximate methods. If sizes of the plants to be allocated are known, an integer programming problem of plant allocation arises (18). If interrelationships of the plants of various types are to be taken into account, optimal assignment is a solution of the quadratic integer planning problem (18). In the latter case restrictions of the type (9) are to be observed for all the regions.

Since utility of a city depends also on the effectiveness of production, the utility curves should be corrected after solving the optimal assignment problem, and new optimal sizes of the cities by the aid of model (7) should be determined. In this way the optimal settlement pattern is determined by the aid of an iterative procedure which consists of sequential solving of social and economic optimization problems (7) and (8),(9).

In the optimal solution marginal utilities of the cities are equal (Fig. 5). The cities whose optimal size is bigger, act as higher order centres in the region. In this way a socially optimal hierarchical settlement pattern is formed. It is to be seen that no universally optimal city size exists. The optimal size for every city depends on its individual utility curve.

Model (8),(9) can be used to observe environment standards in a centrally planned economy. However, most effective in practice would be an economic self regulating pollution control system. In some instances pollution control can be based on the payment for the land which is polluted by a certain factory above the standard. To develop this idea we are next going to show that with certain assumptions central planning and urban land market lead to the same urban structure.

CENTRAL PLANNING AND LAND MARKET

There is a difference between approaches to urban planning in socialist and capitalist countries. In capitalist countries the development of a city is in many respects predetermined by the price of land. The development of cities in socialist countries is determined by central planning. Formally land value is not taken into account. Since the structure of cities is rather similar both in capitalist and socialist countries, the mechanism of urban development should essentially be the same although from the formal point of view they differ considerably. We shall tackle some aspects of that problem.

Let us consider a simple optimization problem of developing potential residential areas of a town. The following symbols will be used:

s_i - area of site i (i = 1,2,...n);

x_i - area of site i which will be developed;

c_i - building costs of one sqm of dwelling space at site i;

p_i - housing density (sqm/acre) at site i (considered to be given);

S - total needed amount of dwelling space (sqm).

We have the problem

$$\left.\begin{aligned} &\min \sum_{i=1}^{n} p_i c_i x_i \\ &0 \leqslant x_i \leqslant s_i \quad (i=1,2,\dots n) \\ &\sum_{i=1}^{n} p_i x_i \geqslant S \end{aligned}\right\} \quad (10)$$

The dual problem is

$$\max\ (Sy_o - \sum_{i=1}^{n} s_i y_i)$$

$$y_i \geqslant 0 \qquad (11)$$

$$-y_i + p_i y_o \leqslant p_i c_i \quad (i=1,2,\ldots n)$$

where the dual variable y_i is the shadow price of land at site i, and y_o is the shadow price of the dwelling space.

Model (10) minimizes the total building costs by fulfilling the given plan of dwelling space S. This is a typical problem in a centralized economy.

The dual problem (11) can be interpreted as follows. Let building be carried out by a firm whose expenditures on the creation of one sqm of dwelling space at site i make a total of c_i. Land price at site i is y_i, selling-price of dwelling space is y_o. Model (11) maximizes profits of the firm.

If land market is perfect, the price of land corresponds to the solution of model (11). Since solutions of problems (10) and (11) are identical, we may conclude that with certain assumptions central planning and land market lead to the same city structure. In this idealized case the difference between city structure formation in socialist and capitalist countries consists simply in that in the former case the primal and in the latter case the dual mathematical programming problem is solved.

However, market mechanism plays a certain role in socialist economy (4). Therefore much attention has been paid to the determination of shadow prices and to their application in planning (19). It has been shown that land value helps to decentralize town planning process, to make corrections to an optimal master plan not running the whole model again, to find optimal allocation for various activities, etc. (20).

AN ECONOMIC METHOD OF POLLUTION CONTROL

Let us consider pollution of air and soil by a factory. For many industries air and soil pollution is highest near the factory and diminishes with the distance from it. At a certain distance from the factory the pollution level equals the standard. The aim of pollution control is to reduce the area which is polluted above the standard to a reasonable minimum. One possibility for that is to use administrative measures. However, the same result can be achieved by making the factory pay the price of land for all the region which is polluted by it above the standard. I.e. the area polluted by a factory will be considered as belonging to this factory and the price of land should be paid by the factory even when all the land is actually not used by it. The price of the polluted area should be paid to the municipal authorities.

In this way the city gets compensation for valuable territory it cannot use or which is polluted, and the factory is forced to choose such a technology that the marginal costs for the treatment of the residuals equals to the marginal cost of land. Fig. 6 explains this simple model.

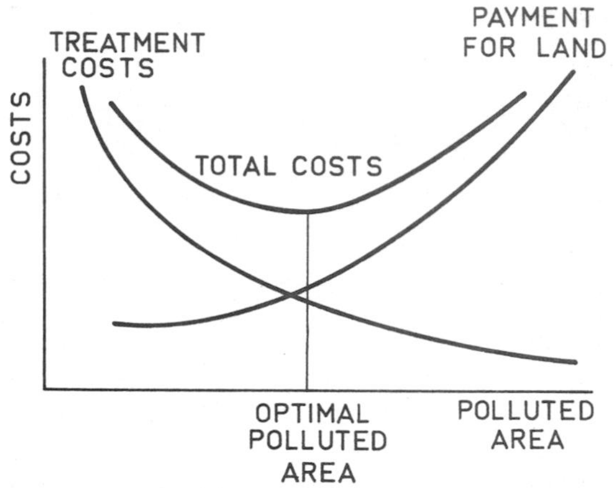

Fig. 6. Optimal technology is connected with optimal polluted area

If the territory surrounding a factory is not valuable, its price is low and the factory may use cheaper technology not paying much attention to the treatment of the residuals. If, vice versa, the territory around a factory is valuable (good access to city centre, attractive area for housing, etc.), then the price of land is high and the factory has to use more expensive technology to reduce pollution and the total costs.

This method of pollution control can be used in countries with market economy as well as in countries with central planning since in the latter case the price of land can be calculated by the aid of special methods (20).

OPTIMIZATION OF THE CITY STRUCTURE

The previous approach leads also to an optimal city structure from the economic and environmental point of view. Here we develop further some ideas of social optimization of the city structure described in (20).

Let us express the total costs q(r,h) of a factory at a distance r from the city centre with technology h as

$$q(r,h)=c(h)+f(r)+s(h)p(r) \qquad (12)$$

Here c(h) are capital investments which depend solely on the type of technology h; f(r) are running costs during the period of functioning of the factory which depend on the distance from the city centre (due to the transport factor); c(h) is the territory which is polluted above the standard with technology h; p(r) is the price of land at the distance r from the city centre.

For optimal technology (h) and optimal location (r) of the factory the following conditions hold

$$\frac{\partial q}{\partial h} = 0, \qquad \frac{\partial q}{\partial r} = 0 \qquad (13)$$

From Eq. (12) and (13) we have

$$\frac{\partial c}{\partial h} = -p\,\frac{\partial s}{\partial h} \qquad (14)$$

$$\frac{\partial f}{\partial r} = -s\,\frac{\partial p}{\partial r} \qquad (15)$$

Eqs (14) and (15) enable us to formulate several principles of economically and environmentally optimal urban planning.

1. For optimal technology the costs connected with further reduction of residuals are equal to the cost of the territory whose pollution is reduced below the standard.

2. For optimal location of a factory its location farther from the city centre increases the running costs as much as the cost of territory decreases.

3. The higher the price of land, the higher additional costs are justified for reducing the polluted area.

4. If two factories have the same running costs then the factory which pollutes smaller area should be allocated nearer to the city centre (where the price of land is higher).

5. If polluted areas for two factories are equal then nearer to the city centre should be allocated the factory whose running costs with the distance from the city centre rise more steeply.

These principles hold for a monocentric city.

REFERENCES

(1) K. A. Fox, Social Indicators and Social Theory, John Wiley and Sons, N.Y. - Sydney-Toronto, 1974.

(2) F. Archibugi, A progress report: the quality of life in a method of integrated planning, Socio-Econ. Plan. Sci. 8, 339 (1974).

(3) Ю. Н. Гаврилец, Социально-экономическое планирование, Экономика, Москва, 1974.

(4) S. S. Angrist, J. Belkin, W. A. Wallace, Social indicators and urban policy analysis, Socio-Econ. Plan. Sci. 10, 193 (1976).

(5) Hiroyuki Kirajima, Ryoichi Sasaki, A dynamic model to analyze the repercussions of urban policies, J. Operat. Res. Soc. Japan 19, 308 (1976).

(6) В. А. Волконский, Модель оптимального планирования и взаимосвязи экономических показателей, Наука, Москва, 1967.

(7) P. A. Samuelson, Social Indifference Curves, Quart. J. Economics 70, 1 (1956).

(8) А. А. Смертин, Предпочтительный план и целевая функция текущего производства, Экономика и математические методы II, 1050 (1975).

(9) Ю. А. Дубов и др., Математическое моделирование развития городских систем, Автоматика и телемех. № II, 93 (1975).

(10) M. Intriligator, Mathematical Optimization and Economic Theory, Prentice-Hall, N.Y. 1971.

(11) Е. В. Гордина, Об учете процессов обезвреживания производственных отходов в региональном межотраслевом балансе, Экономика и и математ. методы II, 900 (1975).

(12) R. J. Chorley, P. Hagget (Eds), Socio-Economic Models in Geography, Methuen, London, 1969.

(13) А. Х. Корбут, В. В. Малинников, Приближенное решение некоторых неоднородных моделей размещения, Экономика и математ. методы I, 425 (1965).

(14) S. T. Jutila, A linear model for agglomeration, diffusion, and growth of regional economic activity, Reg. Sci. Perspectives 1, 83 (1971).

(15) H. K. Aben, Mathematical models in urban planning. Proc. Conf. NORD-DATA 76, Helsinki, 1237, 1976.

(16) H. Aben, Ein mathematisches Modell für soziologische Optimierung der Struktur des Wohnungsbestandes, 4. Internationaler Kongress über Anwendungen der Mathematik in den Ingeniuerwissenschaften (Weimar), Berichte, 1, 313, 1967.

(17) H. Aben, The threshold theory and dynamic programming in town planning, Eesti NSV Tead. Akad. Toimet., Füüsika, Matemaatika 16, 299 (1967).

(18) R. Artle, P. P. Varaiya, Economic theories and empirical models of location choice and land use: a survey, Proc. IEEE 63, 421 (1975).

(19) Л. В. Канторович, Экономический расчет наилучшего использования ресурсов, АН СССР, Москва, 1960.

(20) H. K. Aben, Some problems of mathematical town planning, Soviet-Finnish Symposium "Mathematical Simulation and Operations Research in Economic Planning", Helsinki, 1972.

MULTIOBJECTIVE LINEAR PROGRAMMING MODEL AS APPLIED TO REGIONAL LAND-USE PLANNING

Y. Nishikawa*, Nobuo Sannomiya*, M. Maeda* and Teitaro Kitamura**

**Department of Electrical Engineering, Kyoto University, Kyoto, Japan*
***Department of Agricultural Engineering, Kyoto University, Kyoto, Japan*

ABSTRACT

The first part of the paper discusses a general concept and the authors' fundamental attitude toward a regional land-use planning and its methodological foundation.

The second part develops an interactive method for multiobjective decision making and optimization starting with a model of linear programming type. The linear programming model includes only one index to be minimized (or maximized) and several constraint inequalities. Among these constraints, some could be altered to some extent by planner's intention, so that called soft constraints. Relaxation of the soft constraints usually results in improvement of the objective value, then it generates a kind of trade-off. In our method we start with one objective model instead of setting multiobjectives at the outset, and try to find a point of satsifactory compromise between attainment of the objective and requirement on the constraints. This is advantageous to avoid unnecessary conceptual and computational complexity. The algorithm for the decision making utilizes the idea of the surrogate worth trade-off.

The third part applies the method to a real example on optimum land-use planning in a rural region of Japan. The trial has been a successful one to yield important suggestions for the rational agricultural planning in the region.

1. INTRODUCTION

Basic tasks in applying systems approach to a regional planning problem are first to clarify an actual structure of the region in consideration, second to identify goals and objectives of the regional development, and third to construct a mathematical model suitable for the problem investigation.

A goal structure should reflect various aspects of the regional requirements including economical growth, industrialization, agricultural development, environmental enhancement, and so forth. Such a goal structure could finally be summarized and reflected by the physical status of land use within the region.

In a whole view of regional planning, the planning of the above mentioned goal structure would be called "nonphysical planning", which implies in wide sense the social and economical planning in the associated region. If we think about the actual situation of urban or rural regional planning in Japan, development of new systems methodologies for the nonphysical planning is badly needed.

This paper tries to respond to such a need by proposing a method for multiobjective planning. Mathematically, an extension of mathematical programming concept is investigated. Since, among various mathematical programmings, a linear programming technique is most widely used, the present discussion gives a special regard to it.

The paper consists of three parts. The first part discusses a general concept and the authors' fundamental attitude toward the regional land-use planning and its methodological foundation.

The second part develops an iterative procedure for a coupled business of model modification and preference search. Our procedure starts with a conventional linear programming model consisting of a single objective and several constraint inequalities. The constraints in the model can usually be classified into two groups, i.e., hard (not relaxable) constraints and soft (relaxable) constraints. The hard constraint is the one which is rigidly fixed by physical or other reasons, so that it can not be altered by human intention. On the contrary, the soft constraint is the one which is set according to human intention, more or less, then it might be strengthened or relaxed within some extent. Relaxation of the soft constraints usually yields a better objective value, and consequently allows a kind of trade-off.

In the proposed method we start with one objective linear programming model instead of setting multiobjectives at the outset, and, in the succeeding procedure, try to find a preferred point of compromise between attainment of the original objective and requirement on the soft constraints. This is advantageous in the sense that it can avoid unnecessary conceptual and computational complexity. The algorithm of the iterative search for the preferred point utilizes the idea of the surrogate worth trade-off method.[1)]

In order to demonstrate practicability of our method, in the third part, we have an example of application to an optimum land-use planning in a real rural region in Japan. The experimental use has been a successful one to yield significant suggestions for the rational agricultural planning of the region.

2. METHODOLOGICAL SIGNIFICANCE OF MULTI-OBJECTIVE APPROACH TO LAND USE PLANNING

A meaningful systems methodology, which is sound in theory and in practice as well, would be generated only through its trials of application to a variety of real world problems. This statement is especially true in systems approach to societal systems, because our society is much more complicated both in its structure and in its goal than any other systems such as engineering production systems and industrial management systems etc.

As a regional land-use status summarizes and reflects all the social needs and activities of people being concerned with the region, the regional land-use planning is a typical societal planning problem. The human activity within the region is subject to certain limits of various natural resources existing in the region. It is needless to say that the land is one of the most important natural resources, which is heavily characterized by its time history and limited in space. Under those limitations, the principal aim of regional planning is to create or recreate a favorable balance between the human activity and the use of natural resources.

In mathematical terms, the limitation and balance rule of human existence could be described as follows:

$$Ax - b \leqq 0 \tag{1}$$

x is a vector whose components show levels of various human activities, and b is a vector whose components indicate usable amounts of resources within the region. Elements of the matrix A represent demands for resources per unit human activities.

If we pick out a particular kind of resources, say the one associated with the first row of (1), and want to minimize its consumption under limitations of the other resources, the problem will be reformulated into

$$\min_x b_1 = a_1 x \tag{2}$$

subject to

$$\tilde{A}x - \tilde{b} \leqq 0 \tag{3}$$

In (2), b_1 denotes the first member of b and a_1 denotes the first row vector of A. Inequality (3) describes the limitation and balance rule for the resources other than the first one. The model of (2) and (3) is of a common linear program type in which b_1 is called the objective and inequality (3) the constraint.[2] It is to be noted that value of the objective b_1 is not prescribed but is subject to change, because it is determined by the optimization under the constraint.

If we pick out more than one kind of resources for minimization, a model will be of a multi-objective linear program type. Most of real regional plannings, if they fit the actual sense, would be formulated into this type of the model. A difficulty arises in the multi-objective program to attain a well balanced optimization among non-commensurable goals. The balanced optimization of the objectives is attained, if we look back to (1), by a good choice of values of components of b which might be altered by human intention. Furthermore the components which make (1) active need be considered as is suggested by the equality symbol in (2).

The discussion made so far gives us a conceptual base to the following mathematical development.

3. PROBLEM STATEMENT

Throughout the paper, we use the following notations: For vectors x and y in R^n,

$$x \geqq y \iff x_i \geqq y_i \quad \text{for } i = 1, 2, \ldots, n$$

$$x \geq y \iff x \geqq y \quad \text{and} \quad x \neq y$$

A prime denotes transposition of a vector or a matrix. If $a, b \in R$ and $a < b$, then

$$[a, b] \triangleq \{r \mid a \leqq r \leqq b\}$$

$$(a, b) \triangleq \{r \mid a < r < b\}$$

$$[a, b) \triangleq \{r \mid a \leqq r < b\}$$

Consider the following linear programming problem:

$$\text{(P1)} \quad \min_x c'x \quad \text{subject to}$$

$$Ax - b \leqq 0, \quad x \geqq 0 \tag{4}$$

$$Bx - \beta \leqq 0 \tag{5}$$

where x and c are n vectors, b an ℓ vector, and β an M vector. A and B are $\ell \times n$ and $M \times n$ matrices, respectively.

The constraint in (4) is a hard constraint, that is, the constraint that can not be changed by planner's intention. We assume that the constraint set (4) has a feasible region. On the other hand, every constraint in (5) is a soft constraint, that is, the constraint that could be relaxed, to some extent, by planner's consideration. The value of β in the soft constraint set is ideally wanted to set equal to β^*. But it is assumed that, if $\beta = \beta^*$, the constraints (4) and (5) are inconsistent and the problem (P1) has no solution. Then the problem is how to choose a value of β making a satisfactory compromise between attainment of the objective, min $c'x$, and requirement on the constraints.

4. A PROCEDURE FOR FINDING A SET OF INCONSISTENT SOFT CONSTRAINTS

4.1 Definition of a Bicriterion Minimization Problem

When the number of the soft constraints is too

large, i.e., $M \gg 1$, it is generally a difficult task to find the inconsistent components out of the constraint sets (4) and (5). In order to overcome this difficulty, we define the following optimization problem with two objectives:

$$\text{(P2)} \quad \min_{x,\beta} \begin{bmatrix} z(x, \beta) \\ F(\beta) \end{bmatrix} \quad \text{subject to (4) and (5)}$$

where

$$z(x, \beta) \triangleq c'x \tag{6}$$

$$F(\beta) \triangleq \sum_{j=1}^{M} f_j(\beta_j) \tag{7}$$

$$f_j(\beta_j) \triangleq (|\beta_j - \beta_j^*|/|\beta_j^*|)^p, \quad p \geq 1 \tag{8}$$

The function F defined by (7) and (8) is the measure of total relaxation of β. This is of the same form as a regret function introduced by Yu et al.[3]. We utilize this function in order to pick out the components of β that must be relaxed for getting consistency of the constraint set.

The function F with $p = 1$, represents the simple average of the relaxation quantities of all components β_j. However, as the parameter p increases, much importance is attached to the individual constraint component which deviates significantly from β_j^*. In (8), f_j is normalized in such a way that each relaxation of β_j is equally weighted (If $\beta_j^* = 0$, an appropriate value replaces β_j^*). When the relative importance among the soft constraints is known a priori, f_j will be multiplied by the weighting factor reflecting the importance.

4.2 Noninferior Solution of (P2)

We are now to obtain the noninferior solution of the bicriterion problem (P2). From the problem statement, the value of the soft constraint must satisfy $\beta \geq \beta^*$. This is satisfied by the noninferior solution of (P2):

Theorem 1. The noninferior solution $(\tilde{x}, \tilde{\beta})$ *of* (P2) *satisfies* $\tilde{\beta} \geq \beta$.

Proof: We prove by contradiction. First, if $\tilde{\beta} \leq \beta^*$, the constraints (1) and (2) with $\beta = \tilde{\beta}$ are inconsistent; hence $(\tilde{x}, \tilde{\beta})$ is not a solution of (P2). Second, we assume that $\tilde{\beta} < \beta_i^*$ for some i and define

$$\overline{\beta} \triangleq (\tilde{\beta}_1, \cdots, \tilde{\beta}_{i-1}, \beta_i^*, \tilde{\beta}_{i+1}, \cdots, \tilde{\beta}_M) \tag{9}$$

Since the feasible region of x given by (4) and (5) with $\beta = \overline{\beta}$ includes that with $\beta = \tilde{\beta}$, the following relation is obtained:

$$\left.\begin{aligned} z(\tilde{x}, \tilde{\beta}) &\geq z(\overline{x}, \overline{\beta}) \\ F(\tilde{\beta}) &> F(\overline{\beta}) \end{aligned}\right\} \tag{10}$$

where $\overline{x}$ is a solution of (P1) with $\beta = \overline{\beta}$. This shows that $(\tilde{x}, \tilde{\beta})$ is inferior to $(\overline{x}, \overline{\beta})$; therefore $(\tilde{x}, \tilde{\beta})$ is not a noninferior solution of (P2).

Q.E.D.

The noninferior solution of (P2) is obtained by solving the problem:

$$\text{(P3)} \quad \min_{x,\beta} [\theta F(\beta) + (1 - \theta) z(x, \beta)]$$
$$\text{subject to (4) and (5)}$$

where θ is a parameter varying over the unit interval [0, 1]. The optimal solution of (P3) for a fixed value of θ is denoted by $(x(\theta), \beta(\theta))$. For simplicity, the following notations are introduced:

$$F(\theta) \triangleq F(\beta(\theta)), \quad f_j(\theta) \triangleq f_j(\beta_j(\theta))$$

$$z(\theta) \triangleq z(x(\theta), \beta(\theta))$$

The objective functions and the constraint set of (P2) are both convex. Accordingly, a direct application of Geoffrion's theorem[4] leads to the following theorem which gives the relationship between the noninferior solution of (P2) and the optimal solution of (P3).

Theorem 2 (Geoffrion).

i) $F(\theta)$ *is monotonically nonincreasing on* [0, 1] *and* $z(\theta)$ *is monotonically nondecreasing on* [0, 1].

ii) Any solution $(x(\theta), \beta(\theta))$ *of* (P3) *is noninferior when* $\theta \in (0, 1)$.

iii) Denote the set of solutions of (P3) *for* $\theta = 0$ *by* $\{(x(0), \beta(0))\}$ *and define*

$$x(0+) \triangleq \lim_{\theta \to 0+} x(\theta), \quad \beta(0+) \triangleq \lim_{\theta \to 0+} \beta(\theta) \tag{11}$$

Then $(x(0+), \beta(0+))$ *is in* $\{(x(0), \beta(0))\}$ *and is noninferior.*

iv) Denote the set of solutions of (P3) *for* $\theta = 1$ *by* $\{(x(1), \beta(1))\}$ *and define*

$$x(1-) \triangleq \lim_{\theta \to 1-} x(\theta), \quad \beta(1-) \triangleq \lim_{\theta \to 1-} \beta(\theta) \tag{12}$$

Then $(x(1-), \beta(1-))$ *is in* $\{(x(1), \beta(1))\}$ *and is noninferior.*

It is observed from Theorem 2 iv) that $(x(1-), \beta(1-))$ is the noninferior solution of (P2) when the maximum consideration is given to the relaxation quantity of β relative to the value of z. On one hand, by Theorem 1, we have $\beta(1-) \geq \beta^*$. Consequently, a component j for which $\beta_j(1-) > \beta_j^*$ (or equivalently $f_j(1-) > 0$) is turned out to be the component of the constraint (5) which makes the problem (P1) infeasible. The value of $\beta_j(1-)$ gives the lower bound of β_j for getting the feasibility.

Furthermore, by solving (P3) as θ varies over (0, 1), we can find conflicting components among the inconsistent constraints, that is, the components such that no decrease can be obtained in the set values of the constraints without causing a simultaneous increase in at least one of the other set values. For this business, we investigate the variation of $\beta(\theta)$ as $\theta \to 1-$, and classify the components of the soft constraint as follows:

$$\left.\begin{aligned} J &\triangleq \{j \mid f_j(\theta) > 0 \text{ for some } \theta \in [\hat{\theta}, 1), \\ &\qquad j \in \{1, 2, \cdots, M\}\} \\ J^+ &\triangleq \{j \mid f_j(\hat{\theta}) < f_j(1-), \quad j \in J\} \\ J^- &\triangleq \{j \mid f_j(\hat{\theta}) \geq f_j(1-), \quad j \in J\} \end{aligned}\right\} \tag{13}$$

where $\hat{\theta} \in (0, 1)$ is a number chosen appropriately.

By Theorem 1, the set J is not empty. Further the set J^- is not empty, either. For, if J^- is empty, then

$$F(\hat{\theta}) = \sum_{j \in J^+} f_j(\hat{\theta}) < \sum_{j \in J^+} f_j(1-) = F(1-) \qquad (14)$$

which contradicts Theorem 2 i). As for the set J^+, the following theorem is established.

Theorem 3. If J^+ is not empty, there exists at least a pair of conflicting components, i.e., $j_1 \in J^+$ and $j_2 \in J^-$ such that β_{j1} and β_{j2} can not decrease simultaneously.

Proof: The point $\beta(1-)$ lies on the boundary of the feasible region in the β space†. However, the point $\hat{\beta}$ defined by

$$\hat{\beta}_j \triangleq \begin{cases} \beta_j(\hat{\theta}) & j \in J^+ \\ \beta_j(1-) & j \notin J^+ \end{cases} \qquad (15)$$

does not belong to the feasible region. For, if it does, then

$$\sum_{j=1}^{M} f_j(\hat{\beta}_j) < \sum_{j=1}^{M} f_j(\beta(1-)) = F(1-) \qquad (16)$$

which contradicts that $F(1-)$ is the minimum value of F (as shown by Theorem 2 iv)). Consequently, as the parameter θ varies from $\hat{\theta}$ to 1, for at least one $j_1 \in J^+$, the value of f_{j1} must become larger than $f_{j1}(\hat{\theta})$. In this case, for at least one $j_2 \in J^-$, the value of f_{j2} must become smaller than $f_{j2}(\hat{\theta})$ due to the fact that $F(\theta)$ is monotonically non-increasing (by Theorem 2 i)). Thus, during the transfer from $\beta(\hat{\theta})$ to $\beta(1-)$, the component β_{j1} is in conflict with the component β_{j2}. From the convexity of the β space, this conflict between β_{j1} and β_{j2} holds on the boundary of the feasible region.

Q.E.D.

As a result of the foregoing investigation, we can summarize the strategy for deciding the set value of β as follows: First, the set value of β_j for $j \notin J$ should be given by $\beta_j = \beta_j^*$, because the set value of this component has less influence upon the solution of (P1) than that of the component $j \in J$. Second, if J^+ is an empty set, the interaction among the set values of the soft constraints may be regarded as negligible. Then the set value of β_j for $j \in J^-$ may be determined individually in due consideration of the trade-off between each β_j and the objective function z. Third, if J^+ is not empty, there exists a conflicting relation among the set values of the soft constraints. Therefore, we must determine the preferred value of β_j for $j \in J$ with regard to the trade-off among all the conflicting components β_j and the objective z.

† Note that both x and β are the decision variables in (P3). The β space here implies the projection of the point (x, β) on the β subspace.

4.3 Procedure for Solving (P3)

If $p > 1$, (P3) is a nonlinear problem. To solve the nonlinear problem (P3), we apply a multilvel optimization technique by decomposing the problem into two subproblems. One of the subproblems is a linear programming problem, and the other is an unconstrained minimization. The interaction between subproblems is coordinated at the second level by using a gradient method. The detailed description of the algorithm is omitted here (See Ref. 5).

If $p = 1$, (P3) is just the following linear programming problem:

$$\text{(P4)} \quad \min_{x,\alpha} [\theta w'\alpha + (1-\theta)c'x] \quad \text{subject to}$$

$$\left.\begin{array}{l} \begin{pmatrix} A & 0 \\ B & -I \end{pmatrix} \begin{pmatrix} x \\ \alpha \end{pmatrix} \leqq \begin{pmatrix} b \\ \beta^* \end{pmatrix} \\ x \geqq 0, \quad \alpha \geqq 0 \end{array}\right\} \qquad (17)$$

where $\alpha \triangleq \beta - \beta^*$ and w is the M vector with the components $1/\beta_j^*$. I is the $M \times M$ identity matrix.

Phase I in the two-phase simplex procedure corresponds to solving (P4) with $\theta = 1$. In the present procedure, we solve (P4) with the parameter θ varying over the unit interval.

5. A PROCEDURE FOR DETERMINING A PREFERRED SET VALUE OF THE SOFT CONSTRAINT

5.1 Definition of a Minimization Problem with (m+1) Objectives

Since (P2) is a bicriterion problem, the non-inferior solutions of (P2) are obtained rather easily. However, the solution depends upon choice of the parameter p and the weighting factor of f_j, and then the solution set is restricted one in that sense. Therefore, it is neither reasonable nor persuasive to select a preferred value of β from this solution set. The purpose of Section 5 is to determine preferred values of the inconsistent soft constraints found in Section 4.2.

Let m be the number of the inconsistent soft constraints. The set values of the remaining $(M-m)$ soft constraints are fixed appropriately (for example, set as $\beta_j = \beta_j(1-)$), and these constraints are appended to the constraint set (4). That is to say, in Section 5, b of (4) is changed into an $(\ell + M - m)$ vector, and β of (5) into an m vector. As a matter of course, $\beta > \beta^*$.

In this section, we treat the relaxation quantities of m components of β as independent performance indexes instead of summing them up. Then we define the following minimization problem with $(m+1)$ objectives:

$$\text{(P5)} \quad \min_{x,\beta} \begin{bmatrix} z(x, \beta) \\ f(\beta) \end{bmatrix} \quad \text{subject to (4) and (5)}$$

where $f(\beta)$ is the m-vector function with its components f_j of (8).

We attempt to find a preferred solution of (P5) out of the noninferior set in accordance with an additional criterion induced by the planner.

5.2 Determination of the Trade-off Rate

The preferred solution of (P5) is obtained by an iterative way which utilizes the idea of the surrogate worth trade-off method[1]. In order to derive an information on the planner's preference, the trade-off rate need be calculated for every noninferior solution of (P5). For this purpose, the ε constraint approach is applied to the problem (P5). This is advantageous in the sense that a revised simplex method is applicable even to the problem with $p > 1$.

Then, by replacing m objectives except $z(x, \beta)$ in (P5) with the inequality constraints, we consider the following problem:

$$\text{(P6)} \quad \min_{x,\beta} z(x, \beta) \quad \text{subject to (4), (5) and}$$
$$f(\beta) \leqq \varepsilon \tag{18}$$

where ε, a parameter of dimension m, is so chosen that (P6) has a solution.

As is well known, the noninferior solutions of (P5) are given by the optimal solution of (P6) when the constraint (18) is active. The Lagrangian function of (P6) is

$$L = c'x + \lambda'(f(\beta) - \varepsilon) + \xi'(Ax - b) + \eta'(Bx - \beta) \tag{19}$$

where λ, ξ and η are, respectively, vectors of Lagrange multipliers associated with the corresponding constraints. Note that, when $\lambda_j > 0$, the value of λ_j represents the trade-off rate between z and f_j.

Since all the constraints and the objective of (P6) are convex and differentiable for $\beta > \beta^*$, the Kuhn-Tucker conditions are necessary and sufficient for the optimality of (P6)[2]. These conditions are as follows:

$$\left.\begin{array}{ll} x \geqq 0, & c + A'\xi + B'\eta \geqq 0 \\ \lambda \geqq 0, & f(\beta) - \varepsilon \leqq 0 \\ \xi \geqq 0, & Ax - b \leqq 0 \\ \eta \geqq 0, & Bx - \beta \leqq 0 \\ x'(c + A'\xi + B'\eta) = 0, & \lambda'(f(\beta) - \varepsilon) = 0 \\ \xi'(Ax - b) = 0, & \eta'(Bx - \beta) = 0 \end{array}\right\} \tag{20}$$

$$(\partial f_j/\partial \beta_j)\lambda_j - \eta_j = 0 \qquad j = 1,2,\cdots,m \tag{21}$$

From (20), we have

$$z(x, \beta) = c'x = \xi'b + \eta'\beta \tag{22}$$

It follows from (20) and (21) that the optimal solution of (P6) is a noninferior solution of (P5), if and only if $\eta > 0$. In fact, if $\eta > 0$, $\lambda > 0$ holds from (21), and then the constraint (18) becomes active. This means that there is no improvement in $z(x, \beta)$ without causing further degradation of at least one of $f_j(\beta_j)$. Thus, this solution is in the noninferior set. On the other hand, if some $\eta_j = 0$, the j-th constraint of (5) becomes inactive except for the degenerate case. Then from (22), the objective $z(x, \beta)$ does not depend upon the values of such β_j. Also from (21), $\lambda_j = 0$ holds; thus, the j-th component of (18) is inactive under the nondegeneracy. Accordingly, this solution belongs to the inferior set. The degenerate solution is also considered as inferior one.

In summary, the noninferior solutions of (P5) and their trade-off rates are calculated as follows: The activeness of (18) yields

$$\beta_j = \beta_j^*(1 + \sqrt[p]{\varepsilon_j}) \qquad j = 1,2,\cdots,m \tag{23}$$

By substituting (23) into (5) and solving (P1), we obtain the noninferior solution of x. In addition, from (21) the trade-off rate is given by

$$\lambda_j = (\partial f_j/\partial \beta_j)^{-1}\eta_j \qquad j = 1,2,\cdots,m \tag{24}$$

where η_j is obtained as the simplex multiplier in solving (P1) by a revised simplex method. The above calculation is continued by varying the value of ε parametrically within the domain where (p6) has a solution such that $\eta \neq 0$.

5.3 The Search Procedure for Finding the Preferred Solution

In the surrogate worth trade-off method, an interactive search procedure is used to find the preferred solution with inquiries being asked of the planner at each step of the search in order to assess the surrogate worth at a given noninferior point (z, f). The value of the surrogate worth function W_j represents the planner's assessment of how much he prefers trading λ_j marginal units of z for one marginal unit of f_j. $W_j > 0$ means that he prefers making such trade, $W_j < 0$ means that he prefers not to make such a trade, and $W_j = 0$ implies indifference.

If the indifference band where

$$W_j(f_1^0, f_2^0, \cdots, f_m^0) = 0 \quad \text{for all } j \tag{25}$$

is obtained, then f^0 and the corresponding z^0 give the preferred values of the objectives. Substitution of $\varepsilon = f^0$ into (23) results in the preferred value β^0. Besides, by substituting $\beta = \beta^0$ into (5) and solving (P1), we obtain the preferred solution x^0.

In practice, it is difficult to find at a time a point at which (25) holds simultaneously for all j. Therefore, the following successive approach may be effective: First, vary f_1 alone by fixing the values of the other objectives f_j, $j = 2, 3, \ldots, m$, to attain $W_1 = 0$ at $f_1 = \hat{f}_1$. Second, vary f_2 alone by fixing other f_j, to attain $W_2 = 0$ at $f_2 = \hat{f}_2$, and so forth. After obtaining $W_m = 0$, return to the search for $W_1 = 0$. Repeat the procedure until $W_j = 0$ is attained for all j.

In this procedure, the planner need only evaluate the value of one W_j at each step of the search. Then the trade-off curve shown in the f_jz plane can be utilized to find the point $\hat{f}_j$ where $W_j = 0$. However, the consistency of the planner's preference must be assumed during the successive evaluation process.

6. APPLICATION TO REGIONAL AGRICULTURE PLANNING

This section is concerned with an application of the proposed method to a regional agriculture planning problem. The decision making by the surrogate worth trade-off method requires a model of mathematical programming type. A result derived from the model reflects not only the planner's preference but validity of the mathematical modeling. Therefore, the mathematical formulation has to be checked repeatedly in discussions on the results obtained. As space is limited, a procedure and some typical results in a case study are reported here to demonstrate the use of the present method.

6.1 Model Description

The regional agriculture planning is to decide an optimum policy for the farming management and the land use with the aim of securing sound agricultural income and satisfactory amount of agricultural products in the region. The region considered consists of 340 farm-households and the farmland of 480 ha, and is located at a part of Tokoname City in Aichi Prefecture, Japan.

The problem is originally formulated by Kitamura[6] in the following linear programming problem:

$$\text{(P7)} \quad \max_{x} \; z = c'x \quad \text{subject to}$$

$$b^1 \leqq Ax \leqq b^2, \quad x \geqq 0 \tag{26}$$

$$B^1x - \beta^1 \geqq 0 \tag{27}$$

$$B^2x - \beta^2 \leqq 0 \tag{28}$$

where z represents the gross agricultural income of this region. In the formulation, the type of the agricultural management is divided into seven groups and further divided into twenty-two classes according to their products or combinations of products. The decision variable x is the twenty-two dimensional vector each component of which stands for the number of farm-households in a class of the agricultural management. The details are indicated in Table 1. For simplicity, we remove the restriction that x be an integer vector.

The hard constraint, given by (26), includes conditions on the area usable for farming and the total number of farm-households. On the other hand, the soft constraint of (27) and (28) includes three types of conditions: i) condition on the desired amount of each agricultural product, ii) condition on the number of farm-households in each group of agricultural management, and iii) condition on the number of each livestock. The first two conditions are given by (27) and the third one by (28). The items of the soft constraint, together with the ideal set values denoted by β^{1*} and β^{2*}, are listed in Table 2.

In (P7), the dimensions of the vectors are as follows: $c \in R^{22}$, $b^1, b^2 \in R^{11}$, $\beta^1 \in R^{19}$ and $\beta^2 \in R^3$. Because of limited space, the detailed description of A, B^1, B^2, c, b^1 and b^2 is omitted here (See Refs. 6 and 7).

6.2 Solution of (P4)

The problem has no feasible solution when $\beta^1 = \beta^{1*}$ and $\beta^2 = \beta^{2*}$. Then the procedures of Sections 4 and 5 are applied to (P7) in order to determine the preferred values of β^1, β^2 and x.

In our case study we put $p = 1$ in (5), and solve (P4). Table 2 shows a variation of the set values β^1 and β^2 with the parameter ranging beween 0.3 and 1. By referring to table 2 we know, from (13) of this problem, that

$$J^+ = 5, \quad J^- = \{6, 10, 19, 20, 22\}, \quad J = J^+ \cup J^-$$

where numerals indicate the soft constraints as of Table 2.

That is to say, the set values of β_j with $j \in J$ are too excessive to make the constraints feasible, so that must be somehow relaxed. In particular, note that the amout of chrysanthemum production ($j = 5$ in Table 2) is in conflict with that of the production of carnation ($j = 6$) or Japanese radish ($j = 10$).

6.3 Examples of Search for the Preferred Solution

As an example, β_5 and β_6 are chosen as trade-off parameters out of β; while the remaining β_j are fixed as

$$\beta_{10} = 150, \quad \beta_{19} = 6, \quad \beta_{20} = 500, \quad \beta_{22} = 160$$

$$\beta_j = \beta_j^* \quad \text{for other } j$$

For convenience, let us renumber β_5 and β_6 as β_1 and β_2, respectively. Accordingly, hereafter β_1 implies the desired amount of production of chrysanthemum and β_2 that of carnation. We then define the problem (P5) having three objectives, i.e., the relaxation quantities $f_1(\beta_1)$ and $f_2(\beta_2)$ together with the original objective z.

Figure 1 illustrates an example of the application of the interactive procedure described in Section 5.3. The first quadrant of this figure shows trade-off curves between β_1 and z for various values of β_2. On the other hand, the third quadrant shows those between β_2 and z for various values of β_1. The process of decision made by the first planner is shown on the $\beta_1\beta_2$ plane in the fourth quadrant. Inquiring him starts from two different initial points, and ends at the points A_4 and B_3, respectively. Note that the planner seems to be interested in the points of discontinuity of the trade-off ratios. Hence, it may be conjectured that his indifference band exists along the line connecting two points A_4 and B_3.

The decision process is experimented also with the second planner. This planner seems to have a dominant preference to high value of β_2. Therefore, his preferred solution will be the same point, C_4, irrespective of initial point.

The preferred values of x thus obtained are indicated in Table 1.

7. CONCLUSION

After a discussion on methodological significance of multiobjective approach to land-use planning, a systems method of multiobjective planning based upon a model of linear programming type has been developed. Our approach starts with a problem having a single objective and several soft constraints. Adjustment of the set values of the soft constraints, which is done by extracting a planner's preference, gives us a point of satisfactory compromise between the attainment of the objective and the requirement on the constraints.

For this purpose, first the constraint components that must be relaxed for getting feasibility of the original problem are found out. Second, preferred set values of the inconsistent constraints and the preferred solution of the orginal problem are determined by an interactive procedure utilizing the concept of the surrogate worth trade-off method. A special procedure is invented to deal with more than two objectives.

The proposed method was applied to a kind of optimum land-use planning in a rural region of Japan. The result obtained gives an important suggestion for the rational agriculture planning of the region.

An extension of the method to a more general class of mathematical programming has also been investigated, and will be reported in a separate paper.

References

1) Y. Y. Haimes, W. A. Hall & H. T. Freedman: Multiobjective Optimization in Water Resources Systems, The Surrogate Worth Trade-off Method, Elsevier, 1975.
2) L. S. Lasdon: Optimization Theory for Large Systems, Macmillan, 1970.
3) P. L. Yu & G. Leitmann: Compromise Solutions, Domination Structures and Salukvadze's Solution, JOTA, Vol. 13, No. 3, pp. 362-378 (1974).
4) A. M. Geoffrion: Solving Bicriterion Mathemathical Programs, Oper. Res., Vol. 15, No. 1, pp. 39-54 (1967).
5) N. Sannomiya, Y. Nishikawa & Y. Tsuchihashi: Optimization under Vector Valued Criteria and Its Application, Preprints, 4th SICE Symp. on Control Theory, Tokyo, pp. 109-112, June 1975 (in Japanese).
6) T. Kitamura: Yata District Master Plan in Tokoname City, Inst. of Comprehensive Architectural Planning, Tech. Report, March 1973 (in Japanese).
7) N. Sannomiya: The Surrogate Worth Trade-off Method - III, Research Group on Multi-objective Systems, Japan Assoc. Automatic Control Engineers, Tech. Report No. '76-2, pp. 1-14, Nov. 1976 (in Japanese).

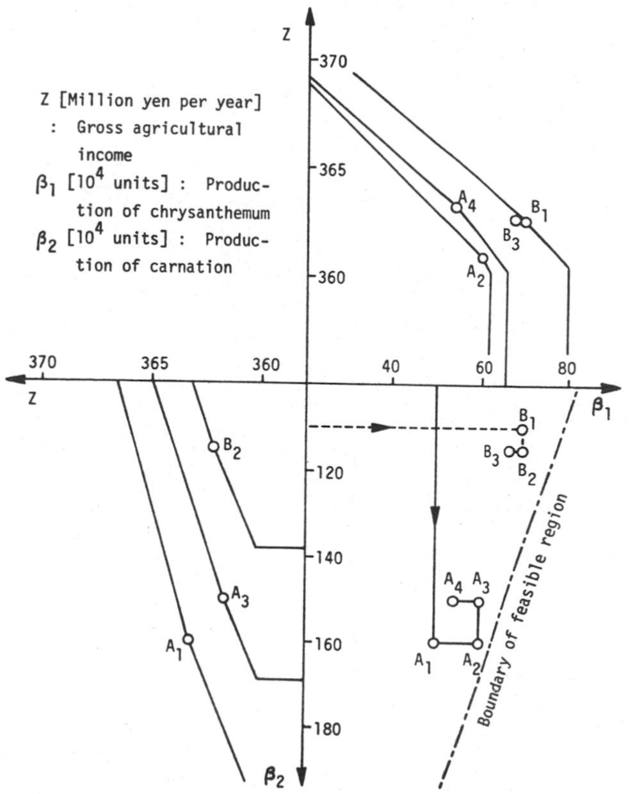

Fig. 1 Decision process made by the first planner.

Table 1 The preferred values of farm-households in class of the agricultural management

i	Class of agricultural management	Preferred solution		
		A_4	B_3	C_4
1	Rice, full-time	0	0	0
2	Rice, part-time I	14	15	11
3	Rice, part-time II	0	0	0
4	Dairy, full-time	17	16	16
5	Dairy, part-time I	0	0	1
6	Poultry raising, full-time	0	0	0
7	Rice & poultry raising, full-time	33	33	34
8	Rice & poultry raising, part-time I	0	0	0
9	Rice & poultry raising, part-time II	6	6	5
10	Chrysanthemum, full-time	4	6	2
11	Carnation, full-time	0	0	0
12	Rice & chrysanthemum, full-time	0	0	0
13	Rice & chrysanthemum, part-time I	53	53	55
14	Rice & carnation, full-time	5	4	7
15	Rice & paddyfield vegetables, full-time	0	0	0
16	Rice & vegetables, full-time	0	0	0
17	Rice & vegetables, part-time I	26	25	26
18	Rice & vegetables, part-time II	85	86	84
19	Rice & oranges, full-time	0	0	0
20	Rice & oranges, part-time I	0	0	0
21	Rice & oranges, part-time II	91	90	93
22	Rice & pig raising, full-time	6	6	6

Note: Full-time farm-households refers to those whose all members are exclusively engaged in their own agriculture. Part-time I refers to the households subordinating jobs other than agriculture; part-time II, households subordinating agriculture.

Table 2 The item of the soft constraint and variation of the solution to (P4), β^1 and β^2, with the parameter θ

Item of soft constraint	Ideal set values β^1*, β^2*	Set values β^1, β^2 θ=0.30	0.50	0.70	0.90	0.99
Agricultural production						
1. Rice	570[t]	570	570	570	570	570
2. Milk	1250[t]	1250	1250	1250	1250	1250
3. Hen eggs	2200[t]	2200	2200	2200	2200	2200
4. Chrysanthemum,hothouse	200[10^4units]	200	200	200	200	200
5. Chrysanthemum	120[10^4units]	107	107	0	0	0
6. Carnation	370[10^4units]	0	0	334	334	334
7. Watermelons	350[t]	350	350	350	350	350
8. Irish potatoes	300[t]	300	300	300	300	300
9. Cabbages	700[t]	700	700	700	700	700
10. Japanese radishes	700[t]	141	141	176	176	176
11. Oranges	740[t]	740	740	740	740	740
12. Pigs	245[t]	245	245	245	245	245
Farm-households by group of agricultural management						
13. Rice	160	160	160	160	160	160
14. Dairy	12	12	12	12	12	12
15. Poultry raising	39	39	39	39	39	39
16. Horticulture	32	32	32	32	32	32
17. Vegetables	39	39	39	39	39	39
18. Oranges	34	34	34	34	34	34
19. Pig raising	8	6	6	6	6	6
Number of livestock						
20. Milk cows	253[Head]	478	478	478	478	478
21. Hens	178[10^3]	178	178	178	178	178
22. Pigs, female	144[Head]	151	151	151	151	151
Gross agricultural income z[Million yen per year]		362	362	353	353	353

A MULTI-OBJECTIVE INDUSTRY ALLOCATION MODEL

M. Ishikawa*, I. Matsuda*, Y. Tamura*, and Y. Kaya**

**The Electrotechnical Laboratory, Tokyo, Japan*
***The University of Tokyo, Tokyo, Japan*

ABSTRACT

Industry allocation problem is one of the most crucial problems in developed countries, especially in Japan. The authors have developed a multi-sector, multi-region optimization model with multi-objective criteria in order to obtain desirable industrial allocation patterns of future Japan. Factors taken into the model are those of economy, population, environment, cargo transport, land, water, and labor force.

Various algorithms have been developed so far for searching the most desirable solution for a decision maker from among a set of non-inferior solutions. The authors propose a new efficient interactive searching algorithm, which the authors employ to determine respective solution or scenario which is the most desirable for each author. The scenarios thus obtained are evaluated in comparison with the present industry location pattern and with the alternative scenario proposed by the Ministry of International Trade and Industry. The results demonstrate that the multi-objective optimization technique introduces a new dimension in the field of industry allocation planning.

1. Introduction

Industry allocation problem is one of the most crucial problems in developed countries, especially in Japan, due to various problems including those of environmental deterioration and a shortage of land and water for industrial use. This paper aims at first obtaining desirable industrial allocation patterns of long-term future Japan taking these problems simultaneously into account by use of a mathematical programming model, and then determining the most desirable one among alternatives.

None deny that industrial siting should be planned, taking into account those factors such as physical, economic, and social ones simultaneously since they are all interconnected in many ways. This complexity inevitably requires the use of models for industry allocation planning, which may roughly be classified into two types: a simulation type model and a planning type model.

It is here to be noticed that the industry allocation problem especially of such a country as Japan with scarce resources involves various kinds of constraints as limits to land and water use and various objectives as prevention of environmental deterioration in highly industrialized areas and narrowing the income gap among regions. Use of simulation type models in this problem to find out desirable and feasible solutions requires exhaustive efforts of cut and try, hence the computational burden may be almost prohibitive if not impossible.

A planning type model or an optimization type one, on the other hand, can overcome this difficulty since the optimization technique is, as it is, a tool for finding optimum solutions in the presence of various constraints.

An argument may arise on how to shape a criterion function to be optimized since various interactive factors are to be taken into account as described before(1). There are two alternatives, the one being to evaluate each factor in common unit such as monetary unit and to shape a scalar objective function, and the other being to introduce multiobjective criteria. The former approach requires a priori knowledge concerning estimation of various factors in terms of monetary unit, which is in many cases hardly possible either because of lack of the data concerned or because of difference in opinions of estimators. The latter approach, on the other hand, avoids this difficulty by refering the decision on what pattern of factors is considered optimum to the player interacting with the model(Henceforce let him be called decision maker or DM) This advantage has motivated the authors to develop a multi-sector, multi-region optimization model with multiobjective criteria, which can generate various scenarios on desirable industrial allocation patterns of future Japan.

The process leading to the final decision is first to present a set of non-inferior solutions to DM and to ask DM to search systematically a solution which he thinks the most desirable among all other non-inferior solutions. Recognizing that DM can hardly express his preference in numerical terms, various kinds of interactive methods have been proposed so far by which DM may search the optimum by cut and try procedure(1). The most useful among them might be the algorithm using the surrogate worth function proposed by Haimes(1). It is however also recognized that the surrogate worth function assigned by DM involves inherent ambiguity, which may make the searching process very inefficient. Desired for multiobjective problem is an algorithm efficient in order to avoid tedious labor of DM in the optimum searching process and also robust from inaccuracy and inconsistency of the decision of DM which are inherent to man. A new algorithm taking this requirement fully into account is proposed in this paper and is applied to the industry allocation problem.

The model structure, the interactive algorithm, and computational results are presented in the following chapters.

2. Outline of the model

The model developed here is a 9-region (Fig. 1), 10-sector(Table 1) linear optimization model including factors of economy, population, environment, cargo transport, land, water, and labor force. A static model is adopted rather than a dynamic one to avoid unnecessary complexity. The problem considered here is to obtain desirable industrial allocation patterns in a specified year, given a framework of product by sectors and total population of Japan. An optimization of 5 objective criteria(Table 2) by use of the ε-constraint method is executed. Basic

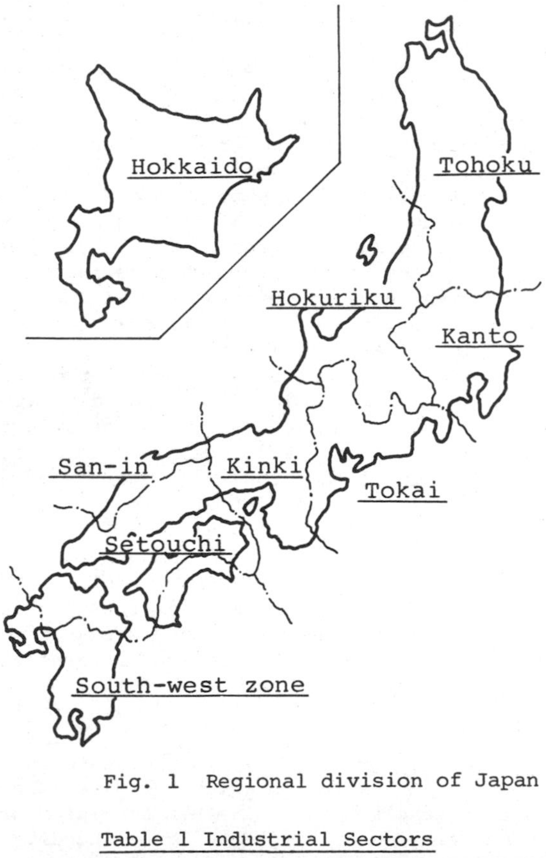

Fig. 1 Regional division of Japan

Table 1 Industrial Sectors

1. Agriculture	7. Heavy and chemical industry I
2. Mining	8. Heavy and chemical industry II
3. Construction	9. Transportation
4. Light industry	10. Services
5. Machinery	
6. Energy	

variables of the model are those of product of value added by regions and by sectors, population by regions, and flow of goods among regions by commodities

Table 2 List of objective criteria

1) Minimization of cargo transport.
2) Prevention of overconcentration of pollutants in some specific regions.
3) Equalization of per capita income.
4) Equalization of marginal cost of water.
5) Minimization of equivalent cost of change in present industry location pattern.

Features of and premises in the model are as follows.

1) The model is of a static type, therefore it cannot reflect the dynamic behavior of the variables as it is. In order to acquire dynamic feasibility as much as possible, the following measures are implemented: feasibility check in terms of capital, by introducing a criterion which penalizes for a change of regional patterns of gross output, and setting of upper and lower bounds to those variables such as product of value added and population in order not to induce excess change from the present pattern.
2) Virtual flows given as solutions of the so-called transportation problem are used in the model in place of real inter-regional flow of goods. This implies flows are the minima of those required due to the imbalance of supply and demand by sectors and by regions, completely ignoring bilateral flow of goods of the same sector. A nonlinear submodel which reflects the real material flows is also developed and linked to the resulting patterns of the industry allocation to estimate corresponding real material flows(2).
3) With regard to the environmental deterioration, only atmospheric one due to sulphur oxides is taken into account in the model because of the limitation of data concerning other pollutants. The authors define two indices. The first is a pollutant discharge index, which represents the amount of pollutant discharge per unit product in each industrial sector. The second is an environmental capacity index, which represents a self-cleansing ability due to wind, rain, and other climatic factors. In the model the level of the environmental pollution in each region is defined as a pollutant discharge per unit area, which is derived from the former index and product of value added, divided by the latter index. The latter index was similar to the one proposed by Sugiyama(3), and the authors estimate this index by use of multiple regression analysis with meteorological and geomorphological parameters as independent variables(4).
4) For each of the following four sectors —— construction, enegy, transportation, and services —— the product of value added is determined according to the premise that the present pattern of export and import in each region will be maintained in the future.
5) The so-called heavy and chemical industry is partitioned into two sectors, of which the

second sector corresponding to iron and steel, and petrochemical industries is supposed to be located from now on in the present site and the predetermined large-scale industrial sites such as Tomokomai, Mutsu-Ogawara and Shibushi.
6) 'Setouchi' region is chosen in the model as a separate region. This is because the environment in Setouchi has been seroiusly deteriorated as compared to neighboring regions.

3. Structure of the model

This chapter describes the structure of the model in some details. Variable with superfix ° designates that of initial year and otherwise that of specified year. And variable with — indicates an exogenous one.

3.1 Exogenous conditions

Government of Japan has made a long range plan of the country economy almost every year. It can be utilized as a framework in which distribution of industrial products among regions is determined through the use of the model. The information thus given a priori is on the product of value added by sectors and the total population.

(1) Product of value added by sectors

$$\sum_{i=1}^{N} v_{ik} = \overline{V}_k \qquad (1)$$

where $\overline{V}_k$: the product of value added in k-th sector

v_{ik}: the product of value added in i-th region and in k-th sector

N : the number of regions.

As was described in the preceeding chapter, sectors of construction, transportation, energy and services do not obey equation(1) but (12), which will be described later.

(2) Total population

$$\sum_{i=1}^{N} p_i = \overline{P} \qquad (2)$$

where P : the total population

p_i : the population in i-th region

3.2 Objective criteria

The criteria here comprise 5 objectives.

(1) Minimization of cargo transport the criterion

$$f_1 = \sum_{i=1}^{N+1}\sum_{j=1}^{N+1}\sum_{k} t_k d_{ij} y_{ij}^k \qquad (3)$$

where

$$\sum_{j=1}^{N+1} y_{ij}^k = v_{ik}/ b_{ik} \qquad (4)$$

$$\sum_{i=1}^{N+1} y_{ij}^k = \sum_{\ell=1}^{M} A_{k\ell}^j v_{j\ell}/ b_{j\ell} + \text{(final demand of k-th goods within j-th region)} \qquad (5)$$

y_{ij}^k: the flow of k-th goods(in monetary unit) from i-th region to j-th region,

t_k : the cost of transportation per unit of k-th goods,

d_{ij}: the average distance between i-th and j-th region,

b_{ik}: the rate of value added in i-th region and in k-th sector.

A^j : the input-output coefficient matrix in j-th region and

M : the number of sectors.

In the above equations, N+1 -th region is the region corresponding to whole foreign countries. The right hand equation of Eq.(4) implies the supply of k-th goods in i-th region, and that of Eq(5) does the demand of k-th goods in j-th region.

The sectors involved in Eq(3) are restricted to four sectors of manufacturing industries, in which transportation costs may affect the location of industrial sites.

(2) Prevention of overconcentration of pollutants in some specific regions

As stated in chapter 2, the level of environmental pollution T_i is defined as,

$$T_i = \sum_{k=1}^{M} e_k v_{ik}/ \theta_i S_i, \qquad (6)$$

where

e_k : the pollutant discharge index in k-th sector,

θ_i : the environmental capacity index in i-th region, and

S_i : the utilizable land area in i-th region.

As is easily seen, $\sum e_k v_{ik}/S_i$ in Eq(6) is an amount of pollutant discharge per unit area. The criterion, f_2, is represented as

$$f_2 = \sum_{i=1}^{N} \theta_i S_i | T_i - T | , \qquad (7)$$

where T : the average of T_i with regard to i. Parameter $\theta_i S_i$ is appended to Eq(7) so that f_2 does not change under different regional divisions.

(3) Equalization of product per capita among regions

It may be an important premise, at least from a political point of view, to narrow the income gap among regions. This criterion is represented as

$$f_3 = \sum_{i=1}^{N} p_i \left| \sum_{k=1}^{M} v_{ik}/p_i - \sum_{k=1}^{M} \overline{V}_k/ \overline{P} \right|$$

$$= \sum \left| \sum v_{ik} - p_i (\sum \overline{V}_k/ \overline{P}) \right|. \qquad (8)$$

In case the product of value added per capita is the same all over the regions, f_3 vanishes. In other words f_3 corresponds to the dispersion of product per capita over regions.

(4) Equalization of marginal cost of water

The balanced use of water in various regions is almost a necessity like Japan with limited availability of natural resources. The penalty of over-exploitation of rivers due to the increase in water usage is then introduced as one of the criteria.

A marginal cost of water in i-th region, w_i, is assumed to be a piecewise linear monotonously increasing function of a net increase in water usage in a corresponding region. The criterion function, f_4, is

$$f_4 = \sum_{i=1}^{N} U_i | w_i - w | , \qquad (9)$$

where w : the average of w_i with regard to i and

U_i: the amount of available water

in i-th region.

Parameter U_i in Eq(9) plays the same role as parameter $\theta_i S_i$ in Eq(7).

(5) Minimization of equivalent cost of change in present industry location pattern

Although the main purpose of the model is to find the desirable pattern of industry allocation, which, in principle, is different from the present pattern, the cost of moving factories and of building new facilities such as railways and roads should be taken into account in the model. This factor, f_5, is expressed as

$$f_5 = \sum_{i=1}^{N} \left| \sum_{k=1}^{M} v_{ik} - \sum_{k=1}^{M} v^{\circ}_{ik} (\overline{V}_k / V^{\circ}_k) \right| . \quad (10)$$

Hereafter in the paper these 5 criteria are abbreviated for simplicity as the criterion of transport, environment, income gap, water cost and cost of change respectively.

3.3 Constraint conditions

(1) Constraints on water usage

Upper limits are set to the total water usage and water usage for large scale manufacturing industries in each region.

(2) Constraints on land usage

Upper limits to the total land usage, to land for industrial use, and to land for large scale manufacturing industries in each region are set a priori.

(3) Constraints on labor force

The total labor demand should not exceed the labor available in that region, and it is expressed as

$$\sum_{k=1}^{M} v_{ik} / \ell_{ik} \leqq \gamma_i p_i \quad (11)$$

where ℓ_{ik} : the product per capita in i-th region and in k-th sector and

γ_i : the participation rate of labor.

(4) Constraints on the change of product and population

Too rapid changes in the product of value added by region and by sector, and the population by region are considered practically infeasible and so upper and lower bounds are set on these variables. As the so-called bounded value variables are employed here, this constraints can be implemented in the linear programming program without increasing a number of constraint conditions.

(5) Export and import pattern of the sectors of construction, transportation, energy and services is assumed to be constant over time.

The product of each sector is determined as follows.

$$g_{ik} \frac{v_{ik}}{b_{ik}} = \sum_{\ell=1}^{M} A^{j}_{k\ell} \frac{v_{j\ell}}{b_{j\ell}} + \text{(final demand of k-th goods within i-th region)}, \quad (12)$$

where g_{ik} is the ratio of total demand, i.e. the right hand side of Eq(12), and total supply, i.e. v_{ik}/ b_{ik}, of k-th goods within i-th regoion in the initial year. This parameter g_{ik} is assumed to be constant over time. A final demand within a region is obtained as a sum of private consumption, private investment, government consumption, and government investment. Details are omitted here only for brevity.

3.3 Computational procedure

The multiobjective optimization of this problem is formulated in the following form.

$$\text{Minimize } \{ f_1(\underline{x}), f_2(\underline{x}), \cdots, f_5(\underline{x}) \} \quad (13)$$

$$\text{Subject to } A\,\underline{x} = \underline{b} \quad (14)$$

where $\underline{x}$ comprises all variables and slack variables hitherto defined.

Eq(14) contains equality constraints, inequality constraints which are converted to equality ones by introducing slack variables, and additional equality constraints generated in implementing equations with absolute signs such as Eq(7) in linear programming problem.

To solve the above problem, the authors adopt the following ε-constraint method, which generates the non-inferior solution when all the constraints of Eq(16) are active.

$$\text{Minimize } f_1(\underline{x}) \quad (15)$$

$$\text{Subject to } f_j(\underline{x}) \leqq \varepsilon_j, \; j=2,\cdots,5 \quad (16)$$

$$A\,\underline{x} = \underline{b} \quad (17)$$

The size of the model, represented in the form of the linear programming, is in the following.

* The number of constraints 228
* The number of variables 661
* The percentage of the number of non-zero elements in the coefficient matrix 2.04%

This percentage is considerably high for this size of the conventional Linear Programming problems.

Computational time required by use of FACOM 230/75(computation speed is 207 ns in terms of Gibson mix) is about 4 minutes from the beginning. When starting from some initial feasible solution, it takes more than 10 sec, depending upon the distance between the initial solution and the optimum one.

In the model, the initial year and the specified year correspond to 1970 and 1985 respectively. The data for the model have been gathered from the various statistical tables of Japan, the details of which are omitted here for space limitations. The long-term vision by the Japanese Ministry of International Trade and Industry is adopted as the macro frame of Japanese economy in 1985.

4. Interactive optimum seeking algorithm

The word 'optimum' here is used in the meaning that it is the most desirable one for a specified DM. Application of the ε-constraint method to the industry allocation model generates various non-inferior solutions. The authors' main concern is how to select the most desirable one for DM from among a set of non-inferior solutions. The key idea of the proposed algorithm is first to determine a broad domain which includes the optimum solution, then to contract it step by step keeping the optimum solution inside. The problem is to find a domain with such a property. The authors overcome this difficulty by developing a modified ε-constraint method.

Here DM's assessment on the solution is presented in the form of the surrogate worth function, W_{ij}, after a little modification of the one originally proposed by Haimes(1). W_{ij} has the following property.

- $W_{i1} > 0$ when improvement of f_i at the sacrifice of f_1 is preferred over improvement of f_1 at the sacrifice of f_i.
- $W_{i1} = 0$ when improvement of f_i at the sacrifice of f_1 is equivalent to improvement of f_1 at the sacrifice of f_i.

and othewise ∘ $W_{i1} < 0$.

Hereafter each criterion, f_i($i = 1,\cdots,n$), is assumed to be already normalized between 0 and 1. Steps of the algorithm are as follows.

(1) To obtain a non-inferior solution { $f_1^{(U)}, \cdots, f_n^{(U)}$ } with positive surrogate worth function $W_{i1}{}^{(U)}$ ($i = 2,\ldots,n$) by use of the ε-constraint method. It is preferable that each $W_{i1}^{(U)}$ is as large as possible.

(2) To obtain the non-inferior solution { $f_1^{(L)}, \cdots, f_n^{(L)}$ } with negative surrogate worth function $W_{i1}{}^{(L)}$ ($i = 2,\cdots,n$) in the same way.

Let the optimum solution be { $f_1^*, \cdots, f_n^*$ }. The following inequality defines the initial domain.

$$f_i^{(L)} - f_1^{(L)} \leqq f_i^* - f_1^* \leqq f_i^{(U)} - f_1^{(U)} \quad (i = 2,\cdots,n) \tag{18}$$

Validity of Eq(18) will be dicussed later. Eq(18) states that an upper bound, U_i, and lower bound, L_i, for $f_i^* - f_1^*$ is expressed as

$$U_i \triangleq f_i^{(U)} - f_1^{(U)}, \; L_i \triangleq f_i^{(L)} - f_1^{(L)} \tag{19}$$

(3) To reduce $U_i - L_i$ iteratively by decreasing the upper bound and increasing the lower bound in turn until each $W_{i1}^{(U)}$ and $W_{i1}^{(L)}$ become zero, in other words $\{f_1^{(U)}, \cdots, f_n^{(U)}\}$ and $\{f_1^{(L)}, \cdots, f_n^{(L)}\}$ become indifferent to DM.

For example the upper bound is reduced as follows.

$$U_i = U_i - (U_i - L_i)\cdot \alpha W_{i1}^{(U)} / (W_{i1}^{(U)} - W_{i1}^{(L)}) \quad (i = 2,\cdots, n) \tag{20}$$

where α takes an appropriate value between 0 and 1 and is temporarily set to 1/3.

Using the new upper bound, U_i, obtained by Eq(20), solve the following modified ε-constraint method.

$$\text{Minimize} \quad f_1(\underline{x}) \tag{21}$$

$$\text{Subject to} \quad f_i(\underline{x}) - f_1(\underline{x}) \leqq U_i \tag{22}$$

$$A\underline{x} = \underline{b} \tag{23}$$

The solution thus obtained is proved to be a non-inferior one in case when all inequality constraints in Eq(22) are active. Let the solution be { $f_1^{(U)}, \cdots, f_n^{(U)}$ }. DM is to assign the surrogate worth function $W_{i1}^{(U)}$ and check that each $W_{i1}^{(U)}$ be positive. The lower bound is increased in the same way.

In general W_{i1} is a function of $\{f_1,\cdots,f_n\}$ among which f_i and f_1 are here assumed to be dominant. Furthermore, it is evident that W_{i1} is an increasing function of f_i, and a decreasing function of f_1. Hence an approximation $W_{i1} \doteqdot W_{i1}(f_i - f_1)$ is adopted here, consider-

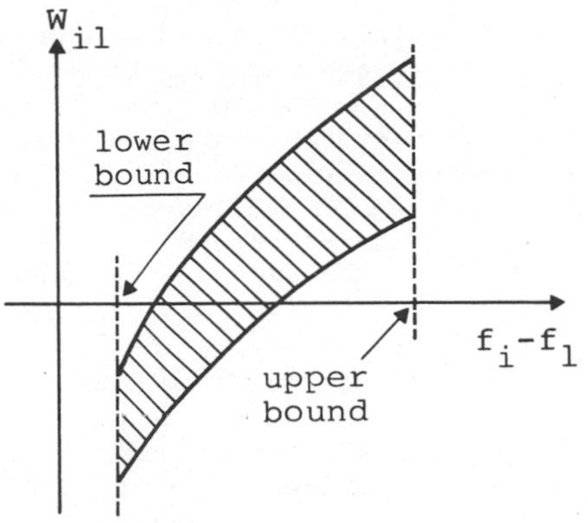

Fig. 2 The shape of W_{i1}

ing that W_{i1} cannot be definitely determined, even if $f_i - f_1$ takes a specified value as depicted in Fig.2. The degree of ambiguity of the value W_{i1} depends on the size of the domain mentioned above, which diminishes as the optimum seeking proceeds. This ambiguity however does affect little the final result as long as the size of the domain is monotonously reduced.

The advantages of the above algorithm are:
(a) the number of iteration required is considerably small compared to the search algorithm proposed so far,
(b) in each iteration DM's assessment on non-inferior solutions can further be divided into separate judgements, W_{i1}($i = 2,\cdots,n$), instead of a comparison between a pair of non-inferior solutions. This reflects the fact that a pairwise comparison is very difficult and is a burden to DM unless the problem is rather simple and considerably tangible,
(c) the judgement required is essentially whether each W_{i1}, is positive or negative, and a value of W_{i1} itself does not directly affect the final solution,
(d) a judgement concerning the sign of W_{i1} becomes increasingly difficult as $|W_{i1}|$ decreases.

In steps (1) and (2) $|W_{i1}|$ is fairly large so that even a DM with relatively little knowledge can decide the sign of W_{i1}. As iteration proceeds $|W_{i1}|$ gradually decreases, during which DM is expected to acquire more exact and consistent views on the problem.

5. Computational results

Two of the authors played the role of DM respectively, following the algorithm described in the preceding chapter, to find his optimum scenario on industry allocation in 1985. In applying the algorithm to the problem DM must be aware of the complexity of each criterion in the model, since each criterion is an aggregate of many variables such as a dispersion of the environmental pollution and the income gap among regions. Therefore DM's assessment of a criterion is made besed not only on the value of a criterion or its deviations, but also on states of many variables which comprise the criterion. The scenario in 1970 corresponding to the present industry location pattern is presented as a reference. Furthermore the industry allocation pattern in 1985 proposed by the

Japanese Ministry of International Trade and Industry(the so-called long-term vision by the MITI) is also presented for the purpose of comparison.

It is important to recognize where each scenario is located in the entire set of non-inferior solution. Upper and lower bounds of each criterion are useful informations for this purpose, and are obtained by the Pay-off table in Table 3. In the table each row corresponds to a non-inferior solution of which only one of the criteria is taken into account in minimization whereas others are completely neglected, and each column represents values of the corresponding criterion. The lower bound of each criterion is the minimum value in the corresponding column elements and is found always the diagonal one. The upper bound of each criterion is approximated by the maximum value in the corresponding column elements. In Table 3, values normalized within values of 0 and 1 are presented. From the Pay-off table thus obtained, one may easily recognize that emphasizing the environmental criterion causes serious degradation of all other criteria.

Fig.3 exhibits changes in upper and lower bounds for $f_i - f_2$ at each iteration(only the case of i = 5 is shown here because of space limitation, and f_2 instead of f_1 is used for minimizing variable in the modified ε-constraint method) brought by two DM's, say DM-A and DM-B. Fig.4 (a) and (b) display changes in f_2 and f_5 respectively.

A major difference between the two DM's is best illustrated in Fig.4 (b): DM-B prefers the criterion of cost of change to other criteria, or in other words he lays more stress on the present industrial location pattern than DM-A.

Table 4 exhibits the normalized values of criteria in 4 cases stated above. One must notice that because the upper and lower bounds are obtained from the Pay-off table in the specified year, values of criteria in the initial year do not necessarily lie between these upper and lower bounds. Values of the first and the third criteria are the ones normalized by GNP. For example the first criterion in case 1 is larger than those in other cases, yet the amount of cargo transport in case 1 is the smallest in all cases. Values before the normalization are also shown in (-).

Comparison of the results of case 2 and 3 with those of 1970 tell that values of the criterion of environment in case 2 and 3 are fairly small compared to that in 1970. It tells that industrial siting cannot but decentralize in the future due to constraints by land and water, and also that both DM's lay stress on this criterion. The values of criterion of the income gap in case 2 and 3 are both about 1/10 of that in 1970. This is due to the inevitable decentralization of

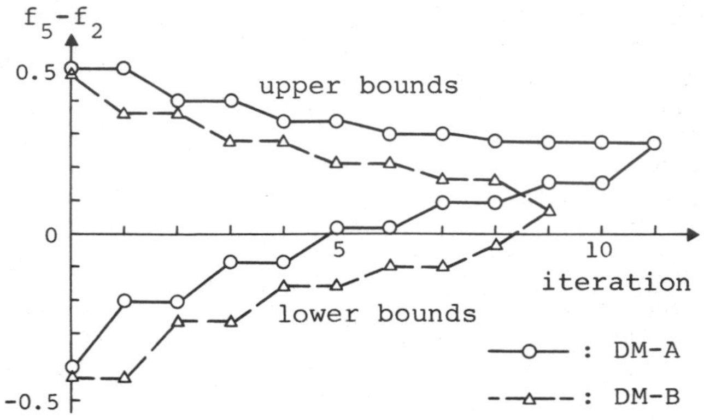

Fig. 3 changes in upper and lower bounds

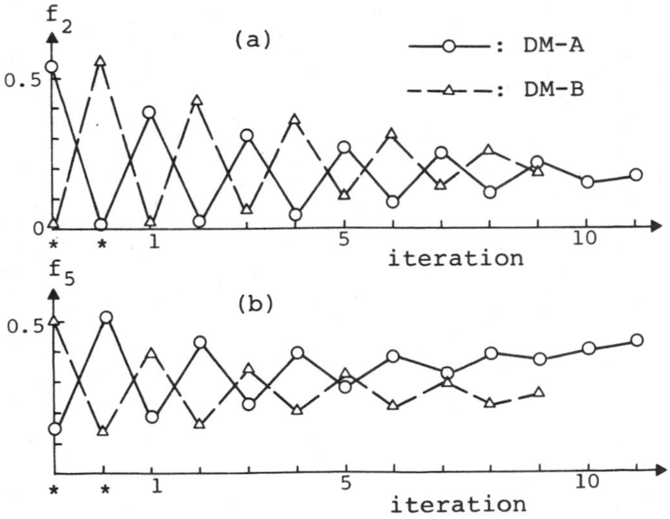

Fig. 4 changes in f_2 and f_5

Table 3. Pay-off table

		values of criteria				
		transport	environment	income gap	water cost	cost of change
minimized criteria	transport	0.0	1.0	0.664	0.577	0.733
	environment	1.0	0.0	1.0	1.0	1.0
	income gap	0.500	0.561	0.0	0.132	0.087
	water cost	0.545	0.279	0.255	0.0	0.162
	cost of change	0.981	0.773	0.439	0.453	0.0

Table 4 Values of criteria in 4 cases

cases		values of criteria				
		transport	environment	income gap	water cost	cost of change
1. actual pattern in 1970		0.348 (-0.148)	0.999	2.296 (0.945)	----	0
2. DM - A	in 1985	0.283	0.164	0.234	0.124	0.442
3. DM - B	in 1985	0.333	0.205	0.290	0.098	0.270
4. long term vision by MITI	in 1985	0.133	0.622	0.993	0.060	0.294

industrial siting and to the decrease in the gap of labor productivity among regions in future.

In the long-term vision by the MITI the amount of cargo transport per unit of GNP takes its minimum among alternatives, showing that a degree of self-sufficiency in each region concerning manufacturing goods is the largest. The criterion of environment and that of the income gap are better than those in 1970, but worse than those of case 2 and 3. From these one may conclude that in the long-term vision by the MITI the amount of cargo transport is decreased at the sacrifice of the criteria of environment and of the income gap.

Other computational results such as those by region and/or by sector are omitted here only due to space limitations.

6. Summary and conclusions

The authors have developed an industry allocation model with multiobjective criteria and proposed a new interactive algorithm for searching the most desirable solution for a decision maker. By applying the algorithm to the model two scenarios have been obtained, which have been evaluated in comparison with the present industrial location pattern and with the long-term vision by the MITI. By all these, it is well demonstrated that the multi-objective optimization techniques introduces a new dimension in the field of industry allocation planning.

ACKNOWLEDGEMENT

The authors would like to express their sincere thanks to Dr. Kurokawa of the Electrotechnical Laboratory for his discussions during the course of this study, and Japan Industrial Policy Research Institute for their sponsorship.

REFERENCES

[1] Y.Y.Haimes, et al.: Multiobjective Optimization in Water Resources Systems, Elsevier, 1975.

[2] Y.Kaya, et al.: Models for Interregional Material Flow, in IFAC Symposium on Environmental Systems Planning, Design and Control, 1977.

[3] K.Sugiyama: Dynamic Simulation on Environmental and Economic Behavior of the Japanese Islands-- Terrestrial Environmentology IV, J. Earth Sci., Nagoya Univ., vol. 24, 1973.

[4] I.Matsuda, et al.: A Macroscopic Approach to Environmental Modelling, in IFAC Symposium on Environmental Systems planning, Design and Control, 1977.

INTEGRATION OF ENVIRONMENT INTO REGIONAL DEVELOPMENT: AN IIASA FRAMEWORK

D. Fischer and S. Ikeda*

International Institute for Applied Systems Analysis (IIASA), 2361 Laxemburg, Austria
**Research Scholars, IIASA*

INTRODUCTION

The consideration of environmental factors in regional development programs has received widespread attention in this decade, primarily because of public awareness of adverse environmental deterioration which can very often be irreversible. Indeed, the larger the scale of development and the more concentrated and complex these development projects and activities, the more massive the environmental changes have been. Despite the wide range of economic benefits that are reaped from development concern for environmental quality has become an important source of activity for attempting to thwart development thrusts. The increase in the amount of literature on the subject and the creation of environmental institutions attest to the fact that the growth of the international character of environmental impacts has proven to be of increasing importance to regional development.(1)

Recently, proposals have been made in the direction of an integrated approach to large-scale development planning.(2) However, it is easy to discuss the necessity of such an approach, but it is extraordinarily difficult to develop an integrated approach or methodology which can be applied in a practical way and to endure the actual demands of real large-scale development projects.(3) Generally speaking, an integrated approach requires the perspective and tools of systems analysis which can deal with a system of interrelated actors and approaches, each representing an individual subsystem such as energy, local economy, water, population, ecology, etc. In this way the development-environment structure and linkages can be analyzed in part and treated in such a way that can be applied in a development program.

IIASA'S USE OF SYSTEMS ANALYSIS AND RESEARCH STRATEGIES

It is not surprising that IIASA has become an institute that has the potential to pursue the above mentioned research objective. IIASA is ideally equipped to examine complex and practical problems from an applied systems perspective. IIASA is at present composed of scientists from East and West from seventeen developed countries and aims to bridge the gap between scientific and technological development in modern societies and the social, cultural and other repercussions on human beings and on the surrounding environments. IIASA has provision for drawing on highly developed research resources and on information from a broad range of disciplines from East and West on the basis of non-political, international cooperation. Taken together IIASA offers five major approaches to the research tasks it undertakes:

- international in scope
- non-political in substance
- systems analysis perspective
- applied to real problems
- multi-disciplinary in structure.

These features have led directly to the role IIASA has defined in its application of systems analysis over the past four years:(4)

1. Exploration of problems of international importance;
2. Comprehensive approach to such problems.

For the first application IIASA has been concentrating on *global and universal issues*. Global problems cross national boundaries, inherently involve more than one nation and cannot be solved without intense cooperation between nations, particularly between East and West. Current global problems which IIASA has tackled are energy systems and food and agricultural systems. On the other hand, universal issues lie within single nations but are shared by almost all nations; these are problems such as planning, management and organization of large-scale regional development programs and the design of national health care systems.

The second aspect is essential to effectively address the above problems of international importance that are confronted by every country. For example, energy problems must be studied from various points of view to obtain a systems perspective: energy supplies, environmental pollution, energy demand, new technological advances, etc. Therefore, IIASA's goal could be briefly described as follows:

To analyze international problems of importance in a comprehensive way and to offer possible solutions to decision makers, identifying and investigating the interrelationships among the pieces of the overall problem.

IIASA's research strategies have been formed on the basis of a matrix organization as shown in Fig. 1.(5) The vertical columns are four major areas of research competence which depend on a solid base of modern science and technology essential to industrial societies. Research activities which cut across these areas of competence at present include Global Energy Systems, Food and Agriculture and Integrated Regional Development.

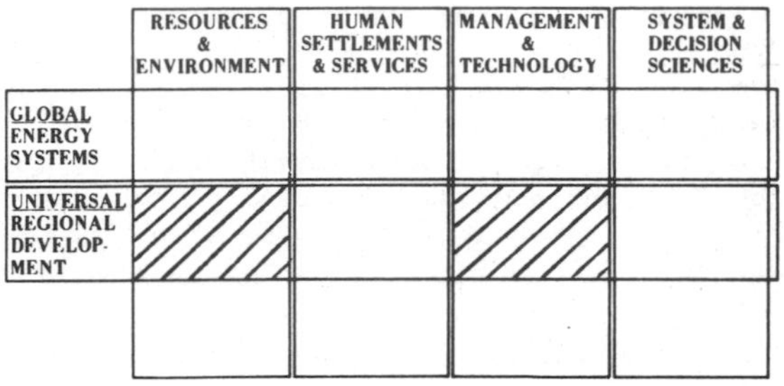

Fig. 1.

In attempting to implement its research program based on the matrix organization shown in Fig. 1 IIASA has experimented with the following three types of systems analysis over the past four years:(6)

Type I: Optimization Simulation
This type of systems analysis, for example, forest pest management, makes it possible to test all possible policies in the model rather than in the real world, as shown in Fig. 2(a). With provision for this kind of information about future consequences, the decision maker is in a much better position to select from the options faced.

Type II: Scenario Exploration
Instead of simulation models in Type I, there is a problem of identifying a range of strategies responsive to different national and international goals and of designing alternatives that satisfy specified demands by selecting from options and constraints as illustrated in Fig. 2(b).

Type III: Case Studies
Large-scale development programs have been internally organized and managed in different ways to achieve a particular program's goals within specific conditions for specific periods. An adequate selection of past experiences could lead to a systems analysis through a careful examination of the potential consequences of different policies of these "natural experiments" which have been under way around the world (Fig. 2(c)).

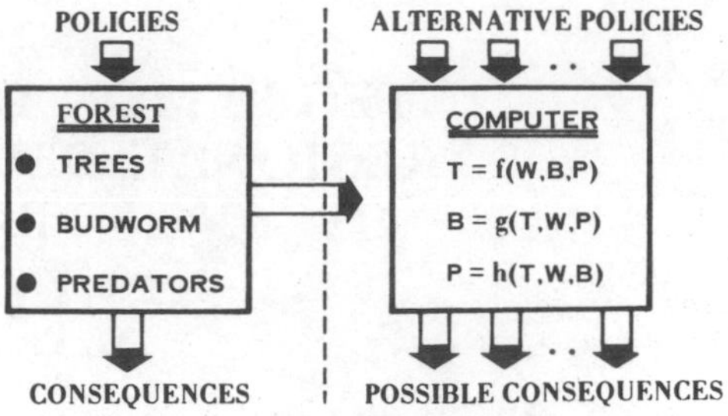

Fig. 2(a). Systems analysis, Type I: forest pest management.

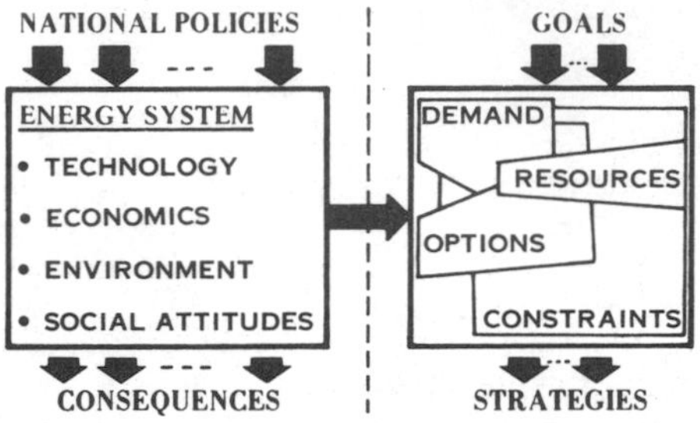

Fig. 2(b). Systems analysis, Type II: global energy systems.

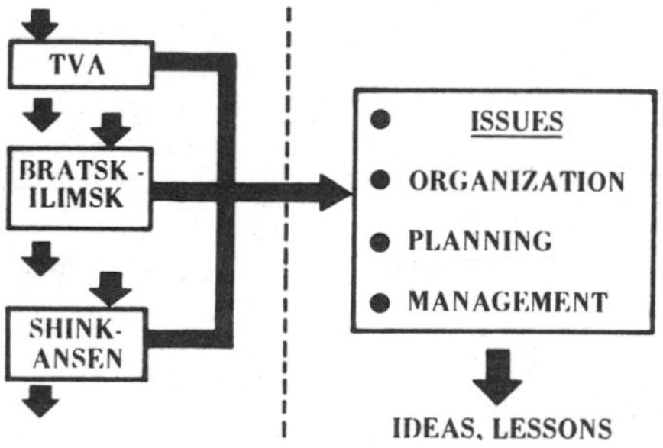

Fig. 2(c). Systems analysis, Type III: regional development.

Approach to Regional Development at IIASA
This paper only deals with the interaction of the shaded areas illustrated in the IIASA research matrix (Fig. 1) which constitute only one of the many research projects at IIASA. In the Management and Technology Area work has been underway which focusses on the analysis of planning, management and organization of present day large-scale development projects. The main objective of this research is the generalization of international experiences from the case studies and in-house research on the methodological aspects. How to plan, manage and organize a large-scale development program is an essential problem which governments, local authorities and corporations face. Such programs include social, economic, technological and environmental aspects as well.

Both the international interest and the relevance of systems analysis encouraged the

Management and Technology research area in IIASA to launch a series of studies on experiences of several large-scale development programs in the world. The first one was the Tennessee Valley Authority (TVA) in the USA. The second study was on the Bratsk-Ilimsk Territorial Production Complex (BITPC) in the USSR. The third study will be on the Super Express Railway project (Shinkansen) in Japan. (See Fig. 2(c)).

The purpose of this Type III systems analysis could be summed up as: (7)

- to learn from a specific case about the management problems of a complex development system;
- to obtain a better understanding of the overlapping conflicts inherent in implementing development in a specific socio-economic environment;
- to develop an integrated methodological experience;
- to ascertain principles and methods which are applicable to the other large-scale regional development projects in the world.

It is readily understandable that one of the major aspects in these studies should be devoted to the integration of environmental factors into such regional development programs. Needless to say, the environmental programs or systems should comprise an important component of overall regional development strategy.

In this context this research is closely connected with another research area, Resources and Environment, as indicated in Fig. 1. Since current concern among publics, regional planners, and decision makers centers on the fact that inherently scarce resources and pollution of the environment may affect the rate of social and economic development in many regions, it is important for the Resources and Environment Area to address regional development and environmental policy considerations. Scientists from both Resources and Environment and Management and Technology Areas worked together in a multidisciplinary approach to the integration of environment into regional development.

RESEARCH OBJECTIVES

In order to obtain a broad view of the environmental integration process, in addition to the past two case studies, TVA in the USA and BITPC in the USSR, more studies were undertaken such as the Shinkansen rail transportation system in Japan, the Kinki industrial region in Japan, and North Sea Petroleum in the U.K. and Norway. Each of these cases offers such complexities as multiple decision makers, conflicting issues and impacts. Specific objectives of these studies are to:

- Attempt to create a framework to investigate and compare the environmental aspects of these various cases.
- Identify and describe the environmental component of the regional development programs.
- Determine the existence and degree of comprehensiveness of the environmental considerations and their degree of integration into the development program.
- Suggest guidelines and processes for performing comprehensive environmental assessments and integrating the results of such assessments into large-scale regional development programs.

The basic approach in these studies is the premise that environment and development are not fundamentally incompatible. In other words, there is or should be an environmentally sound way to develop a natural resource and to achieve conflict resolution. Over time there should be a growing convergence rather than conflict between environment and development goals, activities, actors and strategies.

Research Framework

The analytical framework developed for these case studies is in three stages as follows:

- Identification framework: To identify the perceptions of development-environment actors and impacts through determining what is necessary for development activities to be successfully sustained in an environmental setting of high quality capable of satisfying its traditional users as well as the newer users associated with the development program.
- Interaction framework: The specification of the development-environment interface and responses to include those actor subsystems integral to answering to the environmental management criteria of comprehensiveness and integrativeness.
- Information framework: The development of the environmental management interface of planning, regulation, and monitoring based on the information linkages among the actor subsystems and the necessary environmental management functions for generating a successful decision defined in terms of acceptability and adequacy.

The Identification Framework. Fig. 3 shows the basic structure of the framework and provides the introduction to the figures and discussion that follows. Fig. 3 is divided into two separate policy systems, a development system and an environment system. Society generates a set of demands for a set of development and environment programs. Each system in turn generates its own set of responses based upon existing uses or programs, the nature of the impacts and the degree to which the impacts shift the values inherent to each system.

The key interface between these systems comes first from the development side as a set of development activities impinge on the environment as a set of impacts. The second aspect of this development-environment interface comes from the environmental response to these impacts as thrusts from the environmental side to influence the development activities. This influence occurs through several approaches including standards, sanctions, impact assessments, monitoring, etc. Both the environmental response and the development response are involved in mitigating or eliminating the environmental impacts of development activities. This dual response set comprises the environmental management system. The adequacy of this system is determined via the comprehensiveness of the responses and degree to which they are integrated into the development system.

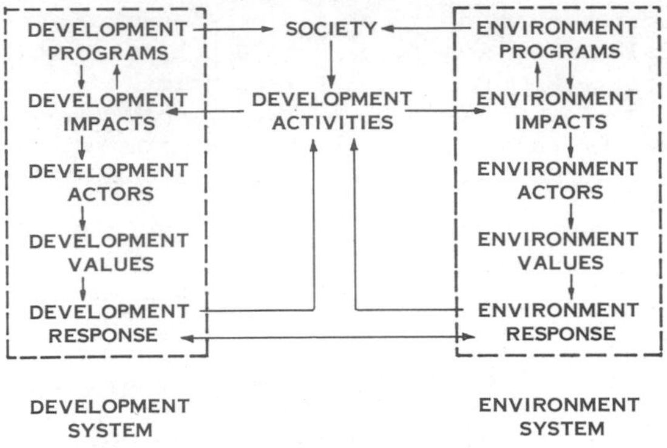

Fig. 3. Basic Structure of the Development-Environment Interface

Fig. 3 contains a basic set of policy variables that comprise and characterize the two policy systems shown:(8)

- program: a decision sphere which defines the set of decision problems within the competence of that system;
- impacts: a set of effects occurring internally and externally which define the changes imposed, experienced and perceived within that system;
- actors: a set of existing user groups or actors and their relationships affected by the changes within that system;
- values: a set of core beliefs, prevailing ideologies, rules and previous policy stances held by the actors that characterize that system and that are challenged by the impacts;
- responses: a set of opportunities, constraints and options created to allow the impacts to be extenuated, mitigated or eliminated within the system.

Together these policy variables comprise a policy system that is capable of responding to a set of impacts that affect that system. One of the reasons the development system has grown so large is the set of positive development impacts that have created and propelled that system over time. One of the reasons the environment system has evolved is the set of negative environmental impacts from development activities that have given rise to the creation of a system to offset development pressures. The scope of the case studies are to ascertain the nature of the development and environment responses connected with large-scale regional development programs. In particular there is an interest in determining the linkages characterizing the interface between the development and environment systems. These linkages would comprise intersystem connections which could be joint responses evolving into a comprehensive and integrated environmental management system.

Both of these core development groups respond to the impacts created by development activities via the kinds of responses required by the environmental system. Different actor groups are associated with each of these general responses even though all groups can engage in each of them as well. The values or premises underlying each of the systems are activated by development impacts. Such values are not by any means totally pure, e.g., within the development policy system some concern would be evident for the environment and within the environment policy system credence would be given to economic values. Once values are affected then the question of favorability toward the development activities is evinced. Should key actor groups be unfavorable then the responses from each policy system are heightened.

One important factor stemming from Fig. 3 includes the concept of actors and associated values as demonstrated via the degree of favorability toward the development and the degree of involvement with it. A complete array of possible actor groups which would influence the outcome of a development program would include:(9)

- Core Actors: This group has continuous and intensive involvement in the technological development program. It is usually the core actors who initiate a program via one or more fundamental decisions.
- Allied Supporting Actors: These actors are characterized by a favorable orientation through the supplying of goods and services, provision of infrastructures, enabling decisions, etc.
- Independent Central Actors: Actors of this type have a degree of independence or autonomy from both the proponents and adversaries of a given development program because of being constitutionally or legally-based or having an "objective" information position, i.e., performing their own research, information-gathering and interpretation.
- Middle Range Actors: This actor type has moderate involvement in the development program and may have favorable, unfavorable or neutral attitudes to the development. An actor is classified middle range for several reasons: (i) chooses only moderate involvement, (ii) has limited legal basis for involvement, (iv) lacks information especially from other key actors, thus position not sufficiently well developed to qualify as another actor-type, or (v) is waiting for decisions by others to determine or declare position.

- Rivals and Adversaries: This group of actors consists of those who, for reasons of expertise, power, resources and information, have only moderate involvement and are declared rivals or adversaries of the development program. Such actors can also develop viable alternate technological programs. Given a fundamental decision against the prevailing program, former "core" or "allied supporting actors" may shift to rival or adversary status.
- Exogenous Rivals and Adversaries: This group of actors is outside the policy system in its day-to-day functioning. Exclusion may be on a geopolitical basis, opposition to the prevailing development program, or support for an alternative program which may or may not differ technologically.
- Exogenous Supporting Actors: (i) Those actors who have definite links to "allied supporting" and "core" actors and who though geopolitically distinct from members of the policy system may indirectly and significantly control their actions (e.g., multinational corporations). (ii) Those actors who are characterized both as marginal to the development program and supporting it. Usually they can only be identified through solicitation or indirect representation of their views (e.g., other countries with similar development programs).

The actors classified as above provide a systems perspective of the basic behavioral structure between the development and envirionment policy systems. This actor linkage and interplay given the descriptions of each position above can be manifested in a variety of ways and strategies.

In an attempt to apply Fig. 3 in a complex and large-scale development program few actors have become so broad in outlook that the decision making system can appear diffuse. What emerges as a central issue is the defining of the boundaries of the decision problem and the means for addressing separate policy systems. Even over time actor values cannot be described as shifting but appear to remain both complex and central to the actors. One clear observation is the deep imbedding of these values over time as the development program proceeds.

Interplay of actors, and therefore interplay of responses, results in indirect relations. For example, ecology itself is not a value in which companies would be directly interested, but environmental bodies may apply certain measures for achieving environmental goals thereby influencing company capital and operating costs (which in turn are of no direct importance to these environmental bodies). While Fig. 3 separated all development and environment actors into different policy systems it is readily seen from the above that the development-environment policy systems are complex, representing numerous decision makers with diverse direct and indirect values often showing conflicting objectives. Therefore, when considering individual environmental problems many of these actors will be deleted or regrouped to demonstrate their essential interactions and interests with the problem at hand.

<u>The Interaction Framework</u>

The responses by the development and environment systems to environmental impacts created by development activities requires a further regrouping. The response systems generated by the development and environment systems can be seen as an environmental management system. It is here that the criteria of comprehensiveness and integrativeness come into play. Comprehensiveness can be defined in two ways:

- a comprehensive set of actor groups or subsystems included in the environmental system, and
- the full range (comprehensive) of environmental management activities to regulate the development activities, including research, planning, regulation, management and monitoring.

Integrativeness can be equally defined in two ways:

- an integrated set of relationships between actor groups or subsystems, and
- an integrated communication pattern giving similar weighting to information generated.

An environmental management system defined as above has some minimal actor configuration required for an adequate solution to the environmental problem of interest. Each of these actor subsystems comes into the environmental management system on the basis of different values and for different reasons. Each actor subsystem within the environmental management system can be seen as an individual decision making unit. The interest of an applied systems analysis is the focus at the interface of these five actor subsystems.

Clearly, a central thrust is to judge the adequacy of response to the development challenges faced. Also, an important consideration is the judgement as to what constitutes an adequate environmental management system. In order to implement this wide-ranging approach to the environment two criteria are important for setting the stage for this analysis. Comprehensiveness is the first criterion and by comprehensive is meant the entire set of environmental responses noted earlier that would comprise a total environmental management system.

To provide balance in a strong development-oriented system this set of environmental management responses should be organized and operating separately from the development actor subsystem. This separation allows for not only a counter-balance to the developers but it provides for a strong source of environmentally sound ideas and information to support, bolster and integrate with the development system. The strengths derived from a comprehensive set of separate environmental responses can then be of great utility to development planners.

To capitalize on these strengths from a separate and comprehensive environmental management system the criterion of integrativeness is important. By integration is meant the complete set of processes and procedures whereby the above environmental responses are given important consideration or even precedence over development considerations where significant environmental disruptions would likely occur. This integration process should exist at each jurisdictional and planning level whose decisions will affect the environment. Its thrust is to retain, promote and protect environmental options in the face of development pressures. To implement this concept of integration would require such factors as are necessary to interlock environment and development activities at all levels. Such devices as models, standards, impact assessments and plans are studied to ascertain the degree of integration. Integration will be determined by such precepts as:

- environment on the same level and status as development;
- environmental alternatives given basic consideration including elimination of planned development;
- future environmental options considered from the beginning of the planning period;
- environment strongly linked to development at each stage in the development process;
- environmental incentives built into the development planning and operational stages, and
- environmental limits and potentials recognized and integrated at each development step.

These items comprise an initial set of environmental planning principles that are necessary for a development planning system to be environmentally sound via integration of environmental factors into the development process. These principles place environment on an integral footing with development and provide for environmental factors to penetrate into and permeate through the development policy, planning and implementation phases. Thus, these two criteria of a systematic comprehensive and integration process comprise the basic approach taken by the IIASA environmental team in evaluating the information obtained about regional development programs. (10)

One key element that combines both a comprehensive view and an integrative approach is that of the reticulist role suggested by Friend, Power and Yewlett.(11) The reticulist actor occupies the role of system assessor of some major technological development system.(12) This role literally means networking judgements which are required in any policy system or decision network that occupies the interface between two contiguous policy systems such as development and environment which can be in conflict.

<u>The Information Framework</u>

The lack of necessary information and information-gathering and supply functions makes the decision making process incomplete, sometimes resulting in serious misunderstandings. Monitoring data with respect to social and physical environments can provide a scientific basis for the decision making process if the information contains proper quality and content for the value-judgements necessary in a multi-dimensional system. To ensure a planning capacity for an environmental management system equal significance must be given to the environmental monitoring scheme and to the design of an environmental information system which must not only enable planners to have access to all necessary data and enable them to use it, but must also allow all development actors and environmental impactees to communicate throughout the entire development process.

In this section a normative framework is developed to analyze and design an environmental system. It will serve to incorporate the responses of impactees or exogenous bodies into the whole environmental planning process as well as to communicate effectively among actors and impactees.

This information system will provide a powerful tool for attaining the comprehensiveness and integrativeness of environmental management policy by using the conversational functions of:

i) feedback and feedforward of information among actors;
ii) learning from internal and exogenous responses;
iii) data gathering and data formation for decision making;
iv) education and consensus formation to public, etc.

Fig. 4 shows an analytical framework which illustrates the information flows for environmental planning, monitoring and regulatory processes. As input into the decision making process three major information sources, P, R and $\tilde{V}$ are shown. The first one, P, consists of: (i) the environmental goals, (ii) administrative guidelines, (iii) legislative framework, and (iv) other top-level policy issues. The second one, R, is the responses from: (i) environmental impactees, (ii) other publics, and (iii) exogenous or international bodies. The third one, V and or $\tilde{V}$ is the feedback information of the environment impact process.

The input $\underline{U}$ to the environmental impact process will be determined within the input decision making process as a challenge to development and environment policy alternatives. These inputs can be classified into different categories such as development inputs (resources, physical and capital requirements, technology and infrastructure), environment inputs (ecosystems, quality of lifestyle, aesthetics), and regulatory inputs (standards, sanctions).

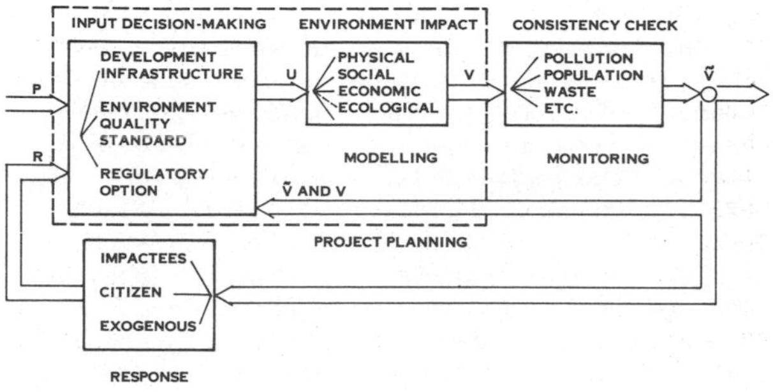

Fig. 4. Information Flow Model in Environmental Planning, Monitoring and Regulation

The block of "environment impact" describes an input-output relation concerning physical, social, economic, and ecological impacts that are projected to adopt some development, environment and regulatory policies as the input vector U. This process will be realized through various efforts in the form of conceptual, experimental, simulative, qualitative and quantitative models.

First, inputs U will be explored among the major three actors and finally, the selected inputs will be integrated and compromised with tandem use of feedback procedures for all processes. The output vector V means the projected status of social, economic and ecologic environments after a set of specified input policies have been applied to a development program which would include pollutants, wastes, social impactees, and biological impactees.

The next process is the monitoring evaluation of the output V. This process is particularly important for both the validation of the constructed model and for the consistency of the selected input policies with the given legislative and administrative guidelines. Therefore, various output items must be checked for complying with the monitoring data or exogenous information.

The outputs $\tilde{V}$ through a consistency check are partly provided to the response system and to feedback as an input into the decision making process, together with the original output V. These responses will be projected in the planning system through various channels between actors, impactees and exogenous bodies.

Appropriate institutional considerations to deal with these responses are crucial in environmental management. In other words, to what degree and in which way should the information of the detailed environmental impact data be provided to the response system? How should the impactees and their participation be realized or reflected in the inputs to the decision making process?

In addition to the above mentioned questions, actual development-environment decision making is supposed to be done by repeated use of a total feedback procedure either in an explicit or implicit way. Moreover, there is a possibility of time discrepancies preventing the procedure from proceeding in the defined order in accordance with the degree of project maturity. This problem suggests the need for a proper interface which serves to promote coordination and to integrate the issues in each time phase of each process. In this sense this interface provides a kind of environmental information system.

An information system usually means a system to ensure a well-organized information flow from sources to users or from users to sources in such a way that it puts a vast amount of available data in order, corresponding to specific purposes. Since a sort of processing, editing, sorting and input-output facility is needed, computer systems may be used but not necessarily. The objective of this interface can be summarized from the above discussion as follows:

- to provide basic information to planning, modelling and monitoring systems;
- to aid data-gathering and data-formation for the decision making process;
- to coordinate the information exchange among actor subsystems;
- to aid managerial efforts to solve inconsistencies or time discrepancies caused in each process;
- to facilitate the publics and the impactees' participation in the decision making process;
- to offer educational and social opportunities for both actors and publics.

The actors, impactees and exogenous bodies that should be involved in the environmental information interface were noted earlier. The necessary functions which combine actors, impactees and the exogenous factors into an interface come from the objectives of the interface within a set of environmental management goals. It is evident that surveillance monitoring of pollution levels is a fundamental information source to allow development actors to comply with existing statutory systems and regulations. Inclusion of impactees can overcome the data protection problem in the decision making process by learning exact information about resource and operational problems from the point of view of industry.

Such an interface as above can ensure an effective performance for an environmental management system. Necessary and sufficient information at the moment when it is needed for decision making is important. In addition, in order to facilitate the data-gathering function, it is essential to allocate resources (manpower, funds, etc.) in such a way so as to get sufficient information at the right time. At least two channels to communicate and make consensus between actors and impactees are required; the first is directed from public authorities to impactees by offering, in principle, all scientific information about environmental issues and assessment results for the purpose of social education. The second is from both impactees and exogenous bodies to public authorities to promote social learning by means of some legislative or regulatory procedures reflecting outside responses.

CONCLUSION

Environmental adequacy then is the joint outcome of a truly comprehensive and integrated environmental system. By adequacy is meant the matching of the environment and development responses to the challenges posed by the development process. These challenges are in the form of environmental problems emanating from the development. The concern here is for a set of satisfactory or adequate solutions for all actors and impactees for resolving the conflicts associated with the development program. An environmental management system that is comprehensive in its approach and integrated into the development decision making process should be adequate in meeting the environmental problems stemming from the development program.

Some kinds of intersystem linkages and responses one could expect to comprise an environmental management system include:(13)

- integrated policy objectives and planning mechanisms: the integration of environmental quality objectives and planning precepts into the development objectives and planning approaches at the highest level.
- systems perspective: the perspective derived from a systems analysis and synthesis for denoting the full range of impacts, actors and responses;
- reticulist role:(14) the creation of a special intersystem role to provide a communications link between policy systems for joint exploration of interlinked responses;
- multi-disciplinary involvement: the involvement of relevant, experienced professionals from a variety of disciplines for generating a broader response spectrum;
- public participation: the participation of a broad spectrum of publics representing the relevant external value dimensions of each system;
- unified monitoring system: the development of a comprehensive and unified system of data collection on the baseline, development impacts, their effects and feedback to publics and actors in the relevant policy systems.

Such intersystem links as these constitute examples of how the development-environment interface can be bridged. Taken together these examples provide a technology assessment system capability for obtaining the broadest possible assessment of the intersystem implications of a major technologically oriented development program.(15) These intersystem linkages can occur through and be integrated into most of the normal operations associated with a development program such as finance, personnel, accounting, etc.

In this paper there is an attempt in each of the sections to draw together the necessary elements for both a comprehensive and integrated approach to environmental management. Through the suggested framework in Fig. 3 the existing environmental responses from each subsystem are tied together into a system as in Fig. 4 to determine if there is a cohesive and consistent pattern of environmental management responses performed in a comprehensive and integrated manner. Should IIASA continue to achieve this goal it will have performed an important service to systems analysis.

REFERENCES

(1) D. Fischer and G. Francis, Water Res. Dev. and Env.: An Approach to Impact Analysis, International Journal of Env'l Studies, 5, 299, (1974).

(2) ECE, Ecological Aspects of Economic Dev. Planning, ENV/SEM.2/3, Sept. (1975); T. Gladwin and M. Royston, An Env'ly-oriented Mode of Industrial Project Planning, Env'l Conservation, 2, 189, (1975).

(3) D. Fischer and G. Davies, An Approach to Assessing Env'l Impacts, Journal of Env'l Mgt. 1, 207, (1973); L. Leopold, F. Clarke et al., A Procedure for Evaluating Env'l Impact, Geological Survey Circular, 645, U.S. Geological Survey, Washington D.C. (1971).

(4) R. Levien, Applying Systems Analysis in an International Setting, IIASA Conf. '76 1, 29, Laxenburg, Austria, (1976).

(5) Ibid.

(6) Ibid.

(7) H. Knop, Large-scale Planning Projects, IIASA Conf. '76 1, 187, Laxenburg, Austria, (1976).

(8) See also J. Friend, J. Power and C. Yewlett, Public Planning: The Inter-Corporate Dimension, Tavistock Pubs. London, 26, (1974).

(9) R. Keith, D. Fischer et al., Northern Dev. and Technology Assessment Systems, Science Council, Ottawa, 168 (1976).

(10) See ECE ENV/R.53/Add.1, 15 Dec. 1976 and the Senior Advisor's adoption of this report 21-25 Feb. 1977 for a legitimization of this criteria dev. by the authors.

(11) J. Friend, J. Power et al.,op.cit.44,356.

(12) R. Keith, D. Fischer et al., op.cit.166.

(13) D. Fischer and G. Francis, op.cit.; T. Gladwin and M. Royston, op.cit.

(14) J. Friend, J. Power et al., op.cit.

(15) R. Keith, D. Fischer et al., op.cit.

OPTIMAL HARVESTING OF A RICKER POPULATION

A.A. Voronov, E.I. Skaletskaya and A.P. Shapiro

Institute of Automation and Control Processes, Far East Science Centre, USSR Academy of Sciences, Vladivostok, U.S.S.R.

ABSTRACT.
This paper is devoted to a search for the optimal strategy of harvesting a Ricker population with random type reproduction.

INTRODUCTION.
Ricker (ref.1) proposed the following interrelation between the biostock and natural increase of salmon population: where y is the number of the biostock and x the number of the natural increase,

$$x = \xi y \exp(-\alpha y). \qquad (1)$$

Coefficients ξ and α were considered constant. However, parametres ξ and α, which represent the ability of the population to reproduce and the natural death rate, are random quantities. And Ricker's formula in reality has the sence of the mathematical expectation of the biostock. In the present work it is assumed that the coefficient ξ is the random quantity having a known distribution function A(z).

For several types of salmon (for example, pink salmon) the spawning school is all the same age. In such a case, the problem of finding optimal harvesting of the population is simplest of all and can be solved completely. The first part of this work offers a precise definition of the problem and a resumé of the basic results. The second part contains proofs of theorems.

RESULTS.
Let us consider a k-aged spawning school. We designate as q_i that part of the generation which is going to spawn at the age of i years (i=1,...,k). Coefficients q_i are assumed to be constant (in as much as some of the fry die immature, $\sum_{i=1}^{k} q_i < 1$). The relation between the biostock and the natural increase is expressed by formula:

$$x = \xi \varphi(y), \qquad (2)$$

where $\varphi(y)$ is a double continuous differential function having a single maximum at point x_0, concave in the interval $[0,x_0]$ and continuously smoothly decreasing for $y > x_0$; ξ is a random quantity with known distribution function A(z), having two first moments. It is easy to see that for such conditions, formula (2) is a generalization of formula (1). We pose the problem of finding a rule for exploiting (harvesting) such a population, the use of which would give a maximum for the function:

$$\psi(x) = E\left\{\sum_{n=1}^{\infty} V_n \beta^n\right\}, \qquad (3)$$

where V_n is the gain achieved in the harvest process in the nth year. A quantity $\beta \in (0,1)$ is the discount factor. In this paper the gain from harvesting the population for one year is taken as proportional to the catch.

If the size of the spawning school this year is x_1, i years ago

x_{i+1}, i = 1,...,k, then next year the size will be:

$$\sum_{i=1}^{k} z_i q_i \varphi(x_i), \qquad (4)$$

where $z_1,\ldots,z_k$ are concrete values of the random quantity ξ. The basic result of the paper (theorem 1) is that: the decision taken in current year depends upon the numbers (x_1, ...,x_k) and is determined by a certain function $y(x_2,\ldots,x_k)$ in the following sence: if $x_1 > y(x_2,..,x_k)$ thenit is reasonable to catch $x_1 - y(x_2,\ldots,x_k)$ units of fish. Otherwise, in the alternative case, fishing must be forbidden. In the particular case where the parameter ξ is assumed constant, $y(x_2,..,x_k) = y_o$ = const, and y_o is the root of the equation

$$\varphi'(y_o) = \left[\xi(\beta q_1 + \beta^2 q_2 + \ldots + \beta^k q_k)\right]^{-1}.$$

In the case of a unoform age of the spawning school (without limiting the generality we may assume the age of the mature fish to be one year), the function y, determining the optimal strategy, is also equal to the constant y_o. It is interesting to note that if we replace the random quantity ξ by its mathematical expectation, the constant y_o decreases.This means that the presence of random fluctuations of the parametre ξ decreases the allowable catch. Optimal strategy is determined by the constant y_o in the following sence: if the number of the spawning school x exceeds y_o, then the harvest should be equal to $x-y_o$ units of fish; in the alternative case, fishing should be forbidden.

For a population with a uniform age of spawning school, the optimal strategy can be found using the criterion of average gain for an infinite time interval:

$$\Psi_1(x) = \lim_{n\to\infty} E\left\{\sum_{k=1}^{n} V_k / n\right\} (6)$$

In this case, such a strategy has the same structure as the strategy for criterion (3), and the constant here y_o is the limit of the corresponding constants for criterion ψ when $\beta \to 1$.

For a population having a spawning school of uniform age, we have determined the optimal strategy according to criterion ψ for directing fishing and fish hateries. The basic supposition in this case was that in the conditions of the hatchery, the relation between the biostock and the natural increase may be expressed by the formula:

$$x = N\xi\varphi(y), \qquad (7)$$

where N is a constant expressing the increase of the survival of the fry in the artificial surroundings(N>1). The cost of raising the fry from y parents is assumed equal to ry, where r is constant and the gain from a catch of y units is y. Here the solution is determined by two numbers y and t, where y is the number of units which are not to be harvested and t the number of units sent to the hatchery.

The optimal strategy is determined by constants $\hat{t}$, y_o, t_o and function t(x) in the following sence: for $x \leq \hat{t}$ all of the fry are to be raised in the hatchery; for $\hat{t} < x < t_o + y_o$ fishing is forbidden and t(x) units are sent to the hatchery; for $x \geq t_o + y_o$ $x - t_o - y_o$ units may be harvested and t_o units sent to the hatchery.

APPENDIX.

Theorem 1. Let the age of fish going to spawn be assigned any integer from 1 till k; from the stock of any one generation $q_i x$ units will go to spawn at the age of i years,i=1,..,k; $\sum_{i=1}^{k} q_i < 1$; the connection between the biostock and the natural increase is established by formula (2). Then there exists a function $f(x_2,\ldots,x_k)$ such that optimal strategy according to criterion (3) consists in harvesting $x_1 - y(x_2,\ldots,x_k)$ units if $x_1 > y(x_2,\ldots,x_k)$ and in the alternative case, no fishing is to be allowed (here x_1 is the number of spawning fish, x_i is the remaining population of spawning fish i-1 last year, $i = 2,\ldots,k$).

Proof. We first consider the finite step process. We designate the maximum value of the criteria for n years of harvesting as $V_n(x_1,\ldots,x_k)$. According to formula (4)

$$V_{n+1}(x_1,\ldots,x_k) = \max_{0 \leq y \leq x_1} \Big\{ x_1 - y + \beta\int_0^\infty V_n(z_1 q_1 \varphi(y) + \textstyle\sum_{i=2}^k z_i q_i \varphi(x_1), y, x_2,\ldots,x_{k-1}) dA(z_1)\ldots dA(z_k) \Big\} .$$

It is obvious that $V_1(x_1,\ldots,x_k) = x_1$ is a continuous convex function. Using the method of mathematical induction, it is possible to show that all functions $V_n(x_1,\ldots,x_k)$ are continuous and convex. In addition there exists such a sequence of functions $y_n(x_2,\ldots,x_k)$ where the gain $V_{n+1}(x_1,\ldots,x_k)$ may be calculated by the formula

$$V_{n+1}(x_1,\ldots,x_k) = \Big\{ \beta\int_0^\infty V_n(\textstyle\sum_{i=1}^k z_i q_i \varphi(x_i), x_1,\ldots,x_{k-1}) dA(z_1)\ldots dA(z_k) \text{ for } x_1 \leq y_{n+1}(x_2,\ldots,x_k);$$
$$x_1 - y_{n+1}(x_2,\ldots,x_k) + \beta\int_0^\infty V_n(\textstyle\sum_{i=1}^k z_i q_i \varphi(x_i) + z_1 q_1 \varphi(y_{n+1}), y_{n+1}, x_2,\ldots, x_{k-1}) dA(z_1)\ldots dA(z_k) \text{ for } x_1 > y_{n+1} \Big\},$$

and where the optimal strategy for the nth step consists of harvesting $x_1 - y_n(x_2,\ldots,x_k)$ units when $x_1 > y_n(x_2,\ldots,x_k)$ and forbidding fishing in the alternative case.

Since the sequence $y_n(x_2,\ldots,x_k)$ is limited for any fixed set, one may select a convergent subsequence $y_{nl}(x_2,\ldots,x_k)$:

$$\lim_{e\to\infty} y_{ne}(x_2,\ldots,x_k) = y(x_2,\ldots,x_k).$$

It is easy to show that the smoothly increasing sequence uniformly converges to the final function $V(x_1,\ldots,x_k)$, and not for any strategy can we get a gain that is greater than $V(x_1,\ldots,x_k)$. Now let us examine the following strategy π for an infinite step process: for $x_1 > y(x_2,\ldots,x_k)$ the harvest is $x_1 - y(x_2,\ldots,x_k)$ units of fish, and for $x_1 \leq y(x_2,\ldots,x_k)$ fishing is forbidden. The value of criterion (3) when using such a strategy is the unique solution of the functional equation

$$\bar U(x_1,\ldots,x_k) = \Big\{ \beta\int_0^\infty \bar U(\textstyle\sum_{i=1}^k z_i q_i \varphi(x_i), x_1,\ldots,x_{k-1}) dA(z_1)\ldots dA(z_k) \text{ for } x_1 \leq y(x_2,\ldots,x_k);$$
$$x_1 - y(x_2,\ldots,x_k) + \beta\int_0^\infty \bar U(z_1 q_1 \varphi(y) + \textstyle\sum_{i=2}^k z_i q_i \varphi(x_i), y, x_2,\ldots,x_{k-1}) dA(z_1)\ldots dA(z_k) \text{ for } x_1 > y(x_2,\ldots,x_k). \quad (10)$$

Going in equation (9) to the limit for subsequence n_e, we find that $V(x_1,\ldots,x_k)$ also satisfies equation (10), from which we get

$$V(x_1,\ldots,x_k) = \bar U(x_1,\ldots,x_k),$$

and, therefore, strategy π is optimal.

QED

Theorem 2. If the spawning school is of uniform age, then the optimal strategy according to criterion (6) consists in harvesting $x - y_0$ units if the size of the spawning school is greater than y_0, and in the alternative case harvesting is forbidden.

Proof. For a population with a uniform spawning school, with $\beta = 1$ formula (9) assumes the form

$$V_n(x) = \Big\{ \int_0^\infty V_{n-1}(z\varphi(x)) dA(z) \text{ for } x \leq y_n;$$
$$x - y_n + \int_0^\infty V_{n-1}(z\varphi(y_n)) dA(z) \text{ for } x > y_n, \quad (11)$$

$V_1(x)$ as before is equal to x. We may prove inductively the following inequality: $y_{n+1} \geq y_n$,

$V_{n+1}(x) - V_n(x) \leq V_n(x) - V_{n-1}(x)$.

As a result of these inequalities and the limitation of y_n, there exist the finite limits:

$$\lim_{n\to\infty} y_n = y_o \quad \text{and}$$

$$\lim_{n\to\infty} [V_{n+1}(x) - V_n(x)] = g(x).$$

Lemma 1. There exists a finite limit $\lim_{n\to\infty} V_n(x)/n = g$ which is the same for all x different from zero.

Proof of lemma 1. It is evident that for all $n \geq 1$

$$\max_{0\leq x<\infty} \{V_{n+1}(x) - V_n(x)\} = V_{n+1}(y_o) - V_n(y_o).$$

Therefore, there exists a finite limit:

$$g = \lim_{n\to\infty} [V_{n+1}(y_o) - V_n(y_o)] = \lim_{n\to\infty} \sum_{i=1}^{n} [V_{i+1}(y_o) - V_i(y_o)]/n = \lim_{n\to\infty} [V_{n+1}(y_o) - V_1(y_o)]/n = \lim_{n\to\infty} V_{n+1}(y_o)/n.$$

In as much as for all $x > y_o$ $V_{n+1}(x) - V_n(x) = V_{n+1}(y_o) - V_n(y_o)$, it follows that for such x the statement of lemma is valid. Let us consider now the x laying the interval $(0, y_o)$. The following equations are relevant:

$$V_n(y_n)/n = g_n = (1/n)\int_0^{y_{n-1}} V_{n-1}(z)\,dA\left(\frac{z}{\varphi(y_n)}\right) + (1/n)\int_{y_{n-1}}^{\infty} [V_{n-1}(y_{n-1}) + x - y_{n-1}]\,dA(z/\varphi(y_n));$$

$$(1/n)\int_{y_{n-1}}^{\infty} V_{n-1}(y_{n-1})\,dA(z/\varphi(y_n)) = g_{n-1}(n-1)/n \int_{y_{n-1}}^{\infty} dA(z/\varphi(y_n)) = g_{n-1}p_{n-1}(n-1)/n,$$

where $p_n = \int_{y_n}^{\infty} dA(z/\varphi(y_{n+1}))$;

$$(1/n)\int_{y_{n-1}}^{\infty} (z - y_{n-1})\,dA(z/\varphi(y_n)) \leq (1/n)\int_0^{\infty} z\,dA(z/\varphi(y_n)) \leq (\varphi(x_o)/n)\int_0^{\infty} x\,dA(x) = \delta_n,$$

where $\delta_n \to 0$ when $n \to \infty$. Therefore,

$$g_n = g_{n-1}p_{n-1}(n-1)/n + \delta_n + \int_0^{y_{n-1}} (V_{n-1}(z)/(n-1))((n-1)/n)\,dA(z/\varphi(y_n)); \tag{13}$$

$$\lim_{n\to\infty}\int_0^{y_{n-1}} V_{n-1}(z)/(n-1)\,dA(z/\varphi(y_n)) = g(1-p), \text{ where } p = \lim_{n\to\infty} p_n = 1 - A(y_o/\varphi(y_o)). \tag{14}$$

From equations (13) and (14), it follows that

$$\lim_{n\to\infty}\int_0^{y_o} [g_{n-1} - V_{n-1}(z)/(n-1)]\,dA(z/\varphi(y_n)) = 0. \tag{15}$$

The relationship (15) together with inequality

$$g_{n-1} \geq V_{n-1}(z)/(n-1)$$

for $z \leq y_o$ is equivalent to the statement of lemma.

It is evident that if for a certain strategy the value of the criterion (6) is equal to g, then this strategy is optimal.

Let $V_n(x, y_o)$ be the mathematical expectation of the gain for n steps when the strategy π described in the statement of the theorem is applied. We prove that the limit of this is equal for all x different from zero:

$$\lim_{n\to\infty} V_n(x, y_o)/n = g. \tag{16}$$

Let us consider an auxiliary strategy λ, determined by the number y_o for N-n stages and by the numbers $y_n, \ldots, y_1$ for the following stages. Let $V_N^{\lambda}(x)$ be the mathematical expectation of gain using this strategy.

$$\lim_{N\to\infty} V_N^{\lambda}(x)/N = \lim_{e\to\infty} V_e(x, y_o)/e.$$

If $y_o - y_n \leq \varepsilon$, then

$V_{n+m}(x) - V^{\lambda}_{n+m}(x) \leqslant m\mathcal{E}$, therefore,

$$\lim_{m\to\infty} V_{n+m}(x)/m - \lim_{m\to\infty} V^{\lambda}_{n+m}(x)/m$$

$$= \lim_{e\to\infty} V_e(x)/e - \lim_{e\to\infty} V_e(x,y_o)/e$$

$$\leqslant \mathcal{E} \quad .$$

The last inequality is fulfilled for all $\mathcal{E} > 0$. The theorem is proven.

Theorem 3. If a spawning school is of uniform age and there exists a hatchery where reproduction occurs according to relationship (7), the cost of raising the fry of y parents equal ry, then the optimal strategy according to criterion (3) is determined by constants t_o, y_o, $\hat{t}$ and function $t(x)$ in the following sehce: when $x \leqslant \hat{t}$ all fry should be rised in the hatchery; when $x \geqslant t_o + y_o$, t_o units are sent to the hatchery; $x - t_o - y_o$ units may be harvested; when $\hat{t} < x < t_o + y_o$ fishing is not allowed and $t(x)$ units are sent to the hatchery.

The proof is based on the following of a recurrent equation connecting $V_{n+1}(x)$ and $V_n(x)$:

$$V_{n+1}(x) = \max_{\substack{y+t\leqslant x\\ y,t\geqslant 0}} \left\{x-y-t+\beta\int_0^\infty V_n(z\,\varphi(y)+ Nz\,\varphi(t))dA(z) - rt\right\}. \qquad (20)$$

The following facts are established inductively: all functions $V_n(x)$ are convex; a maximum in (20) is reached for non-negative y_{n+1} and t_{n+1} which are solutions of the system of equations:

$$\beta\int_0^\infty zV_n'(z\varphi(y)+Nz\varphi(t))dA(z)\cdot\varphi'(y)=1,$$

$$\beta\int_0^\infty zV_n'(z\varphi(y)+Nz\varphi(t))dA(z)N\,\varphi'(t)= = 1 + c\ , \qquad (21)$$

for $x \geqslant y_{n+1} + t_{n+1}$ the optimal solution in n+1-step consists in harvesting $x-y_{n+1}-t_{n+1}$ units and raising in the hatchery the fry of t_{n+1} spawning fish; for $x < t_{n+1} + y_{n+1}$ the optimal t and y equal $t_{n+1}(x)$ and $y_{n+1}(x)$ lie on the straight line $y + t = x$ and $y_{n+1}(x) = 0$ when $x < \hat{t}_{n+1}$; the sequences y_n, t_n, $t_n(x)$, $\hat{t}_n$ increase smoothly and have an upper limit. There limits

$$y_o = \lim_{n\to\infty} y_n,\ t_o = \lim_{n\to\infty} t_n,$$

$$\hat{t} = \lim_{n\to\infty} t_n,\ t(x) = \lim_{n\to\infty} t_n(x)$$

determine the optimal strategy for an infinite process.

REFERENCES

1. Ricker, W.E. Stock and Recruitment, J.Fish Res. Board of Canada, 11, 5 (1954).

2. Skaletskaya, E.I. and Shapiro, A.P. Optimal Exploitation of a Population with Random Increase, Doklady Acad. Nauk USSR, 227, n2 (1976) In Russian.

AN ANALYSIS MODEL OF THE DEVELOPABLE VALUE OF SHIPMENTS OF A REGIONAL MANUFACTURING INDUSTRY

Hitoshi Sakai, Takayoshi Mutoh,* and Chikashi Watanabe**

**Institute for Social Engineering, Inc. Akasaka Palece Bldg. 1-4-21 Moto-Akasaka, Minato-ku, Tokyo 107, Japan*
***Tokyo University of Science, Noda-shi, Chiba-ken 278, Japan*

ABSTRACT

The model proposed in the present study is composed of seven sectors for analytical purposes: population, industry, labor, government funding of transportation, power resources, environmental pollution, and land use. The computation of the model is performed every year, and the model can be used to compute the developable value of shipments of the manufacturing industry for the following year. The outputs of the model include several variables of the industry (the total area of sites, the quantity of water demand, the number of employees, the exhaust quantity of pollutants) as well as some of the regional frame (population, the income per capita, percentage of green coverage, level of pollution, rate of employment, and others as such). The model is useful not only for the harmonious development of the manufacturing industry between regional economics and natural environment, but also for regional planning because it is able to forecast the various impacts created by the industry.

INTRODUCTION

After the Second World War, the activity of the manufacturing industry in Japan has been concentrating upon metropolitan areas in accordance with the free market law. The activity of the industry in metropolitan areas of Japan has been obstructed by serious problems caused by its concentration from about ten years ago, e.g., overpopulation, pollution, traffic jams, housing shortages, draining of power resources and others as such. On the other hand, the out-migration of the youths has been reducing the economic activity of the residents as well as industries in rural areas. To this end, barren land and reservoirs of water for the industry remain unutilized.

The Japanese government is pressured to find a solution to simultaneously solve the two problems stated above. Therefore, the government plans to lead the industry out into the rural areas and distribute them appropriately to well-balance the development of national land. As the industry extends out into the rural areas, however, the supply potential of sites, water and labor for the industry, and the state of the accumulated government stock in transportation must be taken into consideration in advance; at the same time, a study of the influences that will be caused by the industry on the environs of the residents must be conducted. Due to this fact, we have attempted to formulate an assessment model for the industrial location and have developed the systems dynamics model for the analysis of the developable value of shipments of a regional manufacturing industry. Thus, the model takes into consideration the number of employees available, the total area land space, the availability of water, and the amount of pollutants allowed in the water along with the state of the accumulated government stock in transportation in order to determine the local conditions and restrictions for the manufacturing region. It has a feedforward structure so as to be able to forecast the developable value of shipments of the manufacturing industry for the next year in accordance with the above conditions of location and restrictions.
This is the strong point of this model and also the difference between the usual systems dynamics in cases dealing with urban models. This paper briefly describes the model with an example.

BASIC CONCEPT OF THE MODEL

(A) The purpose and input/output relation of the model

A model for the analysis of the developable value of shipments of the manufacturing industry (DVSMI) is required to be able to comprehend and organize the dynamic flux of variables of several conditions of location and restrictions as well as the main variables about a regional frame. The input/output relation of this model is shown in Fig. 1. As input variables, we arranged the planned variables such as the planned value of shipments of the manufacturing industry, the ratio of each value of shipments among seven types of the industry. The planned variables are partly given by a pre-arranged table, and partly by some calculations within the time period. These variables are revised as time goes on from the present to the future. The output variables, the responses to the input variables are computed under various conditions.

(B) Model construction

The present model consists of the following three definitions:

i. Definition of system boundary.
ii. Definition of system elements.
iii. Definition of interactions among system elements.

Because of the fundamental differences among different types of the industry, the detail structures of clasified relations of elements are to be specified for each type of the industry.

(1) System boundary

(a) Boundary of area

A prefecture is adopted as the boundary of area in the present system.

(b) Boundary of time

This model is designed to predict the conditions in the year 1985. The first year was set at 1965 because data can be traced back and the model can be verified back to that year. The verification of the model was conducted in the years between 1965 and 1972; the evaluations of the past records were the inputs to the model to previse the present. From 1973 to 1985, the planned values were input to the model to forecast the future. The time interval was set as one year.

(c) Interactions with the outside of the boundary

It seems that this problem mainly effects the three points stated below:

i. Inflow and outflow of population.
ii. Commuters crossing boundary.
iii. Money and physical distribution extending over boundary.

In this model, item i. was considered but item ii. and iii. were not considered. Item i. was explained by the difference of attractiveness between both sides of the boundary.

(2) Definition of system elements

In this study, the elements considered were population, types of industries, capital stock for industries, environmental pollution and land use. But, this model ignores public finance and living and cultural circumstances in the target region.

(3) Definition of interactions among elements

This model contains a simple subsystem which can be used to estimate the DVSMI of the following year. And according to the estimated value, a situation of the next year can be supposed. That is to say, the model contains a feedforward system. To put it more concretely, the model estimates and calculates the element values of following year which influence the DVSMI in order to compute the value of shipments of the manufacturing industry for the successive year. It may be more common that the feedback structures applied rather than the feedforward structure in this model. Certainly, the feedback structure is suitable to stable or oscillatory systems. But, in this model, the feedforward structure is applied in the calculation of the DVSMI of the successive year because it seems more natural to look into the future when an enterprise intends to plant a factory. However, loops of the migration of population are feedback systems as they respond after becoming aware of the situation.

Being based on the above principles, the systems dynamics method was applied as a modeling method.

STRUCTURE OF THE MODEL

(A) Elements of each sector

This model is composed of seven sectors. The interactions among these sectors are shown in Fig. 2 and described in (C) of this chapter. The main elements of each sector are shown in Table 1.

(B) Function of each sector

(1) Population sector

This sector treats natural increase/decrease (births and deaths) and net migration (in and out). It calculates the total population and the internal and external population by sex and age.

(2) Industry sector

This sector calculates the value of shipments of the manufacturing industry by type for the following year, and the value of production or sales by industry. In addition, it calculates the net prefectural product by industry, the prefectural income per capita, the revenue/expenditure, and so on.

The appraisal of shipments of the industry is shown in Fig. 3. The factors controlling the value of shipments of the industry are the following five elements: the number of available employees, the total area of usable sites, the availability of water supply, the state of the accumulated government stock in transportation, and the permissible quantity of the water pollution. Each limit of the DVSMI of the industry of the following year is calculated in accordance with each condition of location and restrictions. Then, each element is converted into price in accordance with its basic unit. The minimum value of them becomes the DVSMI for the successive year. The value of shipments of the industry is determined by comparing the DVSMI with the planned value for the next year, and adopting the minimum value of the two.

(3) Labor sector

There are two functions in this sector. One is to calculate the number of employees by industry, and the rate of employment. The other is to calculate the limit of the

DVSMI controlled by the labor force for the industry for the year after. Then, the rate of employment is in the ratio of the number of employees to that of available employees and the defference obtained from subtracting the rate of employment from 100 percent does not exactly mean the rate of unemployment.

(4) Government transportational funding sector

This sector refers to the state of the accumulated government stock in transportation and calculates the limit of the DVSMI controlled by the stock for the following year.

(5) Power resources sector

Water demand and supply by major use and demand of electric power for industrial and residential use are treated in this sector. An important function of the sector is to calculate the limit of the DVSMI which is controlled by the availability of water supply for the industry for the next year.

(6) Environmental pollution sector

Air pollution (SOx) and water pollution (COD) are handled and the exhaust quantity of their pollutants by kind is computed in this sector. In addition, the sector calculates the limit of the DVSMI controlled by the amount of pollutants allowed in the water for the industry in accordance with restrictions for the following year.

(7) Land use sector

This sector treats the change of land use by kind every year and calculates the percentage of green coverage. An important function of this sector is the calculation of the limit of the DVSMI controlled by the total area of usable sites for the successive year.

(C) Interactions among sectors

(1) Industry sector --- Labor sector

The number of employees for each industry is determined by its output. And the number of available employees for the industry inversely controls the DVSMI for the following year.

(2) Industry sector --- Government transportational funding sector

The revenue/expenditure calculated in the industry sector influences the state of the accumulated government stock in transportation. And, the government stock in transportation inversely controls the DVSMI of the next year.

(3) Industry sector --- Power resources sector

The demand for water and electricity by the manufacturing industry is decided by the value of shipments of the industry. The revenue/expenditure influences the water supply through its fraction of the investment for development of water resources. And, the capacity to supply water for the industry inversely controls the DVSMI of the successive year.

(4) Industry sector --- Environmental pollution sector

The exhaust quantity of air pollutants and the discharge quantity of water pollutants are determined by the value of shipments of the manufacturing industry. The amount of water pollution for the industry controls the DVSMI of the following year. In addition, the revenue/expenditure increases the number of sewers and consequently controls the amount of pollution flowing into the oceans.

(5) Industry sector --- Land use sector

The area for industrial land is determined by the value of shipments of the manufacturing industry. The increase of the area for public land is determined by the value of construction for public order. This value also influences the change of other areas. In the opposite direction, the total area of sites for the manufacturing industry controls the DVSMI of the next year.

(6) Population sector --- Industry sector

The income per capita calculated in industry sector influences the rate of migration. And the fluctuation of the total population conversely has the effect on the income per capita. That is to say, they constitute a negative feedback loop.

(7) Population sector --- Labor sector

The prefectural population 15 years of age and over controls the labor force.

(8) Population sector --- Power resources sector

The total population in the prefecture decides the water and electric power demand for residential use, and influences the balance between supply and demand of water and electric power.

(9) Population sector --- Environmental pollution sector

The rate in which public sewers are constructed is determined by the internal population which regulate the amount of sewage released.

(10) Population sector --- Land use sector

The number of households calculated in the population sector determine the space for residential land and influences the area for forests, waste land and agriculture.

(11) Power resources sector --- Environmental pollution sector

The electric power demand is a factor decided by the exhaust quantity of air pollution.

(12) Land use sector --- Power resources sector

The demand for agricultural water is decided by the area for agricultural land and it influences the balance between the demand and supply of water.

EXAMPLE

This section presents a simulation result of the standard case of a certain prefecture.

(A) Variables controlling the DVSMI

The transition of variables which control the DVSMI is shown in Fig. 4.

(1) The value of shipments of the industry was suppressed by the restriction of the amount of water pollution from 1976 to 1983. In 1976, it decreased about two hundred billion yen.

(2) The discharge quantity of the water pollutants is reduced from 1981 onward. And the planned value is achieved in 1985.

(3) Other factors controlling the value did not restrict it.

(B) Variables related to the manufacturing industry

The transition of variables related to the manufacturing industry is shown in Fig. 5. The following consequences appeared because the value of shipments of the industry was suppressed by the restriction of water pollution from 1976.

(1) The industrial land area did not increase from 1975 to 1980.

(2) The water demand showed a decrease of twenty percent.

(3) The number of employees showed a decrease of thirty thousand from 1975 to 1976. Though it was mostly constant from 1976 to 1980, it gradually increased and rose to about 180 thousand in 1985.

(4) The exhaust quantity of the air pollution (SOx) was most stringent in 1970; it became lax after this year.

(5) The discharge quantity of the water pollution in 1970 was the strictest and remained the permissible quantity in accordance with the law from 1976 to 1984.

(C) Variables indicating the ecological and industrial conditions

The transition of variables which indicate the ecological and industrial conditions is shown in Fig. 6. Variables except the internal population and the percentage of green coverage were obviously controlled by the water pollution law.

(1) The internal population was fairly constant by 1970 and after this year it monotonously increased. It reached 1,530 thousand in 1985.

(2) The income per capita showed a decrease of forty thousand yen in round.

(3) The percentage of green coverage decreased little by little.

(4) The level of the water pollution showed the maximum value in 1970 and decreased after this point. It stabilized at seventy percent of the value of 1965. This showed that the amount of COD discharge for the industry was tightened.

(5) The rate of employment decreased from 87 percent in 1975 to 74 percent in 1980. At this point, it increased and recovered to the 85 percent mark in 1985.

DISCUSSION

In this study, we considered the aberration degree in terms of the varification of the model. The aberration degree was defined as follows:

$$\frac{100 \times (\ CV - AV\ )}{AV}$$

CV : The computed value in 1970
AV : The actual value in 1970

The aberration degree about the main elements is presented in Table 2. In this table, some values of the degrees were rather large. But there was little influence on the other elements. And some of them were caused by external variables.

Originally, the systems dynamics model was said not to be so useful for a quantitative forecast of the future. However, the model might solve this problem fairly by means of feedforward structure. This structure, however, was not strictly the same one as actual decision-making system of enterprises. As for the restrictions of environmental pollution, it was difficult to estimate whether or not enterprises kept the restrictions. In addition, there are problems concerning the accuracy of the estimation of the pollution. Therefore, the value of the DVSMI in the model should be regarded as an approximated value of the actual one. If a solution to the latter problem is desired, the method of econometrics or Kalman filter should be included in the model. If one more problem is added in the future, it may affect each ratio of the seven industries. In this model, each ratio was fixed to the completed table given at the beginning. Therefore, if the DVSMI is controlled or restricted by a certain element, the model never fails to uniformly control every value of shipments of the seven industries. If a more accurate model is required, each ratio might be changed to meet the restricted conditions.

FINAL REMARK

Systems dynamics has rapidly expanded in the world since 1961 when Industrial Dynamics was developed by J.W. Forrester. Now, even the econometric model is being absorbed by it. It has been said that systems dynamics can treat socio-economic systems which heretofore were too large and complex for other methods to be modeled. In this respect, it has a remarkable feature. Therefore, we harnesed it for this study because of its feature.

The construction of a model is only a hypothesis. Therefore, this paper presents one hypothesis which needs to be proved by the effectiveness of the model. And we think that its effectiveness increases, if it is used not only to forecast the future but also to examine the cause of the problems which may occur in the model. Finally, we expect that this model is useful for regional planning.

REFERENCES

(1) Aida, S., Honda, N., Sakai, H., et.al, The Consigned Study For The National Land Agency: Extremely-Long-Term Time Series Analysis Of Population Distribution In Japan (Population Distribution Forecasts From The Present To 2000 A.D.), Institute For Social Engineering, Inc., 1975. (in Japanese)

(2) Sakai, H., Mutoh, T., Watanabe, C., et.al., The Consigned Research For The Japan Regional Development Corporation: Research Concerning Potential And Methods Of Industrial Site Selection In Shikoku, Institute For Social Engineering, Inc., 1976. (in Japanese)

(3) Forrester, J., Industrial Dynamics, MIT Press, 1961.

(4) Forrester, J., Urban Dynamics, MIT Press, 1969.

(5) Forrester, J., World Dynamics, MIT Press, 1971.

(6) Meadows, D.L., et.al., The Limit to Growth, Universe Books, 1972.

(7) Whithed, M., Sarlv, R., et.al., Urban Simulation : Models for Public Policy Analysis, Sijthoff, 1974.

(8) Mass, N., Readings in Urban Dynamics : Volume I, Wright-Allen Press, 1974.

(9) Bish, R., Nourse, H., Urban Economics And Policy Analysis, McGraw-Hill Book Company, 1975.

(10) Alfeld, L., Graham, A., Introduction to Urban Dynamics, Wright-Allen Press, 1976.

(11) Sakai, H., Mutoh, T., Watanabe, C., An Analysis Model Of The Developable Value Of Shipments Of A Regional Manufacturing Industry, Joint Fall Conference, Society of Instrument and Control Engineers, 1976. (in Japanese)

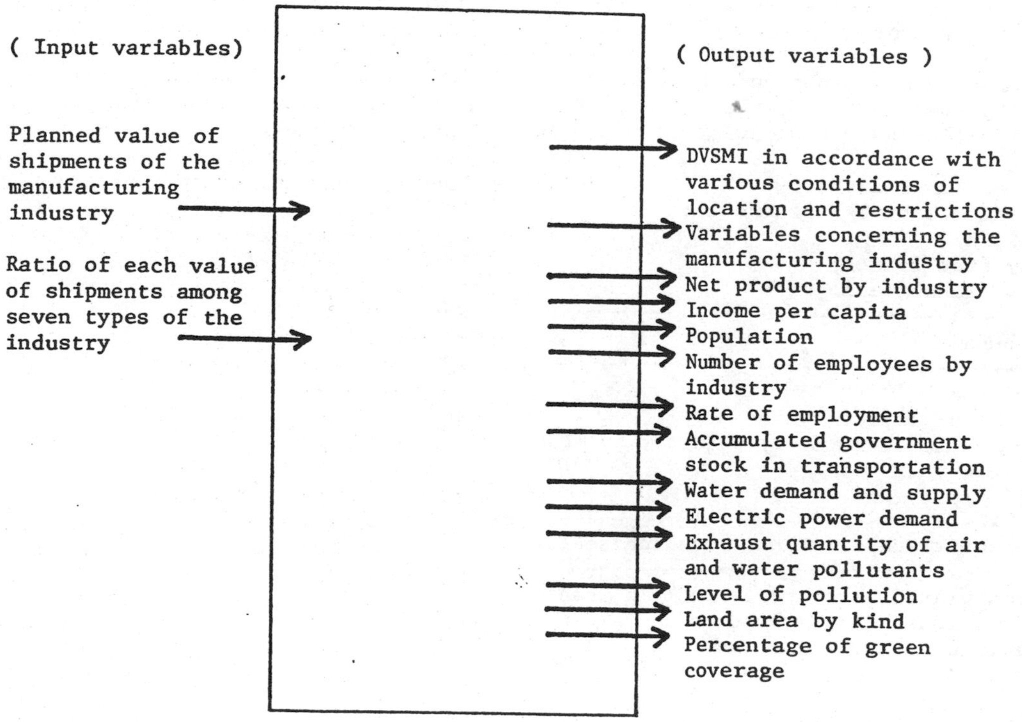

Fig. 1 Input/output relation

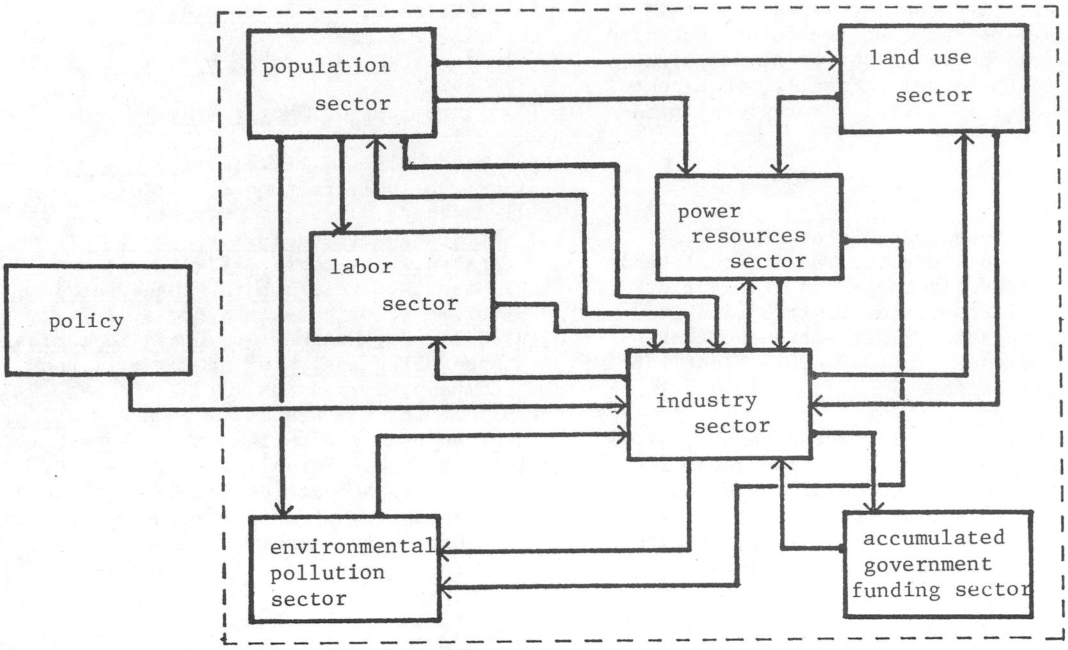

Fig. 2. Interactions among sectors

Table 1. Main elements of each sector

Sector	Main elements
Industry sector	Output by industry Net product by industry Income per capita Revenue/expenditure
Population sector	Population by age group and sex for a prefecture and the outside of the prefecture Migration (in and out) population by age and sex Number of live-births by sex Number of deaths by age and sex Households Density (total area) Density (inhabitable area)
Labor sector	Labor force Number of employees by industry Forecasted labor force by industry for the following year Rate of employment
Government transportational funding sector	The accumulated government stock in roads, Japan national railways, ports and air ports National and prefectural investment on transportation facilities
Power resources sector	Water supplies and demand Water demand of agricultural, residential and industrial use Electric power demand of residential and industrial use
Environmental pollution sector	Discharge quantity of water pollution by the industry and population Permissible quantity of water pollution for the industry Exhaust quantity of air pollution by the industry and electric power demand Accumulated government stock in public sewers Rate of public sewer construction
Land use sector	Land of forests, waste land and lakes Land for agricultural use Land for residential use Land for industrial use Land for public use and others Reclaimed land Inhabitable land Percentage of green coverage

Notes
1. The division of industry is as follows: Agriculture, Forestry, Fishing, Mining, Manufacturing, Construction, Wholesale and retail trade, Services and others, Public administration.
2. The division of manufacturing industry is as follows: Food and beverages, Textiles, Wood, pulp, paper and so on, Chemicals, petroleum, coal products and so on, Basic metal, fabricated metal products and so on, Machinery, Others.
3. The division of age group is as follows: 0 - 14, 15 - 29, 30 - 49, 50 - 64 years old, and 65 years old and over.

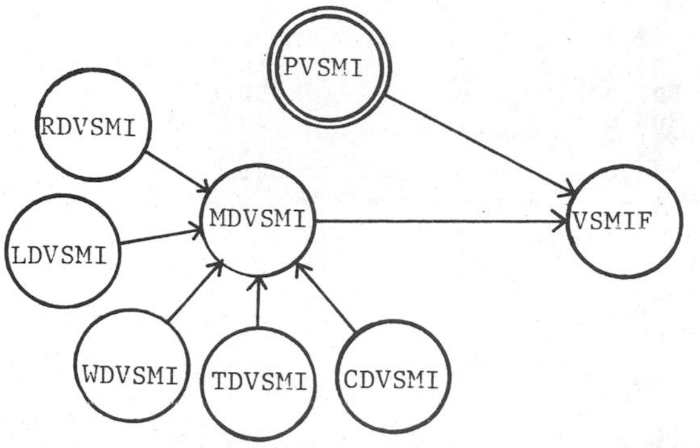

Fig. 3. Appraisal of the value of shipments of the manufacturing industry

PVSMI : Planned value of shipments of the manufacturing industry (G in the Fig. 4.)
VSMIF : Value of shipments of the manufacturing industry for the following year (P)
MDVSMI : Minimum value of DVSMI
RDVSMI : DVSMI controlled by labor force (R)
LDVSMI : DVSMI controlled by land use (L)
WDVSMI : DVSMI controlled by water supply (W)
TDVSMI : DVSMI controlled by the state of the accumulated government stock in transportation
CDVSMI : DVSMI controlled by the restriction of water pollution (COD) (C)

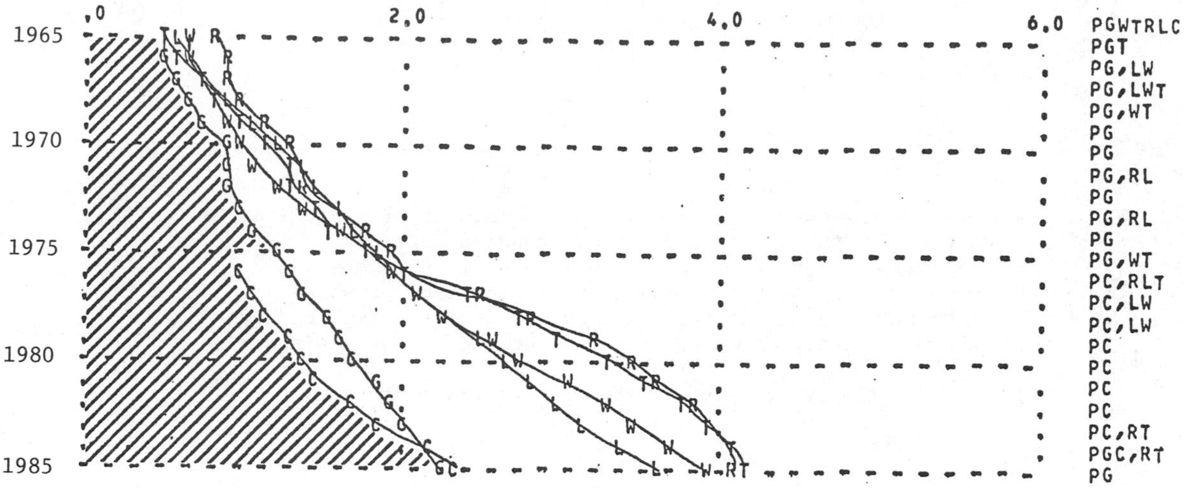

Fig. 4. Variables controlling the DVSMI (Value in billions of yen)

Table 2. Varification of the model

Item \ Variables	Population (in thousands) Total	Male	Female	
Computed Value in 1970 (CV)	1449.50	691.33	758.22	
Actual Value in 1970 (AV)	1418.12	670.98	747.14	
Aberration degree (%) (AD)	2.12	3.03	1.48	

	Net product (in billions of yen)					
	Total	Agriculture	Manufacturing	Wholesale and retail trade	Services and others	Revenue/ expenditure
CV	734.83	58.77	228.04	106.16	237.01	143.39
AV	739.90	62.44	228.38	105.39	237.18	139.18
AD	-0.69	-5.88	-0.15	0.73	-0.07	3.02

	Number of employees (in thousands)					
	Total	Agriculture	Manufacturing	Wholesale and retail trade	Services and others	
CV	691.31	171.85	144.09	118.12	163.90	
AV	705.11	182.67	145.15	117.04	164.27	
AD	-1.96	-5.92	-0.73	0.92	-0.23	

	Land area (in hundred hectare)					
	Total	Forests and waste land	Agriculture	Residential use	Manufacturing industry	Public land and others
CV	5658.40	4025.80	895.38	135.68	17.42	584.12
AV	5658.00	3980.00	894.00	133.00	17.00	634.00
AD	0.01	1.15	0.15	2.02	2.47	-7.87

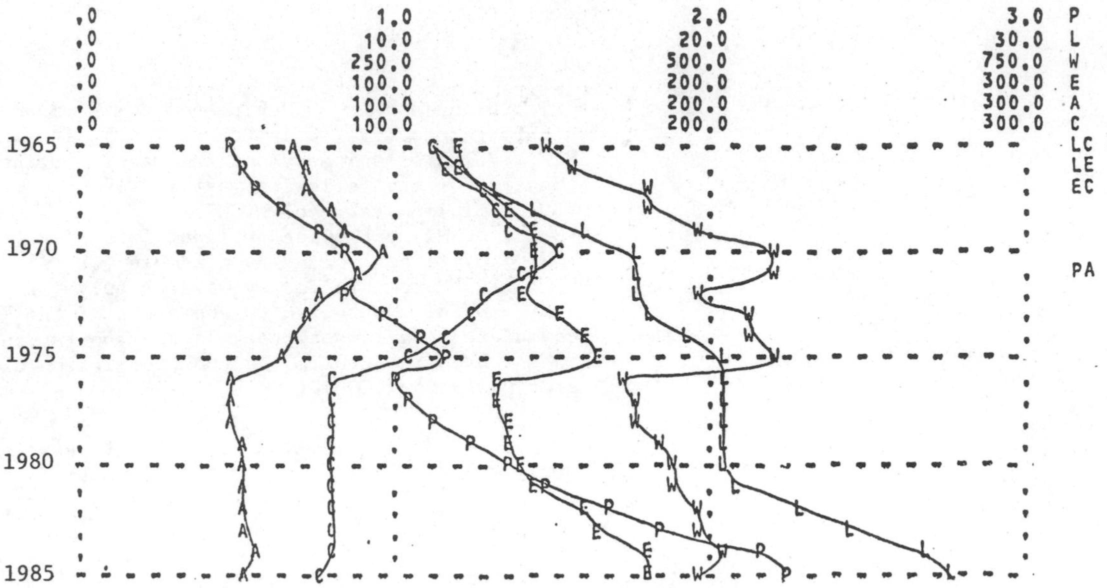

P : Value of shipments of the manufacturing industry (in billions of yen)
L : Land area for the industrial use (in hundred hectare)
W : Water demand of the industry (in millions of cub. meter)
E : Number of employees of the industry (in thousand persons)
A : Exhaust quantity of air pollution by the industry (in ton/day)
C : Discharge quantity of water pollution by the industry (in ton/day)

Fig. 5. Variables related to the manufacturing industry

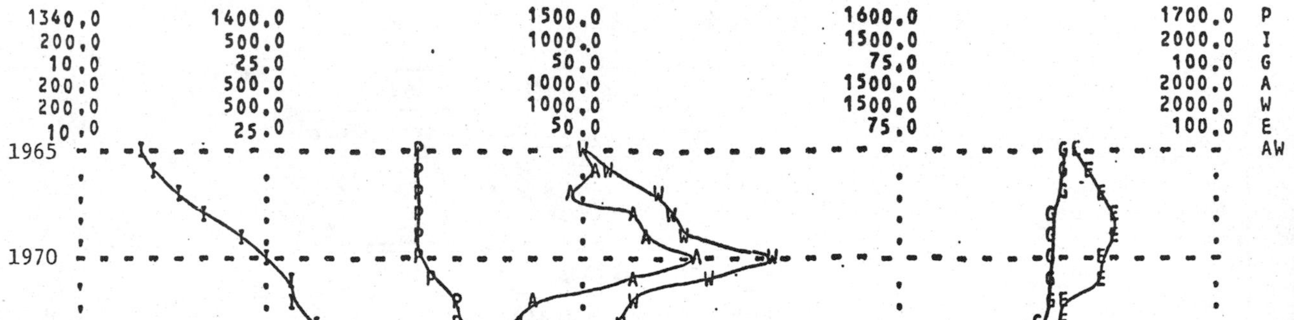

P : Prefectural population (in thousands)
I : Income per capita (in thousands of yen/person)
G : Percentage of green coverage (%)
A : Level of air pollution (figure in 1965 = 100.0)
W : level of water pollution (figure in 1965 = 100.0)
E : Rate of employment (%)

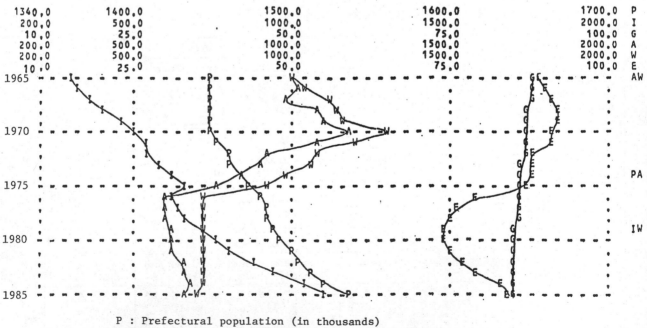

Fig. 6. Variables indicating the ecological and industrial condition

URBAN, REGIONAL AND NATIONAL PLANNING IN INDIA

A. C. Chaturvedi

Irrigation Commission, U.P., Lucknow -226001, India

ABSTRACT

Planning is the most important tool in the battle against poverty and unemployment. Poverty and unemployment are the central problems of our National Five-Year Plan and automatic controls in Urban, Regional and National Planning for Environment. The answer to poverty and unemployment lies in planned development in the sectors of agriculture, power, irrigation, transportation, social life and environment.[1] Planning therefore, is the centre of our lives and should contain the charter for our economic betterment. At present a large percentage of new entrants to our civil services are drawn from the urban background. For an allround development they have to come from the rural lower middle class background. These officers have to be provided training in modern concepts of management orientated towards social, economic uplift of our people. We should no longer play second fiddle to the conventional methods of planning but take up the new concepts boldly. This will give us the opportunity to employ our wholehearted energy and vigour in the vast arena of National reconstruction work. We have to provide whole-hearted support and do everything possible to propagate these new concepts.

We need a revolution in our approach if we have to avoid the catastrophe which awaits us if we continue to be as complacent as we are. The trap of the population explosion-resources depletion pollution is real, serious and universal. The developing countries have yet a further disadvantage; it takes technological organisational capability to solve these inevitable problems. In the context of the objective the seminar is none too early. We have to carry out detailed system studies of the challenging subject which has already attracted the attention of us all. The management issues and implications of the technological problems have been presented to develop a general awareness of their scope and limitations.[2]

INTRODUCTION

Despite 28 years of regular planning through five-year plans and annular plans, much is left to be desired in accelerating the tempo of development.[3] So automation as a principal instrument was adopted in our fifth five-year plan and has been accorded a high priority in the national economic development plan of Mrs. Indira Gandhi.

We have predominantly an agricultural economy with 80% of our population in rural areas, contributing 48% to the national income. Agricultural production subsists on irrigation provided by state and private works besides the insufficient and uncertain rainfall.

There has been an increase in agricultural production and income of the cultivator leading to a chain reaction of overall economic and social development flowing through channels of trade and industry. Development of roads, marketing centres, warehouses and storage facilities have accelerated the agro-industries and allied cottage and ancillary industries have been set up. There has been an increased revenue gain to local and central authorities in the form of Central Government income-tax, supertax from sugarcane factories, cotton and flour mills etc. There is increase in income to the railways on account of movement of agricultural goods and traffic, income from duty on oils, muster goods, employed in the movement of agricultural produce and extra traffic, increased income from posts and telegraphs, income from customs duty on account of increased imports of machinery and material. State income is increased by land revenue, increase in registration and stamps, excise, sales-tax etc. saving in famine and flood expenditure. Markets, mandies etc. are the source of benefits to local bodies.

The Central Board of Irrigation and Power had suggested in 1936 in its annual meeting an economic survey for estimating the direct and indirect benefits to remove the handicap of the restricted view in the values of irrigation. The value of irrigation works is continually on the increase due to two reasons. Most economical schemes were taken up in periods of lowest prices and we are left with intricate schemes now. The utility of the irrigation projects has to be judged in a scientific manner before correct assessment of expenditure of large funds in irrigation, drainage and flood control works and their respective allocations in State and private sectors are sanctioned and correctly determined.

PAST WORK

One of our most celebrated economists Prof. Gadgil completed the studies on socio-economic benefits on the five projects of Sarda Canal, Ganga Canal, Tribeni Canal, Damodar Canal and Cauvery Mettur Project and established the benefits from double cropping, diversification and better quality crops, higher yields, large income and greater opportunities for hired labour, benefits from processing industries, expansion of consumer industries, retail trade, transport and communications. The study on the Sarda Canal was conducted during 1958-1960 by Prof. Baljit Singh of Lucknow University and the report published in 1960. The Planning, Research and Action Division of the State Planning Institute in collaboration with the World Bank conducted a study on State tubewells in 1967-68. Another study on State tubewells was conducted by the Evaluation and Training Division of the State Planning Institute and the report published in 1971. The other studies also covering a limited area of the specific project, viz. Gandak Project, Jaunpur and Muzaffarnagar are in progress.

Assessment of Benefits—a Methodological Problem.

The nature of benefits from multipurpose projects are far-flung and complex and often elusive to measurement. The benefits are primary, secondary and tertiary depending on the primary sequence in which the benefits arrive and the closeness of their connection with the benefits whose uses are being studied. High agricultural production is a direct benefit and the increased economic activity resulting in more employment and trade incomes, which are partly spent, give rise to increased demand for producer goods and services. Measurement of primary benefits is comparatively easier than other benefits.

WATER AND POWER RESOURCES

1.1 The study of our economy has pointed out water and power to be essential elements for all eco-systems and for the development of national activities. Unfortunately water occurs only in a limited quantity on our land surface and is unevenly distributed in space and time. Energy depends on fossil fuels, wind, gas, geothermal effects, ocean, sun.[4] The analysis of our national resources reveals the basin area of our river systems as shown in Table 1.

Table 1.

River Basins	Accessive basin area in Km^2	Annual average discharge $10^6 m^3$
Major basins		
Indus Basin	143 750	41 955
Ganga including Damodar	853 300	493 400
Brahmputra including Basak	238 137	510 450
Sabarmati	20 770	3 200
Mahi	34 120	8 500
Narmada	98 670	40 705
Tapi	63 630	17 982
Subarnrekha	19 296	7 940
Brahmni	39 008	18 310
Mahanadi	139 710	66 640
Godavari	307 840	105 000
Krishna	256 390	67 675
Pennar	54 700	3 238
Cauvery	82 270	20 950
Total	2 351 661	1 405 945
Medium and Minor river basins	2 896 881	1 518 056

HYDEL POWER

2.1. Except in the field of irrigation, we lag behind, especially in hydropower generations. This is revealed by a comparative study of the uses of water in some other countries of the world. Water is deeply related to the water mechanism.[5] We have to tackle the river systems of India. We have fourteen major rivers with a catchment area of 20 000 km^2 and above each. The next group of 44 rivers each with a catchment area between 2000 km^2 and 20 000 sq. km. carries 7% of the total flow. The last group consists of minor rivers each with a catchment area of less than 2000 km^2 and desert rivers which disappear into the sands. The minor rivers are numerous and not put to any substantial use except in Kerala and Tamilnadu. The total flow of all the river systems in India is broadly assessed as 1645 thousand million cubic metres. No adequate or precise measurements of flows are available, though these are essential for planning the precious resources economically. These measurements cannot be carried out by conventional methods as we have been doing so far, and so we have to take recourse to planning, by automatic control. These measurements should be carried out immediately and with sufficient courage.[6]

COMPUTERS

3.1. We have to use the computers and electric analysers for pipe networks. Both the analogue and digital computers are to be used. The McElroy pipe network analyser is an analog type and has been used by us in a number of cities. The flow of electricity in these circuits behaves as the flow of a fluid in a pipe and electric network was set up using resistors that caused a voltage drop analogous to head losses caused by pipe friction, current inputs and take offs equivalent to water inputs and take offs proposed for the water system were made and voltage changes noted. Effects of proposed new systems were also investigated. We have set up such large networks in major towns, five in each state. Some are also available on a rented basis.[7] These analysers are special type of computers and are called electric analysers. Other more general types of analog computers used were more elaborate and depended upon complicated electronic circuits, These computers allowed a wider range of variables to be introduced instantaneously, and the machines solved a wide range of problems.

3.2 Like the analyser it handled varying quantities for a given set of conditions and the answers usually appeared in the form of a plot of varying voltage. The electronic digital computers worked with actual numbers. They made mathematical calculation much faster than the human or desk calculators and with a minimum of errors. They were fed with a programme which broke down the problems into steps involving our basic operations of multiplication, addition and subtraction. These digital computers were used in water department offices. They are being increasingly employed in pipe network analysis. Programmes were written for the reservoir yield problems etc. and faster and cheaper computations resulted; we worked out our utilisable groundwater as 255 thousand million cubic metres most of which occurred in the Ganga Basin. Thus the total water available in India was worked out as 1900 thousand cubic metres. We have to develop the use of water in irrigation, navigation, power production, industry etc., when dealing with development of water; we drew up comprehensive studies of its impact on fish and aquatic life.[8]

3.3. This was also necessary because these played a great part in protecting the air from severe pollution beside being a valuable source of food. The control of pollution, protection of other species of life and prevention of excessive sediment in the river by proper land use are the important objectives kept in view while dealing with water development. Environmental constraints on water development were also considered.[9]

We are passing through a critical period of development in our country and lion share of responsibility has come on our shoulders. About 70% of our annual expenses are in the functional fields like manufacturing goods, irrigation, power, public works and health, family planning etc. The basic approach objectives and policy of our current plan is for growth and stability. The investment allocation has to be heavily weighed in favour of sectors which are critical or for maximising growth potential of the economy. Since the price situation is a matter of grave concern and the terms of trade have turned adverse, fuller utilisation of capacity in sectors which can in particular promote or save in imports has to be given special attention. More specifically the sectors which have to receive special attention are agriculture including irrigation power, coal, oil and fertiliser. These are precisely the areas as envisaged which have to be assigned the key role in investment strategy underlying our plans.

National Resources and Energy Problems

4. The division of natural resources energy in the Planning Commission deals with these issues and at the state level, the State Electricity Boards are in charge of power programmes except for industries which meet their partial requirements for industries from their own end.[29] The generation of power has necessarily to be concentrated in limited areas having potential of their own in water resources, fossil fuels, tide, wind etc. Depending upon other facilities required, role of transmission system in transportation of bulk power from the generating stations to different distribution points has become very important in the power systems. Its role in the form of interconnecting various power stations with a number of sub stations, located at major load centres is the vital one for operations of power systems as a whole.

Development in the field of generation with introduction of larger units in the range of 1200/2000 MW units and transmission of large quantum of power over long distances called for similar development activities in transmission.

Biogas technology has to be developed for providing better and cheaper energy sources for the rural people and the activities of various institutions for better exchange of information has to be coordinated. We have at present more that 18 000 biogas plants in our country but still a lot has to be done for improving and evolving cheaper designs and for fuller understanding of different processes. We need undertaking projects in (i) fermentation kinetics (ii) improvements in the domestic burners and development of industrial and radial burners (iii) corrosion aspect (iv) maintenance of temperature (v) studies on conversion of IC engine (vi) microbiological aspects (vii) production of algae (viii) insulation studies for increasing the gas generation.

We have to undertake a survey of rural energy consumption, to determine the changes in the pattern of consumption including any tendency to purchase fuels rather than collect in the wake of increases in agricultural incomes and meeting the possibilities of meeting domestic needs through village plantations for firewood and gobar gas. The allocation has increased by Rs. 829 million from Rs. 3853.2 million in 1974-75 to Rs. 4682.2 million in 1975-76 and this amount is expected to increase further in the current year. A provision of Rs. 900 million has been made for rural electrification. Taking these outlays into account, the total funds for development of agriculture of Rs. 3300 million would be significantly higher than in the power sector if increased by 44% from the previous year 1974-75 of Rs. 7665.5 million.[10]

MANAGEMENT

5. We should set up management development programmes. These should be thrown open to Managers in industry. These participants should be taught modern management techniques with emphasis being laid on production and man management aspects. The consultancy cells should be established to render assistance to the industry in different disciplines and functional aspects. These cells may comprise of panels of experts drawn from industries, institutes and universities. The areas in which assistance may be provided are production tooling, designs, heat treatment, testing of material and equipment instrumentation, stress and vibration analysis, drainage, sewage, sewage disposal, irrigation, feasibility studies and cost estimates, acoustics and noise control, selection and training etc. Industries should be invited to utilise the services of these cells. The automatica control engineers and experts in management development programmes have to man these cells. These cells may also look after apprentice training and enterpreneuring development.[11]

RESEARCH AND DEVELOPMENT

6. Research and Development in engineering related to environmental control should not only be restricted to one institution of technology or university. These should be taken up in other institutions as well. Agriculture is still our biggest industry, contributing to 55-60% of national income and 76% of our people live in villages and depend on agriculture and even many of our industries are agroliased. The social scientists need the help of technical personnel in order to draw a plan for the well being of our community. Labour should not be considered as an input but a result. Modern technology cannot be applied piecemeal. Policy planning, strategy for development, administration and the political process,[12] efficiency and effectiveness, administration and 25 Point National Development Programme, concepts and Principles of Management, administration as a change agent, communications in management, its influence and activities, culturable variables in administration, managerial effectiveness, principles and techniques of programme evaluation, theory and practice of planning and control systems, Man Management, Practice and problems, Problems of Personnel Management, Administration in Government and Management in business, Management information Service, Administration and programme for weaker sections, theoretical frame of decision making, project formulation and cost benefit analysis, Interpersonal relationships in Management, Administrative Reforms in Budgeting and Financial Controls, Leadership in Administration, Human Relationships in Management, Motivation and Morals, Significance of Public Participation and Response in Public Administration, Decision Making in Government, Authority, Scope and Limitations, Quantitative Techniques in Administration, Techniques of Effective Communication, Application of Quantitative Techniques, followed by Case Studies, Presentation of reports.[13]

6.1. Development of Roads, Marketing Centres, Warehouses and Industries, Storage facilities have accelerated the agro-industries and allied cottage and ancillary industries set up. There has been increased revenue gain to local and central authorities in form of central government income tax, Excise duty from sugarcane factories and mills, cotton and flour mills etc. There is an increase in income to rail-ways on account of movement of agricultural goods and traffic, income from duty of oils, muster goods employed in the movement of agricultural produce and extra traffic, increased income from posts and telegraphs, income from custom duties on account of increased imports of machinery and material. State income is increased by land revenue, increase in registration and stamps, excise sales tax etc. Saving in famine and flood expenditure, markets and mandies are source of benefit to local bodies. We have to take up an economic survey to estimate the direct and indirect benefits. We have to take up the most economical schemes.[14]

INDUSTRIAL PRODUCTION

7. The growth rate in the industrial production was 1.1% between January to June 1975 and is now 11.5% in the half year Jan-June 1976. The increase can largely be affected by accelerating the production of cotton textiles chemicals, paper and paper products, appliances and transport equipment.

7.1. Among the basic industries, production of nonferrous metals, particularly aluminium and copper, have recorded an impressive growth of 53% and 42% respectively. Cement production had recorded a rate of growth of 26%. With the increase in production, capacity utilisation in these industries has also recorded a corresponding increase.

7.2. Among intermediate industries, remarkable growth in production has been achieved in aluminium conductors (plus 144%) polyester staple fibre (plus 75%) viscose filament yarn (plus 44%) and caprolactum (plus 35%). Among chemicals there has been a significant increase in the production of caustic soda, DA gas, oxygen gas, liquid chlorine. Consequently, there has been an improvement in the capacity utilisation in these industries. On the other hand, industries which have shown decline in production during this period were automobile tyres and bicycle tyres, and viscose tyre cord between 2 to 6%

7.3. Among consumer industries, those which have recorded significant increase (between 23% and 50%) in production during the first half of 1976 were room air conditioner, bicycles, wrist watches, electric lamps and matches. On the other hand soaps, synthetic detergents, razor blades and domestic refrigerators have recorded decline in production. Apart from these industries such as baby food, cigarettes, storage batteries, fluorescent tubes and sewing machines has shown higher production as well as higher capacity utilisation.

7.4. Among capital goods industries, machine tools, tipped tools, transmission towers, welding electrodes, agricultural tractors, air/gas compressors have recorded impressive growth in production. Some of these industries and also hand made tools, twisted drills and boilers had shown high capacity utilisation. On the other hand, production of power driven pumps, road rollers and stationary diesel engines have recorded a decline in production ranging between 17 and 63%. Consequently there has been a lower capacity utilisation.

7.5. Among transport equipment, production of three wheelers and scooters have recorded a significantly higher rise in production of 69% and 59% respectively and commercial vehicles have recorded an increase in production of 11%. Railway wagons have not recorded any growth rate and the capacity utilisation of this industry is also at a low level. Passenger cars and jeeps have also recorded a decline in production with a corresponding decline in their capacity utilisation.

HABITAT COMMITTEES

8.1. A beginning has been made in the state of Rajasthan where the government has constituted a six member Habitat Committee headed by the Chief Minister to consider matters belonging to establishment of model Habitat centres in rural and urban areas. It will also plan urban development to eliminate pollution, to create more green areas and to promote amity.

HARYANA SCHEMES

8.2. The first rural Housing project was installed in Haryana on January 11, 1977. The houses are being constructed with modern amenities on residential sites allotted free to citizens belonging to scheduled and backward classes. Haryana had planned to construct 25 000 such houses this year. Within the next four years houses will be constructed for all 215 000 allottees of free residential plots in rural areas. The State Housing Board has prepared a scheme under which every government employee in the State will be ensured a house of his own before retirement.

PUNJAB SCHEMES

8.3 Industrial workers with an income not exceeding Rs. 250 per month would be entitled to one-roomed or small two-roomed tenements under the industrial housing scheme. An industrial worker whose income exceeds Rs. 250 per month but remains below Rs. 500 would be entitled to a two-roomed tenement. In the case of allotment of houses to persons with the income limit of Rs. 351 to Rs. 500 per month, additional charges equivalent to 50% of the interest charges on the subsidy for the houses, over and above the subsidized rate would be recovered. Full economic rent would be charged as soon as the income of an allottee crosses the Rs. 500 per month, until he is evicted.

Urban, Regional and National Planning in Context of Control System

9. So far the planning in India has been done from the top. The planning Ministry has the planning commission attached to it with divisions of Irrigation, Technical Development, Agriculture Division, Urban Housing Construction, Rural Development, Water Supply Divisions, Economics, Finance, Education, Employment and Planning, Village and Small Industries, Expert Committee on Storage, Industry and Minerals, Village reforms, Plant protection to look after central planning. The targets are prescribed according to resources and the National Plan is subdivided into Urban and Regional, District and Block plans.[15] For the first time in 28 years of development planning, the plans are prepared bottom upwards from village to the top level. One hundred beneficiary cultivators of planned benefits are selected from the blocks in villages and similar non-beneficiary villages are selected. A sample site is adopted in the system in the first stage, in which 5 to 10 villages are randomly selected categorising inter se groups of 50% of area subject to restriction of one village in a sub-division. This is used to devise a system on a computer to utilise resources involving men, machinery and materials to attain a definite objective. Yearly plans are worked on the basis of gradually increasing activity.[16]

Evaluation of Existing Planning Procedures

10. The nature of benefits from our plan projects are far flung and complex and often elusive to measurement.[17] The benefits are primary, secondary and tertiary depending on the primary sequence in which the benefits whose uses are being studied. High agricultural production is a direct benefit and the increased economic activity resulting in more employment and trade incomes, which are partly spent, give rise to industrial demand for producer goods and services. Measurements of primary benefits is comparatively easier and we have been planning our evaluation on this basis so far.[18]

Proposal of New Procedures

11.1. Calculation of benefits can be before and after and with or without study designs, but it is not easy to isolate one factor, say irrigation, transport, energy, alone in our command areas. As no reliable data of inputs and outputs of cultivation before the construction of irrigation works are available, the current input relations cannot be compared with those prevailing before. Hence the method of with or without designs was adopted by us in evaluating the benefits of irrigation.[19]

11.2. We elicited information from beneficiary and non-beneficiary cultivators on agriculture conditions like cropped area, irrigated area, average yield of crops, seed rate, organic and chemical fertilisers applied, nature of tenancy etc. Questions of socio-economic conditions including employment, indebtedness, farming nature were also asked.[20]

General Transportation System

12.1. The division of transport, communications has worked out the evaluation of progress and determined the degree of fulfilment of the objective.[21]

12.2. For further planning, analysis of the status of the project has been done. The planning decisions are arrived at after research on data received from the computers and network analysis.[22] The plans are accordingly modified for real locations of resources. In other words, remedial or cost minimising measures are adopted at this stage.[23] Determined and conscious effort to meet the deficiencies of the general transportation system as generated by the accelerated growth began only a decade back.[24]

12.3. Planning effort to bring the general transportation situation to an acceptable level started with electronic control with twin objectives of meeting the existing deficiencies of the system and to make room for future growth without creation of further adverse problems in the field of general transportation.[25] Improved and enlarged physical facilities for general transportation alone will not bring the desired result.[26]

12.4. Transportation management and administration plays an important part in the efficient functioning of the general transportation system.[27] Preparation of the area to accomodate accelerated growth, including provision for an acceptable transportation system, depends on many factors,[28] historical, economic and geographical. When these factors support the growth, problems generated in the field of transportation would be minimum. In the absence of adequate support from these sources, the problem is magnified disproportionately.

Social Life and Environment

13. The divisions of employment and social planning carry out the research programmes and planning in these sectors, but not in isolation. Engineers and technologists work hand in hand with sociologists to work out a viable programme. Depending on the objectives of management, the extent of control desired, and availability of computerised aid, the plan is broken down into physically identifiable and controllable units of activity or work content. This work break-down structure portrays the various group elements or individual elements of activity of the work content in order that a systematic and logical relationship is arrived at amongst these activities. WBS is really the skeleton that is needed for the management to communicate throughout the period of planning. The planners determine the secondary and tertiary benefits to the economy. Account is taken of the land shaping operations and increasing awareness to use of modern amenities.

Socio-Economic Modelling and Forecasting

14. The division of economic finance, management and project evaluation, programming, associated finance, programmers, Electronic computers, perspective planning plan coordination, plan information and publication, programme administration, public cooperation, determine the sectoral plans and monitor the programme in these various sectors. A number of alternatives are considered before making the final choice of the projects. The engineers, lawyers, material scientists, system experts, financiers, land developers coordinate with the government officials and the people to play a pivotal role. This calls for determination, allround development, modelling and forecasting and comprehensive planning from engineering angles with the social economic and legal aspects. Techniques of system analysis are freely used as the problems are stochastic with elements of probability. Benefit cost ratio plays a vital role in selection of projects for development out of various other solutions. Economic modelling studies are conducted under system analysis with the computer for closer and detailed study out of extensive material that is available when the problems are viewed from a number of disciplines. This leads to final best solutions under various restraints.

Conclusion

15. We shall have to change the institutions which create and perpetuate inequality. Inequalities and concentration of income will have to be corrected by fiscal and economic devices like automatic control planning by an intensive system of state intervention and regulation in the vital sectors of our economy and through a progressive expansion of the public sector and the socialisation of the means of production. The special privileged class created during the British rule has to go. There should be a quicker abolition of the urban upper class. The special class was retained on the plea of continuity and for maintaining close touch with different states. We have to change our king. Administrative and national stability with continuing administration is to emanate from the under privileged and economically backward section of our people. The old people had become a class by themselves and completely lost contact with the needs of the masses. We should not allow planning to be done any longer to conventional methods of planning but take up automatically controlled processes.

REFERENCES

1. A.C. Chaturvedi, Planning for water supply in U.P.- a new approach. *Pub. Health. Eng. Ind.* 8, 114, 1976.
2. A.C. Chaturvedi, Pilot survey for area planning and regional dev. *J. of Power Riv. Val. Dev.* 11, 26, 1976.
3. A.C. Chaturvedi, Twenty-five year plan for flood control. *Daily Navjiwan.* 2, 36, 1976.
4. A.C. Chaturvedi, Planning for power in U.P. *J. Std. Chap. Inst. Eng. Ind. U.P. Cent.* 4, 32, 1976.
5. A.C. Chaturvedi, Flood problems of U.P. *J. Inst. of Civ. Eng.-S. Afr.* 10, 267, 1975.
6. A.C. Chaturvedi, Availability of water. *Daily Navjiwan* 2, 19, 1976.
7. A.C. Chaturvedi, Uniformity in irrigation rates. *Daily Navjiwan* 2, 357, 1976.
8. A.C. Chaturvedi, Irrigation development in Bundelkhand. *Daily Navjiwan* 3, 13, 1976.
9. A.C. Chaturvedi, Water resources for irrigation and water rates. *Daily Navjiwan* 2, 360, 1975.
10. A.C. Chaturvedi, Prospects of irrigation development in Bundelkhand. *An. Souv. Nu. J. Inst. Eng. Ind. U.P. Cent.* 27, 55, 1975.
11. A.C. Chaturvedi, Irrigation in hills. *Daily Navjiwan* 2, 335, 1975.
12. A.C. Chaturvedi, Planning for cheap housing. *Civic Affairs* 13, 23, 1975.
13. A.C. Chaturvedi, Planning for rural water supply in backward areas. *J. Inst. Eng.,* P.H.
14. A.C. Chaturvedi, Irrigation development in Rohilkhand. *J. Pow. & Riv. Val. Dev.*
15. A.C. Chaturvedi, Housing for the millions. *Builders Friend.*
16. A.C. Chaturvedi, Planning for water supply. *Navjiwan* 26.2 & 28.2, 1976.
17. A.C. Chaturvedi, Drought affected area policy for iirigation development, 28.4.76. *An. Num. Inst. Engr. Ind. U.P. Cent.*
18. A.C. Chaturvedi, Planning and execution of irrigation works, Dec. 74. *Hindi Sec. Inst. Eng. Ind.* 4, 12, 1974.
19. A.C. Chaturvedi, Irrigation investment criteria. *Hindi Sec. Inst. Eng. Ind.* 13, 55, 1974.
20. A.C. Chaturvedi, Hydel development in U.P. *Hindi Sec. Inst. Eng. Ind.* 4, 25, 1975.
21. A.C. Chaturvedi, Development and future prospects of irrigation in U.P. *J. Hindi Sec. Inst. Eng.* 8, 27,1975.
22. A.C. Chaturvedi, Irrigation acts and codes. *J. Hindi Section. Inst. Eng. Ind.* 2, 12, 1977.
23. A.C. Chaturvedi, Agriculture development in Sitapur-Sitapur Samachar 2, 12, 1975.
24. A.C. Chaturvedi, Irrigation in Bundelkhand-Swatantra Bharat, Lucknow, 2, 1975.
25. A.C. Chaturvedi, Instrumentation and Automation in irrigation. *Papers of Nat. Con. Instr. and Aut.-* Allahabad 2, 12, 1975.
26. A.C. Chaturvedi, Water Resources Council. *Proceedings of Tech. Div. Irrg. Dept. Lucknow.* 2, 10, 1975.
27. A.C. Chaturvedi, Power development in U.P. *Proceedings of Rad. Lucknow* 2, 20, 1975.
28. A.C. Chaturvedi, Water resources in U.P. and their Utilisation. *Papers of Inst. Eng. U.P. Cent. Lucknow* 2, 12, 1974.
29. A.C. Chaturvedi, Environmental management, 12/76. *Papers Inst. Engr. (I), U.P. Centre, Lucknow.*

PLANNING CONSEQUENCES OF TRAFFIC SYSTEMS MANAGEMENT

Paul P. Jovanis and Adolf D. May

Institute of Transportation Studies, University of California, Berkeley, U.S.A.

ABSTRACT

The traffic network model, TRANSYT 6, has been modified to include fuel consumption and vehicle emission impacts, as well as modal and spatial demand responses. Tests on a 5-mile section at Wilshire Boulevard in Los Angeles indicate that the most promising strategies from an environmental and passenger productivity viewpoint appear to be exclusive bus lanes and signal optimization on a passenger basis. Further tests under varying conditions are needed before traffic management guidelines can be established.

INTRODUCTION

Transportation engineers can no longer afford to build a transportation system by reacting to crises. They must manage the development of the transportation system considering the optimum use of natural resources and the protection of the environment. As construction of new facilities becomes less feasible, better operation of existing facilities is seen as a key to better system management. The management should include a view of impacts for three time periods: short term (immediate), longer term (after demand shift but with no growth), and long term (with demand growth).

During 1975-77 the University Research Office of the U.S. Department of Transportation has supported the research project, "Managing the Future Evolution of the Urban Transportation System." One of the five task groups participating in the study was the Traffic Management Group. This group developed and tested a series of models to be used to evaluate the impact of traffic management strategies.

One of the primary areas of concern was the improved management of arterial street operation. By improving the operation a better balance would exist between arterial and collector street flows. The quality of life in surrounding neighborhoods would improve, and more efficient use of existing street space could be maintained. The major thrust of the research was toward improvements in passenger mobility while benefiting society through lower fuel usage, decreased air pollution and more efficient travel patterns.

The development and application of a traffic management model for arterial streets follows. A series of sensitivity tests are described which examine the applicability of test results to varying conditions. Emphasis is placed on the longer term consequences of the strategies tested.

ARTERIAL MODEL DEVELOPMENT

A survey of existing arterial traffic models was undertaken to determine their suitability for use as a traffic management tool. By selecting an existing model, major effort could be directed toward the study of impacts and demand consequences, rather than in traffic model evolution. The investigation led to the selection of TRANSYT, developed at the Transport and Road Research Laboratory (TRRL) in Great Britain by D. I. Robertson (1). The most recent version of the model, TRANSYT 6 was made available for use.

A. The TRANSYT 6 Model

The model provides a macroscopic simulation of traffic flow. Vehicles are represented by platoon shapes which change as the vehicles proceed through signals and disperse along a route. The arterial is represented as a series of nodes (intersections) connected by a series of links. The model requires as input the flows, journey times, saturation flows and link lengths for all intersections in the study section. It produces as output traffic performance measures for each link such as time spent, distance traveled, uniform and random delay, number of stops, and percent saturation. The individual link values are summed to arrive at system performance measures.

The model has been used worldwide in traffic signal timing studies (2). The signal splits and offsets are changes sequentially as specified by the user. The optimization is a hillclimbing technique which searches the response surface for a minimum value of a performance index. The index is the sum of a delay plus a weighted value of stops. The model has been used and calibrated at several sites around the world. Its systemwide traffic performance measures have been shown to be accurate to within 1-3% of field measurements.

In addition to its widespread use, TRANSYT had several other desirable characteristics. The model provides for representation of different classes of vehicles (buses and automobiles) utilizing common or separate stoplines. Bus flows may be designated by specifying a bus freeflow speed and average bus stop time on each link. The speed and stop time are used to compute an equation for bus platoon dispersal which is separate from automobiles. The program also has a feature allowing the weighting of the delay on a link by a specific multiplier. By weighting the delay by the average passenger loads of the vehicles, estimates of delay in passenger-hours are obtained for bus and auto links.

The remainder of this chapter discusses the modifications performed to TRANSYT 6 to obtain the desired traffic management model.

B. Model Modifications

Major modifications to the TRANSYT 6 model included the incorporation of new traffic management impacts and demand responses. After a study of several impacts, fuel consumption and vehicle emissions were selected for inclusion. An additional study determined that spatial and modal demand responses would be incorporated. The following sections describe the impact and demand response additions to TRANSYT 6.

1. Additional impacts. Fuel consumption estimates were obtained from tables of fuel consumption developed by Claffey in NCHRP 111 (3). Three classes of vehicles are considered: auto, gasoline-powered truck, and diesel-powered truck and bus. Two driving aspects are considered: in motion, and stopped. Corrections are applied for roadway gradient, curvature, surface condition and acceleration-deceleration at signals. Traffic performance measures computed by TRANSYT are used to enter the tables to obtain fuel consumption estimates for all links.

A simplified version of a vehicle emissions model was developed from a report by CALSPAN (4) to the U.S. Environmental Protection Agency. It was assumed that the amount of a particular pollutant emitted can be computed by multiplying the emission factor for that pollutant (for each driving aspect) by the extent of driving done in each aspect. The model form is therefore:

$$Q_j\ (R,T) = \sum_k A_{jk}\ D_k\ (R,T)$$

where Q_j (R,T) is quantity of pollutant j emitted by all vehicles in region R during time period T, A_{jk} is the amount of pollutant j emitted per unit of driving aspect k (emission rate), and D_k (R,T) is the extent of driving in aspect k.

Three driving aspects, cruise, idle and acceleration/deceleration are considered. The time in cruise and idle are computed directly from TRANSYT output while acceleration/deceleration is obtained from the estimated stops and an average aceleration/deceleration profile.

Detailed discussions of all model modifications are contained in reference 2.

2. Demand Responses. One of the effects of traffic management strategies could be a diversion of traffic over space, mode, or time, or a change in the rate of trip making. The inclusion of demand responses is essential to the evaluation of alternative strategies. The amount of each type of shift depends upon several factors (trip purpose, change in travel time, trip length, availability of alternate routes, etc.) and can vary substantially from site to site.

Submodels for modal and spatial shift have been added to TRANSYT. Both models apply the general formula that a response is a function of a stimulus times a sensitivity. The stimulus in both cases is the change in vehicle travel time computed by TRANSYT. The sensitivity is user specified and is applied to the demand shifts as described below. While spatial and modal shift vary, the total passenger demand remains fixed.

The spatial shift submodel diverts traffic from or to the studied arterial depending on the change in vehicle travel time resulting from the management strategy. By specifying sensitivity values from 0 to 4, the conditions of parallel routes are changed from no parallel routes available to an unlimited number available or those available having very large unused capacity. The spatial shift is computed iteratively until a new traffic equilibrium is reached. Details of spacial shift model are contained in reference 1.

Modal choice is also a function of trip characteristics, trip maker characteristics and transportation system characteristics. The modal submodel relates modal shift to changes in on-vehicle travel time only. The model was developed from a logit formulation used in the Travel Demand Forecasting Project (5). A range of sensitivities from 0-3 specify very poor to excellent bus service. Modal shift elasticities derived from data in the reference correspond to the sensitivity values.

By varying the values of the modal and spacial sensitivities, different operating environments are being simulated. The flow and design conditions on the arterial remain the same while the impacts of the strategies in a variety of operating environments may be evaluated. The spatial shift is always performed before modal shift as it is assumed that drivers will seek alternate routes before changing mode.

MODEL APPLICATION

The new model was applied to a 5-mile section of Wilshire Boulevard in Los Angeles. Travel in the area is characterized by heavy dependence on the automobile with buses the only form of mass transit. The bus service along Wilshire Boulevard is considered good.

A previous study by Sperry Systems Management for the city of Los Angeles developed data to be used in TRANSYT for this arterial. Flow data were collected and smoothed for all intersections. Approach capacities were computed using the Highway Capacity Manual method. Studies indicated that operating conditions in the p.m. peak were most critical.

A. Establishment of Base Conditions

The evening peak hour was chosen for study with TRANSYT 6B. The study section has the following characteristics used as input to the new model: (1) bus flows averaged between 17-25 per hour in both directions; (2) the average bus occupancy was 45 passengers; (3) average auto occupancy was 1.2 passengers; (4) the vehicle mix was approximately 1% trucks and buses with 30% of those diesel; (5) the roadway was straight and level; (6) the street carries two-way operation, 3 lanes in each direction, on a 60 to 74-foot width.

Conversations with local officials indicated that the average trip length on the study section was approximately 1.5 miles. To obtain reasonable spatial shift estimates, the study section was divided into three segments approximately 1.7 miles long in each direction. Directional split along the study section was approximately 55-45 with predominant flow leaving the Los Angeles CBD.

1. Traffic management strategies. After considering a number of different management strategies, the following were tested:

a. traffic signal optimization on a vehicle basis - each automobile and bus contributes equal weighting to delay.

b. traffic signal optimization on a passenger basis - the contribution to the performance index of the delay on a link was weighted by the average passenger occupancy for that link. Bus delays were thus weighted by 45 and autos 1.2.

c. exclusive bus lane - an exclusive bus lane was conceptualized in the curb lane in both inbound and outbound directions. Capacities were adjusted appropriately. After simulating conditions with the exclusive lanes, the signals were optimized on a passenger basis (as in b) for the new flow conditions.

d. reversible lane - a reversible lane was added in the peak direction by adjusting link capacities along the study section. After application of the reversible lane, signals were optimized on a vehicle basis for the new flow conditions.

2. Demand response. Concerning the demand response analyses that follow, it is helpful to identify three states of traffic conditions:

a. existing conditions - these conditions existed at the time of the Sperry Systems study. The street design, signal timing and flow conditions were those existing at that time.

b. short term - these results represent the impact with the management strategy implemented but no spatial or modal shift occurring. The conditions may be interpreted in two ways: they will exist for the first few days of operation before a new traffic equilibrium is reached, or no parallel routes or alternate bus service are available and these results may remain for an extended time.

c. longer term - these conditions exist after demand shift occurs and a new traffic equilibrium has been established. The conditions represent changes in mode and over space, but total passenger demand remains fixed. In this model application a spatial shift value of 4 was used with a mode shift value of 2. The spatial value of 4 indicates that many parallel routes were available in the Wilshire Boulevard area. The mode shift value of 2 indicates that good bus service was available.

All comparisons which appear in the following sections are with respect to the existing conditions. When applicable, notes will be made of comparisons between strategies. The results of the tests of each strategy will now be discussed.

B. Results of Strategies

Table 1 contains a summary of all strategies tested with results divided into short term and longer term. The impacts resulting from

TABLE 1 Impact Improvements for Base Conditions

STRATEGY \ IMPACT ON	Time Spent (pass-hr)		Fuel Consump. gal.		Vehicle Emission (kg.)		Mode Shift		Product. (pass-mi)		Bus Travel Time		Bus Fuel Consump.	
	ST	LT	ST	LT	ST	LT	ST	LT	ST	LT	ST	LT	ST	LT
Signal Optimization (vehicle-basis)	-9	+1	-6	+3	-9	0	--	0	--	+15	-5	0	-6	0
Signal Optimization (passenger-basis)	-9	+1	-5	+2	-9	+1	--	0	--	+15	-6	-1	-9	-4
Reversible Lanes	-7	+1	-3	+4	-7	+2	--	0	--	+16	-1	0	-1	-1
Bus Lanes	+58	+2	+32	+3	+50	+2	--	+1	--	-2	-13	-13	-22	-23

Definition of Impacts

All % changes with respect to existing conditions

Time Spent	- % change in passenger-hours for all vehicles
Fuel Consumption	- % change in gallons of fuel consumed for all vehicles
Vehicle Emissions	- % change in total vehicle emissions
Mode Shift	- % increase in passenger-miles for buses
Productivity	- % change in passenger-miles on study arterial
Bus Travel Time	- % change in bus travel time
ST	- short term results
LT	- longer term results

signal optimization are virtually the same whether optimization is done on a passenger or vehicle basis. Short term impacts show improvements in time spent, fuel consumption and vehicle emissions. The major difference in the short term impacts is the larger saving in bus fuel consumption for the passenger optimization than the vehicle optimization.

Longer term results are again quite similar; the time spent, fuel consumption and vehicle emissions have returned to values obtained during existing conditions, but arterial productivity (passenger-miles) has increased 15%. The implication is that every seventh street may be closed, or devoted to transit use, if the strategy is implemented. The passenger optimization again yields a greater saving in bus fuel consumption.

The impacts for the reversible lane strategy in the short term are slightly worse than improvements obtained by signal optimization. The longer term results are also similar to signal optimization except no appreciable benefits accrue to buses.

The impacts of the exclusive bus lane were the most difficult to interpret. The short term results indicate very large overall penalties in terms of longer time spent, increased fuel consumption, and greater vehicle emissions. There are, however, significant benefits to buses in terms of decreased time spent and fuel consumption. The longer term results indicate that overall impacts return to nearly existing conditions, with one exception. Many drivers have shifted to parallel routes resulting in a 2% reduction in productivity on the arterial. In the longer term the fuel and travel time savings for buses are maintained since there are few buses added due to mode shift and the bus lane operates far below capacity.

SENSITIVITY ANALYSES

Several sensitivity tests were performed to determine variations from the base conditions. Promoted by an earlier report by Courage and Parapar (6), longer cycle lengths were tested with the existing Wilshire Boulevard flow conditions for the strategy of optimizing signals on a passenger basis. Additional sensitivity tests of the TRANSYT 6B model were performed by varying the K value weighting for stops in the performance index. Again, existing flow conditions on Wilshire Boulevard were used and the strategy applied was signal optimization on a passenger basis. The last series of tests varied the spatial and modal shift sensitivity values. By varying these sensitivities, the study section is conceptually moved to different operating environments. All four traffic management strategies were evaluated to determine the effects of the operating environment on the impacts of the strategies.

A. Sensitivity to Longer Cycle Lengths

Analysis of minimum signal splits due to pedestrian requirements indicated that the existing cycle length (60 seconds) on Wilshire Boulevard is nearly the shortest possible. Additional cycle lengths of 70, 80 and 90 seconds were tested. The TRANSYT subroutine STAR 1 was used to equalize percent saturation on all approaches as an initial starting condition. The same optimization sequence was then applied to the extended cycle lengths as in the base conditions. The short-term results of the tests are summarized in Fig. 1.

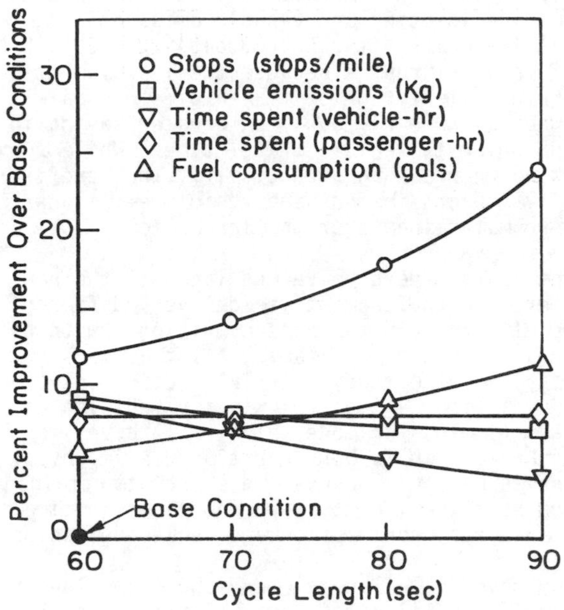

Fig. 1. Impact sensitivity to change in cycle length

The figure indicates a clear trade-off in fuel consumption and stops compared to vehicle emissions and time spent. As the cycle lengths increased, the number of stops per mile decreased as did fuel consumption. The height of the curves indicate improvements from the base conditions but the trends in the improvements are more interesting. The longest cycle length results in fuel savings that are twice as large as for optimization with the 60 second cycle. Stops also decreased but the duration of each stop (as expressed by time spent) increased with cycle length.

It is interesting to note the relatively constant value of time spent on a passenger basis. As the cycle length increased, buses were greatly aided, balancing the increased time spent by autos. While extended cycle lengths result in savings in the other impacts, the savings are not as large as for the shorter cycle lengths. Analysis of the optimum signal timings for the longer cycle lengths indicated that most of the additional time per cycle was added to Wilshire Boulevard. It appears that the minimum split constraint (pedestrian) has forced splits at shorter cycle lengths which do not equalize percent saturation (or delay). These results are specific to existing flow conditions. Lighter flows may not yield the same impacts.

B. Sensitivity Tests for K Value of Stops

By increasing the value of stops in the performance index, it was expected that stops would decrease and benefits in fuel consumption and air pollution would accrue. Values of K of 4, 40, 100, 200 and 1,000 were tested; the results are summarized in Fig. 2.

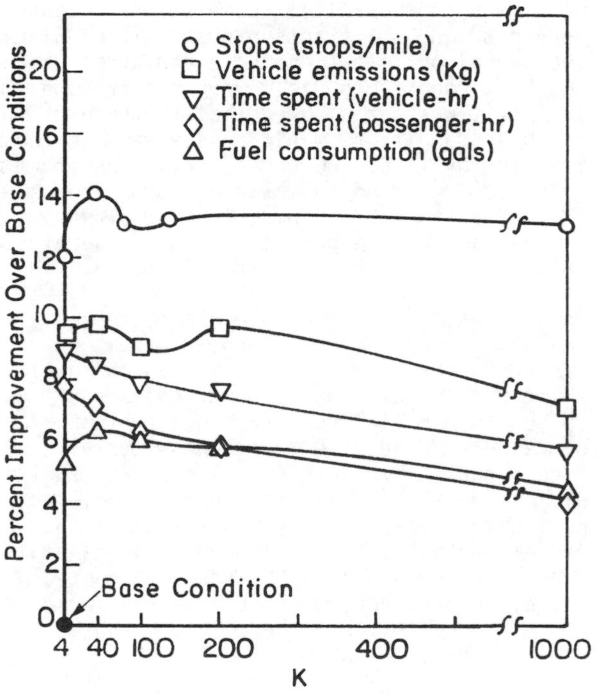

Fig. 2. Impact changes with K value

The initial vertical position again measures percent improvement over the existing conditions. Of greater importance are the trends in the improvements as the K value increases. The stops, air pollution, and fuel all exhibit similar trends.

There are slight variations in all three impacts as K varies from 4-200 and a downward trend at values of 1,000. Time spent on a passenger and vehicle basis both exhibited downward (worsening) trends as expected.

The K value of 40 appears to be the best if primary consideration is given to fuel consumption, vehicle emissions and stops. The commonly recommended value of K = 4 did yield the maximum savings in time spent. The extreme value of K = 1,000 appeared to degrade the optimization process and is not recommended for use.

C. Sensitivity of Impacts to Operating Environments

In order to more fully evaluate the traffic management strategies, they were tested in two additional operating environments. These environments were simulated by changing the spatial and modal sensitivity values in TRANSYT 6B.

The first additional operating environment corresponds to moving Wilshire Boulevard at its existing flow conditions to a corridor with very good parallel route structure but very poor and unattractive bus service. Since the signal optimization tests conducted under the base conditions yield very little mode shift, it was anticipated that the results in the base conditions would be the same as the impacts for these new conditions. Therefore only bus lanes and reversible lanes were tested. (See Table 2). Short term results will be the same as the base conditions, therefore only longer term results are discussed.

The exclusive bus lanes yielded essentially the same impacts in the longer term as occurred in the base conditions. Since modal shift was not desirable, most vehicles diverted to parallel routes resulting in a 2% decrease in productivity on the arterial. Significant savings in travel time and fuel did accrue to buses in the longer term, indicating that the strategy was effective in decreasing bus travel time and fuel consumption. In areas where good parallel routes are available there will be little adverse impact to society but there is also no benefit of improved impacts.

The testing of a reversible lane showed little direct benefit to buses. The sizable productivity increase, if repeated on other parallel routes, means that every seventh street could be closed or used for some special purpose. There were small disbenefits in the way of increases in time spent and fuel consumption in the longer term.

A second series of tests were conducted in an operating environment with no parallel routes and very good bus service. The results are summarized in Table 3.

Both signal optimization strategies yield essentially the same impacts. The short-term benefits accrued to the longer term. There were systemwide improvements in time spent, fuel consumption and vehicle emissions. Very little mode shift occurred despite the lack of parallel routes because the improvement in travel time for priority vehicles was balanced by a nearly equal or greater saving in non-priority vehicle travel time. While there is no increase in productivity, the beneficial impacts in fuel and vehicle emissions were maintained over the longer term.

The tests of exclusive bus lanes in the new operating environment yielded very different results than in the base condition. With no parallel routes available, all travelers stayed on the study arterial. Using only the travel time savings to priority vehicles as the stimulus for mode shift, a 1% diversion occurred. While bus operation was improved, very substantial overall disbenefits remained. The negative impacts were increases in time spent, fuel consumption and vehicle emissions.

The reversible lane yielded short and longer benefits similar too, but slightly less than, the signal optimization strategies. Since the impacts were less favorable than signal optimization in all cases, reversible lanes are not a preferred strategy when very good bus service and no parallel routes characterize the study corridor.

TABLE 2 Impact Sensitivity in Operating Environment with Poor Bus Service and Very Good Parallel Routes

IMPACT ON / STRATEGY	Time Spent (veh-hr)		Fuel Consump. gal.		Vehicle Emission (kg.)		Mode Shift		Product. (pass-mi)		Bus Travel Time		Bus Fuel Consump.	
	ST	LT	ST	LT	ST	LT	ST	LT	ST	LT	ST	LT	ST	LT
Reversible Lanes	-7	+4	-3	+1	-7	+4	--	--	--	+16	-1	-1	-1	-1
Bus Lanes	+56	+2	+32	+1	+50	+1	--	--	--	-2	-13	-13	-22	-23

Note 1: Signal optimization not tested in this operating environment since results would be close to those of the base conditions.
Note 2: Impacts are as defined in Table 1.

TABLE 3 Impact Sensitivity in an Operating Environment with Very Good Bus Service and No Parallel Routes

STRATEGY \ IMPACT ON	Time Spent (veh-hr)		Fuel Consump. gal.		Vehicle Emission (kg.)		Mode Shift		Product. (pass-mi)		Bus Travel Time		Bus Fuel Consump.	
	ST	LT	ST	LT	ST	LT	ST	LT	ST	LT	ST	LT	ST	LT
Signal Optimization (vehicle-basis)	-9	-9	-6	-6	-9	-9	--	0	--	0	-5	-5	-7	-7
Signal Optimization (passenger-basis)	-9	-9	-5	-6	-9	-9	--	0	--	0	-6	-7	-9	-10
Reversible Lanes	-7	-7	-3	-4	-7	-7	--	0	--	0	-1	-2	-4	-4
Bus Lanes	+56	+46	+32	+24	+50	+39	--	+1	--	0	-13	-12	-22	-22

Note: All impacts are as defined in Table 1.

D. Other Sensitivity Investigations

1. Signal timing with heavy bus weighting. In an operating environment with very good bus service and no parallel routes, the passenger-based optimization yielded greater savings in bus travel time and fuel consumption than the vehicle-based optimization (see Table 3). Stimulated by these larger savings to buses, tests were conducted in which bus delay was weighted by 1,000 (rather than 45). The optimization thus yielded signal settings timed nearly exclusively for buses. The impacts in the short and longer term are summarized in Table 4.

Short term results indicate a clear tradeoff. Fuel consumption and time spent for buses were significantly better than for the previous optimization (passenger weight = 45). Overall benefits, however, did diminish as total fuel and time spent figures were less improved than with the earlier optimization and vehicle emissions were nearly as bad as the existing conditions. The benefits in fuel savings and reduced travel time may help the transit operator to cut fuel costs and perhaps provide better schedules and improved schedule reliability.

In the longer term, no significant modal shift occurred. Travel time and fuel savings for buses were diminished compared to the short term but arterial productivity increased by 7%. The study section was unable to efficiently handle the added demand and overall increases in time spent, fuel consumption and vehicle emissions resulted. The improved bus system performance must be traded-off against deteriorated overall arterial operation in the longer term. Due to the macroscopic representation of bus operation, further tests are needed to substantiate these results.

2. Bus lane tests of additional mode shift stimulus. There was considerable congestion remaining on the study arterial, when bus lanes were tested in an operating environment with good bus service and no parallel routes. The large increase in non-priority vehicle travel time could be considered as an incentive to change mode. When the travel time increase for non-priority vehicles was added as a stimulus for mode shift, very significant

TABLE 4 Impact Sensitivity to Signal Optimization (Passenger basis) with Heavy Weight to Buses

STRATEGY \ IMPACT ON	Time Spent (veh-hr)		Fuel Consump. gal.		Vehicle Emission (kg.)		Mode Shift		Product. (pass-mi)		Bus Travel Time		Bus Fuel Consump.	
	ST	LT	ST	LT	ST	LT	ST	LT	ST	LT	ST	LT	ST	LT
Bus Passenger Weight = 45	-9	+1	-5	+3	-9	0	--	0	--	+14	-6	-1	-9	-4
Bus Passenger Weight = 1,000	-2	+5	-4	+4	-1	+7	--	0	--	+7	-9	-5	-13	-7

TABLE 5 Bus Lane Tests with Added Mode Shift Stimulus

IMPACT ON / STRATEGY	Time Spent (veh-hr)		Fuel Consump. gal.		Vehicle Emission (kg.)		Mode Shift		Product. (pass-mi)		Bus Travel Time		Bus Fuel Consump.	
	ST	LT	ST	LT	ST	LT	ST	LT	ST	LT	ST	LT	ST	LT
Normal Mode Shift	+56	+46	+32	+24	+50	+39	--	+1	--	0	-13	-12	-22	-22
Added Stimulus	+56	+3	+32	+.5	+50	+2	--	+5	--	0	-13	-8.8	-22	-17

diversions resulted (see Table 5).

The longer term results show that system travel time, fuel consumption, and vehicle emissions have returned to the existing conditions. The large diversion to buses has offset the 33% decrease in capacity that resulted from the exclusive bus lane. The productivity did not increase but the bus travel time and fuel consumption savings were maintained.

It is important to note that the modal shift returned impacts to existing conditions for the existing flow conditions only. In conditions where buses carry a larger percentage of corridor passengers, it is expected that such a large diversion will result in decreases of systemwide impacts in the longer term. Further tests are needed to generalize these results.

A STEP TOWARD POLICY GUIDELINES

The purpose of this research study is to be able to predict the various impacts of several traffic management strategies under different operating environments. The goal is to develop policy guidelines which will enable the decision maker to select the traffic management strategy for a particular operating environment which will ensure the most desirable impacts. With this goal in mind, the following conclusions are drawn based on this investigation. Additional work will be required to confirm and extend these conclusions.

A. Signal Optimization on a Vehicle Basis

In the short term or in cases with no demand shift occurring, there were significant overall benefits in terms of fuel, air pollution and travel time savings for all operating environments. Buses were only marginally aided under these conditions. In the longer term under all conditions, no significant mode shift occurred. The policy appears useful to decrease overall impacts but did not result in significant mode shifts or significant direct benefits to buses. The weakness of this strategy is its emphasis on vehicle movement rather than passenger mobility.

B. Signal Optimization on a Passenger Basis

The short term and longer term results for this strategy have generally similar implications to the vehicle-based optimization. Some larger improvements in fuel and travel time savings did accrue to buses due to the weighting by passenger load. The improved bus flows could result in increased service reliability-an important measure of bus system performance.

Tests with longer cycle lengths than those used on Wilshire Boulevard also resulted in significant savings in bus fuel consumption and travel time. If the policy is to cut transit operating costs, or improve passenger movement efficiency, serious consideration should be given to use of extended cycle lengths on arterial routes.

This strategy resulted in the least negative impacts and as such is viewed as a safe strategy in a variety of conditions.

C. Exclusive Bus Lanes

The wide range of impacts makes bus lanes the most difficult strategy to evaluate. Moderate mode shift occurred only when no parallel routes existed. While there may be some natural operating environments with no parallel routes, traffic restraint measures can be used to deter spatial shift. A combination of restrained traffic movement, an exclusive bus lane, and very good transit service holds the best hope for significant modal shift of the strategies tested. Good transit service should include good level of service, reasonable comfort and reliability, and short access to and from work.

In areas where the bus service is not perceived as good, and parallel routes are not available, the model indicates severe negative impacts. If no spatial or modal shift occurs, these results of impacts may be extended for a long period. This cautions against the implementation of bus lanes in areas with limited bus service when the bus lane would remove road space currently utilized by other vehicles.

D. Reversible Lanes

Very little direct benefit to buses occurred under any operating conditions. Overall impacts improved similarly to vehicle-based signal optimization. In unbalanced flow conditions the strategy will result in overall improvements, but has little application elsewhere.

REFERENCES

1. Robertson, Dennis I., TRANSYT: Traffic Network Study Tool. Crowthorne, England: Great Britain Transport and Road Research Laboratory, 1969. 37 pages. (TRRL Report LR 243).

2. Clausen, T. J. and A. D. May, The Analysis and Evaluation of Selected Impacts of Traffic Management Strategies on Surface Streets. Berkeley: University of California, Institute of Transportation Studies, June 1974.

3. Claffey, Paul J., Running Costs of Motor Vehicles as Affected by Road Design and Traffic. Washington, D.C.: Highway Research Board, 1971. 97 pages. (HRB NCHRP No. 111)

4. Kunselman, Paul et al., "Automobile Exhaust Emission Modal Analysis Model," EPA Report 460/3-74-005, NTIS, Springfield, Virginia, 1974. 167 pages.

5. Train, K., "TDFP Demand Model," Internal Report, Travel Demand Forecasting Project, Institute of Transportation Studies, University of California, 1976.

6. Courage, K. C., and S. M. Parapar, Delay and Fuel Consumption at Traffic Signals, Traffic Engineering, November, 1975.

A DYNAMIC MODEL OF TRANSPORTATION AND LAND USE

Yoshio Hanzawa* and Takehiko Matsuda**

**Nihon University*

***Tokyo Institute of Technology*

1. Summary

Two Systems Dynamics models have been developed for planning parking facilities and residential environment, respectively. These models should be considered as subsystems of a more comprehensive, dynamic model dealing with the general problems of transportation and land use in an urban area.

Sets of simulations with several policy alternatives have been carried out, and results would seem to indicate the direction of effort to realize a better urban life in the selected model district.

2. Present State of the Model Area

Chiba City, our model area, is located within 50 kilometer from the Tokyo metropolis, accomodates the Chiba Prefectural Government and at the same time is the vantage point as the gate to Boso Peninsula. (See Fig. 1)

1)

Large housing projects, both public and private, have been carried out in this area, turning the area into one of Tokyo's bedtowns with a rapid increase night population. (See Fig. 2)

The present pattern of land use of Chiba City is as follows. The Keiyo (Tokyo-Chiba) industrial belt is deployed along the Tokyo Bay, a commercial district is situated around the Chiba Central Station of J.N.R. (Japan National Railway) Lines, and a residential district is adjacent to the commercial district. Some industries and large housing projects have been developed in the inland area, and other parts are either agricultural or green areas. (See Fig. 3)

Fig. 4 divides Chiba City into 18 zones. Zones 10 and 11 comprise a commercial district with large stores, and the Chiba Central Station is included in this district. This station was built 15 years ago, and the former central station is now the Higashi-Chiba Station. The shift of the central station has created a considerable change in the traffic flows ; the location of transportation facilities influences the pattern of land use.

Zones 17 and 18 are the reclaimed land from the sea ; the Chiba Works of the Kawasaki Iron and Steel Co., Inc., one of the largest steel mills in Japan is located in Zone 17, and public offices, industrial complexes, warehouses and large-scale housing projects are found in Zone 18. According to the triangular chart of land use pattern in Chiba City (Fig. 5), Zones 17 and 18 appear as the mix of the secondary and tertiary industries district, Zones 10 and 11 belong to the tertiary industry district, and other zones are for the primary and secondary

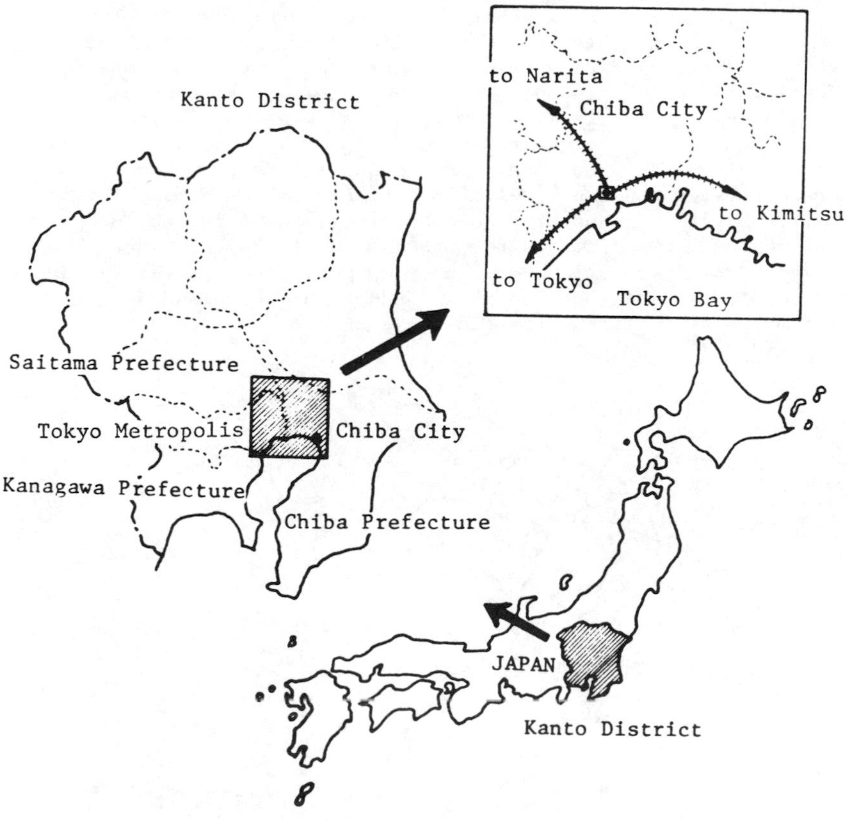

Fig. 1 Study Area

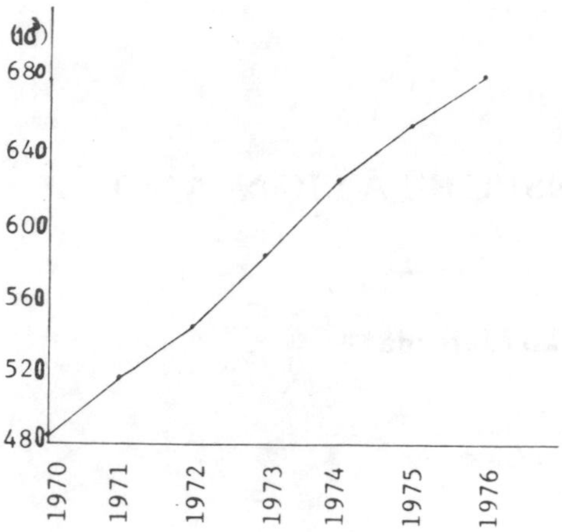

Fig. 2 Change in Night population

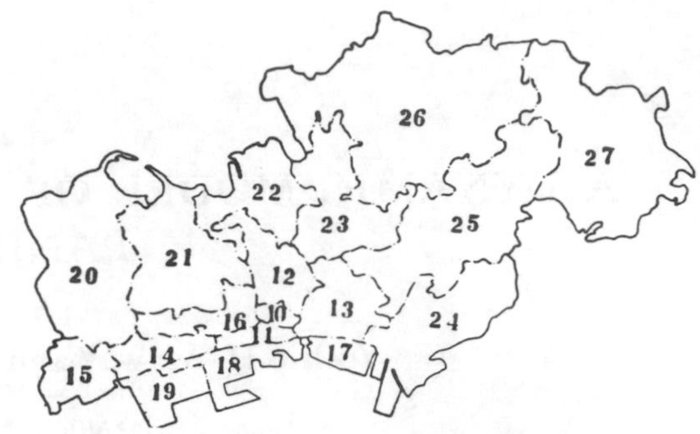

Fig. 4 Zone Map of Chiba City

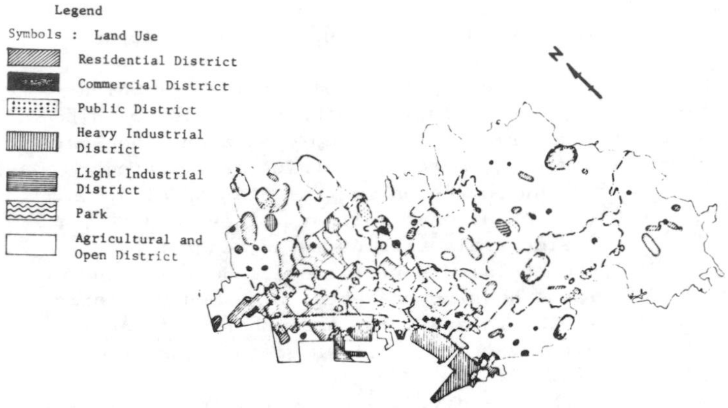

Fig. 3 Land Use Map of Chiba City

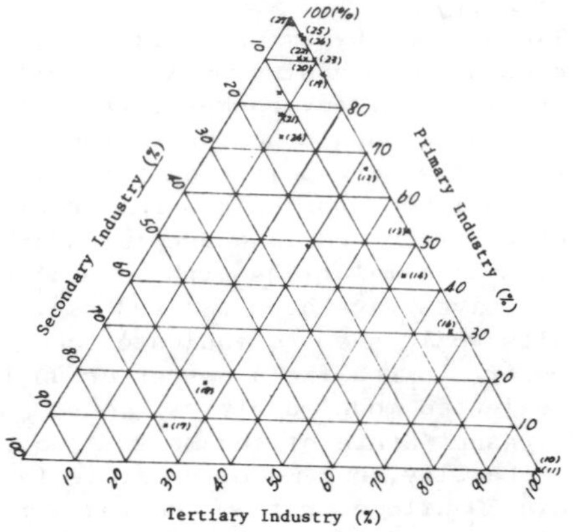

Fig. 5 Triangular Chart of Land Use Pattern in Chiba City

industries. That is, the area of Chiba City excluding Zones 10, 11, 17 and 18 is for agriculture and green, scattered with residencial houses.

Fig. 6 shows the estimated traffic flow map for Chiba City. The map has been derived from the survey of traffic generation by type at each node based on the future land use plan drawn by the city government. The map tells us that the traffic flowing from the inland area into the central commercial district and the traffic flowing into, and passing through, the Keiyo industrial beld are the heaviest. The city with 200,000 households and with car ownership of 1 for 3 households would seem to be confronted with serious urban traffic problems.

In this connection, this paper deals with
(1) the parking facilities planning in the central commercial district including the J.N.R. Chiba Central Station, and
(2) the residential environment planning in the districts adjacent to the central commercial district, since those districts are likely to suffer from heavier passing traffic.

3. Parking Facilities Planning Model

In these days, the parking difficulty due to the increase in urban traffic and the demand-supply unbalance in parking capacity is one of the causes of aggravation of traffic conditions such as conjestion. In order to solve the parking problem, a rational parking facilities planning based on a reliable estimate of the demand for parking must be developed. Although in most cities the parking facilities have been planned under such philosophy, actually more parking areas induce more cars and so make the traffic conjestion more serious.

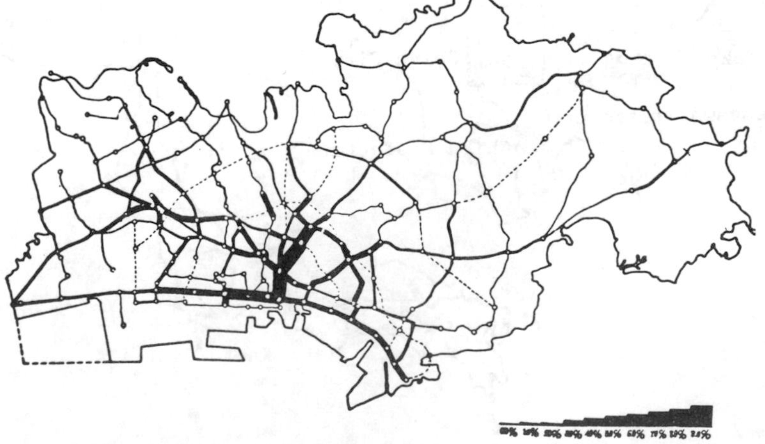

Fig. 6 Estimated Traffic Flow Density

Thus, the problem as to how the investment for public parking supply should be and the problem as to whether or not to stimulate private parking supply are under re-examination. Particulary, the public investment in construction works has been limited since the oil shock and its future fast growth such as experienced in the past would seem to be implausible. Consequently, a long-run parking facilities policy, such as public parking supply planning, and administrative guidance for private parking supply planning, should be developed.

In this study, the Systems Dynamics technique is used to build a model for parking facilities planning. Public investment in parking facilities and plan (capacity) for private parking facilities are taken as the policy variables and the parking phenomena are simulated. Then the effects of alternative policies are evaluated and the problems are examined, so that the future direction of parking facilities planning may be indentified.

The model area is the central commercial district of Chiba City, especially in the neighborhood of the J.N.R. Chiba Central Station.

3 - 1 Model

The model has 4 levels --- number of parked vehicles (PV), private parking supply (CP), business area space (BA) and housing area space (HA) ---, 27 auxiliary variables and 10 parameters, and 6 policies are evaluated. The model contains 2 positive information feedback loops 2nd 2 negative information feedback loops. (See Fig. 7) Explanation of interrelationships among the factors in the flow diagram is in order. First about the levels and rates. The level, private parking supply, is determind by the rates, private parking supply to be built and that to be demolished. The rate of private parking supply building is influenced by the floor space of the building and the firm output. The level, number of parked vehicles, is determined by the rates, increase and decrease. The increase and decrease are determined by the balance between parking capacity and road traffic. The levels, business area space and housing area space, are determined by the rates, building and demolishing. The rate of building is influenced by the number of firms and the number of houses.

Next about auxiliary variables. All ratios are against the preceeding year. Per capita income ratio is determined by firm output ratio; car ownership ratio by per capita income ratio, tax revenue ratio by firm output ratio and per capita income ratio; public investment ratio by tax revenue ratio; road area ratio by pavement ratio and public investment ratio; car utilization ratio by car ownership ratio, pavement ratio, number of firms and parking supply rate; road conjestion ratio by traffic per road area; off-street parking capacity and traffic accidents ratio by road conjestion ratio; parking supply rate by the ratio of number of parked vehicles to public and private parking supplies; ratio of number of grievances against public nuisance by ratio of number of traffic accidents and number of firms; ratio of number of bus and train passengers by ratio of number of firm employees; car traffic volume ratio by ratio of number of bus and train passengers, car ownership ratio and car utilization ratio; firm output ratio by floor space and number of parked vehicles; ratio of number of firm employees by firm output ratio; number of firms by ratio of number of firm employees; night population by ratio of number of grievances against public nuisance and housing space; number of houses by night population; building floor space by business area space, housing area space and building coverage.

Incidentally, public parking supply, off-street parking capacity and building coverage are given as the policy variables.

3 - 2 Simulation

The parking facilities planning model is built around the philosophy that, in response to the need for increase in parking capacity, private parking supply should be built up, since public parking supply increase is difficult due to shortage of public funds. Consequently, policies in this study are capacity of private parking facilities, public investment in parking facilities and parking regulation.

In view of the basic philosophy that private parking supply should be stimulated and in light of the legal requirements to increase parking capacity in proportion to the increase in building floor space, the future building floor space is specified by the building coverage, and private parking supply is geared to the growth of building floor space.

The policy regarding the capacity of private parking facilities is represented by business building coverage (FAR 1) and housing building coverage (FAR 2). The housing building coverage in each policy is held at 80% for each year. The policies concerning public investment and parking regulation are represented by public parking supply (PP) and off-street parking capacity (RP), respectively. Fig. 8 is the result of simulation.

Simulation has been carried out for 6 policy patterns. The policy pattern 1 assumes that building coverage (FAR 1) steadily grows and that public parking supply is to be gradually built up until 1980, and neither building nor demolition takes place after 1980. Parking regulation is supposed to be enforced every 3rd or 4th year, and off-street parking capacity in 1990 is 100. The policy pattern 2 is essentially the same as the policy pattern 1 except that public parking supply is supposed to be built up with a constant number each year until 1990, and packing regulation is to have been abolished in 1974; consequently, off-street parking capacity (RP) is constantly 650 from 1974 through 1990.

Results on public parking supply (PP) and

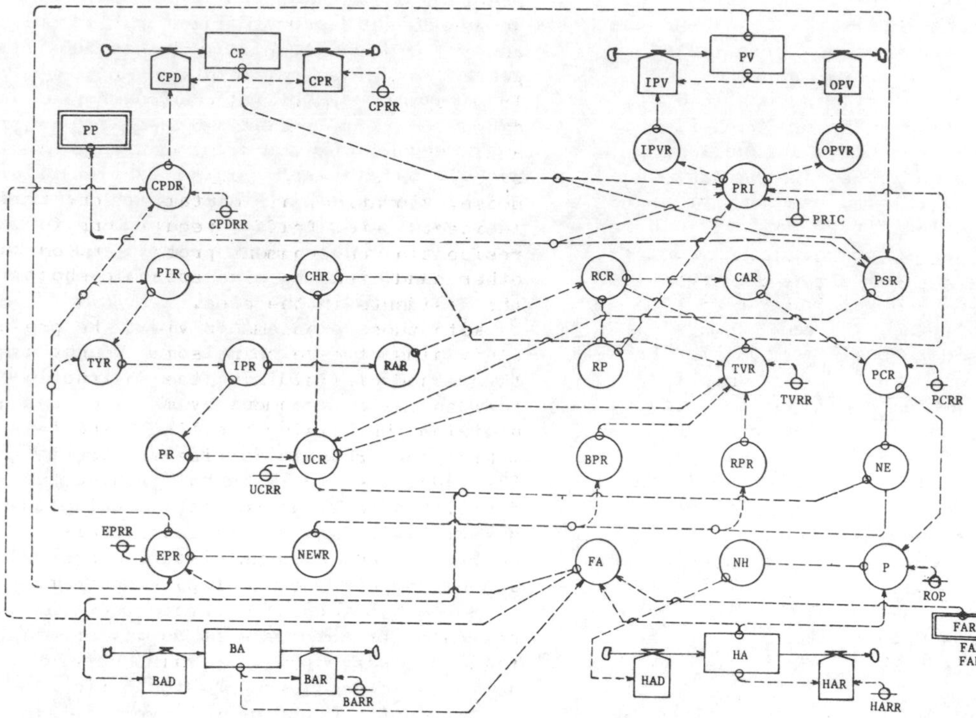

Fig. 7 Flow Diagram of Parking Facility Planning Model

Appendix to Fig. 7 :
Index of Terms for Fig. 7

PP : Public Parking Supply (Number of Parked Vehicles)
CP : Private Parking Supply
CPD : Private Parking to be Built
CPDR : Rate of Private Parking to be Built
CPR : Private Parking to be Demolished
PR : Pavement Ratio
CHR : Car Ownership Ratio
UCR : Car Utlization Ratio
PIR : Per Capita Income
RAR : Road Area Ratio
TYR : Tax Revenue Ratio
IPR : Public Investment Ratio
NEWR : Ratio of Number of Firm Employees
EPR : Firm Output Ratio
BA : Business Area
BAD : Business Area to be Built
BAR : Business Area to be Demolished
HA : Residential Area
HAD : Residential Area to be Built
HAR : Residential Area to be Demolished
NH : Number of Houses
P : Night Population
NE : Number of Firms
BPR : Ratio of Bus Passengers
RPR : Ratio of Train Passengers
RP : Off-Street Parking Capacity
TVR : Traffic Volume Ratio
RCR : Traffic Congestion Ratio
CAR : Traffic Accidents Ratio
PSR : Parking Supply Ratio
PV : Number of Parked Vehicles
IPV : Increase in Parked Vehicles
IPVR : Rate of Increase
OPV : Decrease in Parked Vehicles
OPVR : Rate of Decrease
PRI : Parking Inducement Ratio
PRIC : Contol Value of Parking Inducement
ROP : Parameter
PCRR : Parameter
TVRR : Parameter
FARL : Business Building Coverage
PCR : Ratio of Number of Grievances against Public Nuisance
CPRR : Rate of Private Parking to be Demolished
CPDRR : Parameter
UCRR : Parameter
EPRR : Parameter
FAR2 : Housing Building Coverage

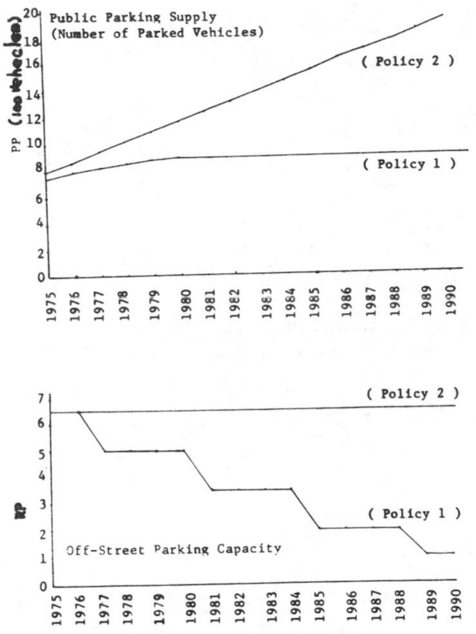

Fig. 8 Result of Simulation

off-street parking capacity (RP) are shown in Fig. 8.

3 - 3 Considerations

Our findings would tell us that parking phenomena, especially number of parked vehicles, would seem to be controllable by meens of some parking policies such as an increase in public parking supply and a regulation of off-street parking. And if we measure the response of residents in the community by number of grievances against public nuisance, such a policy that regulates parking supply through regulating the growth of building floor space might be desirable from the residents' viewpoint.

Problems in this model are as follows.

(1) Some variables used in the model are measured in terms of the city as a whold and others are measured in terms of the model district; here some inconsistency is observed.

(2) Construction of parking facilities within a building is at present being questioned. The model, however, does not consider any policy in this regard.

(3) The model does not take into consideration the physical distribution problem nor civil engineering construction problem.

In view of these problems, we plan to develop a model which is empirically tastable and is conducive to the optimal policy. We further hope to develop a model which indicates the effects upon an urban area of a choice of spot for parking facilities planning from the point of view of the overall traffic system and also with the residents' concern in mind.

4. Residential Environment Planning Model

As human desires diversify, residential environment in the urban area is faced with a multi-faceted problem. Newly developed cities and towns appear to have given reasonable considerations to some aspects of the problem. Older cities, however, suffer from unbalance between rapid growth of the city and its urban functions such as education, public health, transportation, and so on. In particular, road construction cannot catch up with the increase in car traffic, and consequently narrow streets are invaded by cars which create nuisance in terms of noise, vibration, air contamination, traffic accidents, etc. Traffic regulations for residential environment protection, on the other hand, tend to give economic shocks to the residents in the area.

With these problems in view, the present study aims at developing some thought upon the method of minimizing the destruction of residential environment by means of better utlizing the exising facilities and thus making the urban activities more active. The model area is in Chiba City and the district adjacement to the central commercial district. It is a mix of industrial-commercial and housing districts and has a considerable amount of passing traffic.

Here the factors concerning residential environments are taken to be welfare facilities (clinics, hospitals, nurseries, town hall, and other community facilities), educational facilities (Kindergartens, elementary schools, middle schools, libraries, etc.) and, in addition, sports and recreation facilities, waste disposal facilities, park and green areas. On the negative side, air contamination, land subsidence, traffic accidents, etc. may be considered.

The present study focuses on traffic nuisance (exhaust gas and noise) and traffic accidents. And a Systems Dynamics model is built on the basis of mutual relationships between night population and traffic volume, between traffic volume and traffic nuisance and accidents, between traffic nuisance and accidents and night population, night population and day population, traffic accidents and traffic safety investment, and so on.

4 - 1 Model

The purpose of the present study is to find out the optimal residential environment by way of measuring the change in night population induced by alternative policies on the improvement of traffic accidents, traffic noise, exhaust gas, etc. Increase and decrease in night population influence the increase and decrease in night population density, commercial population, industrial population, and so on.

Most traffic accidents are caused by the passing traffic, but here we relate them to car ownership. Car ownership in the model district is divided into that of night population, that of commercial population and that of industrial population. So we multiply each population by ownership ratio and sum them up to find out the total car ownership in the district. The incidence of traffic accidents in recent years shows a tendency to decrease, in spite of the increase in car ownership. This is due to the cumulative effect of ever-increasing invest-

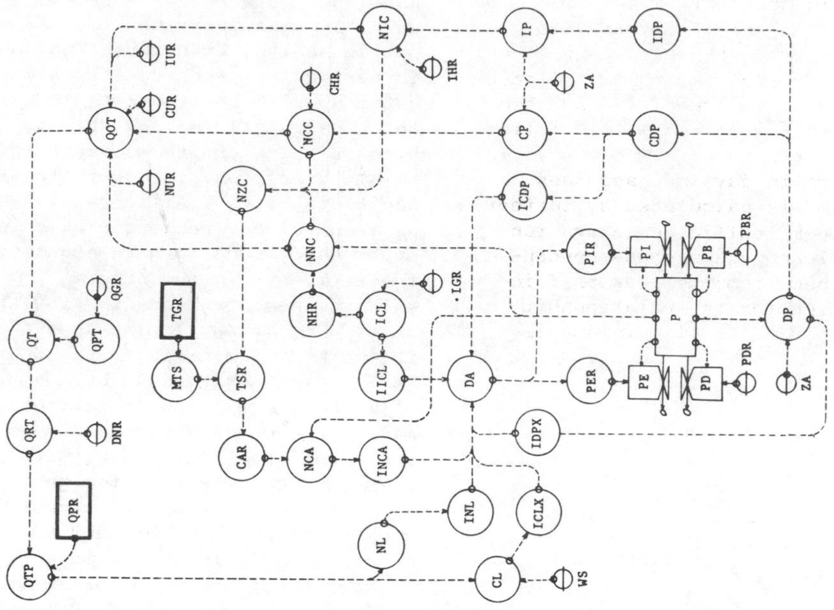

Fig. 9 Flow Diagram of Residential Environment Planning Model

Appendix to Fig. 9 :
Index of Terms for Fig. 9.

P : Night Population
DP : Night Population Dencity
PI : In-Coming Population
EP : Out-Going Population
PB : Number of Births
PD : Number of Deaths
PBR : Birth-Rate
PDR : Death-Rate
CP : Commercial Population
IP : Industrial Population
CDP : Commercial Population Density
IDP : Industrial Population Density
ICDP : Index of Commercial Population Density
NCC : Number of Vehicles in Commercial Population
NIC : Number of Vehicles in Industrial Population
CHR : Car Ownership Ratio in Commercial Population
IHR : Car Ownership Ratio in Industrial Population
CUR : Car Utilization Ratio in Commercial Population
IUR : Car Utilization Ratio in Industrial Population
QOT : Traffic Volume Gerated
MTS : Traffic Safety Investment
ICL : Income Level
TSR : Safety Rate
CAR : Rate of Traffic Accident
NCA : Number of Traffic Accidents
INCA : Index of Traffic Accidents
NL : Noise Level
DA : Degree of Attractiveness
DNR : Day-Night Ratio (ratio of daytime population against night population)
QGR : Growth Rate of Passing Traffic Volume
IICL : Index of Income Level
QTP : Peak-Time Traffic Volume
QPR : Peak-Time Traffic Volume Concentration Ratio
Q12T : Traffic Volume of 12 hour in Day Time
QT : Traffic Volume
QPT : Passing Traffic Volume
TGR : Growth Rate of Traffic Safety Investment
NUR : Car Ownership Ratio in Night Population
NZC : Number of Vehicles in District
NHR : Car Ownership Rate in Night Population
NNC : Number of Vehicles in Night Population
IGR : Growth Rate of Income Level
INL : Index of Noise Level
CL : CO-Density
ICLX : Index of CO-Density
IDPX : Index of Night Population Density
WS : Wind Velocity
PER : Out-Going Population Ratio
PIR : In-Coming Population Ratio
LA : District Area

ment in traffic safety. In view of this, we try to find traffic accidents from car ownership and traffic safety investment.

Noise level and exhaust gas concentration are measured from the volume of passing traffic per hour. In order to find them out, traffic volume (24 hours) is multiplied by the day-night ratio to obtain the traffic volume for 12 hours in daytime, and then peak traffic volume is calculated by further multiplying the peak traffic concentration ratio. Noise level and exhause gas concentration are obtained from the peak traffic volume. The equation for the relationship between noise level and traffic volume is shown in Fig. 10

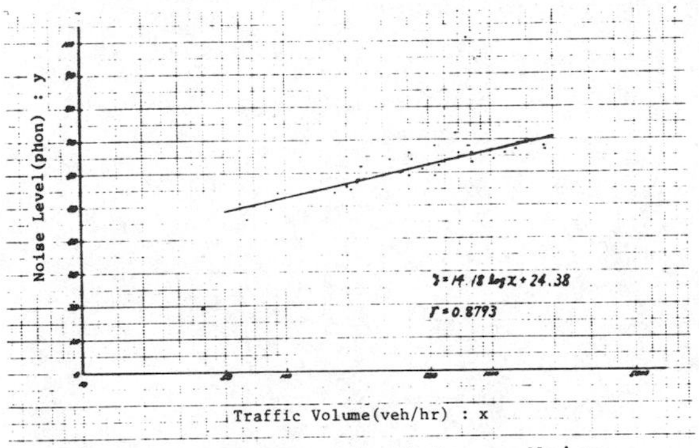

Fig. 10 Relationship Between Noise and Traffic Volume

There seem to be 2 causes for in-coming population and out-going population in the district; namely, job change and environment. Whenever somebody changes his job and moves in Chiba City, unless so restricted as to live in the company-provided residence, he would choose to reside in the model district because of the desirable environment. The model assumes that increase and decrease in the district population are influenced by residential environment. And desirability of residential environment is assumed to be determined by the degree of attractiveness of the district as defined by such factors as noise level, exhaust gas con concentration, traffic accidents, income level, night population, commercial population, etc.

The model is shown in Fig. 9 .

4 - 2 Simulation

Simulations have been carried out by introducing 9 changes in the policy variables, namely, growth rate of traffic safety investment and peak-time traffic volume concentration ratio. And simulation results of changes over time in night population and in the degree of attractiveness in response to alternative policies are shown in Figs. 11 and 12.

In conclusion, if both of the policies (growth rate of traffic safety investment and peak-time traffic volume concentration ratio) are parallelly enforced, the earlier the enforcement of policy to increase the growth rate of traffic safety investment is, the better would become the future residential environment. On the other hand, if either one of the policies is to be chosen,

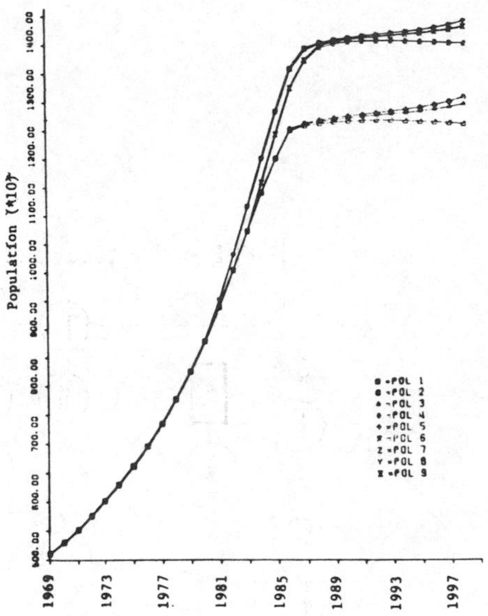

Fig. 11 Night Population

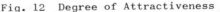

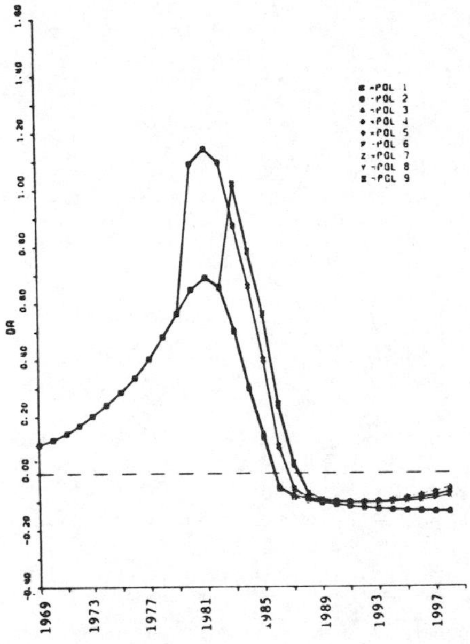

Fig. 12 Degree of Attractiveness

the policy to lower the peak-time traffic concentration ratio is likely to bring about better residential environment.

In the future, we plan to add to the model some considerations on parks, green areas, living environment, and so forth.

References

1) Jay W. Forrester, Urban Dynamics, The M.I.T., Press, 1969.
2) Y. Hanzawa & T. Matsuda, Passenger behavior and system design for urban bus transportation, Traffic Control and Transportation Systems, AFCET, 1974.

OPENING ADDRESS

Takehiko Matsuda

Immediate Past President and Chairman of the External Affairs Committee, International Federations of Operational Research Societies

Mr. Chairman, Ladies and Gentlemen!

May I first of all congratulate IFAC on the successful opening of this Workshop on Urban, Regional and National Planning; Environmental Aspects.

I am here somewhat semiofficially representing IFORS, International Federation of Operational Research Societies; semiofficially because IFORS wished to cosponsor this workshop with IFAC, but some procedural inefficiency on the IFORS side prevented us from doing it. Yet, since I am currently acting as Chairman of the IFORS External Affairs Committee, which is charged with affairs with other scientific and professional organizations, I thought that I should come to convey to you the IFORS' spirit of goodwill and support for this IFAC event.

IFAC and IFORS are "sister" federations, so to speak, under what we call FIACC, Five International Associations Coordinating Committee. We act together in dealing with other international organizations such as UN, UNESCO and others as well as in cooperating in promotion of scientific activities in the areas of common interest.

In fact, IFAC and IFORS have cosponsored many, many conferences and workshops together in the past and will continue such cooperative acts in the future; for example, we are cosponsoring one conference for development in Cairo, Egypt, in late November this year.

IFAC and IFORS share so much in common. As a matter of fact, looking at the program of this workshop I feel as if I were sitting in one of the IFORS conferences; names of the sessions, such as Modeling, Evaluation, Simulation and Optimization are exactly what we use in IFORS, too.

Both IFAC and IFORS are interested and involved in analyzing the structure of environment in connection with planning of urban, regional and national levels as well as in private firms, and such environmental structure is getting more and more difficult to deal with due to complexity, uncertainly and ambiguity.

I hope we can take full advantage of this kind of opportunity to further mutual stimulation and contribution so as to better the future human life.

Finally, let me again pay my deepest respect to the effort and effectiveness of IFAC, its Working Group on UNRENAP and the local organizing committee and I wish you every success in carrying out this workshop.

Thank you.

OPENING ADDRESS

Pieter Eykhoff

Member, IFAC Executive Council

Mr. Chairman, Ladies and Gentlemen,
Dear Colleagues,

The President of IFAC, Mr. U. Luoto , has asked me to bring you his greetings and very best wishes for a successful Workshop. This Workshop has been organized under the auspices of the International Federation of Automatic Control, IFAC. For those of you who are not very familiar with this organization I like to indicate that IFAC is a Federation of National Member Organizations of 39 countries. It has the aim to promote the science of automatic control in the broadest sense. Much of the work is being done through 13 Technical Committees, ranging from Mathematics of Control to Biomedical Applications. During 1977 there are 12 symposia, 7 workshops; in addition there are 4 other events in which IFAC has a cosponsorship.

For this Workshop it is of interest to note that also the socio-economic aspects are within the range of IFAC's interests. Some recommendations formulated during the sixth Congress, Boston, August 1975 underline this aspect (1):

- *"efforts by IFAC members, social scientists, economists, and othersto develop a greater understanding of the world as a dynamic system should be encouraged;*
- *IFAC programs, publications and other facilities are available for presentation evaluation, comparison and advancement of techniques for understanding the world as a dynamic system;*
- *individual IFAC members are invited to participate in this activity to the extend of their interests, capabilities and resources;*
- *IFAC and the general public should engage in a broad and concerted effort to insure the widest possible appreciation of the capabilities and limitations of the concepts and tools of dynamic system analysis and simulation as applied to the study of the world."*

This is quite an assigment, it concerns all of us.......

Note that indeed there have been a number of IFAC events in the area of environmental systems and natural resources:

- Symposium "Automatic Control of Natural Resources and Public Utilities", Haifa, September 1967;
- Symposium "Control of Water Resources Systems", Haifa, September 1973;
- Workshop "Systems Analysis and Modelling Approaches in Environment Systems", Zakopane, September 1973;
- Symposium "Environmental Systems Planning, Design and Control," Kyoto, August 1977;

and now this Workshop.

The purpose of this workshop is to provide the participants an opportunity to have rather informal discussions on their experiences, on new ideas and other valuable informations. The theme is set by the title: "Urban, Regional and National Planning; Environmental Aspects", and especially:

- what kind of model can be constructed to describe environmental aspects of these problems?
- what kind of methodology can be used to solve these problems?

The tables 1 and 2 indicate clearly that it is quite appropriate to have this workshop in Japan - a country with a high population density and a need for intensive industrialization due to a lack of raw materials. In such a situation urban, regional and national planning is very important!

> *Issun - saki wa yami*
> *(One inch in front of us*
> *all is darkness)*

and

> *Kaho wa nete mate*
> *(The best way to wait for events to take a better turn is just to keep on quietly sleeping)*

In 1977 those (old) sayings are completely outdated!
I expect that during these days we will find out, that also in this field of planning Japan has many good examples to offer.
Of course, also in this area the impact of computers is very clear.

On behalf of the IFAC President I like to extend cordial words of thanks to:
- the Organizing Committee for this Workshop;
- the SECOM Working Group;
  both under the chairmanship of Mr.T.Shiina;
- Professors Hasegawa and Inoue for their many activities in organizing this Workshop;
- IBM Japan for the financial support that made this Workshop possible.

IFAC sincerely appreciates their contributions. Also I like to recall the impressive list of contributions that Japan has made under the IFAC auspices to the control engineering community!

The participants/authors present, the preprints available and location of this Workshop provide excellent initial conditions. With the proper inputs of all of us this event is bound to be a success, i.e. an interesting and stimulating event.

To all of you: many good wishes for a successful Workshop.
Thank you for your attention.

REFERENCE

(1) IFAC Information Bulletin, no.88, 1975-11-17.

TABLE 1 Increase in GNP per year

1960 - 1970

	GNP (%)	industrial production (%)	energy consumption (%)
Japan	10.8	14.8	11.6
England	2.7	2.8	2.3
USA	4.2	4.8	4.5
Netherlands	5.3	7.3	8.4

TABLE 2 Economic data per km^2 habitable area

1974 - 1975

	GNP 1975	industrial output 1974	energy consumption 1974
Japan	6.05	2.04	4.12
England	1.04	0.26	1.00
USA	0.32	0.09	0.36
Netherlands	3.10	0.83	2.38

$.10^6$ \$ per km^2 habitable area

OPENING ADDRESS

Manfred Thoma

Member, IFAC Executive Council

Urban, regional and to some extend national planning are in the broadest sense almost as old as mankind exist. It was always the desire of human beeing to do planning in order to achieve optimal conditions in one or the other way. Here, of course, the difficulties start, because it is by no means easy to define what is optimal at all, due to the fact that there exist an infinite number of solutions.

The idea to have a workshop on these subjects shows how much attention is now a days given to planning. The increased interest can be explained by the fact that tools for an effective planning of large scale and complex systems have been developed. Let me just mention a few of them:

1) Increased understanding of modelling of real systems. In this connection the field of control engineering, system analysis and synthesis and so on have to be mentioned.

2) Development of different methodologies to solve the diverse problems. Here applied mathematics, optimization and system theory, for example hierarchical structures and so on, play an important part.

3) Interdisciplinary cooperation, because the problems must be studied from various points of view. Economics, social sciences, operation research and others have contributed to a great extend.

4) Development of reliable and high speed large digital computer systems. Computer sciences, information processing and related fields should be mentioned in this connection.

Already this few topics show that the tremendous progress which has been achieved in applied mathematics, control engineering, system theory, in simulation and optimization and so on was very necessary for successful planning of large scale systems.

In order to discuss in a more informal way, the problems in urban, regional, and national planning it was even necessary to restrict the topic of the workshop to environmental aspects. There is still a great number of impacts to environmental systems which have to be considered, as was clearly demonstrated during the IFAC Symposium on Environmental Systems Planning, Design and Control, which ended yesterday. I am sure that this more informal discussion for the next two days will be very fruitful for all participants since it will bring together scientists of different fields. —

Thank you very much.

KEYNOTE ADDRESS

Takeo Shiina

Chairman, IFAC Working SECOM Working Group on UNRENAP. President, IBM Japan

Ladies and Gentlemen,

It is indeed a great pleasure and honor for me to open this IFAC Unrenap Working Group Meeting this morning in this ancient city of Kyoto. Hundreds of thousands of people from within Japan as well as from other parts of the world visit this city each year. Some of these visitors come to attend international meetings such as this. The majority, however, come to visit and admire the vast number of shrines, temples and other historical monuments for the beauty, culture and historical heritage that they represent.

Kyoto was for centuries on centuries the capital of Japan. Officially made capital in the year 794 A.D., the long line of Japanese emperors resided in Kyoto for virtually the entire period from that year till the meiji restoration of 1868. As in any community in the world, Kyoto had its share of human happiness and tragedy. There were times of place and others of war. There were periods of growth and others of destruction. Love and hate, envy and admiration, came and went in varying degrees of intensity and variety of content. Throughout this multifaceted history of Kyoto, nevertheless, lay the fundamental aspiration of the people for betterment of the human lot. In the serene contemplation of the buddhist statues, and the awe-inspiring structures of great temples and shrines that you may see in this city, I am sure you will feel that impulse coming across to you -- that urge for bettering the human lot.

It is in the sense that Kyoto is in this way a symbol of the perennial aspiration and struggle of the Japanese to realize a better world that I find it particularly meaningful that this gathering is taking place in this ancient capital of Japan. For the subject matter being taken up here is a central one for the betterment of mankind, if not in the environment of centuries ago, certainly in the vastly changed environment of the modern world.

Because of the immensely rapid advance in science and technology in the past half-century, the world has literally been reduced to a small village. One can pick up a telephone in Tokyo and be speaking to a person in New York in a matter of several tens of seconds. A speech by the president of the U.S. can be viewed live on television in Tokyo as well as Rome. Partly because of the time difference, a traveller leaving Tokyo at 10 am will be in New York at 11 am of the same morning. This shrinkage in distance in the world has brought about an immensely enhanced interdependence among nations as well as within each nation. A hundred years back what happened in Saudi Arabia had little to do with life in Kyoto. Today, as you know, it has a great deal to do with it.

The interdependence thus enhanced in human contact has been particularly sharply felt in the field of environment. The vast scale of modern plants using ecologically untested chemicals and technology has threatened the public safety of many communities and regions. Even a prima facie harmless things as the effluence of cooling water from an electric power plant can conceivably inflict irreparable damage to vegetation, marine life and weather.

The close interrelationship among the numerous components of a system make the right decisions extremely difficult to come upon. This situation is further aggravated by the politically activist nature of present day citizens. Because of the greatly enhanced level of education and the rapid dissemination of information in modern society, actions affecting the lives of local residents can in many cases be obstructed by resident environmentalist groups.

In such cases the need arises to enlist the understanding and support of those people. But to do that one can no longer resort to categorical statements that there will be no or minimal damage: the public is now too sophisticated for that kind of treatment. What becomes necessary is thus a systematic, scientific and objective assessment of the action by which the local resistance can be objectively and impassionately overcome.

Moreover, Japan is not the only country where land, clean water and unpolluted air are becoming critically scarce. On top of that there has been a worldwide increase in awareness of the need to conserve energy and other basic resources. Future planning at the urban, regional and national levels must consequently be such as to economize on these limited resources to the maximum extent.

It is from these points of view that the subject of this meeting is particularly pertinent to the problem faced by the human race today. The intricate and complex interrelationships, feedbacks and interaction among the many components that make up the system that constitutes human society today are areas in which the computer, and the simulation and modeling made possible by it, can make an invaluable contribution.

Kyoto today is no longer the Kyoto of the year 794 or of 1868. The problems of Kyoto of 1977 can be resolved only by the use of a tool adapted to the Kyoto of 1977. This awareness, I believe, is appropriately sharpened by our holding this meeting today in this ancient capital. It also brings forth, by contrast, the striking importance of the subject that we will be discussing here in these two days.

For all of these reasons, I am particularly happy to be chairman of this IFAC Unrenap Working Group Meeting. I am convinced that the interchange over the two days of this workshop will prove to be of enormous value to all of us. I wish you all a meaningful and enjoyable stay in Japan.

Thank you.

AUTHOR INDEX